HENRY JAMES,

GERTRUDE STEIN,

AND THE

BIOGRAPHICAL

ACT

CHARLES CARAMELLO

HENRY JAMES,

GERTRUDE STEIN,

AND THE

BIOGRAPHICAL

ACT

 THE UNIVERSITY OF NORTH CAROLINA PRESS   CHAPEL HILL AND LONDON

© 1996
The University of
North Carolina Press
All rights reserved

Library of Congress Cataloging-in-Publication Data
Caramello, Charles.
  Henry James, Gertrude Stein, and the biographical act /
by Charles Caramello.
    p. cm.
  Includes bibliographical references (p.   ) and index.
  ISBN 978-0-8078-2267-8
  ISBN 978-0-8078-5726-7
  1. American prose literature—20th century—History and
criticism. 2. United States—Biography—History and criticism.
3. Stein, Gertrude, 1874–1946—Technique. 4. James, Henry, 1843–
1916—Technique. 5. Biography as a literary form. 6. Narration
(Rhetoric). 7. Self in literature. 8. Autobiography. 9. Authorship.
I. Title.
PS2127.B54C37   1996
810.9'004—dc20   95-34701
                                                            CIP

For Dagmar

CONTENTS

Preface   ix

Abbreviations   xiii

1   Precursors   1

2   The Good American
     Hawthorne   21

3   The Bostonian Type
     William Wetmore Story and His Friends   57

4   In the Heroic Age of Cubism
     The Autobiography of Alice B. Toklas   119

5   Generals James and Stein
     Four in America   169

Notes   201

Works Cited   255

Index   269

A section of illustrations appears following page 101.

PREFACE

Commentators began remarking Henry James's and Gertrude Stein's similarity as early as 1910 and have continued to do so, on a regular but very casual basis, since then; few, however, have explored that similarity in any depth, and virtually no one has explored the issues that concern me or has brought together the series of texts that shape my study.[1] In the singular exception, an anonymous writer of dustwrapper copy for a reprint of James's *William Wetmore Story and His Friends* observed: "Long before Gertrude Stein attracted a flock of young American writers and painters to her famous Paris salon, an earlier generation of American 'expatriates' was drawn to the magnificent Palazzo Barberini in Rome, the residence of William Wetmore Story."[2] The copywriter evidently had not read *Story*, since the next sentence erroneously has the young James meeting Hawthorne at the Barberini. But the serendipitous pairing of our two principals suggests the extent to which James has become a model for the cosmopolitan literary expatriate and Stein a model for the expatriated doyen of an artistic salon; and the fortuitous error about Hawthorne, moreover, suggests the literary genealogy, distortions intact, to which James and Stein laid claim in their biographical portraiture.

James and Stein appear, in the following study, not only as artists, as sophisticated portraitists and autoportraitists, but also as types, as emblems in an ideal history of modernism to which they are central but in which they are not unique. They often performed biographical acts, I shall argue, in two senses of the phrase: they wrote biographical portraiture, but they wrote it, intentionally and studiously, as a cover for autobiography. Specifically, they used biographical portraits of other artists to construct autobiographical portraits of themselves as exemplary modern artists; and, as part of the process, they used those portraits to create artistic genealogies for themselves. With typically modernist fusions of form and function, moreover, they not only used those portraits as occasions for rejecting earlier styles of portraiture and for advancing a contemporary style, but they also used that style, simultaneously and circularly, to depict themselves as ideally modern—James countering Hawthorne's Romance with his own Realism, and Stein countering James's Realism with her Cubism.

Though I shall emphasize James's and Stein's *representations* of exemplarity and genealogy, their imaginative constructions of their precursors and themselves, I also shall treat James and Stein as *representative* moderns, exemplars embedded in an ideal but not unreal genealogy. As portraitists, James and Stein exhibited traits that mark them, however differently, as modernist: their obsessions with their own contemporaneity and with precursivity; their evolutions of a sophisticated portraiture at once autobiographical and autoreferential, whatever its nominal subject; their commitments to a functionalist aesthetics with radical economy as its linchpin, appearances often notwithstanding; and their commitments to the social mission of art, again appearances often notwithstanding. And as serious students of literature in general and of portraiture in particular, moreover, they went to school with writers who, in fact, did influence them: Hawthorne not only influenced James, as everyone recognizes, but James also influenced Stein, to a degree greater than anyone acknowledges. These influences, I shall argue, shaped both the form and the content of their biographical portraiture.

To advance those arguments, I have selected four works that explore themes of artistry and precursivity and that experiment with conventional forms of biographical portraiture, four works, moreover, that reflect a textual genealogy within the larger biographical genealogy. They include James's two book-length biographical studies: *Hawthorne* (1879), a slim life-and-works critical essay, set in the America of two generations back and focused on Hawthorne's art in its place and time; and *William Wetmore Story and His Friends* (1903), a massive life-and-letters group biography, set in the American colony in Rome in the generation immediately preceding James's and focused on social relations between Story and his circle and between Story's circle and James. And they include two of Stein's many works of biographical portraiture: *The Autobiography of Alice B. Toklas* (1933), her famous experiment in autobiographical narration, set in the Franco-American artistic colony in Paris around the Great War and focused on Toklas's relationship with Stein and on their relationship with their circle; and *Four in America* (composed 1933–34, published posthumously 1947), Stein's largely ignored experiment in the brief "life," her serial polyptych portraying Ulysses S. Grant, Wilbur Wright, Henry James, and George Washington, and implying the relationship between those eminent Americans and herself.[3]

I shall approach those works as follows. In a brief opening chapter, I consider James's and Stein's commentaries on biography and portraiture toward the end of isolating the basic premises of their own work in those genres. In chapters 2 and 3, respectively, I treat James's *Hawthorne* and his *William Wetmore Story*, and I show that he meant the two books as a diptych portraying dissimilar but equally romantic artists as his precursors. Though James focused on artistry in both works, however, he also articulated Hawthorne's romantic art with his conservative politics, presented Hawthorne as uncritical in both arenas, and then covertly presented himself as the postbellum expatriate artist of modern artistic principles and of shrewd and even progressive social vision; and he did the same, but with noticeable ideological differences, in the more openly political *William Wetmore Story*. In chapters 4 and 5, I treat Stein's *Autobiography of Alice B. Toklas* and her *Four in America*, specifically the latter's "life" of James, first focusing on how Stein portrayed Toklas portraying them both, and next showing how Stein created, with a series of portraits, a polyptych concealing a self-portrait. Though Stein, too, focused on artistry in these works, she, too, addressed relations between art and politics, exploring in both works how patriarchy produces and enshrines masculine art just as it produces and enshrines masculine cultural icons, and advancing in both works her art and herself as lesbian and feminist.

I must comment further on my examples and approach. Though I shall treat portraits of figures who influenced James and Stein, and shall emphasize precursivity, I claim neither that influence alone drives literary history, nor that Hawthorne alone foreran James or that James alone foreran Stein. And though I shall treat those portraits as central to James's and Stein's constructions of themselves as ideal moderns, I claim neither that my selections represent the extent or the evolution of their work in literary portraiture, nor that points made about their portraiture automatically extend to their work in other genres. In fact, I might have used other selections, or additional selections, to advance my arguments, and I especially regret lacking the space to include chapters on James's *A Small Boy and Others* (1913) and *Notes of a Son and Brother* (1914), what he called jointly his "Family Book," and on Stein's series of portraits, "Picasso" (1909), "If I Told Him: A Completed Portrait of Picasso" (1923), and *Picasso* (1938). Since I take as a premise, moreover, that James generally observed the lines marking nonfiction from fiction, while Stein virtually obliterated those lines of demarcation, I can treat *Hawthorne* and *William Wetmore Story* as imaginative recreations, but I must treat *The Autobiography of Alice B. Toklas* and *Four in America* as creative inventions. And since I focus on James's and Stein's *uses* of biographical portraiture, finally, and frequently make assumptions about intention, my arguments must remain inferential and, especially in Stein's case, often speculative.

Any study owes intellectual and scholarly debts, and I have benefited from several critical conversations. Though work on biography remains scant, with Ira Nadel's *Biography* a robust exception, work on autobiography has become voluminous, particularly that on feminist and modernist autobiography; I owe much to that work, particularly to the idea, often associated with Paul John Eakins's *Fictions in Autobiography*, that autobiographical texts are fictional inventions as well as nonfictional imitations. Precursivity and influence have become hotly contested matters, and Harold Bloom's *Anxiety of Influence* and *Map of Misreading*, together with Sandra Gilbert and Susan Gubar's oppositional *Madwoman in the Attic*, have provided the theories I have attempted to negotiate; Daniel Mark Fogel's prior negotiation, *Covert Relations*, has proven an important model. Leon Edel's still magisterial *Henry James* and Richard Bridgman's groundbreaking *Gertrude Stein in Pieces* have been indispensable sources of background material, more important to me than my notes may suggest.[4] For discussions of James and Stein as portraitists, I owe much to John Carlos Rowe's *Theoretical Dimensions of Henry James* and to Wendy Steiner's *Exact Resemblance to Exact Resemblance*; and for signal insights, finally, I have returned often to Carol Holly's work on James's "Family Book," to Marianne DeKoven's work on Stein's feminism, and to Catharine Stimpson's work on Stein's sexuality.

I began this study some years ago while a fellow at the National Humanities Center, and I want to thank the Center and its staff for their support. I completed the study at the University of Maryland, and I want to thank the College of Arts and Humanities for a Research Award that helped in the initial stages of writing, and the Office of Graduate Studies and Research for a Research Support Award that defrayed the cost of illustrations. I have benefited from the professionalism, patience, and sharp editorial practices of the University of North Carolina Press, and I want to thank, particularly, Sandra Eisdorfer, Barbara Hanrahan, Ron Maner, and Eric Schramm. An early version of chapter 5 appeared in the *Henry James Review*, and I want to thank the editors for their good advice, Leon Edel for his generous public response, and the Johns Hopkins University Press for permission to reprint. I want to thank Anne Carroll, my research assistant, not only for her care in preparation of the manuscript and its index, but also for her sound judgment and good cheer. I want to thank the friends and colleagues who kindly discussed the project with me, particularly Daniel Mark Fogel, Ted Leinwand, John Carlos Rowe, R. Jackson Wilson, and Marjorie Perloff. For constant interest, encouragement, and keen advice, finally, I want to thank my wife, Anne Olszewski Caramello.

ABBREVIATIONS

I have used the following abbreviations in this study; the reader will find pertinent bibliographical information under Works Cited.

HENRY JAMES

AN	*The Art of the Novel*
HJL	*Henry James Letters*, ed. Leon Edel
LC 1	*Literary Criticism: French Writers, Other European Writers, The Prefaces to the New York Edition*
LC 2	*Literary Criticism: Essays on Literature, American Writers, English Writers*
N	*Notes of a Son and Brother*
PL	*The Portrait of a Lady*
SB	*A Small Boy and Others*
WWS	*William Wetmore Story and His Friends*

GERTRUDE STEIN

ABT	*The Autobiography of Alice B. Toklas*
CAE	"Composition as Explanation"
EA	*Everybody's Autobiography*
FIA	*Four in America*
LGS/CVV	*The Letters of Gertrude Stein and Carl Van Vechten, 1913–1946*, ed. Edward Burns
LIA	*Lectures in America*
NAR	*Narration*
P	*Picasso*
TI	"A Transatlantic Interview"

OTHER

HJ	Leon Edel, *Henry James*

HENRY JAMES,

GERTRUDE STEIN,

AND THE

BIOGRAPHICAL

ACT

One

PRECURSORS

Of course James was the precursor alright.

—ALICE B. TOKLAS TO DONALD SUTHERLAND, 1947

Discussing John Singer Sargent, James declared in 1893 that "there is no greater work of art than a great portrait"; discussing Francis Picabia, Stein declared in 1933 that "if you do not solve your painting problem in painting human beings you do not solve it at all" (*ABT* 146).[1] I would argue that James and Stein saw portraiture as the foundational genre, and, in the following study, I shall focus on biographical portraiture as a medium through which they declared their modernity, with which they established their genealogy as moderns, and in which they theorized and practiced, in one and the same gesture, a modern literary art.[2] As prelude to a close reading of texts, though, I first need to consider James's and Stein's views on biography and portraiture. If we attend to their commentaries on these genres, we will see not only that they studied the relevant traditions, but also that they set out, respectively, to advance them from romance to realism and from realism to modernism. We also shall see that James, devotee of aesthetic refinement, foreran Stein, devotee of aesthetic experimentation, and that she portrayed him in that role.

When James and Stein commented on biography and portraiture, they tended to link composition to representation and both to broader issues. Emphasizing questions of composition, each writer framed those questions with a specific generic bias—James leaning from biographical narrative toward portraiture, Stein eventually leaning from portraiture toward autobiographical narration. Recognizing that all portraiture requires negotiation of general and specific, abstract and concrete, or, in their preferred terms, type and instance, moreover, each writer argued that reliance on type not only produced static rather than dynamic composition, but also, in substituting the ideal for the real, produced false rather than true representation—James the Realist focusing on romantic types, Stein the Cubist on the realist claim to having abolished type. Both James and Stein, however, also knew that the question of type exceeded the bounds of sound composition and accurate representation and entered the realms of knowledge and power. Simply put, relying on type meant substituting social conventions for the realities they concealed or distorted and meant substituting received ideas for critical thinking; exploring type, it follows, meant investigating those conventions and those ideas toward some corrective end.

Following Hawthorne's lead in the question of composition as in so much else, James framed the formal problem as one of negotiating the competing claims of incident and character and thus of story and picture; he construed biography as being narrative and devalued it, construed portraiture as containing and focusing narrative and valued it, and, in his fiction and nonfiction alike, he sought to absorb the former into the latter. As a critic, he was severe with writers who went too far toward overly kinetic narrative, too far toward overly static characterization, or too far toward both at once—in a word, toward type in event or person; and he was kind to writers, by contrast, who understood characterization to be the primary—perhaps the only—site of dynamism, and who understood the novel, therefore, as an act of psychological portraiture. As a practitioner, he wed his formal emphasis on picture to his thematic emphasis on analysis of individual psychology and often used both to critique the social construction of the individual. He claimed to have evolved *The Portrait of a Lady* (1881), for example, by beginning with his character and then inventing the "relations" and "situations" that generated her story. Seeking to keep "the centre of the subject in the young woman's own consciousness," he had developed "her relation to herself" while he focused the views of her "satellites, especially the male," on her; among other things, he was exploring the conventions that mediated his heroine's perception of herself and her satellites' interpenetrating perceptions of her, especially the conventions encoded in the coercive social type *lady* (see *AN* 43, 51).

Following James's lead, as we shall see, Stein framed the same basic formal problem at a higher level of abstraction, framed the problem of negotiating story and picture as one of negotiating portraiture and narration; she construed portraiture as "composition" in a multiply punning and idiosyncratic sense of the term, construed modern biography and autobiography as narration rather than as narrative, and, in her later work, sought to conflate them as "portrait narration" (TI 19). Wedding Henry James's aesthetics of individual portraiture to William James's compatible psychology of individual identity, and taking the representation of duration as the key, she evolved an original literary portraiture that eliminated "story" in favor of a cinematic "continuous succession of the statement of what that person [the subject] was"; she disparaged story as so much novelistic remembering of conventions; and she praised those portraitists, like Picasso, who "tried to express things seen not as one knows them but as they are when one sees them without remembering having looked at them" (*LIA* 121–22, 176–77, 181; *P* 15). In her work from *Three Lives* (1909) forward, moreover, she used this portraiture to dismantle type in general, coercive sexual types in particular. Though the titles of "The Good Anna" and "The Gentle Lena," from *Three Lives*, focus on the nominal, on individuals, for example, the two biographical "lives" themselves deconstruct the adjectival, the patriarchal norms of "goodness" and "gentleness"; and "Melanctha," the central "life" of the triptych, I would argue, deconstructs the type "tragic mulatta" in order to get at the less accessible type of the tragic lesbian.

James and Stein, then, both advanced the theory and the practice of biographical portraiture; but they did so in different roles and with different focuses. James began his literary life as a reviewer and a critic, he wrote portraiture throughout his distinguished career as a novelist, and he eventually returned almost exclusively to memoiristic, nonfictional work; he often wrote about other writers, then, and often at great length. By contrast, Stein began as a writer of fictional portraits, she developed highly intergeneric nonfictional forms throughout her career as an experimentalist, and she eventually concentrated on her trademark autobiographical narration; she rarely wrote about other writers, then, and usually only briefly. Because James and Stein commented on biographical portraiture differently, in short, we must approach them differently in this chapter. We might begin with James's reviews of biographical writing, particularly from the 1870s, and then take up some of his essays in portraiture from the 1880s together with his later remarks on his great novel of the period, *The Portrait of a Lady*. We then can turn to Stein's stunning *Three Lives* and to her later comments on its composition, and then return to some of her writings in the 1930s on biography and autobiography. From that vantage, finally, we shall be able to see larger issues of portraiture and precursivity that inform the succeeding chapters.

4 *Precursors*

⤴

When James reviewed regularly for the *Nation* and other periodicals in the 1870s, he wrote a large number of brief, evaluative notices of biographies. He tended to emphasize the kind of life the biographical subject had led, and he did so in two different but, for him, related senses: he established the biographical subject's arena of activity and assessed the biography's relative tilt toward the public or the private; and, perhaps more strikingly if less defensibly, he graded lives as, inherently, either interesting or dull. The biographical subjects in question were almost by definition persons of achievement either in affairs, broadly speaking, or in the arts, and James tended to stress public and often political matters in the former cases and more personal (if not more private) and often aesthetic matters in the second; he also tended to characterize the former cases as excellent subjects for biography, the latter as boring subjects. In short, he often seemed to be identifying lives of action as appropriate for biography, lives of the mind as inappropriate; and, as a generic corollary, he often seemed to be identifying the narration of incident, the telling of story, with biography, rather than the portrayal of character.

As James did when reviewing novels, he divided his attention almost evenly between subject and treatment, though he insisted less strongly on their fusion in biography. In a frequent show of fairness, moreover, he noted and to some degree accommodated two salient differences between novel and biography: biographers, first, had to take their central figures essentially as given, or, at least, as unavailable for total recreation; and biographers, second, not only had to procure, select, and organize documentary material relevant to the life represented, but also, and particularly given the conventions of Victorian biography, often had to shape the written "life" out of such material.[3] In any case, James generally attended both to auctorial point of view (in both the general and the technical senses of the phrase) and to editorial conception and execution; he elaborated a system of values, often implicit, in which a biography either had or failed to have a compelling and coherent narrative point of view and either had or failed to have a compelling and coherent editorial policy for selection and arrangement of documentary material.[4]

In fact, though, James was performing a sustained, if inconsistent, depreciation of biography. In one maneuver, he collapsed his own distinctions between kinds of subject and kinds of biography, intimating, in effect, that all biographies, whether about lives of action or lives of the mind, whether narrative or documentary, depended too much on conventional plot and on character type. In another conflicting maneuver, however, he not only sustained his distinctions between kinds of subject and kinds of treatment, but he also extended them into a generic distinction between biography and portraiture, arguing that an active life can be retold as story, in biography, but that a contemplative life must be portrayed as picture, in portraiture. In both maneuvers, he was generalizing his objections to specific romantic biographies into an indictment of biography as inherently romantic. In the first maneuver, that is, he identified biography with the spirited narration of adventure and with the emblematic depiction of character and thus associated the genre with the features he elsewhere denounced in fictional romance. In the second maneuver, he identified biography with the plotting of active lives, portraiture with the characterizing of contemplative lives, and thus associated the former with the trait he elsewhere pronounced dominant in romance, the latter with the trait he elsewhere theorized as becoming dominant in realism—that is, dynamic characterization.[5]

This does not work out with clarity for reasons having as much to do with James's evolving professional relationship to biography as with his evolving aesthetics of portraiture. Though he had begun by writing brief reviews, that is, the biographical subjects varying widely in vocation, he quickly began using biographies by others as informational bases for his own extended, essayistic critical studies, their subjects almost invariably being writers; relegating the original biographer's treatment of the subject to the background, James brought his own portrayal and evaluation of the subject into the foreground. At almost regular intervals throughout his career, moreover, he pieced together occasional reviews, revised already lengthy essayistic studies, and formed the collections *French Poets and Novelists* (1878), *Partial Portraits* (1888), *Essays in London and Elsewhere* (1893), and *Notes on Novelists* (1914).[6] James began to compare biography unfavorably to portraiture, in other words, at exactly the moment that he was emerging as a literary portraitist of consequence and reputation. And he developed those comparisons, more strikingly, in the genre that he was advocating, in his critical portraiture.[7]

James revealed all these tendencies in a long-running series of reviews and essays about George Sand, and he did so, moreover, in the context of yet another problem in biography. As a reviewer, James dealt with many "personal" biographies, with memoirs or compilations of journals and correspondence that often attended to domestic relations; and, as a purveyor of domestic melodrama, however disguised, in his fiction, he certainly knew that a good biographical subject could be a person lacking public or intellectual consequence but having an exciting, perhaps lurid, intimate life. For aesthetic, ethical, and, one assumes, personal reasons, however, James deplored works of "intimate biography," particularly when an artist or writer was the subject. He wrote in 1875 on "this latest development of literary portraiture. It is the trivial playing at the serious; it is not the masculine way of looking at things" (*LC* 2:278–79); and he elaborated the point in 1882, expressing displeasure "in the growing taste of the age for revelations about the private lives of the persons in whose works it is good enough to be interested" (*LC* 1:214). George Sand had forced these issues not only with her autobiographical *L'Histoire de ma Vie*, but also with her romance *Elle et Lui* in conjunction with the posthumous publication of her intimate correspondence with Alfred de Musset; James found her, then, an ideal case.[8]

At one level in his writings on Sand, James was advancing a complicated argument, inflected by gender, not only about Sand but, implicitly, about biography as opposed to art. Something "very masculine" in Sand's genius, he proposed in 1877, was compromised by her being "a woman and a Frenchwoman," by something feminine that he associated with fluidity, with the "too fluent" quality of her work (*LC* 1:712–13); her "true male inwardness," as he called it in 1897 (*LC* 1:748), her "masculine" qualities, as he elaborated in 1902, accounted for her concentration and intensity, in life as in writing, but something feminine, again, caused both an interest in lovers and a neglect of form, a laxity in sexual and textual proprieties, and accounted for her "vulgarity" (*LC* 1:758–60, 722–24).[9] However circuitously or inadvertently, James was suggesting that Sand the memoirist of *L'Histoire de ma Vie* was feminine, Sand the artist of *Elle et Lui* masculine, that, put differently, femininity, laxity in form, and biography went together, as did masculinity, rigor in form, and novelistic portraiture. And James developed these suggestions most fully, not surprisingly, when reviewing volumes of Madame Wladimir Karénine's biographical *George Sand: Sa Vie et ses Oeuvres* in 1902 and 1914.

In fact, at a second level of this series, James was devaluing biography and practicing portraiture, and he thus was maneuvering, in effect, to outflank both Sand and her biographer. Claiming the high road in 1877, he implied that he disapproved of a fluidity in biographical narrative that ended up producing neither veracity nor verisimilitude. Presumably taking that road in 1897, he would do for Sand what she had not succeeded in doing for herself—make her credible as an artist. Sand had shown how she had converted life into art; James would not reconvert her art into intimate biography—with its lack of masculinity—but would convert her art into different art: critical portraiture. In 1902 and in 1914, moreover, James chastised Sand's biographer Karénine for her prolixity and lack of art, and he implicitly was attempting to show, by the example of his writing, how the thing should be done (see *LC* 1:757, 776). In the latter three essays, however, which James brought together as a unit in *Notes on Novelists*, he himself made Sand the subject of a romantic and tragic portrait. In fact, he treated her in the way that the romantic biographers that he often criticized in the 1870s had treated their subjects; he treated her as a personal example, as a feminine martyr in the sexual wars whose career had the elegant composition of cause (pedigree), effect (search for an adequate male counterpart), and conclusion ("moral tragedy"), as, in a word, *type*.[10]

Years earlier, James had opened *The Portrait of a Lady*, as he would close it, by having satellite characters portray Isabel Archer as type. Soon after this opening passage, however, he returned the narrative to an earlier moment in Albany, and himself portrayed Isabel by entering her consciousness and by having her recount, somewhat romantically, what she remembered of the past and imagined for the future. The scene foreshadows its far greater counterpart, the pivotal midpoint of the *Portrait*, Isabel's "vigil of searching criticism" (*AN* 57), where James painted a conventional genre-study of a woman sitting before a fire, but where, again, he portrayed his heroine by entering her consciousness, by having her, this time, critically examine her past and realistically assess her present situation. He portrayed Isabel twice, in short, in the acts of remembering, imagining, and, in the second case, coolly analyzing; and he modeled these passages thematically and visually, I would argue, on Hawthorne's stylized autoportraiture in "The Custom-House," the lengthy introduction to *The Scarlet Letter* (1850), which James had been studying for his own *Hawthorne* (1879). If I am right, then James may have intended first to compare Isabel Archer as a romantic author of her fate to Hawthorne as a romantic author, and then to compare Isabel as a realistic critic of her fate to himself as a realistic author; he may have intended to show Isabel *seeing* (his term) first as a romancer and then as a novelist and thus to have allegorized a literary succession from Hawthorne to himself.[11]

Whatever the case, James had shifted his critical attention in *Hawthorne* and in the 1880s toward theorizing the proper novel as portraiture—especially in the critical portraits of Trollope, Stevenson, Eliot, Emerson, and others that he collected with "The Art of Fiction" (1883) to form *Partial Portraits* late in the decade. Throughout these essays, he tended to formulate problems in binary terms, returning repeatedly to the cluster of pairs incident/character, plot/characterization, story/picture. Explicitly debunking as specious and old-fashioned such binaries as "novels of plot" and "novels of character," explicitly declaring as transposable such terms as "incident" and "character" and thus such oppositions as "novel" and "picture," he nonetheless repeatedly sustained the binaries, he made the second term in each pair the term of privilege, and, as he had done with "biography" and "portraiture," he essentially absorbed the first terms into the second. In each case, however, he remained ambivalent, and especially so with respect to the more inclusive, and related, elements that, as a reader, he found most familiar and appealing but that, as a theorist, he denounced most vigorously: *type* and *romance*.[12]

Type was James's bogey. He had repeated so often in *Hawthorne*, for example, that his precursor had created type rather than character that even William Dean Howells, allied with James in defense of the realistic novel, tasked him for treating the terms "romantic" and "novel" as if "convertible," for failing to acknowledge that "the romance and the novel are as distinct as the poem and the novel," and for having criticized Hawthorne's figures "because they are rather types than persons, rather conditions of the mind than characters; as if it were not almost precisely the business of the romance to deal with types and mental conditions."[13] Unpersuaded by Howells and unregenerate after Robert Louis Stevenson's similar rejoinder to "The Art of Fiction," James would continue in 1885, in a portrait based on John Cross's *Life of George Eliot*, to compare Eliot's portrayal of character adversely with Balzac's in a way that extended his basic case against Hawthorne's romance.[14] For Eliot, James proposed, the novel "was not primarily a picture of life, . . . but a moralised fable." Eliot erred, in James's estimation, in "proceed[ing] from the abstract to the concrete," in using ideas rather than observations as bases, in "car[ing] for the things she finds in [the personal spectacle] only so far as they are types" (*LC* 2:1003–4); and her characters suffered accordingly.

This all suggests that by the mid-1880s James had repudiated not only a use of type that he earlier had identified in Hawthorne's romance, but also a use that he had come to identify in George Eliot's philosophical realism. Following a discussion of the pedantic quality of *Romola* in the essay on Eliot, in fact, he extended even further his demand for direct observation and, literally speaking, *unconventional* treatment. He portrayed Eliot's later work as marked by coldness—"the coldness that results from most of one's opinions being formed, one's mind made up, on many great subjects; from the degree, in a word, to which 'culture' had taken the place of the more primitive processes of experience" (*LC* 2:1008). Citing Alphonse Daudet on the point that "the personal impression, the effort of direct observation, was the most precious source of information for the novelist; that nothing could take its place; that the effect of books was constantly to check and pervert this effort. . . ; that we were ending by seeing everything through literature instead of through our own senses; and that in short literature was rapidly killing literature" (*LC* 2:1009), James rehearsed the argument that he had advanced allegorically, some years earlier, in *The Portrait of a Lady*—an argument, not incidentally, that Stein later would advance in relation to Picasso and herself.

It should not be surprising, therefore, that we find James revisiting the same issues, two decades later, when prefacing the much-revised *Portrait* for the New York Edition of his works. In the last of this preface's four movements, James explains how he had used Isabel's characterization of her own life not only as the subject of his characterization of her but also as the model for it. He had decided that she would have "mild adventures"—independent "of flood and field, of the moving accident, of battle and murder and sudden death"— but that she would not perceive them as such: the trick precisely had been to make "her sense of them, her sense *for* them," such that they mystically would convert "into the stuff of drama or, even more delightful word still, of 'story' " (*AN* 56). He had wanted to show "what an 'exciting' inward life may do for the person leading it even while it remains perfectly normal." He then points to his exemplary chapter, his "young woman's extraordinary meditative vigil," her "vigil of searching criticism," as a scene that "throws the action further forward than twenty 'incidents' might have done." He elaborates: "It was designed to have all the vivacity of incident and all the economy of picture. . . . It is a representation simply of her motionlessly *seeing*, and an attempt withal to make the mere still lucidity of her act as 'interesting' as the surprise of a caravan or the identification of a pirate. . . . It is obviously the best thing in the book, but it is only a supreme illustration of the general plan" (*AN* 57). And with that analysis, he reveals not only how he had understood character (in both senses) as implying incident and therefore *being* plot and how he had understood picture, as a result, as being narrative, but also how he had understood that principle—or at least now understands it—as allowing him to replay one level of romance in realism while repudiating another.

The keys lie in the subtle allusiveness of James's own retrospective gloss on the *Portrait*. Earlier in the preface, James had contrasted Shakespeare and George Eliot, on the one hand, as writers who created young women as important centers of interest, with such "expert painter[s]" as Dickens, Walter Scott, and, especially, Stevenson, on the other hand, as writers who have "preferred to leave the task unattempted" (*AN* 49).[15] In the same passage, he had cited George Eliot's line, "In these frail vessels is borne onward through the ages the treasure of human affection," an apparently gratuitous citation until one sees that James was portraying himself as one who belongs with Shakespeare and George Eliot in terms of subject, but, at least apparently, with Dickens, Scott, and Stevenson in terms of his treatment of it. He did so by punning on the key words "vessels" and "treasure" and by weaving them throughout his preface until, in the final paragraph quoted above, he converted Isabel Archer of the meditative vigil into a version of Jim Hawkins. Identifying Osmond as a treacherous, indeed piratical figure, based on her having seen him together with Madame Merle, Isabel Archer reenacts Jim Hawkins's identifying Long John Silver as a mutineer and pirate by overhearing him conspiring with his confederates. Isabel's parlor replaces the ship's hold, her mind replaces the apple barrel secreting Jim, and the treasure of affection that she seeks and that Osmond steals (not to mention the treasure of her inheritance) replaces the gold of *Treasure Island*.[16]

James had begun the 1880s, in short, with what would prove his longest novel and arguably his greatest piece of fictional portraiture, *The Portrait of a Lady*. Thematizing in it the issues of romance and of portraiture that he had raised in *Hawthorne* and had gone on to elaborate in the studies collected in *Partial Portraits*, he showed that romantic representations, pictorial and narrative, have aesthetic and ideological ramifications that require the corrective of a more realistic "searching criticism." If he was allegorizing in the *Portrait* a shift from romance to realism and from Hawthorne to himself, however, he went on to complicate the matter in the later 1880s, at least aesthetically, when he associated romance at once with Hawthorne's overly static characterization and with Stevenson's overly kinetic plotting—ultimately not antithetical quantities, of course, but rather complementary ones. By 1907, finally, James had arrived at an ambiguous sense of the difference between romance and realism and, more important, at an unambiguous sense of the virtues of Hawthorne and Stevenson as "painters." With his closing allusions to them in the preface to the *Portrait*, one might say, he was carrying to its terminus a line of argument he had begun in 1879, he was paying homage to two exemplars of romance, and he was continuing to legitimate his preference for realism and for picture by appealing, somewhat defensively, to the value of romance and story.[17]

༄

At the same moment that James was revising and prefacing *The Portrait of a Lady*, Gertrude Stein was composing her highly original *Three Lives*.[18] Influenced by Flaubert and by the Naturalist concern with scientifically derived psychological and sociological types, she seems to have invested in type in a way that would have conflicted, in theory at least, with her proclaimed Realist commitment to direct observation and unmediated representation—a problem faced by Flaubert, as well as by many of Stein's contemporaries.[19] One can argue, however, that Stein was setting the traditionally hagiographic form of the triptych against the grain of her apparently Naturalist premises, that she was elevating to the status of sacred icons three otherwise anonymous "cases," that she was writing, in a word, lives of saints, portraits of three evidently lesbian or bisexual women, portraits that individually depict victims of heterosexist patriarchy and that collectively constitute an indictment of what Adrienne Rich later named compulsory heterosexuality.[20] In this hypothesis, Stein was discovering in Cubism a method for using type compositionally while simultaneously deconstructing type thematically; she was not conducting Naturalist case studies so much as she was conducting Cubist studies *of* Naturalist case studies, Cubist studies, moreover, incorporating second-order discourse about themselves.

Stein was practicing, as William James wrote her upon receipt of *Three Lives*, "a fine new kind of realism."[21] Though James did not elaborate, we might say that Stein had succeeded in extending *Henry* James's procedures for melding incident and character, event and personality, narrative and portrait, into a more modernist idiom, albeit one equally focused on the second term of each binary; she also had extended James's manipulation of perspective into the multiperspectivalism emerging in modern painting. She had employed his techniques, moreover, to attack the problem that he had identified in George Eliot and in others and that the Realists in general had seen in their own work.

The Realists, that is, had been conscious of contradictions in their own program of unconventional representation and had built that consciousness into their work. They were writers, and painters, who strove for undistorted reference to unmediated reality, but who also understood the problems inherent in that goal and, indeed, theorized those problems in their work. Simply put, Realists perceived the distance between their mimetic ideals and any practical attempt to achieve them; and they made that distance one level of their subject matter.[22]

Stein brought that aspect of literary Realism to an extreme of autoreference, to precisely the extreme that the Cubists, rightly understood, were bringing painterly Realism. The Cubists, that is, made art nonillusionistic and nonimitative not by choice but by necessity; they understood that any attempt to reach an objective description of visual reality always occurred within a formal system, a visual language. Put simply, the Cubists began with the premise that one was painting. Their analyses and resyntheses of visual reality, as a result, produced pictures that explored the fundamental shapes of visual reality and the depth of field in which we perceive them; but those pictures also explored the formal language used by artists to combine and to arrange those shapes and to give them an illusion of depth. Cubism directed attention, then, not only to *the* painting in particular but also to *painting* in general—as genre, as idiom, as medium, even as material reality. And this, at least arguably, produced a *third* focus—not *painting* as an ahistorical proposition, but the *history* of painterly representation, including iconography, in its aesthetic and its ideological dimensions. This is certainly a focus Picasso built into *Les Demoiselles d'Avignon*, the quintessential early Cubist painting and the one Stein would associate, albeit ambiguously, with *Three Lives*.[23]

Recognizing the demanding complexity of *Three Lives*, Stein glossed her intentions in it on two subsequent occasions, the first twenty years distant from its composition, the second twenty years distant from the first. In her widely disseminated lecture, "Composition as Explanation" (1926), she named two of her works, *Three Lives* and *The Making of Americans* (completed circa 1911, published 1925), in the context of her describing her quest for a "continuous present" in composition; she then stated the key point of her lecture: "Continuous present is one thing and beginning again and again is another thing. These are both things. And then there is using everything" (CAE 31–32).[24] As I read this subtly cubistic lecture, Stein was assigning "composition" multiple and simultaneous orders of referent; in the key passage, she was referring not only to the artwork *as* composition, as commentators generally infer, but also to the composition *of* the artwork and, more obliquely still, to the historical composition that (circularly) *determines* the compositional process that, in turn, determines the compositional shape of the work. She virtually said as much when she wrote, some years later, "The business of Art as I tried to explain in Composition as Explanation is to live in the actual present, that is the complete actual present, and to completely express that complete actual present"—or, more simply and deterministically put, "the composition in which we live makes the art which we see and hear," but only for those artists with eyes and ears attuned to the contemporary (*LIA* 104–5, 165).

Stein returned to this autoanalysis of *Three Lives* some six months before her death. In the opening exchange of "A Transatlantic Interview" (1946), she claimed that Flaubert and, especially, Cézanne had given her "a new feeling about composition," essentially the idea of a decentered multiperspectival canvas, and that she had practiced it in *Three Lives* and, especially, in "Melanctha." Echoing "Composition as Explanation," and repeating an idea she had proffered often in the interim, she was arguing that a cultural moment decentered politically, militarily, and technologically produced among select artists the awareness that decentering should define the contemporary method, and that artists with this awareness, in turn, with proper consciousness of the contemporary, produced decentered artistic compositions. She then used this specific context of an emergent decenterment in the arts to name Henry James as her "forerunner," while differentiating his atmospheric composition ("he made it sort of like an atmosphere") from her presumably geographic composition ("I made it stay on the page quite composed"), his abstract composition, one infers, from her concrete composition (TI 15).[25]

Stein was encoding an even more significant claim, however, in the awkward syntax with which she then opposed to James's atmospherics and apposed to her concreteness a matter of realism: "it was not solely the realism of the characters but the realism of the composition which was the important thing, the realism of the composition of my thoughts" (TI 15–16). She seemed to be suggesting, with the first "realism," that she still had wanted to depict characters realistically in her compositions; and, with the second "realism," that she also had wanted to imbue her compositions either with verisimilitude or with veracity. In fact, she had produced compositions that did not *look like* reality—as Cubist pictures do not look like visual reality—but that were true to the conditions of contemporary reality; and she had abandoned verisimilitude in order to explore—as Cubist pictures do—the composition itself as a generic, idiomatic, mediumistic, even material reality. With the third "realism" in the series apparently apposite to the second, finally, she suggested that she also had attended to her thoughts as a composition—that is, not only depicted the evolving shape, or composition, of her thoughts, her consciousness, but also depicted the process by which some unnamed agent composed her thoughts, gave them that shape. And that agent, given Stein's sense of determinism, had to be the conformation of her historical moment in conjunction with the conformation of her psyche.

Stein began her career, in a word, with a work in serial portraiture that she subsequently mythologized as the originary point in a lifelong programmatic quest for a "continuous present." In her various commentaries, she depicted *Three Lives* and other works *as composition* in terms that converted Hawthornian-Jamesian story and picture into a more modern cinematic seriality of image, into "continuous succession"; and she depicted the *composition of* her works in terms that made them both a product of contemporary reality and a process reciprocally engaged in the creation of contemporary reality (see *LIA* 176–77). When she specifically formulated, in "A Transatlantic Interview," the history of her career as the evolution of her "composition," she made the crucial point for us that after *Tender Buttons* (1914), she had regained "a new interest in portraiture," but then, following the war, "began to be slowly impressed by the idea of narration," because "human beings are interested in two things. They are interested in the reality and interested in telling about it." Like other humans, Stein not only was concerned with the real and its representation, but also was interested in how the real gets represented, how the duration of the individual life or of the nation, to speak of narrative forms like biography or history, gets told. And at that point in her career, she says, she began "the narration consisting in plays at first," and then, "after the *Four Saints* [*in Three Acts*, 1927], the portrait narration began, and I went back to the form of narration, ... and I was asked to write a biography, and I said, 'No.' And then as a joke I began to write *The Autobiography of Alice B. Toklas*" (TI 18–19).[26]

In addition to being portrait narration, *The Autobiography of Alice B. Toklas* provided Stein many occasions for theorizing this generic hybrid: following the public success of the *Autobiography*, Stein wrote the six lectures with which she toured the United States in 1934–35 and which appeared as *Lectures in America* (1935); while touring, she wrote four additional lectures published as *Narration* (1935); and following the tour, she narrated its events in the sequel *Everybody's Autobiography* (1937). In these and in shorter pieces, Stein repeatedly worried two issues, the nature of biography and autobiography, and the nature of the novel and the detective story; and she evolved a general argument about genre in tandem with a specific argument about her presumably exemplary use of genre.[27] In essence, she argued that biography resembled the novel, that autobiography resembled the detective story, and that autobiography, largely for that reason, had replaced the novel as *the* modern narrative genre; as a corollary, she implied that her own massive novel, *The Making of Americans*, however modern as a novel, had been superseded by *The Autobiography of Alice B. Toklas*, itself superseded, in accordance with Stein's mythology of her "continuous present," by *Everybody's Autobiography*.

Addressing narrative at length in the *Lectures*, Stein explained that, in her portraits, she "had tried to tell what each one is without telling stories," and then, in her early plays, she "tried to tell what happened without telling stories"

(*LIA* 121–22); and she later explained that she had done the same thing in the novel, that *The Making of Americans* tells no story and accrues its exemplary modernity from that fact (*LIA* 184). She was claiming, in effect, that she first had depicted character in portraiture, then had conveyed incident in plays, and finally had negotiated character and incident in the novel, all without recourse to narrative; instead, she had converted narrative into the seriality of increment and compositional sum, and in the process, she also implied, she had shifted attention in each genre from reference to autoreference, to the "composition" in its multiple senses. In a brief and highly elusive passage built with repetitions of the verb "happens," Stein then distinguished novels from autobiographies on the grounds, apparently, that autobiographies tell "what happens" in two positive senses: novels relate inventions, while autobiographies relate actualities; novels, even if about their own composition, relate a virtual past of a narrator, while autobiographies, inherently about their own composition, relate the actual, or continuous, present of the author (*LIA* 184–85). She had reformulated the problem of narrative, in short, as a problem of narration.

Addressing that problem in *Narration*, Stein extended her inquiry to include the narrative genres of novel, history, biography, and autobiography (see *NAR* 43, 53). With reference to Defoe's *Robinson Crusoe* and to Boswell's *Life of Johnson*, for example, she revised distinctions tested in the *Lectures* by now stressing similarities in all forms of narration; perhaps more important, she was revealing the eighteenth-century precursors of *The Autobiography of Alice B. Toklas*, and she was exploring a key problem in its composition (see *NAR* 45, 60). In contrast to James emphasizing that novelists invent subjects while biographers and historians find them, that is, Stein emphasized the fact that, models notwithstanding, all three *construct* the subjects that they finally present. Invoking Vasari and Plutarch, she notes that biographers "make them [subjects] up so completely that if they are not invented, they might as well be they do not really feel that any one of the ones about whom they tell had any life except the life they are given by their telling"; biographers thus resemble historical playwrights or novelists (*NAR* 61). With an opaque reference to the *Autobiography*, however, she then went on to suggest that, like Defoe's Crusoe and Boswell's Johnson, her Toklas and her Toklas's Stein displace their real models. Not only did she *construct* the Toklas she presented, then, a Toklas who "might as well" have been invented, but, in so doing, she occluded the Toklas who lived prior to that construction and precluded Toklas's thereafter existing independently of it; in effect, she erased the real Toklas from history.[28]

That morose theme of erasure pervades *Everybody's Autobiography*. In its dense introduction, Stein professes her affection for Dashiell Hammett and for detective stories—though "I never try to guess who has done the crime"—and recounts a meeting in which the two writers had discussed autobiography (*EA* 4).[29] They seem to have concurred that nineteenth-century male writers, having confidence, could invent characters, while their female contemporaries, lacking confidence, could produce only conventional portraits based on conventional types; the situation reversed itself in the twentieth century, however, a reversal that Stein then connects, through an apparent non sequitur, to modern autobiography in general and to *Everybody's Autobiography* in particular (*EA* 5–6). Later recounting a similar conversation with William Seabrook about autobiography, Stein advances the parallel argument that "novels now cannot be written" because nineteenth-century writers could create "personalities"—could "dream" them and make them credible through Realist aesthetics—but twentieth-century mass media create personalities that seem more real, "and since there is so much publicity," she adds, no one "dream[s] about personalities. . . . And so autobiography is written" (*EA* 69).[30] Putting aside the question of criminality for a moment, it would follow from these conversations that a properly twentieth-century female writer should invent characters but, paradoxically, in the nonfictional genre of the autobiography; in the metadiscourse that traverses *Everybody's Autobiography*, Stein allows that she is doing just that.

In two passages in that metadiscourse, in fact, Stein redraws the comparison she had made in *Narration* between Defoe and Boswell, only now as a comparison between herself as autobiographical novelist in *The Making of Americans* and herself as autobiographical memoirist in *Everybody's Autobiography*. In the first passage, Stein notes that she had begun *The Making of Americans* with the idea of composite characters, but quickly had moved to the idea of "describing every one, every one who could or would or had been living" (*EA* 69)—with a radically Realist idea, that is, of enumerating "every one," as opposed to postulating an "everyone," in a process, as she had explained in *Lectures in America*, like that of "the cinema and series production."[31] In the second passage, she invokes a different mode of "series production," one she previously had invoked with reference to Henry Ford in the first *Autobiography*, and she likens *The Making of Americans* to "making automobiles" (*EA* 251). She was explaining, in effect, that she had used careful observation and representation of instances in an attempt to evade type, but inevitably had *created* type in the process, much as the projection of frames in cinema produces a continuous image and the line assembly of automobiles produces, say, the Model T. As she had said in the *Lectures*, a writer of novels "had to be remembering" (*LIA* 181) and thus, among other things, inevitably produces composites, types, models; but, paradoxically and simultaneously, as she says in *Everybody's Autobiography*, a writer of autobiography "do[es] not believe" herself (*EA* 68), and thus, among other things, inevitably *invents* whatever types she produces.

In the course of another discussion of *The Making of Americans*, Stein had argued that the lack of connection between individuals "is what makes detective stories such good reading, the man being dead he is not really in connection with any one" (*EA* 99). She regards this lack of connection as "why the only novels possible these days are detective stories, where the only person of any importance is dead"; and she infers from this that "the novel as a form of writing is dead, ... [because] characters in books do not count in the life of the reader the way they used to do and if they do not the novel as a form is dead" (*EA* 102). She regards epics, too, as dead because in epic "the death of the man meant the end of everything and now nothing is ending by the death of any one" (*EA* 213). Working backward toward origins, in other words, Stein finds detective stories contemporary because predicated on the death of *an* individual (and thus, by implication, *the* individual), novels outmoded because predicated on the life of the individual, and epics perfectly antique because predicated on the centrality of the heroic (masculine) individual. She previously had argued in *Narration*, moreover, that newspaper stories focus on the victim of a crime, but that detective stories, by contrast, merely use the victim to initiate the real textual process, the revealing of the killer (see *NAR* 40). And she now implies that autobiographies, appearances notwithstanding, likewise focus *not* on the past self—who is "dead," a victim of time who is unavailable to the present self—but on the revealing of the present self as the "killer" of that past self, as that self's successor.

Stein considered biography, in sum, to resemble the novel, and autobiography to resemble the detective story: the former tells a tale of the education of the central character, the latter a tale of the process of discovering who murdered the central character—who, put differently, effaced that character and thereby decentered the narrative. She told the first tale doubly in *The Autobiography of Alice B. Toklas*, its generic designation notwithstanding; the second tale in *Everybody's Autobiography*: "The first autobiography ... was a description and a creation of something that having happened was in a way happening not again but as it had been which is history which is newspaper which is illustration but is not a simple narrative of what is happening not as if it had happened not as if it is happening but as if it is existing simply that thing. And now in this book I have done it if I have done it" (*EA* 302–3). In the two autobiographies together, she advanced the genre that succeeded the novel by resembling the detective story; she represented the actuality of "what is happening" in the process of narration by telling, especially in the second text, a tale not only of missing persons and, in effect, of dead models, but also of their killers.

↩

In *The Marble Faun* (1860), Hawthorne used a crime story, the murder of an artist's model, to explore the relationship of representation to reality. In his preface to this romance of American expatriate artists, moreover, he first noted that he had "appropriated" for his sculptor-protagonist Kenyon "a magnificent statue of Cleopatra, the production of Mr. William Wetmore Story, an artist whom his country and the world will not long fail to appreciate"; but he then warned his reader, in the next breath, not to confuse Kenyon with Story.[32] He thus created a tension that can serve as a departure point for our inquiry into similar biographical appropriations. As a portraitist, James may have begun with a Realist aesthetics of close observation and accurate representation, but he went on to appropriate real persons as models in an increasingly stylized biographical portraiture; and, in his later phase, he produced intentionally experimental works of uncertain genre that verged on losing the biographical subject in an atmosphere of subtle perspectival shifts and autobiographical narration. Pushing much further in this direction, Stein began with the Cubist rejection of imitation and naturalistic representation, and she expressly declared the death of the model as the birth of modern painting (see *ABT* 55; *EA* 29; *P* 1, 7–8, 10); she produced radically experimental, multiperspectival portraits, and, in her later phase, also turned to a portrait narration whose apparent simplicity conceals a deeper complication, literally, of biography and autobiography.

James and Stein both understood the issue to be nothing less than the murder of reality by representation. As theorists and practitioners of portraiture, they explored two distinct but closely related aspects of that crime through two distinct but closely related senses of the term *model*. First, they knew that a representation always could resemble its real model but never would be identical with it, in part because the very composition that enabled artistic representation also compromised it. Second, they knew that conventions in the form of abstract models or types always compromised observation and representation, and that representation, in turn, inevitably generated new models and types. In effect, they explored how the effort to represent the real model with accuracy collided with the need to use abstract models in the representation. They also appear to have felt that the stakes were very high in portraiture, and that portraiture, consequently, provided not only the best venue for exploring the issues theoretically, but also a necessary venue for resolving them practically. The stakes were so high, of course, because the models in question were human subjects; and the stakes became extremely high when those subjects were the portraitists themselves.

Characteristically modern in worrying these questions, James and Stein also seem differently, successively, modern in how they posed them. With such succession in mind, we shall examine four works of biographical and autobiographical portraiture that James and Stein constructed along the principles, often inconsistent, put forth in their various commentaries. We shall see not only that they built narrative into each work of portraiture, for example, but also that they fit these portraits into larger intertextual narratives about themselves; and we shall see not only that they shifted from biography to autobiography in both intratextual and intertextual narrative, but also that they effected a more profound shift through *narration*—that they used "portrait narration," in Steinian parlance, to represent themselves as modern artists, while, simultaneously, embodying textually their claims to artistic modernity. We shall see, finally, that they took themselves as real models and constructed themselves as abstract models, as types, and that they did so with all the ambivalence encoded in the idiom "executing the model"—an ambivalence that passes genealogically from Hawthorne's *Marble Faun*, through James's *William Wetmore Story*, to Stein's *Autobiography of Alice B. Toklas*.[33]

To take up the cases at hand, James wrote *Hawthorne* and *Story* as works of romantic portraiture, studies in type, that together tell a narrative of the generations born in 1800, 1820, and 1840, with the Civil War as its climax and with James, first the young vanguardist, then the old veteran, as its hero. Portraying Hawthorne as exemplar of antebellum American critical naivete, and Story and friends as romantic sentimentalists, as antebellum provincials with cosmopolitan pretensions, moreover, he used the fact and the form of his narration to portray himself first as the ideal postbellum critic and critical thinker, and then as an inveterate cosmopolite with a shrewd eye for the real but a fond memory for the romantic. Stein wrote the *Autobiography* and *Four in America*, in turn, as studies in autobiographical and biographical "composition" that together coordinate gender wars, artistic wars, and the Great War of 1914–1918 in a generational narrative with the Great War as its crisis, the creation of modern art as its climax, and Stein as its hero. She first portrayed Toklas recalling, among other things, Picasso's constructing Stein as an icon in contrast to the public's ignoring Stein as an artist, and, through this portrayal, Stein offered the counterconstruction of herself as artist that, in itself, proved her artistry; she then used a serial group portrait of famous Americans, public icons of genius, to suggest the genealogy of her portraiture and thus, in the very same act, to claim her place as American genius.[34]

Needless to say, James and Stein rooted those portraits in precursivity. Commentators frequently have noted James's sense of Hawthorne as his precursor, but rarely have noted Stein's sense of James as hers. Not only did Alice B. Toklas observe, however, in a letter to Donald Sutherland written soon after Stein's death, that "of course James was the precursor alright," but she also added, in a subsequent letter, that "she [Stein] always liked to use his word—the *precursor*—in speaking of him."[35] I can find this word conspicuously *as James's* in only one place: titled "The Precursors," the opening chapter of *William Wetmore Story* expressly fixes the precursivity of the first generation of American expatriate artists as the book's central theme; moreover, it figures this company of precursors as a "picture"—"the sitters are all in their places, and the group fills the frame" (*WWS* 1:7–8, 16). Acutely conscious of genealogy, James pictured Hawthorne, Story, and friends as national and artistic precursors who enabled his expatriation and his art, while also necessitating the very different form his expatriation and art took; though severely critical, however, his pictures also glow with nostalgia for antebellum innocence. Equally conscious of genealogy, Stein pictured James, in effect, as her primary American precursor, and, with others like Cézanne, as a principal artistic precursor; thus, she could figure him as *the* American writer culminating the nineteenth century and herself, by implication, as *the* American writer inaugurating and defining the twentieth century.[36]

In *The Theory of the Avant-Garde*, Renato Poggioli has argued that the acute consciousness of *transition*, the conviction that one lives in a moment of political and cultural upheaval, generally entails an acute consciousness of precursivity, a preoccupation with predecessors and successors and with oneself as successor and predecessor. Poggioli calls transition "the agonistic concept par excellence, favorite myth of an apocalyptic and crisis-ridden era, a myth particularly dear to the most recent avant-gardes and, despite all appearances to the contrary, bound up with the futurist attitude"; and, with reference to precursivity, he argues that the myth of transition actually makes decadence and futurism two faces of the same coin. The decadent sees himself or herself as " 'being the last of a series,' " the futurist sees his or her function "to be the opening of a new series, or at least the preparing of its way," and so both, as exemplars, represent "lost generations."[37] Though we should not follow Poggioli too quickly to his tough conclusion and should not characterize James and Stein too easily as respectively decadent and futurist, we can use Poggioli's sound insight not only to compare James and Stein as characteristically modern in their shared consciousness of transition and precursivity, but also to contrast them as differently, again successively, modern in their specific formulations of transition and precursivity.

James lived from 1843 to 1916, Stein from 1874 to 1946. They strode a turbulent century, they saw its political crises as marking moments of cultural transition, but they differed sharply in their responses to those crises. In *Hawthorne* and *Story*, James declared the Civil War the end of American innocence and the Civil War together with the Franco-Prussian War the end of Euro-American civility; in his posthumous *Within the Rim and Other Essays* (1918), he took August 1914 not only as their final issue, but also as signaling perhaps the final moment of western civilization. In the *Autobiography* and *Four in America*, by contrast, Stein pronounced the Civil War the beginning of American modernity and the Great War of 1914–1918, its horrors notwithstanding, as the validation of American modernity abroad; in final works like *Wars I Have Seen* (1945) and *Brewsie and Willie* (1946), she took World War II not only as the grim fruition of those germinated horrors, but also as the premonition of a new democratic spirit. While James generally invested in edenic myths, in short, Stein generally invested in utopian myths, and their visions of cultural genealogy matched those investments: James was preoccupied with his *predecessors* and with himself as their terminal point, Stein with *herself* as successor and as originator of a new lineage.

We can focus the issues that we have raised in this chapter on that exact point of similarity and difference. Finding narrative or portraiture alone inadequate to the representation of reality, James and Stein sought ideal convergences, James absorbing narrative into the portrait, Stein portraying the act of narration, and, at a concurrent second level, James directing attention to the process of portraiture, Stein virtually restricting attention to that process. Finding representation itself inadequate to reality, moreover, they shifted emphasis from mimesis to semiosis, James exploring the nature and possibility of art, Stein exploring the nature and, increasingly, the impossibility of art, and, at a concurrent second level, James worrying the social utility of art in general and of himself as artist in particular, Stein proclaiming the social utility of *writing*, in the broadest sense of the term, in general, and of herself as *writer* in particular. Like other moderns, to put this differently, James and Stein each pushed art not only toward obsession with the moment and with the means of artistic production, but also toward obsession with the identity of artistic producers, pushed art, that is, toward the autoreferential and the autobiographical, a double push perfectly fitted to portraiture. But they played out this obsession with the present and with their roles in it, paradoxically, as a preoccupation with genealogy, a preoccupation, as Poggioli argues, that reveals a desire to "transcend the self" toward either the past or the future—a desire that James admitted but Stein denied.[38] And they did all this, finally, in works of portraiture overtly biographical but covertly autobiographical, works that purport to represent other subjects as real models but that inevitably recreate their authors as ideal models, works we now shall examine.

Two

THE GOOD AMERICAN

Hawthorne

> The good American of which Hawthorne was so admirable a specimen was not critical, and it was perhaps for this reason that Franklin Pierce seemed to him a very proper President.
>
> —HAWTHORNE

The year was 1878, and John Morley had just launched the English Men of Letters, a series of books designed to portray writers as "representative men, representative of great social, historical or philosophical forces." As his publisher Alexander Macmillan had noted, each book would be "a sort of Essay—biographical and critical." Prepared to regard Americans as English for purposes of this series, Morley commissioned the young novelist and critic Henry James to do Hawthorne, and James reluctantly obliged.[1] Drawing much of his material from Hawthorne's posthumous Note-Books (1868–72), and, especially, from George Parsons Lathrop's biographical *Study of Hawthorne* (1876), James delivered his *Nathaniel Hawthorne* (1879), a brief book that unfolded Hawthorne's life chronologically and that addressed his works, in turn, within that chronology.[2] It would be James's longest work of conventional literary portraiture and his major statement on his predecessor, extending a long review of Hawthorne's *French and Italian Note-Books* published in 1872 and anticipating another general essay, really a redaction of *Hawthorne*, published in 1896.[3]

At first glance, James met all terms of the assignment. He characterized antebellum America as a culture lacking history and social texture and, therefore, able to produce romantic but not realistic art; and he treated Hawthorne, the romantic artist of genius, as its representative figure. He did so by telling a biographical narrative, very heavily interleaved with literary criticism, from a single, apparently disinterested point of view. As the chapter titles suggest, he moved in general from Hawthorne's national and local heritage through his biographical particulars to the work that presumably emerged from them. Thus, he moved from biographical chapters on Early Years and Early Manhood to a critical chapter on Early Writings, focused on *Twice-Told Tales* and *Mosses from an Old Manse*. He brought a biographical chapter on Brook Farm and Concord to a discussion of *The Blithedale Romance*, and then segued to a critical chapter on The Three American Novels, about *The Scarlet Letter*, *The House of the Seven Gables*, and, again, *The Blithedale Romance*. Concluding that chapter with an extended comment on Hawthorne's campaign biography, *The Life of Franklin Pierce*, James next took up Hawthorne's resulting consulate in a chapter on England and Italy, with critical attention paid his Note-Books, *Our Old Home*, and, most especially, *The Marble Faun* (which James calls by its English title, *Transformation*). He concluded, finally, with a chapter on Last Years, emphasizing Hawthorne's response to the Civil War and noting his unfinished works.[4]

Put differently, James produced a work of emblematic literary portraiture that comprised biography and literary criticism and that focused on times, life, and work. He established the field of New England and America in the first half of the century and placed the biographical figure of Hawthorne on it; and, simultaneously, he established Hawthorne's biography as field and placed the figure of Hawthorne's art on it. Specifically, he elaborated a geographical and historical background—local, regional, and national—by articulating the spatial arc Salem–New England–United States with the temporal arc Colonies–American Revolution–Civil War. He placed on this background Hawthorne the man—solitary rather than social, provincial rather than cosmopolitan; and he merged this image with one of Hawthorne the writer, no true man of letters, though truly possessed of genius, no theoretician, but an empiricist and experimentalist. And, finally, he attributed to this artist-figure an art pure but cold, brilliant but *démodé*—an art romantic and allegorical rather than realistic and verisimilar, an art, therefore, dependent upon static characterization rather than dynamic narration.

At the same time, though, James complicated that picture in ways that prevented his *argument* about antebellum America as a thin culture from aligning with his *portrait* of Hawthorne as a romantic artist of genius. For one thing, he never established the extent to which he was arguing that antebellum cultural conditions produced Hawthorne and thus, indirectly, his work, or the extent to which he was simply depicting those conditions by using Hawthorne as an adequate exemplar. Further skewing that ambiguity, he was following Morley's and Macmillan's lead and was using as his representative man a genius—that is, someone by definition anomalous; and, even worse, he was using as representative of an essentially nonliterary culture a figure he regarded as a *literary* genius. In sum, James equivocated conceptually on the causal or noncausal relations between times and life and between life and work. Correspondingly, he equivocated compositionally between Hawthorne as a product of his times and Hawthorne as exemplar, and, moreover, between Hawthorne the product *or* exemplar and Hawthorne the anomaly. As a result, he presented Hawthorne's work sometimes as a product of his background, sometimes as a product of his genius, sometimes as a product of the very friction between them.

These complications largely owe to James's evolving sense of literary portraiture as combining biography and analytical criticism and to his equally evolving and complex senses of each of those disciplines. He understood biography, that is, to have cultural and social historiography as its proper context, and literary analysis to have evaluative criticism as its proper subtext. To be more specific, James had graduated in the 1870s from brief reviews to the essayistic portraits of *French Poets and Novelists* (1878). Though he considered Sainte-Beuve his exemplary critic, moreover, he remained deeply engaged with, and deeply influenced by, two thinkers with superficial resemblances but profound differences in orientation: Hippolyte Taine, the French historian on whom James wrote six pieces between 1868 and 1876, and Matthew Arnold, the English poet-critic whose *Essays in Criticism* James had reviewed at length, and with fervor, in 1865 (he would not essay a full portrait of Arnold until 1884).[5] Considered together, these reviews suggest not only that James was divided between Taine and Arnold as intellectual models, but also that he was divided about each one as an appropriate model.

James found Taine especially vexing. He characterized him in 1868 as "materialist," and "no sentimentalist," as a thinker who "studies man as a plant or as a machine. You obtain an intimate knowledge of the plant by a study of the soil and climate in which it grows, and of the machine by taking it apart and inspecting its constituent pieces." But, for James, "the question remains . . . as to whether [Taine's] famous theory of *la race, le milieu, le moment* is an adequate explanation of the various complications of any human organism" (*LC* 1:829). Some four years later, reviewing Taine's *History of English Literature*, James characterized him more explicitly as "a man with a method, the apostle of a theory," namely, that "the race, the medium, and the time . . . shape the phenomena of history" (*LC* 1:893). At this point in the piece, however, James's prose clots and his assessment becomes evasive and ambiguous. He argues, in essence, that no observer of literature would dispute that "a group of works is more or less the product of a 'situation,'" but that only M. Taine holds, first, that the situation accounts for all elements of the work, and, second, that his theory provides the methods for analyzing and explaining those elements (*LC* 1:843).

Arnold held very different principles, and James found him far more agreeable. James began his 1865 review by stressing the "inferiority of the English to the Continental school of criticism," he ascribed to Arnold's style "a decided French influence," and he used the fact that Arnold's essays had been "deemed little else than a wholesale schooling of the English press by the French programme" to justify Arnold's "remarks upon the 'provincial' character of the English critical method"—a point that foreshadows, uncannily, the aftermath of *Hawthorne* (*LC* 2:711–12). Though James suggests that Arnold himself may seem a bit too English, someone in whom "critical feeling and observation" were more in evidence than was any practice of "the science and the logic" of the analyst, James concludes that his program has precisely the virtues of treating both "plain facts" and "exalted fancies" and of taking "*high ground*, which is the ground of theory" (*LC* 1:713, 717). Throughout the review, in fact, James characterizes Arnold's critical method less as analysis than as reasoned and principled evaluation: the function of criticism in Arnold's program, he approvingly paraphrases his subject's key idea, is "simply to get at the best thought which is current,—to see things in themselves as they are,—to be disinterested" (*LC* 1:715).

As an ersatz literary historian under the influence of Taine, James was analyzing Hawthorne's culture to advance an argument about the sociological determinants of his life, and, through his life, his work; he also was analyzing Hawthorne's life itself to advance an imbricated argument about psychological determinants of his work. To the extent that he actually did so, he faced (or created) one problem. He had to distribute causes between Hawthorne's almost static "racial" predisposition as New Englander and as American, on the one hand, and the fluid and mutable cultural conditions of Hawthorne's epoch, on the other hand; and he also had to distribute them between heredity and cultural circumstances *together*, on the one hand, and Hawthorne's unique power as an artist of genius, on the other hand. But the fact remains, of course, that James followed the Tainean program only to a limited, and deceptive, extent, treating *race*, *milieu*, and *moment*, as I have intimated, less as necessary and sufficient causes of the Hawthorne phenomenon than as the conditions for which he would use Hawthorne as adequate exemplar.

James, that is, did not employ Taine's theory as explanatory device so much as he deployed it as rhetorical device, and this owes, in large part, to his commitment to Arnold's program. As an Arnoldian critic, James not only was observing and analyzing but also was evaluating Hawthorne's culture, not only was explaining but also was evaluating Hawthorne's capacities as an artist, not only was elucidating but also was evaluating Hawthorne's individual works. In doing so, however, James had to contend with a culture whose actualities he found incommensurate with the potential of Hawthorne's genius, on the one hand, and a culture whose possibilities he found sometimes to exceed Hawthorne's capacity to imagine, on the other. He also had to contend with a literary genius he found to exceed many of its own productions, a man of whose genius, he would write in 1887, "*The House of the Seven Gables* and *The Scarlet Letter* gave imperfectly the measure" (*LC* 2:269). To add to the problem, moreover, James wanted to treat Hawthorne on the latter's own historical terms, to grant him his *données*, but he also wanted to treat him in terms of the best thought current: Hawthorne the romancer, in effect, had to survive in the modern atmosphere of realism.

Though more than enough in themselves to produce complications, James's ambivalences over the substance of literary portraiture combined with his ambivalences over its form. Though he construed the genre, again, as conjoining biography and criticism, he generally was inclined, as we have seen, to devalue biography in favor of criticism—to the extent, in the case of *Hawthorne*, that Morley evidently had to remind him of his contractual obligations.[6] James obviously had no intention of writing a biographical narrative about an essentially boring life, but set out, instead, to produce a portrait of an interesting mind—or, more properly, "genius." To the extent that he employed biographical sequence, he did so as would any subtle narrativist—he did not unfold the linear chronicle of events that his chapter titles might suggest, but rather wove a complex, multilinear fabric of different orders of event.[7] And that generated a picture that he elaborated as would any subtle portraitist—he handled figure-field relationships not as static, partitioned concentricities of times, life, and work, but as dynamic, interpenetrating elements in a complex composition.

In addition, James employed a rather more complex point of view than first appears. In essence, *Hawthorne* moves chronologically from 1804 to the 1860s, while also counting from fifty years ago, to forty years ago, to thirty-five years ago, and so on, along an overlapping chronology either descending or ascending, depending upon one's historiographical bent, to what James frequently calls "the present day" (see, e.g., 331, 340–41, 371, 380, 381, 397). James dates events, then, from two distinct counterpoints of reference and narrates them accordingly. He tells an indicative narrative of events, as it were, with reference to the chronology of Hawthorne's life, while simultaneously telling a subjunctive narrative of what experiencing them must have been like to Hawthorne, as James now can imagine that. He thus layers events, imagined responses to them, and commentary on that imagining. And this suggests that James already was taking the function of retrospective portraiture to be one of recovering, sympathetically, points of view rather than incidents in a way that foreshadows the techniques of *The Portrait of a Lady* and even, distantly, the radical impressionism of his late fiction and nonfiction.

In sum, then, James had accepted a commission to write a conventional kind of biographical essay, one that required him to have a thesis about American society that he could illustrate, systematically, with a discussion of Hawthorne's life and work. To a large extent, he complied with his charge, but his current influences and his general aesthetic preferences determined the nature of that compliance. Taine provided him a comprehensive cultural theory, one attractive by virtue of its scope and its theoretical, rather than empirical, basis; Arnold provided him, similarly, a comprehensive literary critical program. Yet Taine's theory also repelled James precisely in its claim to comprehensiveness and in its pretense to scientific principles, while Arnold's program pleased him precisely to the extent that it leavened its imported French theoreticism with an English practicality. Always less devoted to promulgating social theory than to painting social effects, always less interested in historical explanation than in aesthetic evaluation, always less persuaded by deterministic philosophy than committed to the power of will, James inevitably leaned from Taine toward Arnold, and, for this and other reasons, leaned from biography, historiography's stepchild, toward the art of criticism.

He bent the lines of his biographical narrative, consequently, to shape a critical portrait, and he shaped it around a schematic that set simplicity against complication. He already had fixed this leitmotif in his 1872 review of Hawthorne, which he concluded on the note that Hawthorne's response to Europe, as evidenced in his Note-Books, attests to "his loyalty to a simpler and less encumbered civilization" (313–14). He later opened *Hawthorne* on the same note of Hawthorne's "simple life" and of his "simplicity" in general (319–20), the effect of his origin and upbringing in "a simple, democratic, thinly-composed society," and, again, he came around to Hawthorne's European Note-Books: "the simplicity which is on the whole the leading characteristic of their pages is, though the simplicity of inexperience, not that of youth" (430). The distinction, a crucial one, allowed James to use Hawthorne as a metonymy for Americans, and Americans as a metonymy for America, for an event such as the Civil War could confer experience but not age, and it was James's central point, as we shall see, that the Civil War inaugurated "a social revolution as complete as any the world has seen," that the Civil War "introduced into the national consciousness a certain sense of proportion and relation, of the world being a more complicated place than it had hitherto seemed." The "good American," having thus "eaten of the tree of knowledge," gained through the war the capacity for critical thought (427–28).

James, of course, was also using Hawthorne as a means to portray himself as just such a postbellum "good American." As most commentators now agree, James suffered a considerable anxiety of influence with respect to Hawthorne, and *Hawthorne*, as a result, reveals as much about its author as about its subject.[8] Commentators have proffered only partial and disarticulated answers to the questions of precisely *what Hawthorne* reveals about James and precisely *how* it reveals him, however, because they have tended to take Hawthorne's mastery of literary romance as James's central point of resistance. If we consider, rather, Hawthorne's imputed *incapacity for critical thought* as the most inclusive trait that James ascribes to him, then we can attend, and indeed must attend, to the substantial portion of *Hawthorne* that does *not* treat its subject as artist. We will find, I believe, that the issue for James, with broad ramifications, was not primarily romance versus realism in art, but, more comprehensively and profoundly, romantic naivete versus realistic criticism in cultural and political values and in cultural and political figures, as evidenced by one's choice of literary mode for expressing the former and representing the latter.

Such a focus, moreover, will allow us to rearticulate James's conceptual and compositional conflicts with his anxiety of influence, will allow us to see that his conflicted senses of cultural theory, of literary criticism, and of the genre of literary portraiture not only led to complications in *Hawthorne* but also became, explicitly and implicitly, part of its subject. We shall consider, first, that James constructed Hawthorne as a type of American and, more specifically, as a type of American man of letters; second, that he employed this typical figure allegorically, his incessant carping at Hawthorne's own allegorism notwithstanding, and that he was allegorizing not only antebellum aesthetics, as is commonly understood, but also, if less obviously, antebellum politics; third, that he was merging, albeit gingerly, his picture of Hawthorne with one of himself, and once again, not just in the realm of aesthetics but also in that of politics; and, fourth, that he elaborated this merger in a series of texts that included *Hawthorne*. We shall see, in short, that James was using Hawthorne to figure not only the romantic artist that he had to surpass, but also the romantic portraitist that he *was surpassing* in *Hawthorne*; we also shall see, however, that while he sought to reveal that, unlike Hawthorne, he *was* thinking critically, he also revealed, doubtless inadvertently, that he too had fallen into romance and, in fact, had done so in *Hawthorne* itself.

⤺

The conceptual problems in James's text surface immediately, in two long opening paragraphs in which he sets out an expository thesis as prologue to the biography proper. Hawthorne "has the importance," he argues in the first, "of being the most beautiful and most eminent representative of a literature"; he is "the most valuable example of the American genius," a genius not primarily literary; he "has the advantage of pointing a valuable moral," namely, and famously, "that the flower of art blooms only where the soil is deep, that it takes a great deal of history to produce a little literature, that it needs a complex social machinery to set a writer in motion," but that "American civilization has hitherto had other things to do than to produce flowers" (319–20). In each instance, James specifically attributes Hawthorne's command on his and our attention to Hawthorne's status as exemplar: he is *important* as a *representative*, *valuable* as an *example*, *advantageous* in pointing a moral *lesson*. At the same time, however, he has presented this representative man as an example of precisely what the culture did not typically produce: a literary figure.

He appears to resolve these problems in the second paragraph, where he uses local typicality to mitigate that national anomalousness. Despite "the absence of the realistic quality," James argues, Hawthorne remains "intensely and vividly local" and, indeed, "testifies to the sentiments of the society in which he flourished almost as pertinently (proportions observed) as Balzac and some of his descendants . . . testify to the manners and morals of the French people." Hawthorne lacked theory, system, and a capacity for realism; he had not essayed "an account of the social idiosyncrasies of his fellow-citizens"; yet he "virtually offers the most vivid reflection of New England life that has found its way into literature" (320–21). In effect, James slides the key term *reflects* from its meaning of "depicts" to that of "exemplifies," and through this slippage, he generates a thesis: antebellum American culture could produce only a romantic artist; Hawthorne depicted New England life romantically and, therefore, he exemplifies American culture. *Why* this is so remains, at this point, moot, and James continues to beg the issue with the even more egregious manipulation of terms with which he closes the paragraph and the argument.[9]

In fact, moreover, James has fused—or confused—the alleged typicality of Hawthorne's romantic genius with the atypicality, as it were, of his genius for romance. That is, James ambiguates the key word "genius," just as he had the term *reflects*, by using it here and throughout *Hawthorne* to mean not only prevailing spirit of time and place, but also, and without clear differentiation, transcendent talent. He asserts, in effect, that the antebellum American genius—the *Zeitgeist*—was a fundamentally romantic one, that Hawthorne *had* a fundamentally *romantic* genius and *was* fundamentally a *genius* at romance. A typical New Englander and, especially, American by virtue of *having that genius*, Hawthorne also remains atypical by virtue of *being a genius*: Hawthorne as "representative" thus connects to Hawthorne as "genius" by way of a non sequitur, and James, through this second lexical slippage, generates the paradoxical aspect of his primary thesis: a nonliterary culture can throw up a literary genius as its representative. In much the same paradoxical way, New England typifies America by being its oldest and originary section—at least in the Jamesian view—but it also remains anomalous precisely by virtue of being the section with the most history in a nation that has virtually none.

Not surprisingly, James replays these conceptual problems in the metaphoric pattern of the same two paragraphs. Figuring Hawthorne as an element in nature before allowing him to emerge as a human in culture, James lifts straight from Lathrop's biography the image of Hawthorne as a flower of American genius—Hawthorne's name, of course, facilitating the trope.[10] Unlike Lathrop, however, James stresses that the sweetly fragrant flower remained delicate because grown in a soil too thin to nourish robust flowers: what James calls, already metaphorically, "the general flatness of the literary field," becomes further and clumsily metaphorized as the thin soil that seems to cause the flatness (319–20). James can add relief to that flatness and a curious kind of depth to that soil, however, by localizing Hawthorne as a New Englander: "Out of the soil of New England he sprang—in a crevice of that immitigable granite he sprouted and bloomed" (320)—a crevice apparently deep enough for Hawthorne to be "deeply rooted in the soil" (322).

The tortured trope has as many tensions and conflicts as does the abstract argument it presumably serves to make concrete. Simply put, a brief history cannot produce realistic art any more than a thin soil can produce robust flowers; but a small pocket of accumulated history *can* produce romantic art just as a small pocket of soil *can* produce a modest, even exquisite, flower. Neither the general history nor small pocket, however, produces culture, any more than untended soil—thin *or* accumulated—produces horticulture. In fact, the small and isolated pocket of history will produce a distorted and isolated effusion of culture, just as a small and isolated pocket of soil will produce inbred and isolated flowering shrubs. This would all seem to suggest that the art so produced would be uncultured art, just as the flowers produced would be wildflowers. And *this*, finally, seems to allow James to claim that New England could produce a natural romantic genius, but that America could not produce a powerful artist and a realistic art.[11]

In this opening argument, then, James has tried to make Hawthorne a representative, simultaneously, of a regional part and of a national whole—a representative of New England and of antebellum America—in order to make him, ultimately, representative of the best that antebellum America could offer. And he carries precisely this uneasy simultaneity into the third paragraph, where he begins his biography proper: "Hawthorne sprang from the primitive New England stock; he had a very definite and conspicuous pedigree. He was born at Salem, Massachusetts, on the 4th of July, 1804, and his birthday was the great American festival, the anniversary of the Declaration of national Independence" (322). Once again embedding the local in the national, he begins his narrative by moving here and in subsequent passages from Hawthorne's colonial and, thus, *prenational ancestry* to Hawthorne's own postrevolutionary and, thus, *national identity*. In the same rhetorical maneuver, he shifts metaphorically from floriculture to animal husbandry (*stock, pedigree*) to human history, while he shifts generically from the pastoral to the historiographical. Though he also seems to shift from the allegorical to the biographical, he reconverts instantly, in the very same sentence, biographical fact—birthdate—into an emblem.

James himself intimates that he was constructing this concentricity of Salem, New England, America (341) and, though he never entirely resolves discrepancies between these places as synecdoches for broader forces, he does manage to produce a coherent picture of the result—Hawthorne the man. He presents a youth in his "small and homogeneous society," in his "provincial, rural community," with little contact "with what is called the world" (319). The youth becomes a "sceptic and dreamer and little of a man of action" (325), "a man but little disposed to multiply his relations, his points of contact, with society" (339), a man who ignored "the good society of his native place" (354). James seems so intent on carrying forward into Hawthorne's adulthood his depiction of him as a lonely, provincial boy, in fact, that he depopulates the story, places Hawthorne virtually alone on the canvas. In effect, he allows the mature Hawthorne only two relationships—his marriage to Sophia Peabody and his lifelong friendship with Franklin Pierce—and, as we shall see, James employs both relationships emblematically, the first to figure community and the second to figure polity.

In accordance with his larger designs, James also converts his solitudinous Salemite and New Englander into an equally solitudinous but additionally provincial American. He sets up and then executes his portrayal of a much older Hawthorne, making his first trip abroad when in middle age. This Hawthorne becomes a traveler "exquisitely and consistently provincial" (430), a man who remains in England "an outsider," "a stranger," "a man who remains to the end a mere spectator (something less even than an observer)," who "lacks the final initiation into the manners and the nature" of the English (433); and a man who remains in Italy, similarly, an "ordinary tourist," his observations "superficial" and, in essence, those of a foreigner (439). He becomes James's "intense American" who looks "at all things, during his residence in Europe, from the standpoint of that little clod of western earth which he carried about with him as the good Mohammedan carries the strip of carpet on which he kneels down to face towards Mecca" (448). And this clod, James would make clear in his redaction of 1896, was that of his "old Puritan consciousness" (465).[12]

Hawthorne the man, in short, emerges from a nexus of *race, milieu,* and *moment* that Hawthorne the exemplar must represent—and here the portrait becomes complicated. When James begins the biography proper, reminding us that Hawthorne was born on Independence Day, he adds that on this holiday "the great Republic enjoys her acutest fit of self-consciousness" (322). He then shifts, almost immediately, from biographical narrative of Hawthorne's lineage to portrait of Hawthorne's mind assimilating that lineage, shifts from Hawthorne's ancestry to Hawthorne's consciousness of it. He quotes Hawthorne on the "figure of that first ancestor" haunting him (323) and, more important, quotes him imagining one of his "forefathers" complaining to another that their descendent had become "a writer of story-books!" (325). James breaks in to observe that "a hundred years of Salem would perhaps be rather a deadweight" for a family such as the Hathornes to carry (326) and concludes that Hawthorne's response to that burden included a feeling of intense "continuity" with his "predecessors," a feeling James regards as peculiarly American in its obsessiveness (327–29).

Though James later concocts an ingenious hypothesis about how Hawthorne the romantic artist employed fancy to disemburden Hawthorne the man of this "old Puritan consciousness" (365), he depicts him, more generally, as proudly absorbed in his ancestry, "as any New Englander must be, measuring the part of that handful of half-starved fanatics who formed his earliest precursors, in laying the foundations of a mighty empire" (368); that absorption, indeed, defines Hawthorne's "historic consciousness" (370).[13] James then converts Hawthorne's consciousness, however, into *self-consciousness*, converts his obsession with the past into an insecurity about it and about his place in the present. He finds Hawthorne "mistrust[ful] of old houses, old institutions, long lines of descent"—of *continuities* in general—and finds him "an American of Americans" in this mistrust (417). He extends that putative mistrust of historical continuity, moreover, to one of present community, to "his constant mistrust and suspicion of the society that surrounded him, his exaggerated, painful, morbid national consciousness" (434).

In his review of 1872, James had characterized Hawthorne as "the last pure American" (313), and the idea, already ambiguous in 1872, remains equally so in 1879. He apparently wants to take the racial characteristics that Hawthorne inherited from his New England ancestors and to isolate them in the form in which they appeared in Americans of a particular generation, the one he identifies as "that generation which grew up with the century, . . . [with] the young Republic" (426). He makes Hawthorne, then, the product of the Puritan *race*, the New England *milieu*, and the antebellum *moment*. He makes him emblematic, then, of that particular nexus as part of American experience. Yet he also makes him emblematic of that nexus as synecdochic for American experience more broadly defined geographically and chronologically—Hawthorne having been born on the early birthday of the Revolution that established the Republic and having died during the Civil War that threatened its existence. And further complicating this picture of Hawthorne as terminal, he again shifts point of view from his own to Hawthorne's own, reminding us that Hawthorne had *seen himself* as "the last of the old-fashioned Americans" (441).[14]

At the crux of this portrayal lies *self-consciousness*. James first had suggested that New Englanders especially, Americans generally, lack as individuals the social confidence, the sense of proper social place, that history confers on the typical Englishman or Frenchman (356–57). He eventually abstracts individuals, however, into exemplars of national identity, converts individuals into types for *race*:

> Americans are, as Americans, the most self-conscious people in the world.... They are conscious of being the youngest of the great nations, of not being of the European family, of being placed on the circumference of the circle of civilisation rather than at the centre, of the experimental element not having as yet entirely dropped out of their great political undertaking. The sense of this relativity, in a word, replaces that quiet and comfortable sense of the absolute, as regards its own position in the world, which reigns supreme in the British and in the Gallic genius. (434–35)[15]

That abstracting has no small consequence for the point of his essay, for it means that he has abstracted Hawthorne, mistrustful of history as of society, and marginal to his society, into a United States likewise distrustful of world history and global society, and marginal to the late nineteenth-century society of states—an awkward position for "a mighty empire," though perhaps not surprising for "the youngest of the great nations."

We should recall, however, that James was writing *Hawthorne* for a series called English Men of Letters, and that his assignment required him to portray Hawthorne not, generally, as representative *man* but, specifically, as representative *man of letters*. This must have proved challenging, since he had argued in 1872 that Hawthorne had "written from the impulse to keep up a sort of literary tradition in a career singularly devoid of the air of professional authorship," but that "never, surely, was a man of literary genius less a man of letters. He looks at things as little as possible in that composite historic light which forms the atmosphere of many imaginations" (308–9). Rather than risk advancing an argument, in 1879, based wholly on a negative proposition, he elects to argue that antebellum conditions enabled only a certain type of man of letters, Hawthorne being the exemplar, and he derives these conditions by extending his points of 1872: American culture failed to supply either a continuity of past authors or a community of living authors, and, as cause and consequence, antebellum American society failed to make possible the profession of authorship.[16]

He argues, specifically, that American literary men of Hawthorne's generation did not form a class and that "the best things come, as a general thing, from the talents that are members of a group." The conditions that conspired to produce Hawthorne the solitary and provincial man, in other words, also conspired to make him a solitary and provincial worker, and "the solitary worker loses the profit of example and discussion; he is apt to make awkward experiments; he is in the nature of the case more or less of an empiric" (342). Moreover, though he now revises his view of 1872 by characterizing Hawthorne as one of the few Americans "who had taken up literature as a profession" (343), he stresses the facts that American society in Hawthorne's era would not support that profession and that Hawthorne, in any case, was inept in the business aspects of such professional authorship as did exist. He rehearses Lathrop's "sorry account" of Hawthorne's brief editorship of *The American Magazine of Useful and Entertaining Knowledge* and of his compiling a *Universal History*, and he goes on to suggest, with some condescension, the "pitiful" and "touching" aspects of the episode: "The simple fact was that for a man attempting at that time in America to live by his pen, there were no larger openings; and to live at all Hawthorne had, as the phrase is, to make himself small" (346-47).

It is difficult to imagine what kind of community Hawthorne's contemporaries, as James depicts them, *could* have formed. Though he characterizes Hawthorne's classmate and friend Longfellow as one "who divides with our author the honour of being the most distinguished of American men of letters" (333), the utterly ambiguous, left-handed quality of the compliment certainly diminishes its force. Poe, less ambiguously, was "a man of genius," but one whose "collection of critical sketches of [his fellow] American writers is probably the most complete and exquisite specimen of *provincialism* ever prepared for the edification of men" (367); and Thoreau, his "genius" likewise beyond question, "was worse than provincial—he was parochial; it is only at his best that he is readable" (391-92). James's point is clear: the antebellum period could produce isolated geniuses, but isolated geniuses cannot become true men of letters. In the postbellum period, by contrast, "an American as cultivated as Hawthorne, is now almost inevitably more cultivated, and, as a matter of course, more Europeanised in advance, more cosmopolitan." And that is why James will allow that "the last of the earlier race of Americans Hawthorne was ... far from being," but also why he will continue to "think of him as the last specimen of the more primitive type of men of letters" (442).

James was using the phrase, clearly, not to denote professional authorship but, rather, to connote cosmopolitan and critical authority. Such authority implied that a man of letters thought broadly, thought systematically, wrote critical commentary as well as imaginative—or fanciful—literature, wrote with a consciousness of belonging to an aristocracy—or republic—of letters, and wrote within the advanced intellectual currents of his moment. Such a man of letters, it follows, had to exist not only within a social and historical context that would sponsor the production of letters, but also within one that could sustain a confraternity of the lettered; such a man, like Arnold, had to have theoretical and critical capabilities, and he had to have equally and coordinately the critical and the imaginative—not just fanciful—faculties. Since his earliest reviews of the mid-1860s, in fact, James had been opposing to his type of the European artist as socially gregarious and theoretically initiated, his countertype of the American artist as isolated experimentalist and empiric. Hawthorne was the countertype *en fleur*.

The self-consciousness that marked Hawthorne as human type, moreover, also marked him as artistic type. As a New Englander and antebellum American, Hawthorne could be only solitary and provincial; as a solitary and provincial man, he could be only a certain type of writer: he was not a proper man of letters but a romancer, not a theorist but an experimentalist. James had opposed to the social certainties of the French and British an American insecurity, and, in parallel fashion, he opposed to the aesthetic certainties of French theoreticism (read: Realism) and of English empiricism the aesthetic insecurities of American experimentalism (read: Romanticism). And just as he had abstracted Hawthorne as an asocial being in America into America as an asocial entity within the family of nations, so did he abstract Hawthorne as isolated romantic artist in America into antebellum American romantic artistry as isolated in the world—abstracted Hawthorne into the figure, that is, of a young nation with a young culture and a jejune aesthetics. What James characterized as the positive experiment in democracy could produce, in his view, only a negative experimentalism in art. We soon shall see, though, that the question of democracy, more than that of art, formed his real subject.

Before doing so, however, we must note that James *did* treat Hawthorne's art at great length, elaborating, in essence, two fundamental, and endlessly repeated, propositions. First, Hawthorne practiced romance rather than realism; though James waffles a bit, he clearly intends by Hawthorne's failure to be realistic Hawthorne's dissimilarity from the specifically Realist program then associated with the French and defended, albeit with ambivalence, by the young vanguardist James.[17] Second, Hawthorne's romance has "coldness" as its primary feature—a metaphorical equivalent, of course, for "fancy." Coldness is both the psychological cause and the aesthetic effect of fancy, and it is fancy that James attributes to Hawthorne's background and describes, variously, as his fundamental virtue and fundamental fault.[18] But "fancy" itself turns out to be only a middle term. It leads one, that is, to picturesqueness and to symbolism and, finally, to allegory; and these compromise the kind of portraiture that James, in this period, was beginning to theorize as the central aspect of the novel and to practice as the central element in his literary criticism.

Indeed, James's opening comments about Hawthorne's lack of realism pertain directly to *portraiture*—the term is used three times (321); and they lead to an odd pattern in James's use of the cognates "picture" and "picturesqueness." He finds picture appropriate to the genre of the short tale, for example, and he does not object to Hawthorne's having used gloomy subjects in his tales for their "picturesqueness, their rich duskiness of colour, their chiaroscuro" (364). That is why he speaks positively of "Young Goodman Brown" as "not a parable, but a picture, which is a very different thing" (396). At the same time, though, he disapproves a tendency of picture *when picturesque* to become allegorical, for "allegory, to my sense, is quite one of the lighter exercises of the imagination" and "has never seemed to me to be, as it were, a first-rate literary form" (366). This all suggests, of course, that he approves emblematic picture only to the extent that it approaches verisimilitude from the side of treatment and does not stray far from it on the side of subject—though "Young Goodman Brown" barely meets the latter criterion. And he approves it, moreover, only in the short form, for the long form, for James, must become novelistic.

James makes the term "picture," in fact, a pejorative when discussing Hawthorne's longer works. Though Hawthorne *had* "cared for the deeper psychology" (368), even his "masterpiece" *The Scarlet Letter* reveals "a want of reality and an abuse of the fanciful element—of a certain superficial symbolism" (404). In *The Scarlet Letter* and, especially, *The House of the Seven Gables*, Hawthorne presented "figures rather than characters," "pictures rather than persons," "types, to the author's mind, of something general." Hawthorne gave us drama "not . . . for the dry facts of the case, but for something in it which he holds to be symbolic and of large application, something that points a moral and that it behooves us to remember" (413; and see 414–15). He transcended this in *The Blithedale Romance*, achieved particularity in characterization, even "a certain human grossness" and concreteness (see 419–20). But he backslid in *The Marble Faun*, which James wishes had fewer "picturesque conceits" and *more* of "real psychology"; Hawthorne had pushed the "unreal" too far, had entered "a vague realm of fancy," had practiced "quite a different verisimilitude" (447). And that is precisely what James was doing in his *Hawthorne*.

༄

Lacking history and social texture, as James proposes, antebellum America had no culture to display and could neither produce nor sustain a novelist and realist to represent its actualities; but it did have nature to display and could produce and sustain a primitive romancer and fantasist to convert its actuality into ideality, to use its surface to symbolize a different depth. That argument informs the infamous passage in *Hawthorne* that incensed many contemporary reviewers—James's portrayal of New England and America as marked by absence, his claim that "one might enumerate the items of high civilization, as it exists in other countries, which are absent from the texture of American life, until it should become a wonder to know what was left." Echoing Hawthorne's preface to *The Marble Faun*, though actually reversing its point, James then famously enumerates those missing items of culture while never specifying the "good deal [that] remains" (351–52). What remains is a meager past that an artist of fancy must make "picturesque" in order to make interesting (368), and what remains is the self isolated on an unpopulated landscape, the self that an artist must look *into* for material.[19]

In essence, as James again would make explicit, a new culture lacking history, a rural culture lacking metropolis, a democratic culture lacking etiquette, left an author with only retrospection and introspection—the former, moreover, into a past in need of romantic transformation because so lacking in historical density, and the latter into a self in need of romantic construction because so lacking in social relations. The antebellum period in America, that is, was a time when "there were no great things to look out at (save forests and rivers)" and when, as a result, "the cultivated classes" would have appreciated "a writer who would help one to take a picturesque view of one's internal possibilities," who would "find in the landscape of the soul all sorts of fine sunrise and moonlight effects" (383). It is to the point of James's own sense of aesthetics and politics, of course, that he fails to associate the democratic with *prospection*, as Whitman famously had done, for example, in *Democratic Vistas* (1870)—precisely the point over which James and Howells would argue with specific reference to Hawthorne (and *Hawthorne*) and with broader reference to the appropriate program for Realism in America.[20]

Following the crucial passage on American absences and their effects on romance, in fact, James associates Hawthorne's "story-telling faculty" and his affection for observation of small things with "a democratic strain" in his personal disposition (354).[21] His articulation of a general aesthetic tendency with a general ideological tendency surprises, for he repudiates, soon after, any direct linkage between Hawthorne's aesthetics and his specific politics, his "cast[ing] his lot with the party of conservatism, the party opposed to change and freshness. The people who found something musty and mouldy in his literary productions would have regarded this quite as a matter of course; but we are not obliged to use invidious epithets in describing his political preferences" (373). James, however, is being either ironic or disingenuous, for throughout *Hawthorne* he associates his subject's literary simplicity with an ideological simplicity—that is, with an untheorized practice; and, as we shall see, he almost explicitly identifies Hawthorne's allegiance to romance, denigrated from the start as an antiquated aesthetics, with his allegiance to the Democratic Party and, by implication, an antiquated politics.

James's weave, however, is even denser, for just as he correlated Hawthorne's life with his aesthetics, so does he correlate his life with his politics. In essence, he overlays two distinct couplings of personal relationship and public action: first, Hawthorne's marriage and his sojourn at Brook Farm, and, second, his friendship with Franklin Pierce and his conservative position on slavery before and during the Civil War. James links Brook Farm as an institution of progressive social experimentation to the Civil War as the event that convulsed but ultimately redeemed the great national experiment in democracy; and, more broadly, he links marriage as the paradigmatic sacrament of personal union to the Civil War as the paradigmatic and, for James, traumatic ritual of public disunion and reunion. Though he roots this, of course, in Hawthorne's biography, he explicitly is using Hawthorne here to represent the postrevolutionary and antebellum American—the American who seemed to prefer the experimental and the empirical over the theoretical in all aspects of life, but who, as James figures him, maintained a conflicting and powerful affection for the conventional.

As a young man, James notes, Hawthorne "was not expansive, he was not addicted to experiments and adventures of intercourse, he was not, personally, in a word, what is called sociable" (339). He engaged Sophia Peabody in his thirty-fifth year, however, and married her in 1842. James attributes the connection to Hawthorne's need (as a self-conscious American) "to be drawn within the circle of social accidents" (370); he tells a rather impersonal anecdote about Hawthorne's meeting his future wife, an anecdote designed to typify "the lonely frigidity which characterised most attempts at social recreation in the New England world some forty years ago" (371); and he ties Hawthorne's need to finance his desired union to his taking his position at the Custom House and to his subsequent sojourn at Brook Farm, the latter of which temporarily delayed but ultimately enabled that union. Indeed, he uses Hawthorne's prior courtship and subsequent marriage only as prelude to his discussion of Brook Farm; he is otherwise silent on the relation.

Since Hawthorne was rather famously married, that relative silence stands out. At one level, it reflects the general lack of scholarship in *Hawthorne*; Lathrop barely had mentioned Hawthorne's marriage and James follows suit.[22] At a second level, it reflects the intent of the English Men of Letters series to present writers in public rather than in domestic or personal contexts—an intent that reflects the patriarchal bias of the series. At a third level, it reflects a tendency already at work in *Hawthorne* and endemic in James's later nonfiction—his tendency to manipulate biographical-historical elements to serve his compositional ends.[23] James neither falsifies Hawthorne's marriage nor, strictly speaking, misrepresents its importance to Hawthorne; he treats it, rather, in the manner most consistent with his portrayal of Hawthorne as a solitary figure, an alien onlooker, disengaged and unencumbered by all save the weight of his Puritan ancestry. And, at a fourth level, James needs only this perfunctory treatment to serve what I take to be his purpose—to link Hawthorne's conventional domestic and marital relations via the ambiguities of his stay at Brook Farm to his conservative political allegiances.

James begins this linkage, actually, with a model woman. He rehearses Hawthorne's disapproval of the estimable Margaret Fuller, the probable model for Zenobia of *The Blithedale Romance*, though James softens Hawthorne's tones and himself equivocates.[24] James first calls her "a very remarkable and interesting woman, ... the apostle of culture, of intellectual curiosity," but he also uses her to make his broader point about America: "a glimpse of her state of mind—her vivacity of desire and poverty of knowledge—helps to define the situation" (372). Though he next calls her a "brilliant, restless, and unhappy woman—this ardent New Englander, this impassioned Yankee" (377), he eventually will leave her with an almost patented Jamesian left-handed compliment: she was "the most distinguished woman of her day in Boston" (420). Invidiously, James seems to compare Margaret Fuller to Sophia Peabody, and, more important, to accord her far more respect than did Hawthorne. Indeed, he comes around to argue that "very much the same qualities that made Hawthorne a Democrat in politics would operate to keep him out of active sympathy with a woman of the so-called progressive type. We may be sure that in women his taste was conservative" (379). And so, James will show, was his taste in institutions and in political figures.

James follows Lathrop in characterizing Brook Farm as a "socialistic community" of the kind that Hawthorne distrusted; but he also figures it as a "would-be happy family" that, as such, he imagines would have attracted Hawthorne (375, 379–80). As he goes on, he opposes "experiment" and "theory"—and, implicitly, Anglo-American and French—when he describes Brook Farm as "devised and carried out by shrewd and sober-minded New Englanders, who were careful to place economy first and idealism afterwards, and who were not afflicted with a Gallic passion for completeness of theory." He refers this lack of completeness specifically to the Brook Farmers' conventionalism in domestic matters, to there being "no interference whatever with private life or individual habits, and not the faintest adumbration of a rearrangement of that difficult business known as the relation of the sexes"; Brook Farm was "thoroughly conservative and irreproachable" in such matters (380). Though he characterizes Brook Farm as a community based on experimental social relations, then, he also uses "family" to figure those relations—uses, that is, the theoretical model for and the practical basis of *conventional* social relations. If Hawthorne parodied Brook Farm, James tames it, makes it available for good Americans.

It may not surprise, then, that James again adverts to his original soil-flower metaphor. "Transcendentalism," James here writes, "could only have sprouted in the soil ... of the old New England morality," but, in this instance, it is soil "gently raked and refreshed by an imported culture" (380).[25] The native soil gave the Brook Farmers their "moral ardour" and kept them from "the lightest breath of scandal" (381), but foreign influences cultivated that soil and enabled something other than wild hawthorns to grow. Lacking that influence, a foreign cultivation of his soil, Hawthorne remained conventional as well as provincial, and conventional not only as an artist in relation to his material but also as a man in relation to women and to proper institutional relations with women. The name "Brook Farm," indeed, proves an *objet trouvé* as useful as was "Hawthorne," for James uses it to suggest how the agricultural had become the cultural on a farm for Europeanized American intellectuals. In his text, correspondingly, the pastoral becomes the historical, as a Hawthornian description of nature gives way to a Jamesian assessment of Brook Farm as comprising "many products that could not very justly be called natural" (375).

In this context, it is worth recalling a lengthy review of Charles Nordhoff's *The Communistic Societies of the United States* that James wrote in 1875—one in which he focused on the two native sects, Shakers and Perfectionists, rather than on the six other sects of foreign origin that Nordhoff also visited and treated. Indeed, James focused on "intersexual" relations in these sects, contrasted at length the celibacy of the Shakers with the "interchangeableness of husbands and wives" of the Perfectionists (versions of the phrase appear twice: *LC* 2:561, 567). While the tenets of the first sect suggest a "wholesome conservatism" that had become "grotesque and perverted" (*LC* 2:566), those of the second suggest something "singularly grotesque and unlovely" that becomes, in James's heated rhetoric, "morally and socially" something "simply hideous" (*LC* 2:561, 567). Though he wonders with approbation how twenty-five hundred Shakers could have been forced to "embrace a life of such organized and theorized aridity" (*LC* 2:565), he uses the Perfectionists' familial relations together with their practice of communal self-criticism as a synecdoche for "the detestable tendency toward the complete effacement of privacy in life and thought everywhere so rampant with us nowadays" (*LC* 2:567).

James was nowhere so harsh on the Transcendentalists in general nor on the Brook Farmers in particular. Hawthorne's sense of them was built into the ambiguity of the title of *The Blithedale Romance*: he was writing a romance about Blithedale, but Blithedale communards collectively had written romance about social relations, a romantic social text. Following Hawthorne's lead, James treated them in *Hawthorne* with the same light irony that he would in his 1887 review essay based on James Elliot Cabot's memoirs of Emerson, where he called them critical thinkers whose "criticism produced no fruit" essentially because they were engaged in "decent and innocent recreation," their experiment "the amusement of the leisure-class" (*LC* 2:267). The real issue with respect to experimental communities, then, the real area of contention, would seem to be that of sexual relations as related to the integrity of the family and that integrity, in turn, as related to the sanctity of the private sphere. Hawthorne and even the Brook Farmers subscribed to conventional familial values, their "experimentalism" notwithstanding, and James clearly was affirming those values, his ironies notwithstanding, if only by expressing nostalgia for them in the current "critical" age.

Sexual relations, however, also function emblematically here, whether by intention or not, of an abstraction, for James actually contrasts not only values but also *kinds* and *degrees* of commitment to them. In his review of Nordhoff, James used the word "experimental" countless times in reference to the sects treated, and in *Hawthorne* he uses it several times in relation to "the little industrial and intellectual association," Brook Farm (e.g., 376, 377, 380). In both cases, he not only opposed experimental to theoretical as a way of formulating ideas, but he also opposed experimental to conventional in terms of the ideas formed as the latter relate to prevailing opinion. The Shakers and Perfectionists formulated ideas theoretically, and those ideas were, themselves, highly experimental, highly unconventional; the Brook Farmers, by contrast, recognized the limits of social theory and formulated ideas experimentally, and their ideas were, in fact, rather conventional. From James's perspective, then, the Shakers and Perfectionists suffered not only from their tendency to theorize but also from their singlemindedness in putting theory into practice, however much it collided with realities; by implication, the Brook Farmers actually redeemed themselves through aristocratic aloofness, just as Hawthorne redeemed himself through his playfully parodic treatment of them, just as James, presumably, redeems himself through irony.

The implications of James's discussion are manifold. First, James makes marriage a central value in *Hawthorne*, though he barely mentions it—marriage, however, as the paradigm for the values of stability and privacy in social relations. Experiments in marriage lack value not because they necessarily fail but because they violate beneficial conventions. Second, he values and devalues experimentation differently in the arts than he does in social relations, though he seems, ultimately, to uphold conservative—if not precisely conventional—values in both.[26] On the one hand, that is, he faults Hawthorne's aesthetic experimentation and empiricism and virtually holds him up to ridicule for lacking a theoretical system; while, on the other hand, he applauds the Brook Farmers' experimentation and empiricism as that which saves them from their theory. But, on the one hand, Hawthorne's theoretical naivete actually allowed his natural genius to operate unimpeded; while, on the other hand, the Brook Farmers' theoretical savvy gave their experiments direction and some originality. In essence, then, third, James seems less troubled by the contents of radical ideas than about the radically systematic formulation of *any* ideas—seems less troubled by romantic fancy or emblematic portraiture, less troubled by institutional celibacy or interchangeable spouses, than about the ideologies driving them, than about ideology, in fact, itself.

James plays a variation on these marital and communal themes when he links Hawthorne's friendship with Franklin Pierce to the Civil War. He can use friendship as the middle term between the private and the public, indeed, because Hawthorne's primary and lifelong friendship was a public and a political one. James first raises Hawthorne's friendship with Pierce when discussing the former's college days at Bowdoin (333), which institution James paints as arcadian and which he contrasts to the great European universities. He raises it again when discussing Hawthorne's much latter Italian sojourn, when he was visited in Italy by then–former president Pierce. He uses the latter occasion to allow that "the sentiment of friendship has on the whole been so much less commemorated in literature than might have been expected from the place it is supposed to hold in life, that there is always something striking in any frank and ardent expression of it" (439–40). James no more inclines toward frank expression of its intimacy, however, than he had done in his treatment of Hawthorne's marriage nor, perhaps more to the point, than Hawthorne had done in his campaign biography. Indeed, just as James had used Hawthorne's marriage to reach Brook Farm, so he uses Hawthorne's friendship with Pierce to reach each of two extended discussions of slavery and the Civil War.

James first discusses the immediate antebellum period and the shift in Hawthorne's relations to Pierce from private affection to public alliance. And he uses the manifestation of that alliance, Hawthorne's *Life of Franklin Pierce*, to move from presidential campaign to presidential election in 1852 and, ultimately, to the Civil War. It is in *this* discussion that James expressly identifies Hawthorne with "that generation which grew up with the country, [and which] witnessed during a period of fifty years the immense, uninterrupted material development of the young Republic," that innocent generation unsuspecting of their future, unaware of the "faint shadow in the picture—the shadow projected by the 'peculiar institution' of the Southern States," that conservative generation who failed to see coming "a social revolution as complete as any the world has seen." This was the "great convulsion" that produced the fundamental change in the American consciousness that forms the crux of *Hawthorne*. After it, the "good American" would be more "critical," would be, "without discredit to his well-known capacity for action, an observer," would be sufficiently critical, indeed, *not* to have mistaken Franklin Pierce for "a very proper President" (426–28). Hawthorne, of course, was not such an American, could not have been; and James, of course, is.

James moves toward that implicit self-assertion through his second extended discussion of Hawthorne, Pierce, and the Civil War; it again interweaves the very private and the public, and it occupies his final chapter. James begins this chapter with Hawthorne's return to America in 1860 and his taking occupancy of a previously purchased house in Concord, birthplace of the Revolution. He first sociologizes the "explosion" of the Civil War as the "fatal blow to that happy faith in the uninterruptedness of American prosperity which I have spoken of as the religion of the old-fashioned American in general, and the old-fashioned Democrat in particular" (449). But he immediately moralizes Hawthorne's response to that blow. He portrays Hawthorne's fulsome dedication of *Our Old Home* (1863) to Pierce and his otherwise continuing to defend Pierce "manfully" (449) as Hawthorne's refusal to abandon his friend in order to curry popular favor—as a matter of personal integrity and loyalty, or, in a word, friendship. He treats likewise the controversial *Atlantic Monthly* article of 1862 in which Hawthorne, in James's words, refused to "pretend to be [an abolitionist] at the eleventh hour" when he had not been one before the war (451). Picking up the chapter's opening, he finally comes to Hawthorne's last, unfinished works, especially *Septimus Felton*, which James criticizes for using "a great historical event—the war of the Revolution"— merely as a pretext for plot (454–55).

James had concluded his treatment of the *Atlantic Monthly* article by quoting at length Hawthorne's argument that "the vast extent of our country" causes sectional allegiance to supersede national allegiance and that, as a result, an *understanding* Union would allow a rebel "an honourable burial in the soil he fights for." This, James adds, exemplifies "the way an imaginative man judges current events—trying to see the other side as well as his own, to feel what his adversary feels, and present his view of the case" (452–53). And when such a man—or woman, as he will say of Elizabeth Barrett Browning in *William Wetmore Story*; when such a *person* fails to do so he or she fails to be imaginative and becomes a zealot—not unlike John Brown, described by James as "the dauntless and deluded old man who proposed to solve a complex political problem by stirring up a servile insurrection" (452). With his cited reference to the honorable burial of rebels, outsiders, in their native soil, James has set up his closing passage, has prepared for his burial of Hawthorne.

He closes with this death scene: Hawthorne had planned a trip to England but instead traveled to northern New England with Franklin Pierce; they reached Plymouth, New Hampshire, Hawthorne died in the night, Pierce found him dead in the morning; Hawthorne's body was returned to Concord for burial. It is an allegorical *tour de force*. Hawthorne dies not in England but in New England, and specifically, in Plymouth, New Hampshire—in a town whose reference to England is mediated by its reference to Plymouth, Massachusetts, the town of the Pilgrims and, at least mythically, the birthplace of permanent English settlement in America. Moreover, Hawthorne dies in the last year of the Civil War, dies in the company of the penultimate antebellum president, is laid to rest in the town of the birth of the Revolution and, at least mythically, of the birth of the national experiment in democracy. Hawthorne, then, represents *not* just this generation, but, more broadly, America from its first colonial stirrings through its national independence to its convulsive disunion and reunion.

Taking the themes of marriage and friendship together, we can see that James showed Hawthorne's taste in women to accord with his taste for marriage, which accorded with his taste for conventional social institutions; Hawthorne's taste in men to accord with his taste for lifelong friendships, which accorded with his taste for conservative political institutions. Specifically, he muted Hawthorne's marriage in order to heighten his portrayal of Hawthorne as loner; but he used that marriage, obviously unavoidable, to portray Hawthorne as a sexual and social conservative who preferred the conventional family to even the prudishly experimental commune of Brook Farm, itself a very American experiment with only light European influence. Though he did not mute Hawthorne's friendship with Pierce to the same degree, since it was public, he colored it to highlight his portrayal of Hawthorne as a man unsophisticated in the world of affairs; and he further used that friendship to portray Hawthorne as a conservative who preferred the conventional politics of the Democratic Party to the more radical program of the Republican.[27]

Finally, James embedded those themes and their allegorical implications within yet another allegory—rehearsed the histories of Hawthorne's ancestry and of their story-telling descendent in order, ultimately, to abandon the historiographical. He had brought forth Hawthorne from the "vast" (320) American landscape in the two opening paragraphs that preceded biography proper; he ultimately fulfilled Hawthorne's charge that a "vast" America should bury its rebellious dead in their native soil, and he did so not only by recounting Hawthorne's actual burial in the New England soil, but also by conducting his own obsequies in the closing paragraph that follows the biography proper. In it, fifteen years after Hawthorne's death, he delivered his eulogy to the American Adonais, to this "beautiful, natural, original genius" (457). James used Hawthorne, then, not only as an emblem of the artist and man of letters in antebellum America, but also as an icon of the artist figure in a timeless realm: Hawthorne sprang from a prehistorical New England soil in James's opening paragraphs and was reinterred in it, honorably, in a posthistorical closing paragraph.

James purported to do for Hawthorne what he would criticize Cabot, several years later, for failing to do for Emerson; in James's view, Cabot had neglected "the social conditions in which Emerson moved, the company he lived in, the moral air he breathed.... We know a man imperfectly until we know his society, and we but half know a society until we know its manners. This is especially true of a man of letters, for manners lie very close to literature" (*LC* 2:251).[28] As I have suggested, James not only addressed Hawthorne's social conditions, but he did so from a narrative point of view that allowed him to imagine what Hawthorne's *experience* of them must have been like. We now can see that he did both things in order to produce an essay in which biographical text carries autobiographical subtext, in which the naive and fanciful Hawthorne makes way for the critical and imaginative James. In his concluding passage, to take an important instance, James strove to see Hawthorne's side and, metaphorically, he returned Hawthorne to his native soil; but his doing so made *James*, too, an instance of the type that the passage honors—the "imaginative man."

For at least two reasons, however, this subtext could not fully emerge. First, Morley had required James to approach Hawthorne from something resembling a detached perspective and to do so with reference to large public forces; as a result, James could neither indulge in impressionistic criticism nor present an otherwise personal assessment that might shift focus from Hawthorne as object of perception toward himself as perceiver. Second, though their chronologies overlapped, Hawthorne and James never actually met; as a result, James could not employ biographical memoir either to include himself as secondary object of memoration or, again, to shift focus away from Hawthorne and toward himself as memoirist. Despite these limitations, however, James managed not only to infuse compassion into his perspective but also to thematize its necessity; he managed to include commentary on the biographical act that aided his self-portrayal as the exemplary postbellum man of letters; and he managed to introduce two recollections of his own childhood apparently designed to thematize his generational difference from, and improvement upon, Hawthorne. Whatever their intent, however, these last also serve to underscore resemblances between the two men.

James first raises the necessity for compassion in the specific context of historical relativism. In considering Hawthorne's life, he tells his reader, we must exercise compassion as our dominant sentiment, though "we may safely assume that [Hawthorne] was not to his own perception the object of compassion that he appears to a critic who judges him after half a century's civilization has filtered into the twilight of that earlier time" (341). We must exercise compassion, he goes on, for the reasons he elaborated in the infamous passage about American "absences." Quoting Hawthorne on the difficulty of writing romance in America, James notes that Hawthorne's American Note-Books confirm the sentiment, though an English reader might find this less obvious than would an American, who "reads between the lines—he completes the suggestion—he constructs a picture." Having thus situated himself in time and, as such an American, in *race*, he goes on to argue that "if one desire[s] to enter as closely as possible into Hawthorne's situation, one must endeavour to reproduce his circumstances." Following his mandate, he constructs the picture of blank provincialism that, he claims, compels compassion—"compassion for a romancer looking for subjects in such a field" (350–52).

He complicates this plea for compassion, however, when he addresses his predecessor's works and converts "compassion" into *appreciation*. He calls *Twice-Told Tales* things "to enjoy, but not to talk about," argues that "not to read them would be to do them an injustice," but that "to bring the machinery of criticism to bear upon them would be to do them a still greater wrong." Though he allows that "to carry this principle too far would be to endanger the general validity of the present little work" (348–49), he evidently regards the danger as an acceptable risk. Speaking of himself in the third person, he first says that "he has been trying to forget his familiarity" with *Twice-Told Tales* in order to imagine "what impression they would have made upon him at the time they appeared," before "the particular Hawthorne-quality," as he terms it, had become a "fact" (361); and he later adds that he prefers to "trust my own early impression" of *The Wonder-Book* and *Tanglewood Tales*, that he has "been careful not to read them over" so as not to spoil his recollections of how he had lost himself in them as a child (417). Though James equivocates here on the *availability* of childhood impressions, he states unequivocally their *desirability*. Moreover, he not only seems to come out against criticism ("not to talk about"), but also, as Leo Marx might put it, seems to associate critical analysis with the anti-edenic ("machinery").

Unlike James's reviewers, then, we must see his plea for compassion as something more than mere condescension. Though he was arguing, to be sure, that the antebellum Hawthorne suffered a meagerness of environment that he, the postbellum James, had not, he also casts that environment in prelapsarian terms and expresses a deep nostalgia for it. To some extent, James was using nostalgia, thematically, to raise issues of partiality and of relative perspective while arguing, ultimately, that one had to exercise compassion without sacrificing rigor.[29] Specifically, Hawthorne could not know that he was missing virtually everything, and neither could the child James; but the adult James can know that, must acknowledge that, and so must do Hawthorne the kindness of granting him his *données* while not failing to be critical about the causes and effects of those *données*. James presented this necessity, moreover, as the problem facing a critical biographer, who has to temper sympathetic story of the life with dispassionate analysis of the conditions of the life and of the importance of the work; and he developed his theme through commentary on Lathrop and Hawthorne as biographers.

Lathrop had opened his *Study of Hawthorne* by claiming that "this book was not designed as a biography, but is rather a portrait"; and James opens *Hawthorne* by claiming that he must give his "sketch" the "form rather of a critical essay than of a biography," because Hawthorne's life was "deficient in incident, in what may be called the dramatic quality" (319)—a formulation he had approximated in his correspondence and would repeat almost exactly in the opening line of his redaction of 1896 (458).³⁰ Having been outflanked by Lathrop, as it were, James proceeds to comment in an extended reference to him that "his tone is not to my sense the truly critical one," and, thereafter, he refers to Lathrop as Hawthorne's "biographer" (e.g. 322, 379, 387). The claim James makes for *Hawthorne* accords with his then general sense of subjects less suitable for biography than for portraiture, but it rings oddly here since James actually gives his "sketch" (his portrait) the *form* of a biography and the *content* of a critical essay. Obviously, he wants to imply that Lathrop wrote mere biography while *he* is writing critical biography, and that the difference is what makes portraiture.

Speaking of himself generally as an "American commentator" (347), for example, James notes, first, that "a biographer has of necessity a relish for detail; his business is to multiply points of characterisation" (347–48), as Lathrop, indeed, does have and has done; second, that "the attitude of the biographer is to desire as many documents as possible" and that James is "thankful, then, as a biographer, for the Note-Books" (349); but, third, implicitly, that his role as biographer differs from his role as critic and that, as critic, he finds such documents of little relevance. James may be an ersatz biographer, a "compiler" (381) using secondhand material found in Lathrop, but he is more importantly a critical essayist, a "writer" (361, 402) examining the firsthand material of Hawthorne's works. Making the distinction, James sharpens his focus on proper portraiture and, simultaneously, advances his subtextual claim to being Hawthorne's successor. Distinguishing himself from Lathrop as biographer, that is, James also distinguishes himself from Hawthorne, for both Lathrop and Hawthorne were biographers: Lathrop of Hawthorne, Hawthorne of Franklin Pierce.³¹

To the extent that James pursues this implicit comparison, he suggests differences in motive despite apparent similarities in effect. Specifically, he makes a virtue of Hawthorne's loyalty to Pierce, but also characterizes that loyalty as uncritical: "Our hero," James writes, "was an American of the earlier and simpler type" (425) who "takes the license of a sympathetic biographer in speaking of his hero's having incurred obloquy by his conservative attitude on the question of Slavery" (427). As Hawthorne to his hero, so James to his: he had taken the license of an "appreciative critic" (348) in speaking of Hawthorne's tales and, in fact, had acted the sympathetic biographer in speaking of Hawthorne's having incurred obloquy on the same question of slavery. If his point, however, is that Hawthorne's loyalty, like his other traits, springs from his uncritical, naive, antebellum character, then his implicit corollary must be that his own loyalty springs from a critical, sophisticated, postbellum character—that his loyalty is conscious, indeed *self-conscious*, though not ironical.

James's capacity for writing a "critical essay" in *Hawthorne*, clearly, becomes the point. As a member of the uncritical generation, Hawthorne was drawn to romance, to biography, to Franklin Pierce; as a member of the critical generation, James is drawn to realism, to literary criticism, and decidedly *not* to Franklin Pierce. Not just about romance versus realism in imaginative literature, *Hawthorne* contrasts romantic naivete to realistic sophistication in one's choice of subjects for portraiture, and in one's sense of portraiture; in one's choice of political and artistic heroes; and, finally, in one's choice of models of culture. In James's schematics, Hawthorne lacked not only literary theory and critical system, but also a capacity for astute social analysis; not surprisingly, he was a romancer, a naif, and a conservative Democrat; James, by contrast, has not only a literary theory and a critical system, but also a capacity for astute social analysis; and, not surprisingly, he is a realist, a sophisticate, and—the inference seems unavoidable—a liberal Republican.

At the source of Hawthorne's limitations, of course, lies his antebellum provincialism, and, by implication, at the source of James's strength lies his postbellum cosmopolitanism. Both terms are essential. America before the war militated against critical thought—literary, political, or generally cultural—and the war made subsequent Americans, precisely, critical. But it takes a proper culture to produce a man of letters—critic, portraitist, novelist—and America after the war still could not do that. Such a man has no place, for "even to the present day it is a considerable discomfort in the United States not to be 'in business' "—"the so-called practical order" still provides the only basis for one's rank in the social system (342).[32] Though "Europeanised in advance" (442), as James has it, the postbellum American who wants to be the proper American *literary* type must be Europeanized *in fact*. More specifically, a Europeanized antebellum figure such as Story would remain, by virtue of *moment*, finally uncritical, while a Europeanized but repatriated postbellum figure, such as Howells, would remain, by virtue of *milieu*, finally unartistic. Only a *postbellum expatriate* could fit the bill.

Only James, in fact, could fit the bill in 1879. Many commentators have pointed out that James, in this period, triangulated exemplars of French, British, and American literature from the preceding generation in order to position himself as the successor of each, and, it would follow, as the unique composite of these traditions—Balzac, Trollope or Eliot, and Hawthorne are the usual candidates.[33] We could say, more precisely perhaps, that he melded the genre of the first, the home or *milieu* of the second, and the nationality or *race* of the third to position himself as unique composite in his time or *mo-*

ment. Antebellum America, however, could produce no *critic* whatsoever—Poe, the only candidate, being "pretentious, spiteful, vulgar," and so on (367)—so a national triangulation for literary criticism had to take a different form: Taine and Arnold formed a trio with James, who becomes the *first* American critic, a critic even more at home than Arnold with the French school.[34] If James was superseding Hawthorne as a writer, he was superseding Hawthorne's contemporary, Sainte-Beuve, as a critic. That he was doing so as an American in England, as an expatriate, brings us to the deepest level of James's subtext, where nostalgia rules.

That nostalgia becomes explicit in the two brief moments of autobiographical memoir in *Hawthorne*, both concerning Hawthorne's major American romances. In the first, James plays Hawthorne's skepticism about Brook Farm and his acute sense of alienation from his contemporaries against James's own warmer feelings. He notes that Hawthorne has given the modern reader, in *The Blithedale Romance*, "a few portraits" of a generation that "at this time of day [should] be spoken of very tenderly and sympathetically," and then adds (speaking of himself in third person) that he, "though his recollections date only from a later period, has a memory of a certain number of persons who had been intimately connected, as Hawthorne was not, with the agitations of that interesting time" (381). Though writing a little homage, a Hawthornian set-piece on the virtue of sympathetic memoration, James turns it to his own advantage. Implicitly invoking his father's early and still extant relations with such luminaries as Emerson, James is claiming that paternal history and personal recollection together give him more purchase on Transcendentalism, on mid-century experimentalism, than Hawthorne's actual but jaundiced observation had given him.

More melodramatic in content, the second recollection plays the dark gothicism and lingering sexualism of *The Scarlet Letter* against the response of an admiring, but still prudish, public. James notes that he, "a child at the time, remembers dimly the sensation the book produced, and the little shudder with which people alluded to it, as if a peculiar horror were mixed with its attractions." Indeed, he recalls having seen a painting of Hester Prynne and Pearl and having been told "that when I grew older I might read their interesting history." Though he mentions this, he says, only to suggest the degree to which the success of *The Scarlet Letter* had made it "an actuality" (402)—nicely applying to *The Scarlet Letter* Hawthorne's term for what a romance did not treat—we can see another purpose.[35] James the adult may be using James the child as the symbol for a public not yet ready for mature fiction, but James the adult is also treating, with subtle irony, his own desire to recapture his youthful innocence, to recapture initial longings for a literary experience that would prove less lurid, though perhaps more profound, than he had anticipated.

Something murkier than condescension or nostalgia, however, suffuses the prelapsarian quality of *Hawthorne*—the endless floricultural and pastoral imagery, the elegiac tone and form, the ironic recollections of once "scandalous" literary and social events embarrassingly tame in retrospect, the attribution, in general, of childlike naivete to antebellum culture. It comes into focus when we see that James's view of Hawthorne reenacts Hawthorne's view of his forebears. A good American made critical by the Civil War, that is, James looks across that chasm to find the most significant artist of the uncritical generation, that which grew up with the young republic, looking across the chasm of the Revolution to the generation that grew up with the founding and settling of the Colonies—that generation, finally, as in *The Scarlet Letter*, itself looking across the chasm of transatlantic separation. At the origin, as in so much nineteenth-century American literature, lies England; and, if we reverse direction and move *from* that origin, we find initial separation, revolution, ultimately civil strife.

We find the clue in James's use of the word "experimental." As we have seen, he yokes the terms experimental and empirical and opposes the pair to the term theoretical. In the realm of aesthetics, he uses experimental and empirical with general disapproval, theoretical with general approval. In the realm of politics, however, he uses the same terms in the same opposition, but reverses their value: experimental and empirical appear to be more positive, theoretical more negative—he prefers the experimental and empirical Brook Farmers, for example, to the more theoretical, more systematically ideological, Perfectionists or Shakers. Ignorant of tradition because isolated from a continuity or a community of writers, his exemplar Hawthorne became an experimentalist with mixed results; similarly ignorant of tradition because isolated from the continuity or community of nations, the United States too retains an experimental quality in its social structure. And this all seems to imply an allegory, intentional or not, of the value of social experimentation that issues neither *from* nor *in* radical social theory—he prefers the American Revolution, for example, to the French Revolution. At the same time, the allegory implies the cost of any revolution: civil strife begets more civil strife.

We find a paradigm, in short, that can be applied to the artistic, the domestic, and the public realms and that James, in fact, applied to all three—as we could begin to see in his portrayal of Hawthorne's romantic aesthetics, of his marriage in conjunction with his association with Brook Farm, and of his friendship with Franklin Pierce in conjunction with his stand on slavery and the Civil War. Since it is my point that the applications are largely unconscious, they will not read out with consistency and clarity; but they will make sense. In the artistic realm, in the view of James and his contemporaries, Hawthorne had pioneered if not *the* American romance, certainly one type of it—the type James most admired. In that realm, then, Hawthorne was a revolutionary of sorts—at least someone who broke with and wrote against the English model.

In the domestic and political realms, however, Hawthorne was the epitome of conservative decorum. He lost his father in childhood, as James notes, so escaped the need for filial rebellion; he also escaped fraternal conflict, finding, instead, connubial concord. Likewise, he eschewed abolitionism and Republicanism, and though his conservative politics made him, in a distant sense, a colluder with the Rebellion, they also made him, in a direct sense, someone quietist and passive with respect to entrenched authority.

We cannot press the analogies very far, however, for at this level of James's text, Hawthorne ceases to be the issue; James is. He is playing out anxieties deeper than those concerning Hawthorne's priority, and he is concealing every bit as much as he is revealing. In the artistic realm, James's taking up Realism in fiction and the French school in criticism are, indeed, revolutionary acts for an Anglo-American writer; and one might say, indeed, that his self-irony about doing so confirms rather than denies his sense of rebelliousness. In the domestic realm, James already was troubled about having a father not "in business" and certainly already had a history of fraternal conflict with William—if we can believe at all his *Small Boy and Others* and *Notes of a Son and Brother*. There can be little doubt, moreover, that Hawthorne's ability to sustain both a marriage and a literary career vexed the James who would examine, in countless fictional and nonfictional passages, the apparent incompatibility of those actions. It is in the third, the public, realm, however, that James confronted his deepest anxieties and in regard to which, in *Hawthorne*, he showed himself to be very like the retrospective, conservative predecessor he portrayed.

James expressly condemned slavery in *Hawthorne* as the evil that led to the Civil War, just as he would condemn it in *The American Scene* (1907) as the folly that had destroyed the South; he treated the war, moreover, in conventional, essentially Miltonic terms—the rebellion in Heaven ultimately leading to the fall in the Garden. As George Frederickson has shown, northern conservative intellectuals before and during the Civil War were faced with the problem of damning the Rebellion while still defending the Revolution, a particularly vexing problem once southern theoreticians had legitimated the Rebellion by appealing to the precedent of the Revolution.[36] James's metaphors here reveal that, a decade and a half after the war, he could disclose a far more conservative attitude than his northern conservative predecessors could have done in the preceding decade—though I doubt his awareness of the disclosure. His metaphors, that is, do not distinguish the Rebellion from the Revolution but, in fact, consider it as a reprise and condemn both events.

If this is so, then something else lurks perhaps even deeper than distrust of any and all revolution. James identified Hawthorne's New England with racial and social homogeneity, and he introduced the disruption of this homogeneity, significantly, while discussing the opening shots of the American Revolution at Concord—while discussing, in other words, the primal rupture with

England and the birth of the democratic experiment. As he luridly notes, "Forty years ago the tide of foreign immigration had scarcely begun to break upon the rural strongholds of the New England race; it had at most begun to splash them with the salt Hibernian spray" (389). He would worry this inundation again at great length in *The American Scene*, but we already can see the implication of James's prelapsarian America having grown critical, having entered culture and history, through its double fall. He identified a fall (Revolution) with a flood (immigration), second fall (Civil War), in *The American Scene*, with a second flood (second-wave immigration). Linking the fall of the Revolution to the fall of secession, to the act of disunion that inaugurated "a social revolution as complete as any the world has seen," that produced in Americans the capacity for critical observation (427–28), he also has linked both to the diffusion of Anglo-Saxon social homogeneity and hegemony. And as fearsome as that diffusion may strike him, it is also what made a space for the Scots-Irish James.[37]

╰╮

James apparently had not relished the commission for *Hawthorne*. He wrote to his sister Alice in February 1879 that he was "busy with the little book upon Hawthorne," but the following week to his brother William that he was putting off his "little book upon Hawthorne," that "there was no imperative hurry," and that he had met with Julian Hawthorne, who "gave me little satisfaction or information about his father" (*HJL* 2:215, 216). He resumed the study in August 1879 and, while still engaged in September, described it to Thomas Sergeant Perry as "a difficult task, from the want of material and (as I think) slenderness of the subject" (*HJL* 2:255).[38] Following publication, he allowed to Grace Norton that he had written it "sadly against my will"; and he wrote his father that Macmillan had offered him $1,000 to do a Dickens volume but that he would decline this offer "owing to want of time," that he wished his "hands free to work upon my forthcoming long novel"—his very Hawthornian *Portrait of a Lady* (*HJL* 2:262, 263). "It is from that," he declared to Perry, "that I myself shall pretend to date—on that I shall take my stand" (*HJ* 2:402).

The American press, of course, went after the "little" *Hawthorne*, as James habitually called it, though with less hostility than one might expect.[39] Most reviewers found James condescending or patronizing—the recurring terms—toward American life, American literature, and Hawthorne as American writer; they found the book written from a variously named French, English, or more generally "foreign" point of view, and found it written toward an English audience—a point not only obvious but, indeed, acknowledged by James. At the same time, most found it less a biography than a work of criticism—also a point acknowledged by James—and, on the whole, *praised* it as criticism—praised James's analytical powers in general, his analyses of Hawthorne's works in particular, and, indeed, his clarity of style. The reviewers, in short, found James the cultural commentator at worst offensive and at best negligible but found James the literary critic fair and astute. For his part, James found them less agreeable. He declared himself civilly, to Howells, "prepared to do battle for most of the convictions expressed" in what he now called, without diminution, his *Hawthorne* (*HJL* 2:266); but, to Perry, he counterattacked his detractors for their "vulgarity, ignorance, rabid vanity and general idiocy" (*HJL* 2:274).

His comments suggest a self-image, related to *Hawthorne* itself, both defensive and divided: on the one hand, he was a harried artist of genius forced to do hackwork and then unfairly vilified for having met his professional obligations; on the other hand, he was, precisely, a professional man of letters practicing his métier and unfairly vilified by a vulgar American public still overly fond of the sentimental and fanciful. If the first half of the image corresponds with the Hawthorne, James's Hawthorne, forced to take up editorial and encyclopedic work, the second half contrasts with the Hawthorne, again James's, incapable of executing such work professionally and successfully. It is a self-image that James would recreate almost exactly when commenting, years later, on the narrative nonfiction of his last phase: the assigned subject posed difficulty because too thin; circumstances, however, forced him to accept the assignment, which he really preferred to decline; he preferred to write fiction, his real work, which the commissioned nonfiction was preventing; but, having accepted the job, he did solid professional work either ignored or, in this case, disparaged by Philistines.[40]

James's decision to decline further biographic work and his spirited defense of his professionalism suggest an unease, already adumbrated in *Hawthorne*, with activity he had been associating with femininity and with dependency. As we saw earlier, in the 1870s James was identifying systematic thinking with masculinity, the "story-telling" faculty with femininity—a specific inscription, of course, of the broader patriarchal distinction between reason and intuition. He was disapproving intimate biography, moreover, as unmasculine (*LC* 2:278–79), and was associating George Sand's penchant for biography, for example, with a vulgar, feminine streak. It is somewhat striking, then, that James had called Taine "a man with a method, the apostle of a theory" (*LC* 1:843), in the April 1872 *Atlantic Monthly*, a month after his first article on Hawthorne—striking because it sheds contrasting light on his calling Hawthorne in 1879, with an odd syntax, "not a man with a literary theory" (*LC* 2:321). Without pressing too hard, we again can suggest that James was feminizing biography and romance, masculinizing theory and realism, and was identifying, therefore, Hawthorne as feminine and himself as masculine. Yet he must have recognized, uneasily, that he had written in *Hawthorne* a biographical romance, not a work of critical realism.[41]

These associations also might account, in part, for James's interest in Hawthorne's dependence on patronage. Hawthorne had obtained his job at the Custom-House, in 1839, James reminds us, "through political interest," as patronage from President Martin Van Buren: "it appears that the Democratic Party, whose successful candidate he had been, rather took credit for the patronage it had bestowed upon literary men" (372). Some years later Hawthorne again basked in "the golden sunshine of Presidential patronage" by virtue of his campaign biography. "The mouth-pieces of the Whig party spared him, I believe, no reprobation for 'prostituting' his exquisite genius," James adds, "but I fail to see anything reprehensible in Hawthorne's lending his old friend the assistance of his graceful quill" (425).[42] Though it would be far-fetched to press the (refuted) analogy with prostitution, and wrong-headed to invert James's refusal to censure Hawthorne, James not only is suggesting Hawthorne's limited range of choices in attempting "to live by his pen," but also is casting, clearly if unconsciously, the antebellum literary man as dependent helpmeet of men of affairs. James himself had other choices, he implies, and has taken another role—that of man of letters.

In any case, James wrote two more autonomous pieces on Hawthorne: his essay of 1896, whose biographical and even covertly autobiographical themes essentially repeat those of *Hawthorne*; and a letter to the Honorable Robert S. Rantoul, mayor of Salem, Massachusetts, occasioned by the celebration of the Hawthorne Centenary in 1904.[43] Mannered and highfalutin in the style of the last phase, the latter begins on an uneasy note of expatriation that James then recovers. Having begun by lamenting his unavoidable absence from the festivities, that is, he goes on to argue that he could "not wish to be better placed than at this distance for a vision of the lonely young man that Hawthorne then was . . . in the place that Salem then was" (469). Conflating space and time, equating spatial distance from contemporary Salem with temporal distance from antebellum Salem, James strikes the Hawthornian note that actualities compromise romance and he reenacts the Hawthornian task of memorially reconstructing a Salem of the past. He goes on to draw, in fact, a more overtly romantic picture of Hawthorne than he had in 1879 or in 1896.

The odd letter in which he elaborates this picture comprises three interminable paragraphs in which, first, he praises Hawthorne for his romantic art; second, defines Hawthorne's romantic art; and third, argues that Hawthorne's romantic art has become classic because subsequent art contrasted with it. A nice argument, it suggests that an artist becomes classic by having intrinsic merit *and* by affecting subsequent art—either directly or, in this case, inversely.

Though essentially a repetition of the opening paragraph of *Hawthorne*, it is, in 1904, more obviously an expression of James's continued concern with surpassing Hawthorne—a concern now coupled with a prepossession about becoming, himself, not just a classic but an *American* classic. James is still writing about Hawthorne *from England*, that is, and he extends and transforms the theme of expatriation adumbrated in *Hawthorne*.

As interpreted by James in 1879, as we have seen, the "good American" had to live abroad to be lettered, to become the postbellum literary type. Specifically, as James later wrote in "London" (1888), any "man of letters" wishing to work in the medium of Shakespeare and Milton, of Hawthorne and Emerson, would have to live in London; belonging to the *race* of the latter, as it were, one needed to live in the *milieu* of the former in order to contribute to the English language and, thus, to Anglo-American culture.[44] One then might become truly transatlantic, mixing new world sensibility with old (and mixing the influence of the Continent with both); one might become the appropriately modern emissary to the English, who, presumably, would reciprocate with welcome and appreciation. As he would say of a proper ambassador, James Russell Lowell, in 1892: "His new friends [the English] liked him because he was at once so fresh and so ripe, and this was predominantly what he understood by being a good American" (*LC* 2:535). It was certainly what James understood by being one a decade later.

Following the turn of the century, one might say, James was cutting his international theme very close to the bone. He had just published *The Ambassadors*, he already had in mind the trip that he would make to the United States in 1904–5 and that would eventuate in *The American Scene*, and he soon would name his collected works the "New York Edition," which, he wrote Scribners, "refers the whole enterprise explicitly to my native city—to which I have had no great opportunity of rendering that sort of homage" (*HJL* 4:365). His two remaining extended comments on Hawthorne, one in *William Wetmore Story and His Friends*, the other in *Notes of a Son and Brother*, not surprisingly focus on the question of the American artist living abroad. The first addresses what it meant to be a good American before the Civil War who, unlike Hawthorne, did settle abroad; the second readdresses what it meant to be the Hawthorne who remained on native ground. Though we will note James's comments on Hawthorne in *William Wetmore Story* in the next chapter, we need to conclude here with James's treatment of Hawthorne in *Notes of a Son and Brother*.

Like most of the writing in James's memoirs of the post-1910 period, the passage on Hawthorne in *Notes* has a prolixity and an obliquity that make its point difficult to discern and nearly impossible to fix in paraphrase. It occurs in the context of James's memorial associations with his former home in Ashburton Place, and it occupies a single four-page paragraph. James moves in it from comments on "General Grant (no light-handed artist he!)" and on Lee's surrender, to his own memorial *fusion*, to use his word, of having heard the news of "Lincoln's death by murder" with having heard the news that "Hawthorne was dead"—presumably not by murder (*N* 406–7). James then recalls reading Hawthorne's tales when a child and later reading straight through Hawthorne's works when a young man, "during certain last [*sic*: lost?] and otherwise rather blank months at Newport," namely, those of his recovery from the back injury that exempted him from service in the Civil War (*N* 408). Finally, he recalls an incident abroad, from a much later period, in which one H. B. Brewster, an American expatriate "who had spent most of his life in Italy," had airily dismissed Hawthorne's treatment of Rome as meaning to him "nothing at all"; James had not defended Hawthorne, as he should have, for being "ever so appreciably American" (he virtually chants the national name, repeating it five times in eight lines), but he now, in effect, will so defend him (*N* 409–12).

The fusions here are dense indeed. Not only does James equate the exemplary antebellum American statesman, Lincoln, with the exemplary antebellum American artist, Hawthorne, but, in so doing, he equates a national icon beyond critical reproach with a personal icon he wants to place beyond critical approach. In fact, he develops the paragraph with a leitmotif on his having decided to forego "harsh inquiry" of Hawthorne. Following his read through the Hawthorne *oeuvre*, he had left Hawthorne's romances on a shelf, "unvisited by harsh inquiry"; he had decided, instead, to "stand in *between* them and harsh inquiry"; but, he tacitly confesses, he took "the note of harsh inquiry" from Brewster and *failed* to "stand in." James recalls that it would have served no purpose to have told Brewster that he, James, had decided "in the gentle time" that he would eschew such criticism and, instead, would choose to appreciate Hawthorne's "*tone*." Though James did not say so to Brewster, Hawthorne had proved "to what a use American matter could be put by an American hand," a proof that gave up, in turn, the "happiest moral": "an American could be an artist, one of the finest, without 'going outside' about it, as I liked to say; quite in fact as if Hawthorne had been one just by being American *enough*," by missing nothing in "the ambient air."

In this passage, then, James redeems Hawthorne from his association with Franklin Pierce and from his conservative stand on slavery by identifying him, ironically, with Grant and then, unironically, with Lincoln. If James does not also redeem himself for his own failure to have served the causes of emancipation and of the Union, and he has not done so in this passage, he does atone for what becomes an equivalent lapse in his service to the now iconic Hawthorne and to American culture. The news of Hawthorne's death, that is, had made James "positively and loyally cry," but he had betrayed that loyalty by failing to deflect the harsh inquiry of Brewster, the latter "the clearest case of 'cosmopolitan culture' I was to have known"; he had been beguiled, he owns, by the "culture" Brewster had offered. Brewster, of course, not only stands in opposition to Hawthorne in this anecdote, but also *stands for* the James of *Hawthorne*, stands for the young expatriate and *soi-disant* cosmopolitan who himself had sounded a tin note of harsh inquiry with regard to Hawthorne's antebellum American provincialism. Yet James, we must add, does not atone here for his expatriation: though one might become an artist without going outside, one still cannot become a proper man of letters.

In closing, finally, we might recall that the autobiographical persona in Hawthorne's "The Custom-House" had been buried "as a politically dead man" but had risen "again a literary man."[45] In *Hawthorne*, James repeated the resurrection, at least ostensibly exhuming the politically suspect Hawthorne of the 1860s in order to honor him as artist and man of imagination and to rebury him as such. In the Centenary Letter, James continued his celebration of Hawthorne as artist, elevated him to the status of American classic, and, a decade later in *Notes*, he returned to unfinished business and virtually erased Hawthorne's political deviationism from the record by conflating him with the Great Emancipator. This constitutes, of course, a romantic hagiography, one in which Hawthorne attains apotheosis and in which antebellum America becomes sacralized. Needless to add, the sequence of texts also favors James: the young expatriated Turk of 1879 becomes the transatlantic classic of 1904 becomes the "man of imagination" celebrated in 1914 (*N* 371). James had not reached this autohagiography in *Notes*, however, without first having tried his biographical hand on another American romancer, a romancer in stone: William Wetmore Story.

Three

THE BOSTONIAN TYPE

William Wetmore Story and His Friends

> The whole matter, at the present hour, is rather phantasmagoric; the artist-life, in the romantic conditions and with the romantic good faith, is a thing of the past.
>
> —WILLIAM WETMORE STORY AND HIS FRIENDS

The James and Story families had connections in Newport and Cambridge before mid-century, connections that James exploited when he traveled abroad in the 1870s.[1] As a young man visiting Rome in 1873, specifically, he came within the social orbit of the older expatriate William Wetmore Story and frequently enjoyed the latter's hospitality at his Palazzo Barberini apartment. James first met Matthew Arnold at the Barberini, in that year, and he endured there, at about the same time, a recitation of Story's *Nero: An Historical Play*. Soon after, he wrote Charles Eliot Norton about having seen Carlyle, about valuing "the company of a man of genius," and, obviously by way of contrast, about just having attended Story's recitation. "The performance," James wrote, "was the result much less of an inward necessity" than of "a most restless ambition" tinged with "vanity"; it made him wish for "half an hour of Carlyle's English and Carlyle's imagination" (*HJL* 1:353).[2] Though James's correspondence shows that he maintained a social acquaintance with Story, in Italy and England, until the latter's death in 1895, James never came to regard him with any higher esteem.[3]

Immediately upon hearing of Story's death, however, James sent an odd note to their mutual friend and fellow exile, Frank Boott. Writing that he wanted to add but a p.s. of three lines to an earlier posted letter, he wound up sending a long letter in which he remarked rather lightly "a certain sense of historic mutation in the thought that Casa Story is no more," recalled having seen "poor W.W. in Rome sixteen months ago and he was the ghost, only, of his old clownship," ridiculed Story's "great unsettled population of statues" that "will be loose upon the world," but added that Story, despite his fate, "had had fifty years of Rome; and that is something." He changed tone perceptibly, however, when he next recalled Constance Fenimore Woolson and Kitty Emmett, both recently deceased, and he closed on this note: "How ghostly must Newport be! But I see ghosts everywhere. You are the only solid substance" (*HJL* 4:23–24). He would sound the same note two years later, when he wrote his British publisher, Blackwood, that he would "live—with it"—the newly commissioned *William Wetmore Story and His Friends* (1903)—"among many old friends and old ghosts" (*HJL* 4:59).[4]

For reasons financial and otherwise, James just had contracted, in 1897, to write a memorial biography of Story—a decision he immediately regretted. After then stalling for two years, he traveled to Rome, in 1899, visited Story's son Waldo, and examined the family archives; on the same trip, he visited Story's son Julian and Story's daughter Edith, the Countess Peruzzi, at her summer house, Lago di Vallombrosa; he then returned home, pronouncing the trip "haunted" (*HJ* 4:317). Following yet more delay, he organized the family's documents and his own recollections in the summer and early autumn of 1902, and he fashioned his biography of Story from them that fall and winter (*HJ* 5:129, 143). While doing so, in December 1902, he declined a request from Houghton Mifflin, the American publisher of *Story*, to do a life of James Russell Lowell. He gave several reasons specific to Lowell and then, citing *Story* as his example, went on to complain more generally of the problems in writing "biography without a real Biographic subject." Echoing a distinction he often had made in reviews of biographies in the 1870s, he allowed that a biographer can "do something" with a man who "has had a quiet life, but a great mind," or with a man who has "had a small mind and great adventures," but when the man "has had neither adventures *nor* intellectual, spiritual, or whatever inward, history, then one's case is hard." Story, evidently, had had neither.[5]

This letter to Houghton Mifflin epitomizes James's correspondence about *Story*. In some dozen published letters written between 1897 and 1903, we find him whining to friends about his predicament but also, more important, using them as sounding boards for an evolving biographical strategy of boldness; we find him, moreover, not only thinking through possibilities for the *Story* biography but also thinking through biography in general—in the letter to Houghton Mifflin, just cited, and in one to Henry Adams, to which I shall return. We also find him, after the fact, reminding old and mutual friends of Story and himself what a chore the book had been, accepting their compliments for a job well done, and, more generally, reminiscing with them about Story, Rome, and the Golden Age of only a few decades earlier. If we read this correspondence thematically rather than chronologically, indeed, we find James telling the same two tales he had woven around *Hawthorne*: in the first tale, he outlined circumstances that forced him to accept an unwanted assignment that, in turn, interfered with his fiction, but he also boasted that he acquitted himself professionally and admirably despite his difficulties; in the second, a technician's tale, he told how he turned a meager and boring subject into a biographic *tour de force*.[6]

Without rehearsing the details of the first tale, we might mention that James often had declined assignments in the 1890s for other than "'creative work,'" but that he also found himself, in 1897, in need of funds to secure a long leasehold on his residence, Lamb House, and to furnish it properly.[7] A genteel man obsessed with privacy, he not surprisingly kept this financial exigency to himself when discussing his acceptance of the commission, focusing instead on the social claims the Story family had made on him. But he also modulated his complaints about those claims, again not surprisingly, to fit his various addressees: very sharp-tongued about them to fellow professional, male intimates like Howells and Adams, he exercised more discretion with nonprofessional, female friends like Sarah Butler Wister and Millicent, the Duchess of Sutherland.[8] In addition, moreover, he modulated his expressions of his commitment to the project itself: presenting himself to Blackwood and to Houghton Mifflin as a sensible professional who was sensitive to the niceties of authorized biography, he struck, again, a more cynical pose with Howells and Adams, a gentle one with Sarah Butler Wister, and an unctuous one with Mrs. Waldo Story.[9]

In his second tale, in this instance to Howells, he emphasized that "There is no *subject*—there is nothing in the man himself to write about." He continued: "There is nothing for me but to do a *tour de force*, or try to—leave poor dear W.W.S. *out*, practically, and make a little volume on the old Roman, Americo-Roman, Hawthornesque and other bygone days, that the intending, and extending, tourist will, in his millions, buy."[10] Nearly a year later, to another correspondent, he presented a different version of the plan. Though the material she had sent him, he wrote Mrs. Waldo Story, was "indispensable . . . [,] all of it put together was not material for a Biography pure and simple"; he had "had to make out . . . what my material *did* lend itself to," and that was a picture:

> I have looked at the picture, as it were, given me by all your material, *as a picture*—the image or evocation, charming, heterogeneous, and a little

ghostly, of a great cluster of people, a society practically extinct, with Mr. and Mrs. Story, naturally, all along, the centre, the pretext, so to speak, and the *point d'appui*. This course was the only one open to me—it was imposed with absolute logic. The Book was not makeable at all unless I used the letters of other people, and the letters of other people were useable with effect only so far as I could more or less evoke and present the other people.

He thus *seems* to have found a simple and obvious solution consistent with his long held theoretical positions: lacking not only an exciting life to narrate, but also an exciting mind to portray, he would render that life in its rich social relations; he would portray a group.[11]

We must qualify doubly, however, the apparent simplicity of his solution. First, in the letters to Howells and to Mrs. Waldo Story, James proffered different versions of his basic solution to Story's meagerness, his shifting emphasis from Story's life to Story's circle and times; and we must accord those letters, differently but equally motivated, equal weight. Second, the James of this period would not have been stymied by Story's meagerness as primary subject; as H. G. Wells snidely put it, as William James soberly put it, and as James himself both ceded and boasted, he had the will and the ways to embroider endlessly around an absent center.[12] He told a half-truth, in sum, when he said he had found his needed "angle" in the decision to write a group biography that also would tap the wider interest of the group's place and time. Though he eventually wrote such a book, he also knew that he could not solve his problem simply by adding, in any empirical sense, *more* subject; he knew that he was not choosing between leaving Story *out*, on the one hand, and putting Story's friends, or even himself as friend, *in*. He had found his angle, rather, precisely in angle—in *perspective*—his forte as a novelist.

He intimated this, indeed, when he stressed that he would not "write" the book so much as *make* it—compile and compose it from documents and recollections. He spoke to Adams, for example, of having "seemed to see a *biais* of subjective amplification—by which something in the nature of a *book* might be made."[13] But he could not have meant here, either, that he simply could *add* the subjective, simply could supplement documents with recollections. The James of this period knew that he could not present Story's documents, even as editor, uncontaminated by his own recollections; he also knew that he could not portray Story, the American colony in Rome, and the Rome of "ancient days" except through those recollections. Though he had considered, as early as the 1870s, risks inherent in experimental archival and memorial volumes, he still would run them: he would meld documentary biography with group biographical memoir, and, being the James of the late phase, he also would incorporate a running commentary on the procedure, implicit and explicit.[14] Ultimately, moreover, he would fix on the spectral as the central trope for his book, a choice made almost inevitable by his previous writing on Story, his theories of memorial representation, and his deep nostalgia and morbid sense of generational isolation.

James had reviewed Story's *Nero* for the *Nation* in 1875. Characteristically diplomatic when reviewing an acquaintance, he began by noting that Story had given in *Nero* "another proof of his remarkable versatility and facility," and that the play "is especially clever for a man who has found so much besides to do with his imagination." Adding that Story, primarily a sculptor, "has made a specialty of the picturesque," and in *Nero* "has painted a picture, in fact, rather than written a play," James then referred repeatedly to the play with such terms as "picturesque," "picture," "portrait," "panorama," and he imagined, with apparent gratuitousness, how differently Robert Browning might have handled a dramatization of the subject. Story, James proposed, had constructed a panorama, "a rolling chronicle," a work that is "sometimes too diffuse" and that "would have gained by compression and by occasional cancellings on a final revision. The dramatic point is sometimes diluted." On the positive side, however, "Mr. Story has breathed for many a year that densely-weighted Roman air," and has so steeped himself in the past of Rome that he habitually sees "imperial ghosts in the sunny stillness of the Palatine," ghosts that "may have come to haunt and importune him."[15]

James rewrote that review on a grand scale nearly three decades later. He argued in his mammoth life-and-letters *Story* that his subject met life, as he did art, with versatility and facility, but that the distinctive and largely enviable activity and ease of Story's life found reflection in a busyness and, at the same time, laxity in his art. He argued that Story lacked a coherent theory of art, certainly lacked a modern sense of representation and of composition; as a result, Story was overly narrative as a sculptor, insufficiently "sculptural," while being, conversely, overly pictorial as a dramatic poet, insufficiently literary. And he argued that Story lacked "insistence," the sustained concentration of the true artist, and lacked it in life as in art. James regarded Story a dilettante, in short, and uninteresting as such. But he also found him quite interesting as one of the "precursors" who made Rome, indeed Europe, available to James's generation; as one of those Victorian travelers—and, in Story's case, expatriates—"without whose initiation we settled partakers of the greater extension should still be waiting for our own" (*WWS* 1:7–8); as one of those who sought the ghosts of the European past and who were sought by the ghosts of an abandoned America; as one of those ghosts, in turn, who had come to haunt and importune James.[16]

Vexed by his commission, in short, James took Story's own cue: Story had conjured the ghosts of imperial figures from ancient Rome, and James conjured the ghosts of "colonial" American figures from a modern Rome that he treated as though it were ancient. Shifting attention from Story as biographical subject to the now "vanished society" of expatriates (1:16) who inhabited a now equally vanished Rome, he used the documentary and memorial resources available to him to construct a vast necrology, to make a book of that society's dead; and he did all of this from the subjective perspective of one not precisely *of* them but, rather, pursuant *to* them—one who retrospectively imagined them, moreover, precursively anticipating their successor. He converted a conventional assignment into an unconventional documentary memoir whose title, rendered graphically tripartite in the first edition, distinguishes the three aspects of his composition: *William Wetmore Story / And His Friends / From Letters, Diaries, and Recollections*. Despite the unconventionality of his approach, however, he met his contractual obligations, for he focused more obviously on Story and his friends as precursors than on himself as successor, much recent commentary to the contrary notwithstanding.[17]

James attended closely, that is, to the life, opinions, and work of his nominal subject. He described Story's activities, and he carefully arranged and edited Story's own utterances—formal documents ranging from biographical and autobiographical extracts to poems and political tracts, informal documents ranging from notebooks and diaries to voluminous correspondence. With these, he fashioned his picture of a man *divided*, divided between abandoned and adopted lands, divided between publicity and privacy, divided between the claims of society—public and private—and those of art. And not only did James portray Story the man as divided between the social and the artistic, but he also portrayed Story the artist as *scattered* rather than concentrated, his attention to anything never fully "there" (2:217). Hypothetically attributing these tendencies to Story's heredity as a young Brahmin from Boston and to his circumstances as an aristocratic expatriate in Rome, James sought to reveal the mechanism of the Story history, the lesson of the Story case. From the specific, he generalized; from the concrete, he abstracted: he treated instance, in a word, as type.

He also treated Story the artistic type, however, as instance of the more inclusive type *romantic exile*, with other cases having other occupations. Placing Story and his wife among their friends, especially the James Russell Lowells and the Robert Brownings, he tracked them all along the axis of Boston-London-Florence-Rome—an axis whose points he elaborated and whose length, he reminds us, he too had traveled. As in *Hawthorne*, moreover, James not only described persons and places in *Story*, but he also advanced an argument about the influence of *race, milieu*, and *moment*. Those influences more complex here, James attended to several "races," and, crucially, to the key condition of *cosmopolitanism*, the condition of ambiguous *race* (that is, nationality). Finally, he attended to America and to Europe as cultures and, crucially, to the United States and to Italy as unified, modern nation-states emerging on what we would call the geopolitical stage; and he attended, accordingly, not only to the familiar divide of antebellum versus postbellum America, but also to the less familiar divide, in his work, of pre-1870 versus post-1870 Europe.[18] His principals had been engaged in contemporary political affairs and had produced ceaseless epistolary commentary on them; James not only cited his principals' documents, but he also used their personal relations as tropes for broad social formations, and he used those, in turn, as emblems in a virtual allegory of history.

While James broadened historical scope, however, he also, paradoxically, narrowed the historical to the deeply personal, recovered the public realm into the private. With Rome as the constant, he explored generation as the variable; he used Story and himself, specifically, to represent overlapping generations. He melded biography and memoir into a tale of the young Story as James's precursor, of the older Story and younger James as contemporaries, and of the older James, Story's successor, trying in the present to limn from other sources the young Story he did not know while also finishing that portrait with recollections of the older Story he did know. In the inward-turning manner of his concurrent late novels, and in anticipation of all his subsequent narrative nonfiction, he represented himself *in the process* of documenting and remembering the antediluvian time and *in the process* of trying to isolate, to order, and to compose those remembrances. Putting geography into historical motion, history into memorial motion, and memory into narrational motion, he produced a truly kaleidoscopic text—one that expressly damned artistic allegory and cultural modernism alike, but that itself verged, with perhaps ironic intention, on modernist allegory.

Obviously aware of those textual complications, James repeatedly allowed that the composing of *Story*, and *Story* as composition, hung on the edge of chaos; and, perhaps to impose some external order, he opted for stage business. While essentially following the chronology of Story's life, that is, he also divided his double-decker *Story* into four main parts—Early Years and Early Work, Early Roman Years, Middle Roman Years, Last Roman Years; he subdivided these parts, in turn, into clusters of numbered and titled chapters; and he outfitted these chapters, finally, with individual page headlines, which, we can infer, he chose with care.[19] Put differently, he seemed to know what we soon shall see—that *Story* had all the complexity of the late novels, but had very little of their elegance. James had made an extraordinary effort to compensate for the fact that biography lacked the freedom of invention that he had been claiming for the novel since the 1880s, but his effort, inevitably, did not wholly succeed. Beside the problem of genre, he had to contend with the problem peculiar to this commission—the various problems: not only did he have to satisfy Story's family, but he also had to confront and placate his own ghosts, public and private.

In order to do James's effort justice, we must avoid two errors common in recent commentary on *Story*—minimizing the documents themselves, and ignoring the previously cited letter to Mrs. Waldo Story.[20] We need to attend, first, to the *documents* James edited and arranged, not just to his own connecting prose. He himself had attended closely to editorial matters when reviewing documentary works; he eventually would compose his own most intimate memoir, *Notes of a Son and Brother*, on documentary lines virtually identical to those of *Story*; and it seems obvious that he neither chose, altered, nor arranged the *Story* materials haphazardly.[21] And we need to take seriously, second, James's description of intent to Mrs. Waldo Story. James may have "decentered" *Story*, as some current commentators maintain, but he neither left Story out nor relegated him to a minor role; the distinction matters, for we shall see that James did not attenuate Story either in favor of another biographical subject, Browning, or in favor of himself as autobiographical subject, in any conventional sense.[22] In my reading, James neither *ignored* Story to write about himself, nor even *used* Story, in precisely the way he used Hawthorne, to write about himself as successor; rather, he used Story and his friends, together, as *points d'appui* for an essay on social history and historiography, and, in the process, he revealed deep anxieties about social history, about the possibilities for representing it, and about himself as social being and social historian.[23]

James made strategic decisions about subject matter, in other words, that allowed him to explore a great range and density of issues while, simultaneously, avoiding unpleasant censure of a man he did not like and of mutual friends he did like. With an equally strategic turn to the hyperconscious, moreover, he could repress, and his text would mask, his very public, and his very private, anxieties. He may have essayed, as he claimed, a study of expatriation to Italy as the fatal trap set for romantic antebellum artists. But he also portrayed a Story *betrayed* by heredity, by circumstances, by his romantic temperament, by his gregariousness—his ease in making "friends"; and he used that Story as the type of a generation and, at the far reaches of biography, as the emblem for an entire epoch of American and European history, an epoch that suffered the betrayals of rebellion and revolution, the betrayals, ultimately, of the *modern* in all its aspects. It almost goes without saying, moreover, that he also portrayed a shadow figure, himself, likewise *betrayed*— the conspirators and assassins various—and used that figure, too, as the type for another moment, one "late in the day" (1:111), betrayed even more cruelly. In order to chronicle these betrayals, I shall take James's cue, and shall advance from Story and his friends, through their *races, milieux*, and *moments*, to James himself and the implications of his query.

Repeating the opening of *Hawthorne*, James characterized Story's reaction to his native New England as lacking the stuff for good "biography" or "drama" (1:14); he proceeded to characterize Story's subsequent years in Italy, moreover, as having unfolded with such monotony, however happy, that their potential "interest" must lie in the "circumstances" that produced his "lively response" to life—those circumstances being all the elements, enumerated by James, that compose "the vanished society that I began by speaking of" (1:35). As he had said, he would have to use his hero as an "existing instance" of a type (1:7).[24] He would employ him to typify the American pilgrim of the early times, specifically the young Bostonian who sought the artist-life in Rome; the pilgrim who, on the one hand, carried his "American consciousness . . . about with him as the Mohammedan pilgrim carries his carpet for prayer" (1:28), but who, on the other hand, also breathed too deeply of the Roman air, imbibed too much from the Borgia cup; who, as a result, succeeded in the pioneering of Europe but also failed to produce significant art; and who either returned home, repatriated but nostalgic for Europe, or remained an "American absentee," expatriated and nostalgic for home.

As an instance, however, Story needed fleshing out, and James did so with at least superficial kindness. The biographical data and the epistolary evidence reveal a well-born, well-bred, well-heeled, well-married, and very well-connected Brahmin; a man talented but not especially gifted, bright but not brilliant; a man capable of deep and lasting love and friendship but given to self-indulgent, morbid sentimentality; a man open to the world of experience but fundamentally bigoted (see, e.g., 1:211–13). In short, Story was a typical Victorian gentleman of a certain class, one of the "handsome young men of leisure, of fortune, of 'artistic taste,' of clever conversation, of filial piety" (2:126), whom James knew in numbers and whom he regarded as lacking substance. Even by those standards, moreover, Story's life had a smooth course—it was a "simple" life that "unfolded itself altogether from within, and was at no moment at the mercy of interventions or shocks" (1:34).[25] That smoothness characterized not only Story's salad days, but also his mature years: a man who "liked the 'world,' and the world also thoroughly liked him," the mature Story had neither inclination nor time for "solitary brooding" but gave himself over to "the human, the social panorama" (2:164–65); his "extremely peopled Roman life," James noted, unrolled like a "pleasant scroll" (2:310). This all left James with the double problem not only of converting a bland individual into type, but also of raising a bland type into interest.[26]

He approached the problem by highlighting the most intriguing feature of Story's personality—his romantic sense of his artistic alienation, a sense both cause and consequence of his beguilement by Rome. James observes, for example, that several of Story's letters written from Boston in the early 1840s show the young jurist "leading without reserve the life the time then imposed on him" (1:60). He later proposes, however, that two winters in Rome apparently had persuaded Story that he "might live as an anxious, even as a misguided, artist, but he could not, apparently, live as anything more orthodox"—that he could bear the anxiety of the artist-life but not the "habit of conformity" (1:295); and, soon after, he says of Story on his last return to Boston before permanent exile that, "with an alienated mind, he found himself again steeped in a society both fundamentally and superficially *bourgeois*" (1:303–4). At the same time, however, James almost compulsively adverts to double negatives, subtly worded left-handed compliments, and situational ironies—all of which reveal Story's romantic self-image as his fatal flaw. He portrays a man himself fundamentally bourgeois: a man who lacked a clear sense of the artistic vocation, who confused the artist-life with artistry; a man who prized marriage and friendship above art, James also implies, and who thus failed as an artist.[27]

Elaborating Story's vocational self-delusion, for example, James quotes an autobiographical extract his subject prepared later in life, one fulsome with references to the young lawyer's initial claim "to give up everything for Art" (1:32). In effect, James uses Story's own words to portray his subject as a winsome amateur who headed toward professionalism but who never reached inspiration—who remained uninspired because unprofessional, and unprofessional, ultimately, because never inspired. James then augments this portrayal when he discusses the anomaly at the start of Story's career, namely, that he was commissioned to sculpt a memorial to his father, Justice Joseph Story, before he had become a sculptor—that he was "to learn the trade in order to make the statue. . . ; he was not to make the statue because he had learned the trade" (1:81–82). James praises the "native cleverness" that allowed Story to pull off the commission—"the latent plastic sense, the feeling for the picturesque in attitude, for the expressive in line, for emphasised, romanticised character, in short, which was to befriend him" (1:82); but he also blames that cleverness for abetting Story's affection for the passional and his inclination "to see sculpture as, above all, expressional" (1:194)—for abetting, in a word, Story's egregious romanticism.

James gives us a young lawyer, in sum, who set out to sculpt, went to Italy to learn how, became discouraged, lost faith, and so returned to Boston to ponder his future. Using the occasion of that return to point again to Story's self-delusion, James contrasts Lowell's successful preparation in Germany for the Harvard professorship he came back to assume in the 1850s with Story's concurrent preparation in Italy for a sculptorship he came back only tempted to abandon (1:291). Story seemed not to realize, seemed never to realize, that he had "to go . . . to school, in the simplest meaning of the term. He had served no apprenticeship to his craft and mystery" (1:294). He remained perpetually divided between the model of the sensitive amateur and that of the skilled professional, never deciding which he was nor, for that matter, which he should aspire to be.[28] The year 1856 thus found him decisively expatriated but still trying to decide if he should "turn his back upon the plastic arts" (1:316). Though James flattered the Story, likewise, who "spent his life in the happy condition of never being without a *subject*" (1:240), he added more equivocally that "nobody in fact moved more, from subject to subject, interest to interest and relation to relation" (1:331–32). As a result of all this, Story lacked intensity, concentration, and insistence, and "it was his fate, inevitably, to be interrupted and scattered" (2:83–84, 217, 222).

When James noted that Story's first commission, the memorial bust of his father, foreshadowed his last work, a memorial bust of his wife, that Story was "happiest" as a sculptor "when inspired by the closest of his personal ties" (1:23), he also launched the theme of familial relations, particularly connubial relations, that inform his portrait from beginning to end. Employing conventional pastoral touches, for example, he notes early on that Story married when relatively young, he develops Story's marriage as not only the central relationship, but also the central fact, of his life, and, eventually, having noted that the Storys lived to celebrate their golden wedding anniversary, he suggests that Mrs. Story's death in 1894 so devastated her husband that it was "practically his own deathblow" (2:316); in fact, Story died within the year. He even closes his biography, finally, with a line contrived to stress not only that Story was fundamentally *related*, but also that his relatedness was fundamentally marital: "Death came to him . . . ," James concludes, and "he was laid to rest near his wife" (2:338).[29]

These few citations, however, fail to convey either the degree to which James used Story's marriage as a technical device or the complexity with which he elaborated it as a theme—literal and figurative. Compositionally, that is, James used it as a way to step from his *point d'appui*, the meager Story, to the Storys together, a slightly richer matter. Correspondingly, and more important, he also used it to step from Story as his point-of-view character: anticipating his strategy in *The Golden Bowl* (1904), he doubled primary perspective by presenting almost as much from Emelyn Story's journals and letters as from Story's, and often by presenting in counterpoint their accounts of the same persons or events (see, especially, chapter 3).[30] Thematically, he documents Story's marriage as part of his portrayal, presents Story as devoted, bourgeois husband—indeed, presents the Storys as devoted, bourgeois couple. He also elaborates a theme present by its absence in *Hawthorne* and common in his tales of artists, namely, the apparent incompatibility of marriage and the artistic vocation. And he does this, paradoxically, while he also appears to contrast Story's marital monogamy and evident fidelity with his artistic polygamy—his equal devotion to many arts and genres—and, even, his willing seduction by "the wanton Italy" (2:226). Finally, again as in *Hawthorne*, he uses marriage as a conventional emblem for union and stability, one he applies by analogy to large social formations.

Nevertheless, James did not title his book Story and *His Wife*, but Story and *His Friends*. He used the terminal noun and its cognates literally scores of times, and he used amicable relations, moreover, to govern his portrait.[31] Next to Story (after Emelyn Story), he placed Lowell, Story's "lifelong friend and his closest" (1:39); and, at a slight remove, Charles Sumner and Charles Eliot Norton. Though emphasizing the Harvard origins and man-to-man character of these early friendships, James chronicles their evolution, particularly in Lowell's case, into friendships between married couples. Of the latter kind, however, that between the Storys and the Brownings serves as exemplary, to the extent that James introduces the Brownings into his text before he does the Storys (1:10), though it was not until 1848 that the Storys met the Brownings and "laid the foundation of the most interesting friendship of their lives" (1:96). Keeping the theme of marriage closely tied to that of friendship throughout, in fact, James not only directs considerable attention toward the Lowell and, especially, Browning ménages, but he introduces many of Story's friends (and other individuals) with reference to their marital status (see, e.g., 1:221, 231). As we have seen, however, James deplored intimate biography and never would have scrutinized real marriages as he did fictional; almost naturally, then, he not only abstracted those marriages, but also subsumed them into the "friendships" that he likewise abstracted.[32]

James made central, that is, his use of friendship as device and his elaboration of it as theme. Compositionally, he would step very far from Story by treating the "friends" who "were friends too of each other's friends," by treating "the whole little society" (1:39). He had told Mrs. Waldo Story, moreover, that he needed both to picture these friends and to present their letters, and, in so doing, he also stepped from the Storys as point-of-view characters: as he would do in *Notes of a Son and Brother*, he allowed a society to present itself, at least superficially, from its own collective but variegated perspective. Thematically, he used these friendships to flesh out his biographical portrait, puzzling quietly, for example, over the dull Story's ability to attract brilliant friends; and he also used a metaphor of friendship, as we shall see in a moment, to figure Story's relation to the arts. Finally, he used these friendships to picture a coherent, cohesive, homogenous society, or, more precisely, a cosmopolitan society in which class homogeneity—barely specified by James as such—counterbalances national heterogeneity, a society moreover, in which international marriages and friendships—his preferred specifications—counterbalance international political disputes.

Perhaps most important, James uses tropes of friendship to figure Story's essential division as man and artist. Throughout this very social book, he distinguishes among different types of social being, particularly between those who flutter, restlessly, from circle to circle, and those who confidently, authoritatively, define "circles" (a ubiquitous word) simply by being, wherever they are, centers. He not only suggests that Story resembled the former more than he did the latter, but he also identifies some of Story's "circles" with nationalities and thereby suggests that Story's expatriation and cosmopolitanism contributed to the problem.[33] In a parallel use of friendship, James suggests that Story made friends more successfully than he made art, that his success in the former, indeed, helped cause his failure in the latter, and he simultaneously used Story's gregariousness as a trope for his lack of discipline.[34] In an importantly placed passage, James tells us that Story failed to discriminate between artistry and friendship, and he implies that Story also failed to choose which art would be his closest friend—a point he makes explicit some pages later (see 1:317; 2:84). Story's enviable richness in human friendships, in short, translates into the division and scatter of his art.

James's full picture of Story's art rests on that division and scatter. As a sculptor, Story did three kinds of work: genre studies, portraits, and monuments. As a belle-lettrist, he wrote not only romantic, expressional verse and historical drama, but also public, occasional verse. And, as an essayist, he wrote not just on art and theater, but also on current political issues. Though James approaches Story's sculpture largely from the perspective of aesthetics, he seems more interested in the public nature of much of it and in the commissioned nature of nearly all of it—he seems, that is, more interested in the sculptor as a public and, perhaps, hackney artist than in the sculpture itself. James not only characterizes Story, moreover, as divided between sculpture and letters and, in each medium, as divided between mythological-historical subjects and contemporary subjects; he also characterizes him as divided in the purposes toward which he directed subject matter, as divided, ultimately, in his sense of the role of the artist and of the proper application of art.

In "Siena and Charles Sumner," the chapter that follows Story's establishment abroad, James quotes a letter from Story to Charles Eliot Norton, dated 1861, in which the sculptor characterized his *Libyan Sibyl* as his "best work" and then described it at length as an allegory of "Slavery on the Horizon" in the form of an Africanized Sibyl foreseeing her future in the Slave States (2:71). Showing it and his *Cleopatra* in the London Exhibition of 1862, Story intended to send a message to the English on their misapprehension of the Union cause and on their misguided sympathy with the Confederacy, a message he underscored by concurrently publishing an antislavery pamphlet on "the American question" (2:73). For the first fifteen pages of "The Cleopatra and the Libyan Sibyl," the chapter on Story's sculpture that follows, James appears to abandon the documentary method he had employed to that point, speaking, instead, in his own voice. In fact, however, he was using Story's two most successful sculptures as his documents, and he was using them to develop points not only about Story's own divisions but also about the appeal he held for an uncritical audience.

Approaching these works from the early 1860s as indexes of "taste, the aesthetic sensibility of the time" (2:76), James reprises in substance and in form his argument from *Hawthorne* about the antebellum and wartime generation's unsophisticated affection for romance:

> The sense to which . . . the work of art or of imagination, the picture, the statue, the novel, the play, appealed was not, in any strictness, the aesthetic sense in the general or the plastic in particular, but the sense of the romantic, the anecdotic, the supposedly historic, the explicitly pathetic. It was still the age in which an image had, before anything else, to tell a story, and that had much to do with the immense welcome offered to the Sibyl and the Cleopatra of the new American sculptor. (2:76)

Both reflecting and catering to his age, in James's view, Story had aesthetic preferences dangerous for a literary portraitist, disastrous for a visual artist, and ruinous for a sculptor. Reflecting his own age, however, certainly reflecting his own aesthetic preferences, James neither explored the didactic purposes nor assessed the possible social effects of Story's sculptural messages—at least not, in any event, in his own voice.

In point of fact, James took pains to recover *Cleopatra* and *The Libyan Sibyl* for his own aesthetics and, by implication, for his vision of the artist's vocation. He sees Story as having worked as a true sculptor in these cases, as having created figures whose composition ordered the narrative elements, as having balanced type and instance by fleshing out type with plastic and thematic detail. And he sees the figures as having "calm intensity," as being "tranquil in their beauty in spite of the quantity of story they were addressed to telling. The Cleopatra in particular is admirable for this, for the way in which line and form, a composition inherently interesting in itself, control and condense the historic, the romantic hints" (2:80). Alluding to Hawthorne's commentary on the *Cleopatra* in *The Marble Faun*, applying to the *Cleopatra* and *The Libyan Sibyl* his own principles for literary portraiture, James essentially views from the perspective of form works that Story had intended as political allegories. As he had done in *Hawthorne*, moreover, he commented earlier in *Story* that "great poets," in this case Barrett Browning, do best when they keep their "saving and sacred sense of proportion, of the free and blessed *general*," that "distinguished spirits" do best when they "keep above" the fray; that, to put it less preciously, true artists should stick to art (2:54–55). As his commentary here suggests, Story succeeded in these two sculptures because he did so, and only to the extent that he did so.[35]

It is in this context that we must interpret James's concluding "The Cleopatra and the Libyan Sibyl" with four impassioned letters written from Charles Sumner to Story between May 1863 and October 1864. In the first, Sumner exhorted Story to "make in marble the record of our national regeneration, which is now at hand. Let that be your contribution" (2:157). Some months later, he repeated that charge: "You will be happy to know that the fate of Slavery is settled. This will be a free country. Be its sculptor. Give us, give mankind, a work which will typify or commemorate a redeemed nation. You are the artist for this immortal achievement" (2:158). Following yet another such exhortation, he finally lavished praise on Story for "the poem of Leonardo in 'Blackwood' [and] the criticism on English neutrality in the 'Daily News,'" doubted "if anybody has ever lived before who could have produced these *two* things, which testify to equal eminence in jurisprudence, art and poetry.... You have done a patriotic service" (2:161). However polite James may seem to be in giving these letters prominence, they have the effect, in context, not of enlarging Story but of diminishing Sumner.

Following a chapter devoted largely to politics, "England and Society," James turns in "Graffiti d'Italia" from Story as sculptor to Story as writer, primarily as poet, and treats Story largely by quoting copious passages from the latter's self-damning verse. Though James credits Story with some success, he finds that his general "disposition" as sculptor and poet "was to project characters, individuals, states of mind and feeling," to do in the latter medium what his friend Browning did, but, regrettably, with "a very much lower degree of intensity" (2:232–33). He brings this chapter, finally, to a discussion of *Nero*, which he essentially dismisses as "but a scenic chronicle" (2:253–54), and he extends this note on drama to a concluding discussion of Story's "Shakespeareolatry," his "uncritical adoration" of the Bard (2:258). James had begun "England and Society," however, by characterizing "the twelve or fifteen years from 1862" as the "happiest" of Story's life (2:164), in part because, he adds under the page headline "The American Commissions," Story won so many commissions in this period to "commemorate eminent Americans" (2:167). And following "Graffiti d'Italia," finally, he devotes his penultimate chapter, "American Commissions," to Story's own public memorials and to Story's opinions of those of his peers.

Throughout these chapters, James damns with faint praise Story as sculptor and memorialist, poet and pamphleteer, and damns him, once again, because his interest in everything prevented his concentrating on anything.[36] With regard to the former of those roles, the one praised by Hawthorne and Sumner alike, he develops some chilling ironies: in "American Commissions," he implicitly contrasts Story's winning the commissions for relatively minor monuments to his rivals' winning those for very important ones; and in the final chapter, "Vallombrosa," he details Story's designing and constructing a mountain villa in St. Moritz. Not the sculptor of American history, of the national redemption, that Sumner exhorted him and, evidently, expected him to be, Story ends up, in this narrative, the builder of his own retreat in exile.[37] Though not an extreme distortion of facts, this remains an extremely unflattering portrait, particularly when one sets it, once again, against that of the secondary "character" Browning, and when one sets it in the context of James's overall thesis about Story's inevitable, almost necessary, failure.

Since Ross Posnock, Joseph Solimine, and Karen Wadman have analyzed James's depiction of Browning at length, we need note here only James's key point of distinction: like Story, Browning had a "double identity," but, unlike Story, he had "mastered the secret of dividing the personal consciousness into a pair of independent compartments." Rather than suffer division by the presumably conflicting claims of art and life, Browning had *divided himself* between them (see 2:87–90). As James goes on to explain, moreover, Story and Browning may have shared subjects, even may have shared a taste for diverse subjects, but *treatment*, not subject, defines the artist—"it is to the treatment alone that the fact of possession attaches"—and "the treatment," he proceeds to paraphrase Buffon, "is the man himself" (2:235). Using treatment to mean artistic style, and artistic style as metonymy for style of life, he was performing the same conflation of logical argument and emblematic representation that he had done in *Hawthorne*. Because a specific combination of heredity and circumstances had shaped Story's temperament, and his temperament had shaped his art, his art could stand as emblem for his temperament, and his temperament for his heredity and circumstances.

James advanced an overall thesis, in fact, in which *race, milieu,* and *moment* caused Story's expatriation to Italy, specifically Rome; his expatriation there, in turn, exacerbated his temperamental habits of division and scatter, his lack of "insistence" (2:216); those habits, that lack, kept his art mediocre—neither inspired, on the one hand, nor steadily professional, on the other. James propelled that causal sequence, moreover, through a set of overlapping dichotomies that posed life against work, the work of jurisprudence against that of art, the art of the professional against that of the enthusiast, the enthusiasm for sculpture against that for letters. Divided between each pair, Story was scattered across them all; he pursued so many interests, worked in so many media, treated so many subjects, that he had no controlling interest, medium, or subject. And it was precisely the lack of controlling center in Story's life that James made the controlling center of Story's portrait.

James's thesis holds. He first argued that Story's evident need to "justify" his turning from Law to Art may have been "the secret of [his] multifarious aesthetic activities, his variety of experiment and expression" (1:25); he then argued that the culture demanding that justification also mandated Italy as the place for art; and he later referred to Story's variousness, his "plenitude in feeling," to his expatriation, adding, ominously, that "a man always pays, in one way or another, for expatriation, for detachment from his plain primary heritage" (1:333). He also argued, as the corollary, that Story's "mind begot ideas about everything," and that he was never "without a *subject*" (1:240); that Story "was not with the last intensity a sculptor," and that, had he been, he would not have been "so many other things; a man of ideas—of *other* ideas, of other curiosities," of ideas and curiosities that drove "him into almost every sort of literary experiment and speculation" (2:83–84). This argument, finally, brought James back to his central question about Story, namely, how Story could be "so restlessly, so sincerely aesthetic, and yet, constitutionally, so little insistent," so incapable of focusing "the whole weight of the mind" on a single point, such insistence being, "on the part of most artists . . . an instinct and a necessity, . . . in fact the principal sign we know them by" (2:216–17).

With that question about insistence, James opened the late passage that reaches the crux of the Story case. Seeking "to extract from the case—the case of the permanent absentee or exile—the general lesson . . . latent in it," James found, once again, that "Story *paid*" for trying to become an artist under the conditions made available to him (2:222–23), paid, specifically, the double price of *subject* and of *insistence*. Living "in alien air, far from their native soil," Story and his fellow pilgrims found themselves "the prey of mere beguilement"; and James himself found "the formula of Story's Roman years": Story's career was "a sort of beautiful sacrifice to a noble mistake," and the mistake was his "frank consent to be beguiled" (2:223–24). The "golden air" of Rome beguiled Story and all the others, but particularly beguiled those with Story's temperamental disposition "to flit rather than to rest," made them, to repeat a citation, the particular "victims" of "the wanton Italy" (2:226–27). Story's moral, then, teaches that those who left Boston for Rome had *paid*; but Browning, who left London for Florence, apparently had pointed a "quite opposed moral," for "the writer's 'relation to his subject' " was as strong in him as was his "insistence." Browning was "neither divided nor dispersed, . . . was devoted to no other art" than writing, and, as cause and consequence, did not *pay* (2:226–27). In order to see how James arrived at those moral points, and how he applied them to himself, we need to trace his argument about *races, milieux,* and *moments*.

Despite such extensive treatment of Story, James did not mention his eponymous hero until page twelve of the latter's ostensible life, when he spoke of "the many Italian years of William Wetmore Story, sculptor and man of letters" (1:12). However accidentally, he captured in the syntax of this introduction the relative weight of his emphases throughout on time, place, and person, foreshadowed the degree to which he would oscillate between writing a life, on the one hand, about Story as individual and as type of the antebellum American pilgrim, and making a book, on the other hand, about the American colony in Rome at mid-century as an example of the broader experience of expatriation. *Type*, of course, enabled the oscillation, for James was again assuming, as he had in *Hawthorne*, that heredity and circumstances shaped the individual or group and thus made the individual or group an available literary emblem for that particular constellation of heredity and circumstances. That assumption, in turn, enabled James's quick shift of register from an extremely clotted, autoreferential opening argument, to which I shall return, to his clearer and looser narrative about Story.

Specifically, James formed part 1 of *Story* from two chapters, "The Precursors" and "Cambridge and Boston," intimating with the title of the former that he would treat Story the precursor and the precursors of Story, and with the title of the latter that he would set two provincial American cities against the cosmopolitan city to come, Rome. In this first part, he portrayed at some length Story's paternal progenitor, Justice Joseph Story, portrayed him as an innately worldly though largely untraveled man, an Emersonian cosmopolitan of the mind; and he portrayed Story, generously, not only as having inherited his father's curiosity of the world but also as having acted upon it (see 1:13). Under the page headline "Story's Heredity," James argued that Justice Story possessed all the "*light*" the "Puritan tradition undefiled had to give"—"culture, courtesy, liberality, humanity, at their best, the last finish of the type and its full flower"; that he had the "note" of his "race," that of "active virtue, virtue cultivated and practiced, as the aim and meaning of life"; that he was, in short, "a thorough New-Englander of his time who was yet also, to his great gain, a man of the world" (1:21–22). Having earlier noted that "the best elements of the New England race" had conspired to form his son, paradoxically, as one who would react "from them" (1:14), James elaborates that his hero had "to react [not] against the ugly, the narrow or the cruel, but against an influence that had everything in its favour save its being the right one for *him*" (1:21).

Similar influences, of course, were at work on Story's peers, and, under the page headline "Early Friends," James introduces the most intimate members of Story's American circle, his Harvard chums and lifelong friends Lowell and Sumner. Essentially characterizing their collective sojourning as a fortunate fall impelled by heredity, James ties the question of their "racial" origin to that of their virtually fated destination. They shared a "good faith" (1:10, 28) that he patronizingly and almost reflexively ascribes to them throughout, "the good faith of the young American for whom Europe meant, even more than now, culture, and for whom culture meant, very much more than now, romantic sentiment" (1:188). But James also differentiated these romantic travelers to

Europe, used Lowell and Sumner throughout *Story*, in fact, to develop variations on his theme of romantic exile. Lowell the later ambassador and Sumner the later senator, that is, figure almost too emblematically service to one's nation abroad or service to it at home, the choice that Story, jurist-turned-artist, had to negotiate with respect not only to kind and place of service, but also to length. Though all three retained their dubious "good faith," that is, Story alone left the world of his father to remain abroad, to take up the *permanent* exile of the expatriate.

The *race* that formed Story, James suggests, was Anglo-Saxon and decidedly not Latin, but the *milieux* that formed Story, he also suggests, included not only the America–New England–Boston cluster that Story abandoned, but also, and more important, the Europe-Italy-Rome cluster that he adopted. Though James focuses part 1 of *Story* on the native side of the cis-Atlantic divide, he elaborates in it what would become his governing trope for expatriates. Story and friends, he writes, had gasped at home for the "vital air" that would inspire their artistry (1:9); sought in its absence to breathe elsewhere "the air itself of the world of art, with which the air [they] found [themselves] breathing had so little in common" (1:26); fixed on Rome as its source and went there thinking that they needed only to breathe it in, only to "partake" (1:83); found, instead, the ceaselessly beautifying but also too soothing "golden air." Making the point explicit in the late key passage about the price paid by Story in particular, by "the American absentee in general," James "allude[s] to those existences . . . that, in alien air, far from their native soil, have found themselves . . . the prey of mere beguilement" (2:223). In terms reminiscent of *The Marble Faun* and borrowed directly from *Hawthorne*, he stresses the fatality of uprooting oneself from even thin soil.

James complicated that rather simple America-Europe dichotomy, however, when he introduced into the question of *race* the third of Story's closest friends, Robert Browning. He quotes Story characterizing Britons as stubborn and opinionated, as a "race" unable to "speculate," to manage "theory" or "philosophy," as a race of empirics wholly unlike Italian visionaries, as a race of the "earth" as the Italians are one of the "air"; "Browning," Story adds, "is by nature not an Englishman" (2:69). Though we might be tempted to dismiss the tirade as irony at Story's expense, we cannot ignore that James, as we already have seen, generally subscribed to attributions of national type and specifically subscribed to stereotypes of English empiricism, French theoreticism, and Italian visionary aestheticism. In this instance, then, he would seem to have been suggesting not that Story erred in adverting to national type, but that he got the type wrong; that it was precisely Browning's *being* a typical Briton that enabled him to sojourn abroad, to Italy in particular, without being beguiled. As I have been suggesting, James used Browning throughout *Story* as his hero's *contemporary* countertype, as the figure who not only could negotiate the two competing arenas of life and art, specifically marriage and poetry, but who also could manage the general condition of cosmopolitanism, specifically that of living in England and in Italy.

In other words, James further complicated the trope that he previously had borrowed from Hawthorne for use in his own *Hawthorne*. He was using earth and air as racially and geographically specific signs for England and Italy, while, at the same time, he was using soil and air as general signs for home and abroad—more complexly, for nativism and cosmopolitanism—whatever the particular locales. In a distinct but related thematic, moreover, he was using earth and atmosphere to figure the difference between realism and romance— a trope he had introduced in *Hawthorne* and would elaborate in the prefaces to the New York Edition (see *AN* 33–34). He obviously was using these metaphors to shape a complex cluster of hereditary causes in which the thin pedologic condition of antebellum America conduced to a romantic worldview that caused barely rooted young Bostonians (as opposed to deeply rooted Britons) not only to sever those roots but then to waft, specifically, toward Italy; the heady atmospheric conditions of Italy, in turn, allowed them to believe their worldview confirmed, and, in concert with that confirmation, prevented their rerooting themselves. Moreover, those same conditions prevented their rooting their art in reality, or, put in the positive, caused them to continue to produce romantic art abroad.

Thus, James not only figured the *hereditary* causes of romantic exile, but he also set up several polarities—exile of Americans as opposed to Britons, exile to Italy as opposed to elsewhere, exile in the antebellum period as opposed to the postbellum, and permanent exile as opposed to extended sojourn—that show some slippage but that obviously were meant to portend, together, the fated doom of poor Story, *antebellum American permanently exiled in Italy*. As we have seen, moreover, he then went on to show one of the consequences of that exile—a romantic art made even more egregiously romantic, as *The Marble Faun* had been, as Story's *oeuvre* was. Apparently to emphasize the force of fate at work, James intimated nearly all of this before his narrative reached the point of Story's choosing permanent exile. Anticipating the various divisions both abetting and abetted by that choice, he deftly concluded part 1 with a letter from Sumner in Boston to the Story newly installed in Rome, concluded with an epistolary link from the American world to the European that itself concluded on a reference to the *Revue de Deux Mondes*: the journal of European culture that had beckoned young Americans while never promising, in essence, that their welcome would be hospitable.

James aligned the major divisions in his book with Story's decisive journeys between those worlds, and he turned in part 2, Early Roman Years, to his hero's *milieu*, his place of expatriation, by tracing a vast concentric space comprising Europe, Italy, and Rome. Working with associations and within oppositions that were conventional and that he had employed in his many writings about the continent, he set a broadly brushed, metaphoric Europe against the broadly brushed America already introduced, while he began to set a less broad and less metaphoric Italy against a parallel United States developed a bit later in his text. Using this double schematic, he could set Europe against America as cultural entities, while also setting Italy against the United States as national entities. This was an important maneuver in a book concerned not only with the demise of romantic conceptions of exile and art, but also with the rise of romantic conceptions of nation—conceptions important to the development of the modern nation-state in the 1860s and 1870s, important to the development, that is, of the entity in command of the geopolitical field by 1902–3.[38]

In this most urban of books, however, James focuses neither on Europe nor on Italy but on Rome—Rome not only as eternal city, holy city, imperial city, not only as *city* essentialized, *civilization*, but also as dangerously seductive city.[39] And near the center of that city stood the Palazzo Barberini, Story's residence, to which James devotes a full chapter placed precisely at the midpoint of *Story*. Approaching the Barberini with characteristic slant, James actually speaks *first* of Story's studio, located elsewhere, noting that "there could be no better centre for the comings and goings of the imaginative *maker*," and only *then* names the Barberini as "the main scene for [Story] of an overflowing personal and social life" (1:336–37). Having thus opposed studio/making and residence/living, James then observes that the palatial residence was "built by Urban VIII. 'out of the quarry of the Colosseum,' on the design of Bernini" (1:337), an observation that conjoins a site of bloodletting, the Colosseum, with an institution of absolution, the papacy. With that opposition and that observation, he introduces distinctly allegorical elements that he eventually brings around to "the plash of the great fountain [that fronts the Barberini], that babble of water from somewhere which is ever the most Roman note of all: as if, precisely, in one of the most bloodstained of cities, fate had provided for it a proportionate washing away" (1:343).

In the ensuing allegory, James acts as a tour guide, first approaching and then entering the Barberini, with "its noble scale and mass," and eventually leading us up the "great staircase" to "a voluminous apartment of the second floor," *casa* Story (1:336–42). Along the way, he pauses to consider "the old mystery of the strong effect that resides in simplicity and that yet is so far from merely consisting in it," instancing the "great lines, great spaces, great emphasis, great reserve"—the "grand style" altogether—but again stressing that the apparently natural and simple are really effects of artifice and complexity, "a wrought refinement, a matter of the mixture of the elements, a question . . . of the mutual relation of parts" (1:341). He then escorts us into "an adorable little old *rococo* apartment . . . that was a minor master-piece of early eighteenth-century *tarabiscotage*, of contorted stucchi, mouldings, medallions, reliefs of every form, a small riot of old-world elements," the apartment of Story's neighbor, the American painter J. Rollins Tilton (1:344–45). Using movement through space as an exponent for movement through time, James appears to be figuring architectural degeneration. He guides us from Romanesque monumentality, through Renaissance nobility and lucidity, to baroque chaotic effects; he guides us, in other words, from *elegance*, simplicity that conceals complex unification of elements, to *floridity*, complexity that reveals a lack of such unification. He declines, however, to take the next step to the Victorian *ostentation* practiced by Story and valued by his contemporaries, the pseudo-complexity of merely complicated elements and effects.

In a concurrent motif in the allegory, our tour guide entertains us with a lurid tale. A previous occupant of the Storys' suite, an English noblewoman, had been "stabbed . . . by a treacherous servant," had been found lying "in her blood," but also had turned the blade on her assailant and had "inflicted a wound by which [he] was identified." Making the most of this low-grade stuff, James calls it a "somewhat sinister fact" that gave rise to "a proper weird legend" (1:339); and he eventually notes that the Barberini's fountain at least "plash[ed] enough . . . to cleanse, for the fancy, the threshold on which poor Lady Coventry bled" (1:343). He appears here to be using his Anglo-Saxon aristocrat stabbed by a treacherous, evidently Italian, servant to figure the two American gentlemen-artists Story and Tilton, done in, *betrayed* by Italy and its promise of the artist-life; he appears to be using her story, made legend, to figure Story's story, now being made art by James. The Barberini "overflowed" with Story's life, as it were, and his studio, as a result, overflowed with bad art; like the Barberini's fountain, however, James's text can cleanse the scene of this metaphoric crime, and perhaps absolve or redeem the crime itself.

James links lucid architecture to lurid story rather simply, with the claim that buildings of the Barberini type have an aesthetic self-confidence that allows them to admit "even to such family secrets as are matters of the back-stairs" (1:337). He is making the point, fairly obviously, that other institutions—Rome, the papacy, *biography*—either have or should have the same self-confidence; but he also is allowing, whether by intention or not, something more elusive to materialize in his text. He appears to be making a case against modernity by shaping an allegory of architectural and cultural degeneration, an allegory that joins the history of his exemplary palazzo to the history of events occurring within it; in this allegory, public bloodlettings over political and spiritual issues of great moment recur as private bloodlettings over matters unspecified though evidently more venal, and the latter, in turn, recur as metaphoric bloodlettings over failed artistry. He appears to be creating an allegory, in short, that contrasts the great historical and architectural scale of the Barberini with the puny crisis of Story's life, that contrasts the grandeur and passion of the past with the smallness and fussiness of the present, the momentousness of the public to the inconsequence of the private—and in creating such an allegory, of course, James is writing romantic historiography.

At the same time, however, James joins the Barberini to the other architectural object introduced, the fountain whose flow of water explicitly washes away blood, and absolves crime. Along with an allegory of cultural degeneration, then, James would seem to be elaborating an allegory of aesthetic absolution; in it, the architecture of the Barberini orders and redeems the bloodletting of the Colosseum, the weird legend orders and redeems the bloodletting of the Barberini, and James's book orders and redeems the bloodletting for which the Barberini stands, that of the betrayal of Story. And this would suggest that architecture as art—thus architecture *and* art—redeem experience in precisely the way James meant when he later spoke in the prefaces to the New York Edition of "the sublime economy of art" as that which orders and redeems the waste of "clumsy Life again at her stupid work" (*AN* 120–21). In its simplest aspect, then, James's whole discussion of the Barberini seems to point to the moral, whether by design or not, that history betrays but that art absolves and redeems, that life degenerates but that art regenerates—ultimately, that time and change mean decay but that timelessness and immutability, precisely, do not. As we shall see, however, that moral remains far from clear.

Whatever the case, when James shifted the setting from America to Italy, he also shifted it from nature to culture; he shifted, specifically, from the America of his *Hawthorne*, associated with largely uncultivated soil, to the Rome of Hawthorne's *Marble Faun*, associated with the highly wrought stonework of architecture and sculpture. As I have said, Hawthorne had identified his sculptor Kenyon with Story, and had implicated Kenyon and, metaphorically, sculpture with murder; James followed suit with a critical difference. If he was using blood and water as conventional emblems for such antinomies of experience as crime and absolution, death and life, then the Barberini housing the flow of blood and its fountain housing the spring of water are *together* implicated in those antinomies, together murder and redeem. And that paradox informs not only James's view of Story's art and of *Story* itself as artwork; it also informs the depiction of historical institutions and events that occupies the middle sections of *Story*—a depiction that reflects, in turn, the nostalgic, even morose, vision of history that James held at the turn of the century.

In addition to *race* and *milieu*, put differently, James focused on *moment*—and the moments that formed Story's life included not only his pre-1848 American phase but, more important, his post-1848 "Roman days." Following the lead of his correspondents in these sections, James coordinated Italian political history from late eighteenth-century stirrings of nationalism to the

Risorgimento with American political history from the Revolution to the Civil War.[40] He did so within a schematic, however, at once geographically broader and chronologically narrower than that, one in which he correlated a European history comprising the Revolutions of 1848, Italian Unification in 1860–61, and the Franco-Prussian War of 1870 with an American history comprising the antislavery and secessionist tumults of the 1850s, particularly 1856, and the Civil War of 1861–65. Concentrating this material in the middle chapters of *Story*, as chronology dictated, James focused "The Siege of Rome" on the Revolutions of 1848 and on the French assault on Rome and restoration of the pope in 1849; in "Siena and Charles Sumner," he correlated the movement of Italian politics of the 1850s toward the crisis producing unification with the movement of American politics in the 1850s toward the crisis of secession and, thus, disunification; in "The Cleopatra and the Libyan Sibyl," he used Story's allegorical sculpture exhibited in England as a way to approach the issues of the Civil War and to explore English response to them; and, finally, he turned in "England and Society" from the fall of the Confederacy and the establishment of Union to the Ecumenical Council of 1869 and the Franco-Prussian War.

Opening "The Siege of Rome" with an epistolary exchange between Story and Lowell, James shows them gushing over Italy in the abstract, finding Italians contemptible in the concrete, gushing over freedom and equality in the abstract, finding it unnerving in the concrete: Story, the artist figure, appearing as aesthete, Lowell, the political figure, showing less than ambassadorial tact.[41] For the remainder of the chapter, he deftly juxtaposes Emelyn Story's and William Story's lengthy diaristic accounts of Italy and of the siege. Emelyn Story portrays Italians as dirty, thieving, cowardly, lazy, and shameful, as does Story, who, like Lowell, also regards them as predisposed to treachery. Each diarist records the French landing at Civitavecchia, each recalls watching the barricade-making in Rome, and each recounts the couple's "assistance" at the siege itself from the balcony of Frank Heath's rooms in the Casa Dies, rooms which "commanded the finest view" (1:135). While Emelyn Story emerges as vulgar and trivial, Story again emerges—for better or worse—as vulgar, trivial, and aesthetic, sketching lazy barricade-makers "leaning picturesquely on their spades," commenting on Margaret Fuller's report of the wounded: "This is the shocking reverse of the picture of glory; these are the bloody ends of the threads that work up the tapestry of honour and war" (1:152–54).[42]

James portrays the Storys throughout these pages as a dull, supercilious young couple with little actual interest—in the deeper sense—in the outcome of proximate political upheavals, a couple *whose own words* suggest a tendency to trivialize events, and a tendency to trivialize the statesmen to whom their station gives them access (see, e.g., 1:119, 157). With *his words*, moreover, James depicts them as taking revolution in stride so long as it does not interfere with the artist-life, and as most compelled by Italian politics when they become spectacle—a speech, say, by Mazzini (see 1:117, 126). He depicts them as passive within history—"history continues to sweep our friends along" (1:120)—and depicts them as mistaking history for theater: they take Mazzini and Pius IX, for example, as actors, as Ristoris on a grand stage; indeed, they find the absence of the pontiff offset by Ristori's being "restored to them" (1:132). To say the least, it is a damning characterization, and James makes it more damning by contrasting the Storys, in these matters, not only to the Brownings, but also, at considerable length, to Margaret Fuller and to the Princess Belgiojoso, the latter of whom James calls an "extraordinary woman" and with whom he concludes this chapter.[43]

Ultimately, there may be nothing remarkable in wealthy, Protestant, American aesthetes at mid-century expressing contempt for the mob while espousing republican principles, disdaining the papacy and church liturgy while adoring the art (the Barberini included) patronized by the former or generated by the latter, and failing to see inconsistency in their behavior; nothing remarkable in their approaching battle as spectacle, the wounded as occasion for sentimental metaphor, revolution—*history* itself—as theater. However regrettable the fact may be, James could stress precisely the *typicality* of persons for whom the martial was scenic and the political social—public spectacle and private intrigue. And he portrayed them, moreover, as typical of a *generation* predisposed to those attitudes, trained to them by the thin, uncritical culture in which they had grown. He was reminding his postromantic readers that the romantic American precursors had found Italy "a sort of poetic or fairy precinct" *before* Hawthorne had called it that in the preface to *The Marble Faun*; he was suggesting that they not only had fed on the Hawthornian imagination, but also had fed *its* production of *The Marble Faun*.[44] They had served Hawthorne as models for American artists abroad, and they were serving James here, more broadly, as models for American colonists abroad, victims not only of artistic illusions, but also of political delusions—as amused, aloof, racist, and, in their ignorant innocence, dangerous.

In these same middle chapters, as I have said, James concurrently developed events leading to the American Civil War and brought the war itself into the foreground. He also complicated even further the allegorical relations between characters. Having named the war, straight off, as opening the "chasm" between the precursors and their successors (1:10), James used a set of letters between Justice Story and Story, dated 1842, to establish the relationship between slavery and the war not yet on the horizon, to suggest Story's "conservative" skepticism toward abolitionism, and to advance a convoluted defense of that skepticism.[45] Following Story's removal abroad, James picked up the thread with letters between Lowell and Story in the late 1840s and early to mid-1850s, letters in which Lowell's evident (and, in 1903, well-known) affiliation with abolitionism absolves Story by association.[46] Simultaneously and paradoxically, however, Story's earlier comments also serve to stain Lowell slightly and, thus, to place the *two men* on more ambiguous terrain. Overall, James portrays them as two Brahminic men of letters, rather conservative though persuaded of their liberalism—a portrayal he extends, in "Siena and Charles Sumner," even to the more obviously radical senator.

The only person named in a chapter title, Sumner plays a large but ambiguous role in James's book. On the one hand, Sumner often sounds like Story, tending toward flourishes such as characterizing Austrians as "barbarous" and southern slave-masters as "barbarians" (2:41, 48), Italians and northern abolitionists, by implication, as civilized; and, of course, he often seems beguiled by Story, or by his own vision of Story, regarding him "the first American sculptor" (2:47), and, as we have seen, exhorting him to witness in stone the Union cause and, later, to commemorate its victory and the national regeneration.[47] On the other hand, Sumner often looks unlike Story: Story, we recall, watched the violence in Rome, suffered an "assault" on his sensibilities in Venice and Berlin, came home to the United States uncertain of his career, and returned abroad to take, "in 1856, his final Roman stand" (1:337). Sumner, meanwhile, suffered a *physical* assault in the Senate, in 1856, by a representative of the tyrannical slave-system, had to travel abroad for his health, as a consequence, and then, in a crucial distinction revealed in a sequence of letters dated 1857 through 1860, expressed a ceaseless desire, a virtual *need*, to return to the United States "to fight the battle" against slavery (see 2:32, 33–34, 45, 46, 48).

This distinction seems the true point, indeed, of "The Cleopatra and the Libyan Sibyl," not only the key chapter on Story as sculptor, as we have seen, but also the key juncture of art and politics in *Story*. James opens the chapter, in fact, by contrasting the zenith of Story's career as a sculptor with the nadir of the career of the Union: 1862 was "*the* date, in Story's life," his success at the London Exposition, but also the date that inaugurated "the dark days of the American Civil War, that weary middle period of anxiety almost unrelieved, especially for spectators at a distance whose sympathies were with the North and to whom it sometimes seemed that the issue scarce hung in the balance" (2:75). One cannot fail to note the unflattering juxtaposition: in his "Middle Roman Years," the absentee thrives, while in the middle period of its crisis, the abandoned nation nearly perishes; and however unrelieved the anxiety of the absentee, it remains spectatorial, and, by implication, theatrical. Picking up the opening theme of *Story*, anticipating the dramatic climax, James again shows how Story paid, *what* he paid, for his expatriation: he had been no more than a spectator of his adopted country's crises, his views and actions literally inconsequential; and, Sumner's mandates notwithstanding, he had become no more than a spectator of his abandoned country's crisis, his views and actions—*as James presents them*—equally inconsequential.

James made clear in his clotted opening paragraph, however, that he would proceed to his larger issues not directly from biography, but, rather, indirectly through memoir. Simultaneously establishing theme and perspective, he argued that his predecessors created the conditions in which "we are contentedly cosmopolite to-day" (1:3), that they put into play relations and situations "that we late-comers take all placidly for granted" (1:4), that "Europe, for Americans," in sum, "has ... been *made* easy; it was anything but easy, however much it was inspiring, during that period of touching experiment ... in which the imagination of the present introducer must thus betray at the outset an inclination to lose itself" (1:4). Subsuming past action into present awareness, he sets up his subsequent specification of his subject as "the dawn of the American consciousness of the complicated world it was so persistently to annex" (1:6), while he also implies that he will trace *that* emerging consciousness in tandem with another emerging consciousness, itself a double one: his consciousness, as a young expatriate, of the Europe to come, together with his consciousness, as a memoirist in his middle years, of the Europe long gone.[48]

As he had done in *Hawthorne*, he would focus on "the first sixty years of the century," an "unadministered age" for pilgrims (1:8), but he would concentrate here on the "artist-fraternity," on the "young Americans aspiring to paint, to build and to carve," and who went abroad to do so (1:9). Theirs had been a Europe of little amenity but of a "celestial cheapness" (1:11)—a hyperbole that accrues its meaning through the later Dantean and Miltonic allusions. He exaggerates how little they paid to *live*, however, in order to stress how much they paid to make conditions for artistry possible not only for themselves but, especially, for their successors in his generation (1:9–12). Identifying this beguiling material cheapness as part of the Roman spell, he claims to be searching for that moment in the past when the "spell" of the artist-life abroad had begun to weaken, for his "subject," he says, there "would find its dramatic climax" (1:10). And though he finds that moment elusive, he still will think of "the American who started on his *Wanderjahre* after the Civil War quite as one of the moderns divided by a chasm from his progenitors and elder brothers" (1:10). He is able to find, that is, the moment that separates Story and the precursors from himself, the climactic moment when "good Americans" became critical and, like James, went abroad with clearer heads.

Having signaled that his subject and its presumed climax would be simultaneously biographical and autobiographical, James then seemed to back off; he went on to identify the "subject," more simply, as "the *period*—it is the period that holds the elements together, rounds them off, makes them right. They partake of it, they preserve it, in return; they justify it, and it justifies the fond chronicler. Periods really need no excuses" (2:16). Extending into group portraiture his long tested formula for individual portraiture, he would seek the event that defined a period, the salient incident that established a generation's character; he was backing away from the phenomenological implications of his earlier specification of "subject" in order to simplify the biographical act. He knew, however, that this claim itself was an act, that he could not avoid the phenomenological implications of his endeavor, and so, in that citation as in the earlier one, he turned from object to subject, from *period* to its *chronicler*, and, in so doing, he suggested that periods, no less than persons, would be treated in relation to each other. As good as his word, he explored relations throughout *Story* between the old order and the new, between the Roman period of the earlier years, however beguiling it was, and the modern age, tawdry as it is: Story's was a "stouter age than ours" (1:225, 233), and it functions here as it would throughout James's nonfiction after the turn of the century—as contrast to the lateness of the present hour, or, as he elsewhere would call it, "the fag-end of time" (see *N*).

Even these early expressions of intent, however, fail to suggest the degree to which James actually turned *Story* toward the autobiographical and the auto-referential—as means, again, to get to larger issues. Because he had not known Hawthorne personally, for example, and because his commission had required him to appear detached and objective, he could embed only two brief moments of autobiographical memoir in *Hawthorne*; because he had extensive personal knowledge of Story and his friends, by contrast, and because his commission virtually mandated that he exploit it, he could compose *Story* as a biographical and autobiographical memoir. He included signal recollections not only about himself as a child destined for artistry and, perhaps, exile, but also about himself as the young artistic pilgrim fulfilling that destiny; in addition, he included a good deal of comment, indirect and direct, not only on himself as a seasoned artist and exile confronting Story's history and his own, but also on himself as a memoirist faced with the literary task of making sense of his archives and his memories.[49] He joined recollection and autoreference, finally, in the ubiquitous trope of the spectral, a trope that suggests how this "entertainment particularly subjective" (1:15) became less entertaining, and more disquieting, than he had anticipated.

At one point, for example, James slides from an adult memory of seeing the actress Pauline Cushman in her later Roman years to a far earlier memory from his own "antediluvian" and "prehistoric" New York years, specifically to an evening when his father rushed home during the intermission of a Cushman performance "to snatch up and carry off my elder brother," leaving little Henry "as near as I came in infancy to seeing the celebrated actress in 'Henry VIII.'" James adds, however, that "the scene, that evening, at which, through my being inadequately estimated, I did not assist, is one of the most ineffacable in my tolerably rich experience of the theater." He had kept "a vivid vigil in which the poor lonely lamplight became that of the glistening stage, in which I saw wonderous figures and listened to thrilling tones, in which I knew 'Shakespeare acted' as I was to never know him again, in which, above all, I nursed my view of paternal discrimination" (1:259–60). The first of three related childhood memories, this extraordinary passage fairly bristles with suggestions.

Selecting one of them, we can read the little tale as a testimony to the power of artistic imagination and as James's testament to his early acquisition and understanding of that power—the power that enabled a small boy to stage a uniquely memorable Shakespeare in his skull. At heart, the power both requires and entails solitude—even loneliness—and Story, gregarious exemplar of the precursors, failed to pay precisely that price. As a result, the "infant" James, embryonic man of imagination, could call forth a vibrant staging, could *do* Shakespeare, not just adore him, while the mature Story only could concoct wooden, unstageable dramas like *Nero*, and only could wallow in Shakespeareolatry. James certainly employs some irony at the small boy's expense, since the drama did occur, finally, *only* in the boy's imagination; but he directs the force of the passage toward more sober and serious ends. James suggests, first, that he had developed the power of imagination beyond the infantile and self-pleasuring to the adult and social, for he had used it as an adult to meet the likes of Pauline Cushman and Fanny Kemble on common ground— his father's inadequate estimation and "discrimination" notwithstanding. Second, he is using it even now to imagine another drama at which he was not able to assist, the drama of "the American initiation in a comparative historic twilight" (1:7), the drama he is staging in *Story*.

He sharpens the point considerably, moreover, when he immediately slides from Pauline Cushman to a second recollection, to an equally antediluvian recollection of Grace Greenwood and Fanny Fern, to the moment, specifically, when "that incipient discrimination which is the soul of criticism attached itself to the intelligent consciousness that Grace Greenwood must be somehow finely differentiated from Fanny Fern"--"a perception of which truth," James adds, "may well have represented, in a small mind, the earliest stir of literary discernment" (1:262–63). Even if unconsciously, then, James slides across different connotations of "discrimination" to the deeper connection between his two recollections. His father discriminated against him, but his father also lacked the subtlety of discrimination that he was acquiring: while Henry Sr., that is, failed to discriminate properly between Henry Jr. and William, Henry Jr. would soon discriminate "finely" between Grace Greenwood and Fanny Fern. And given that James likewise imputes to Story and the other precursors an inability to discriminate, we can begin to see how the filial rage, ironic but explicit, directed toward his father becomes part and parcel of a filial rage, however implicit, directed toward Story and the precursors. As he had said, they were his "progenitors" and "elder brothers."

Having thus linked his acquisition of the imaginative faculty to that of the critical faculty, in any case, he later links his being "a young mind just waking up to a sense of contemporary history," just coming to his "first dim apprehension" of the impending Civil War, to his being "a critic in the groping stage" (1:306–8). And, over a hundred pages after that, he ties the imaginative, critical, and historical faculties into one package. Freezing his account of Story, in 1859, to return for three impassioned pages to "the furious assault made upon [Sumner] in the House of Representatives [sic]," in 1856, James notes that "the impression of the event . . . is one that memory has kept, for this careful chronicler, even though the years of a life have overlaid it." What memory has kept, however, is a "recollection" of the news reaching James in Paris, of its inflaming his parents, and of their receiving Sumner socially on a subsequent visit. Since James allows that a young mind, "inflamed by . . . 'Uncle Tom's Cabin,'" might have taken Sumner's assault as the true outbreak of hostilities, he is recollecting by his own admission his failure to have assisted at them, acknowledges his absence as an embryonic expatriate from the first stirrings of the war. And since he recalls that Sumner, during his visit, fit "one's very earliest apprehension, perhaps, of 'type,' one's young conception of the statesman and the patriot," he also is recollecting not only the familial station that enabled his contact with political figures of the moment, but also his juvenile inclination to be swayed by romance and to apprehend reality in terms of romantic art—two traits, of course, that he also attributes to Story (2:29–31).[50]

With those recollections of boyhood, James anticipates thematically related recollections of early manhood; and, in two of the latter, he undertakes a purposeful upstaging of Story. In the first instance, he sets up a near meeting of Story and himself in the postwar Newport of 1865, "the Newport of the ancient days": the Storys were in Cambridge assisting at the famous Harvard Commemoration at which Lowell presented his "Ode Recited at the Commemoration to the Living and Dead Soldiers of Harvard University"; John Field was in Newport reading Emelyn Story's epistolary account of the event; and the young James, our author obliquely reveals, was among Fields's assembly (2: 176–80). In the second instance, James reproduces a letter from Story to Fanny Kemble in which the former (in James's summary) "recalls the occasion of his having, during the winter of 1873–74, read [*Nero*] aloud to three or four friends, of whom Mrs. Kemble had been one." Demurely adding that "the author of these reminiscences happened to be another," James then proceeds to deflect attention from Story as reader-performer to Mrs. Kemble as listener-interpreter, and concludes by "recall[ing] that, though my ears, on the faraway evening in question, were all for Story, my eyes were for our distinguished companion, in whom the whole matter was mirrored, commented, silently *re*presented" (2:254–55; James's emphasis).⁵¹

James is employing these recollections of boyhood and early manhood autobiographically, portraying himself as a displacer of precursor figures and linking displacement to his emergence as an artist. In the first three scenes, he presents his father and his juvenile self (the child as father to the man) before the war, stressing the discontinuity between his father and his adult self while stressing the continuity between his own past and present selves; in the last two scenes, he presents Story and his young adult self after the war, again stressing the discontinuity between Story and himself while stressing the continuity between himself as a young artist and himself as the present older memoirist. In these last two scenes particularly, James turns the autobiographical toward the autoreferential, deflecting attention from his appearance as a character toward his presence as the narrator-author. He directs the Newport scene, for example, toward medium—the medium of epistolarity that he is using in *Story*; and he constructs the *Nero* scene around reaction—Story reads a document, James portrays an interpreter *re*presenting that document. He creates the *mise en abîme* for Story's having left an archive, and James's acting as the interpreter *re*presenting it; and if our ears are for Story, by implication, our eyes should be on James.⁵²

In fact, James conflates the autobiographical and the autoreferential throughout *Story*, with the culmination occurring in his concluding passages. He first takes up a photograph of Story, at his villa in Vallombrosa, entertaining the Shakespearean actor Tommaso Salvini. Recalling Story's Shakespeareolatry and Salvini's professional forte, and recalling the specific focus of Story's essay on "Distortions of the English Stage," James infers not only that Story and Salvini were discussing Shakespeare, but that they probably were discussing faulty stage interpretations of the relation between Macbeth and Lady Macbeth. He then uses the photograph to prompt a recollection of *his* having met Salvini at Story's Florentine home and his having discussed with "the potent old actor" precisely the question of the Macbeths' relations (2:326–30). In a neatly done trick, James has moved in two paragraphs from documentary evidence of one scene to memorial evidence of a second, then "reads in" the known substance of the second for the suspected substance of the first. Where history fails, fancy serves.⁵³ The trick, moreover, also allows him to launch his conclusion with a final reference to marriage and to bloody betrayal, with a final reminder of his own theatrical connections, and, not least, with an almost perfect emblem for the documentary memoir—a faded photograph, ghosted product of an already ghostly process.⁵⁴

In the body of that conclusion proper, James mentions a "short idyllic novel entitled 'Fiammetta' " (2:330) that Story wrote in Vallombrosa, and thus recalls his own opening chapter with its arcadian fantasy of the virginal Storys at Harvard. He then refers to a monograph that Story wrote about Vallombrosa; he quotes Story's complaint in it about "the present Government, caring little for the picturesque, and apparently seeking rather to obliterate than to preserve the traces of the past" (2:333); and he shifts from this to his own "most intimate recollection" of Vallombrosa, of a time when the monastery there had already been "transformed into a State School of Forestry" (2:333–34). Though apparently gratuitous, the reference actually recalls James's very early comment that his documents would allow him to "repeople the States of the Church—how I remember the crooked, coloured spots so stamped in my school-atlas!" (1:11–12); indeed, it encapsulates the themes of temporal power and of national unification that he had developed throughout *Story*: the great shift from Church to modern State. Strikingly, however, James's metaphors displace political modernization into technological modernization, specifically, that of ox-carts being replaced by trains, the latter a technology that replaces animals with machines, and beaten paths with iron tracks, a technology that thus separates humans from the nature it simultaneously blights, a technology, finally, that provides "for access without contact and acquaintance without knowledge" (2:332).[55]

James had begun this passage, moreover, by invoking Milton, and he obviously intends to recover the romantic sentimentality of a *Fiammetta* into the romantic sublime. Circling yet again to his opening, to his opening sentence about the precursors who "made out the road" (1:3), James closes by imagining Story—"imagine[s] our friend"—traveling this arcadian landscape and feeling, at the end, a kind of "beautiful" sadness, "listening to its voices," voices telling him "how far he had come from the primary scene," what he had lost, what gained (2:338).[56] Having likewise traveled his imagined landscape and having listened to its voices, the documents in his boxes and the memories in his mind, James comes to a final reminiscence of "the road connecting Vallombrosa with Lago"; he then journeys imaginatively on that road from Vallombrosa, with its undertone of monastic community, to Lago, with its overtone of "sociability" (2:336–37). As this conclusion suggests, Story may have failed as an artist, but he also redeemed himself through sociability, a sociability expressed by the marriage invoked in the biography's final word: wife. As this conclusion also suggests, his biographer must redeem himself through a different sociability, a sociability expressed by the artistic but lonely evocation of Roman shades. Story had his society and his wife; James has his documents and memories and, ultimately, his book.

In his subtitle to that book, he had indicated that he would construct his group portrait from letters, diaries, and recollections—as though these were like quantities. Though he never did pursue, in fact, potentially interesting distinctions between the epistolary and the diaristic, he thematized from his opening paragraphs the implications of working with "old records, spared by time and mischance" (1:3–4). Indeed, he pursued at great length distinctions between documents and recollections, between the archival and memorial genres, distinctions he neither could fix theoretically nor sustain in his own application. And from his earliest recollection of his own childhood to his melding, some seven hundred pages later, Story's description of Vallombrosa with his own "reminiscence" of a visit there after Story's death (2:336), he pursued these distinctions in the context of his own roles as disinterested editor but interested historian, as one who "observed" perhaps "too fondly" and who, therefore, could claim neither to having observed from a detached perspective, nor to be narrating from one.[57]

When James said at the start that he intended to chronicle "the dawn of the American consciousness of the complicated world it was so persistently to annex," he added that "the interest is in its becoming perceptive and responsive, and the charming, the amusing, the pathetic, the romantic drama is exactly that process" (1:6). In *Hawthorne*, James had sought to reproduce Hawthorne's circumstances and to glimpse imaginatively this precursor's perceptions of them; in *Story*, he would reproduce his precursors' documents in order to reconstruct literally their perceptions of their circumstances: "To live over people's lives," he adds in a key passage, "is nothing unless we live over their perceptions . . . since it was *by* these things they themselves lived" (1:125). Yet he just had intimated that such perceptions could interest us only by having come into being, or *as having* come into being, and that, as a consequence, he had to *reenact* that process, *stage* that romantic drama. This all presupposes, however, that he would be able to read his documents correctly, and that he would be able to provide them with the correct narrative movement—neither task easy for an author increasingly implicated by memory in the materials at his disposal.

He confronted this problem in his central statement of method, a three-page paragraph that seems, at least initially, to contradict itself. In it, he equates his letters with "ghosts and echoes" whose "interest . . . is a matter of our own memory, our own fancy, to say nothing of our own heredity; I take it indeed for an entertainment particularly subjective." To enjoy this entertainment, he continues, he has to "read [meanings] into" the names invoked, the ghosts raised, and to do this, in turn, he has to commit an "act of remembrance lively almost to indiscretion." He makes this problematical, however, when he later adds that "everything in a picture . . . depends on the composition; if it be the subject that makes the interest, it is the composition that makes . . . the subject"; and when he elaborates that his documents " 'compose,' hang together, consent to a mutual relation, confess, in fact, to a mutual dependence," and, thereby, as we have seen, establish "the *period*" as the subject (1:14–16). In a word, he presents documents that simultaneously *give out meanings* and *allow meanings in*, that simultaneously *compose themselves* and *must be composed*—ghosts that consort freely with one another while simultaneously needing the conjurer to bring them forward. Put differently, he proposed two distinct and not clearly complementary sources of interest.

In terms of aesthetics, his point seems clear. Persons historically related wrote documents, mainly epistolary, to and about each other, documents subsequently collected in an archive. Thus doubly "composed," hung together, *before* they reached James's hands, they formed a potential group portrait. As even thusly *related* elements, however, they needed animation for that portrait to become a drama. To those letters as *character* studies, in short, James had to add *incident*, from *picture* he had to create, if not novel, then heavily *novelized biography*—particularly since, as we have seen, he thought the principal writer of the documents, and by implication the documents themselves, so dull. He achieved this by rearranging the documents according to his own lights, by using memory to elaborate the incidents they mention, by adding his own recollections of related characters and incidents, and, finally, by layering over the narrative thus generated a character study of himself as narrator, unfolded through and revealed in the duration—the extended incident—of narration. In a word, he deflected a good deal of the reader's attention from narrative to narration and, in the process, from period to *period mediated* by himself.

In terms other than the aesthetic, however, his point seems less clear. In his fiction, James frequently had employed the reading of documents as a metaphor for the conundrum of inherent versus applied meaning in any phenomenon: one must read out the meanings that phenomena have to give, while reading in the meanings that one needs or chooses to give them. In *Story*, he did the opposite: he used another phenomenon—the spectral—as a metaphor for written and visual documents and for the hermeneutical problems they raise. He had said in his statement of method that " 'a vanished society' is a label before which . . . the man of imagination must inevitably pause and muse" (1:16–17), a particularly difficult task, he would add later, for the "historian" with "memory and imagination always at his heels" (2:196). Figuring at once the elusiveness of meaning in general and the absence of the past in particular, ghosts prove especially troublesome to a writer inclined toward fiction in general, a writer related memorially to the past in particular. He was facing the central problem of his last phase, the problem, as he put it here, that a "fond embroiderer" can read almost any meaning into any "faded sketch" (1:245), can "at need find worlds"—and James repeats the phrase with variation—in even little *carnet* entries of a half dozen words (1:321–22).[58]

It is not surprising, then, that ghosts, shades, and apparitions overrun *Story*; not surprising that James variously figures himself as Ulysses in the underworld, as Dante among purgatorial shades, and most often as a generic conjurer at his rites. These ghosts, moreover, tend to resist James's will, despite the differing degrees of control suggested by the tropes for himself just cited. When unbidden but encountered alone, for example, or when bidden, they tend to materialize and to speak, to fix a stare, or otherwise to importune; but when unbidden, or when bidden as a group, they tend to "swarm"—and to do so threateningly (see, e.g., 1:222, 257; 2:119). James was using these ghosts to figure a problem in *documentary editing*: historical documents seem not only willfully intractable in the face of one's imaginative desires, but also willfully autonomous in the face of one's imaginative designs. And he was using them, simultaneously, to figure a related problem in *memorial writing*: involuntary memory threatens, anarchically, to destroy the controlling and the ordering processes of voluntary memory. He was suggesting metaphorically that objects of scrutiny seem to multiply themselves and their relations, while the scrutinizing subject, like it or not, complies in the act. He was suggesting, to use a different language, that intertextuality and intersubjectivity entail and exacerbate one another.

James relentlessly pressed this theme not only with spectral metaphors, but also with sylvan and marine metaphors; whatever the vehicle, however, the tenor remained the same: James could not take control of his subjects because he could not stand apart from them.[59] He was so implicated with them, indeed, that he frequently recalls moments in his own past when he had recalled moments in either his own or someone else's past, when, as he says, he starts "the ghost of a ghost" (1:173), hears "the echo of an echo" (1:241–42). But he also acknowledges something perhaps even more fearful than the presence of ghosts, namely, their absence—for that would be absence doubled to absoluteness. And that fear explains why he not only recollects ghosts, but also, in odd moments of prolepsis, has those ghosts anticipate him as their future conjurer (see, e.g., 1:122). To put this in less metaphoric language, his documents may have resisted him, may even have overwhelmed him, but they also connect him materially to his past. Precisely because his memory gives those documents meaning, though paradoxically rendering their materiality immaterial, it becomes a power of extreme value: it, too, may resist and overwhelm him, but its lapse would leave him marooned, alone, in the present.

In the 1890s, both Henry and William James wrote often of the spectral, Henry's investigations culminating, arguably, in "The Turn of the Screw" (1898). So much critical commentary has focused on this theme that I wish to note here only how James used the spectral, in *Story*, to figure the presence of an absence as opposed to a simple absence—to figure, that is, that which exists at least as an occasion for interpretation, as opposed to that which exists only as interpretation in search of an occasion—in a word, solipsism.[60] That use of the spectral, moreover, serves to figure the nature of documentary memoir, and vice versa: the desired if still fearsome meaning of the spectral as the presence of absence could stand for the circumstances of James's task in *Story*, while those circumstances could stand for the meaning of the spectral that James, late in life, seemed desperately to need to believe in. He wanted and needed to be haunted, that is, not only by his precursors, but also by himself as precursor—as child, young man, and even very recent voyager to Italy—for only through such a haunting could he establish a continuity for *his* life and his times.

❦

The first two parts of James's tripartite strategy, clearly, turned out neither so kindly nor so disinterested as he had let on to his correspondents. With respect to "the Biographic subject," William Wetmore Story, he inverted the terms he had used when writing to Houghton Mifflin: he narrated a life that had lacked adventure but that already had been romanticized by the man living it; and he portrayed that man as having failed to find, though he diligently had sought, intellectual distinction. With respect to his compensatory biographic subject, moreover, his portrait of a vanished society, he had adhered to the logic of his inherently unflattering *donnée*: having proposed the dull and mediocre Story, the vain and self-romanticized Story, the illuded and deluded Story, as *instance of a type*, he then could present neither other instances, nor the type itself, as anything fundamentally different—and, in fact, he did not.

None of this was lost on Henry Adams. Writing James in November 1903, he praised *Story* as "*a tour de force*" that exposed "*Type bourgeois-bostonien!*" Adams's entire "New England generation," he wailed, had been "in actual fact only one mind and nature; the individual was a facet of Boston." They had been shallow, ignorant of the world, pretentious in their professional aspirations, and, ultimately, had suffered a "self-distrust [that] became introspection—nervous self-consciousness—irritable dislike of America, and antipathy to Boston." He then drove his point home: "So you have written not Story's life, but your own and mine,—pure autobiography,—the more keen for what is beneath, implied, intelligible only to me, and half a dozen other people still living; like Frank Boott: who knew our Boston, London and Rome in the fifties and sixties."[61] Acknowledging by return post Adams's "so ingenious expression of the effect on [him] of poor *W.W.S[tory]*," James coolly shifted the matter to an indictment of genre. "The truth is that any retraced story of bourgeois lives," he observed, "throws a chill upon the scene, the time, the subject, the small mapped-out facts," because "the art of the biographer—devilish art!—is somehow practically *thinning*. It simplifies even while seeking to enrich" (*HJL* 4:288–89).[62] And, keeping his tone consistent, he concluded on the technical note I cited early in this chapter.

Having measured the third, the memorial, aspect of James's strategy, and having assessed its creator's own "nervous self-consciousness" and "irritable dislike of America," Adams had made Story, James, and himself all partners in folly by absorbing James into his New England generation and into the Bostonian type. Perhaps hungering for company in self-abasement, however, Adams had failed to gauge accurately the distance James had wanted to put between the type and himself, as well as the distance he had needed to; Adams had not really misread his man's text, but he had misread its intent. If we return briefly to the themes of cosmopolitanism, marriage, and public art in *Story*, we can see not only how James was distinguishing his situation from Story's, but also how his attempt to do so concealed anxieties about those three matters as they pertained to him. If we then return to the larger historical issues that James approached through Story and friends, we can see how he was distinguishing Story's generation—indeed, Story's epoch—from his own, while he was intimating throughout his book that just as Story's friends and times had suffered betrayals, so had James's. If Story and his friends had been betrayed by their romantic illusions, James and his friends, he implies, had been betrayed perhaps even worse by their presumed capacity for realistic, critical thought.

Though James had treated the Roman seduction of American painters in "The Madonna of the Future" (1873) and that of American sculptors in *Roderick Hudson* (1875), he still was using cosmopolitanism as a positive quantity, four years later, in *Hawthorne*. Long exiled by 1902–3, however, he took a more louche view in *Story*. Having admitted himself "almost extravagantly disposed, for reasons of my own," to read meanings into the precursors' exile (1:5); having presented as his exemplar a Bostonian who decamped for Rome before the great historical divide of 1865; he could have pictured himself, by simple contrast, as the New Yorker who decamped for London after that divide. He did so, but he also quoted Browning declaring, "I distrust all hybrid and ambiguous natures and nationalities" (2:91), and, as we have seen, he went on to distinguish between persons who could do or be two things at once, successfully *self-divided*, and persons who hovered *between* two things, becoming, in effect, nothing but that state of division.[63] It takes no great insight to see that James wanted to believe himself the former, but feared he had become the latter. With respect to ambiguous nationality, in fact, he expressed precisely that fear to such friends as Edith Wharton and Hamlin Garland, and he expressed it, of course, in *Story*, in "The Jolly Corner" (1908), and, terminally, in *Notes of a Son and Brother*.[64]

Despite James's sentimentalizing of marriage, moreover, he also implicated it in Story's artistic failure. Reprising a theme explored in "The Lesson of the Master" (1888) and in similar tales, James portrayed marriage as the primary manifestation of Story's gregariousness, and his gregariousness as the treacherous enemy of his art.⁶⁵ Here and elsewhere, as I read him, he seemed to suggest not so much that choosing marriage was to choose against art, but rather that the true artist could not choose but to choose against marriage—that his so choosing, perhaps, becomes a sign we can know him by. He had finessed the issue in *Hawthorne*, and he did the same here with the vexing case of Browning, brilliantly domestic and artistic, a case he simply did not attempt to resolve. He did link marriage, however, including Browning's, to uxorial and filial loss—to loss itself—more insistently in *Story* than even in his novels. His actual cases allowed him to imply, however obliquely, that to enter a marriage means to create a situation in which one spouse must endure the death of the other (and in which one or both spouses might endure the death of a child), and that such endurance often entails the survivor's loss of wits . . . or life.⁶⁶

Finally, James suffered no anxiety of influence over Story the artist; though he had regarded Hawthorne the epitome of original romantic genius, he considered Story the exemplar of negligible romantic sentimentalism. At most, he seemed to be entertaining himself with an extended literary *amusette* in which Story's *Nero*, as we have seen on different occasions, functioned as an ironic *mise en abîme* for *Story* itself. If we reread the passage about James's childhood "vigil," however, in the light of his later remarks that (1) Story's "fondest dream in a poetic way would have been to write some play susceptible of presentation" (2:247), and that (2) Story spoke of his *Nero*, specifically, "as if it might have been placed on the stage; yet it is in fact but a scenic chronicle" (2:253–54); then we find not an anxiety of influence but an anxiety based on similar dreams and fates. The "vigil" scene makes sense, that is, against the backdrop of James's traumatic failure as a dramatist in the early to mid-1890s; and it makes equal sense, one must add, against that of his successful return as a novelist afterward, in the "half a dozen years of experimental writing," as Leon Edel has put it, "in which [he] assimilated the techniques derived from the theater."⁶⁷

In fact, the scene cuts precisely in both directions. On the one hand, James was creating Story, by intention or not, in the image of his own fears: the Story reading *Nero* to inattentive friends reenacts the abandoned boy imagining Shakespeare, the boy who later became a dramatist without an audience; and the Story who wanted to write stageable plays, but could not, foreshadows the James who was attacked for lacking theatricality. On the other hand, however, James was creating Story, again by intention or not, as the counterimage to his own glories: Story the dramatist and romancer never could have succeeded as James the *novelist* had done and even was doing, in fact, in *Story*; James was not writing merely "scenic chronicle" but was fusing the pictorial and the romantic in what he pointedly called "drama." Moreover, James had added the literary element that Story, despite his fondness for narrative, lacked; the element that Browning, presumably, would have added had he essayed a *Nero*; the key novelistic element of James's post-theatrical fiction: *narration*.⁶⁸ Those differences provided the basis for the negative genealogy that James treated, however ironically, throughout *Story*: Story's sculpture, including his portraiture, had too much narrative, and his narrative writing, his drama and his poetry, had too much picture; by contrast, James had balanced character and incident in the group picture of *Story*, and he had enlivened the blend with memorial narration.

If Story's art triggered no real anxiety, however, his *commissions*, dwelt on by James, might have done. R. Jackson Wilson has pointed out that the professionalization of authorship in Victorian culture encouraged a particular distinction—"the distinction between the works of persons of 'genius' driven by the love of truth and beauty, and the sordid productions of hackney artists driven only by the love of profit and the tawdry celebrity that might come with it."⁶⁹ Though James was deconstructing that very distinction in such tales as "The Death of the Lion" (1894) and "The Next Time" (1895), and though he was treating Story's own investment in it as one of his hero's romantic illusions, he himself had invested heavily in a related distinction, as Wilson has argued, a distinction between the artistic *amateur* driven by passion, but capable of expressing only himself or his private experience, and the *expert*, driven by financial necessity, but capable of sublimating himself and his private experience. As we saw, the young James praised Hawthorne's genius, while he reproached that precursor's lack of professional expertise; as we have seen, the older James slighted Story as an unschooled amateur, while he also reproached him as a hack who primarily executed commissions. James had joined two sets of binaries, in other words, in a way that left Hawthorne his genius but Story virtually nothing.⁷⁰

In this period, James was writing a good deal of fiction about professionalism, about the commerce of art, and, in the earlier but signal case of "The Aspern Papers" (1888), about the commercial exploitation of biographical documents. In *Story*, he seemed to suggest not only that his subject's active social life left him unsuited to the lonely rigors of art, but also that his active professional life, his seeking and winning commissions, compromised his artistic freedom. Though James applauds Story's refusal to enter competitions (see 2:299), he makes clear that Story did adapt to other circumstances. Evidently, then, James was using Story's career choices, not just his life choices, to comment on his own—simultaneously to puff the integrity that made him a less "popular," less successfully commercial, artist than Story, *and*, more covertly, to justify his occasional need to relax his aesthetic vigilance. This seems neither accidental nor minor, given the complaints he voiced repeatedly in his correspondence about the commission at hand: he obviously knew that *Story* itself constituted a breach of his artistic, if not his professional, ethics. To the extent that Story the professional foreshadowed James, then, he bothered him.

Yet something else about Story's career seems to have nettled James even more, something we can sight through an omission. As lengthy and pivotal as are James's discussions of *Cleopatra* and *The Libyan Sibyl*, he neglects to mention Harriet Beecher Stowe's article, "Sojourner Truth, The Lybian Sibyl," published in the *Atlantic Monthly* in 1863—an article in which the romancer most famously associated with the cause of abolition and the effect of emancipation linked Story's two sculptures directly to the life of Sojourner Truth.[71] Assuming James simply didn't know of the piece, we still might comment on his general handling of Story's involvement, as artist and essayist, in the public sphere: he treats that involvement, in essence, like Story's gregariousness, his residence abroad, and his commissions—as another beguiling distraction from true artistry. Assuming James *did* know of the essay, however, and it is likely that he did in 1902–3, we have a more vexing problem of interpretation. On the one hand, James may have been, crudely put, envious: he could absorb his own bachelorhood, expatriation, and professionalism into the model of himself as artist that he had been developing since *Hawthorne*, but he could not so easily absorb his own failure to be a public artist into his concurrently evolving model of himself as a man of letters. On the other hand, he may have passed, simply put, on a good opportunity: he could have used Stowe's appreciation of Story, like Sumner's, to support his more general if more ambivalent point that Story's artistic romanticism exemplified the social and political romanticism of the great causes of the earlier day.

In order to gauge the ambivalence of that point, we might return to James's childhood "vigil" yet again. The scene suggests that Henry Sr. betrayed Henry Jr. by taking *William* to *Henry VIII*—the betrayal underscored by the shared name of father, younger son, and subject of the drama. Though James doubtless was rehearsing the incident to even the score with his father—demonstrating, one might add, a certain disregard for "filial piety"—his joining it to the passage about his acquiring the critical spirit adds resonance. Henry Sr. lacked the same critical judgment that Hawthorne, Story, the antebellum American in general lacked; and since the young James also lacked it, the older James was using himself as a child, as he had done in *Hawthorne*, to represent a young, an immature, a jejune generation. That same representative young boy abroad, fired up by Harriet Beecher Stowe, uncritically and romantically took Sumner as type of proper statesman—just as Hawthorne, Stowe, and Sumner were taking Story for a proper sculptor. James seems to be suggesting, as he also had done in *Hawthorne*, that his older self in possession of the critical spirit, the self who represented the postbellum generation, had come to see more clearly both literary *and* political culture. Yet when he had acquired the critical spirit, he also makes clear, he had fallen, as had his generation; and it is precisely his fall from the "good faith" of his predecessors that he laments "at this time of day . . . in the age of criticism" (1:115–16).

That "good faith," that is, had allowed Story considerable latitude. It had allowed him to believe that he could live in permanent exile from his native land, permanently resident in an older and alien culture, with only salutary effects on his art; and it had allowed him to believe that he could lead a full and rich domestic life as a paterfamilias, and a social life as a generous host, with no ill effects on that art. It had allowed him to believe that someone with neither training nor genius could become not only a professionally successful sculptor and man of letters, but also a socially and politically effective one—that such a person could put chisel and pen not only in the service of clientele, but also in that of great public causes. In James's depiction, however, Story's good faith betrayed him on all counts: *cosmopolitanism* had robbed Story of the native subject that James came to believe essential to art, and *domesticity* had absorbed the time and attention needed for artistry. Moreover, *professionalism* and *political ideals* had equally, though differently, militated against artistic integrity. James goes much further, however, for the "good faith" that betrayed Story the individual artist stands for the related forms of good faith that betrayed Story's type and Story's generation. And since James was using that generation, at the furthest reaches of his text, to represent an epoch, it seems difficult to avoid the conclusion that the good faith of the epoch had betrayed it—and the epoch had placed its faith in emancipation and in liberation.

James opened his treatment of the Siege of Rome, to be more specific, by jumping from the Storys' arrival in 1849 to his own in 1869. "Story and his wife," he notes, had known "the Rome of the old order, the Rome of which the rough hand of history has so grievously deprived the merely modern pilgrim"; James himself "can remember but the last winter before the deluge, and only a portion of that." Old Rome herself, in that winter, had foreseen "the great assault to be suffered," had "gathered herself up, for her last appearance, her last performance" (1:93). The Ecumenical Council of 1869 "was the making at least of a perpetual many-coloured picture—the vast, rich canvas in which Italian unity was . . . to punch a hole that has never been repaired. The hole today in Rome is bigger than almost anything else we see, and the main good fortune of our predecessors in general was just in their unconsciousness of any blank space. The canvas then was crowded, the old-world presence intact" (1:93–94). He broadens this Roman context to the European when he speaks, some four hundred pages later, of the Franco-Prussian War as "the hitherward limit of the *liveable* era, the age that had not wholly thrown up the sponge of Selection" (2:166).

Taken together, these passages suggest a private history in which the antebellum American Story had ventured from a culture of absence to one of old world presence, but never had gained the experience needed to become conscious of the growing blankness of that latter world; a private history in which the postbellum "good American" James, by contrast, had ventured from an emerging culture of criticism to a declining culture of selection, already had fallen into the experience that enabled him to see the growing Roman blankness, the growing European indiscriminateness. Having had America before the fall and Rome, if only for a winter, before the deluge, he *had been* both prelapsarian and antediluvian, but *became* irrevocably postlapsarian and postdiluvian. On that basis, he expressed a nostalgia—as deep as that in *Hawthorne*—not only for antebellum America, but also, and more centrally here, for Rome before its architectural and institutional transformation into a modern capital, for Italy before its unification and emergence as a modern nation-state, for Europe before its emergence, after 1871, as a contentious family of such national entities. He seemed to use the private histories of Story and himself, in sum, to figure the social and political histories of America and Europe.

Specifically, James seemed to approve the establishment of the republic in 1849 and unification in 1861 as forms of union that preserved, or, at least, did not destroy, the old Rome; but he also seemed to suggest that the subsequent establishment of Rome as capital in 1871, and the changes made to it, left a great absence for the pilgrims of James's generation. The "absence" that had characterized antebellum America, according to *Hawthorne*, would seem to have recurred, in this vision, in the "blankness" of post-unification Rome; just as the "uncritical" state of antebellum America, likewise, would seem to have recurred in the *unselective* state of post-1870 Europe. Without doing so explicitly, James not only was establishing the 1860s as the crucial decade for both sides of the Atlantic, but he also was confirming, from the vantage of 1902–3, a common notion he had been advancing in his fiction since *The American* (1877): as Europe was retreating, the United States was advancing; old world powers were giving way to new on the geopolitical stage.

As I suggested in my previous chapter, we can find beneath the obvious and strident critique of secession in *Hawthorne* a more muted critique of the Revolution. And we likewise can find beneath James's lamentations over the costs of the Civil War there a latent horror over other consequences, a horror that would become manifest in 1907 in *The American Scene*. Similarly, we can read beneath James's aestheticized nostalgia for old Rome, old Italy, old Europe, in *Story*, an even less latent horror at the revolutions of 1848, Italian unification, and the Franco-Prussian War.[72] These not only had robbed James, as a young pilgrim (and, of course, as an exemplar of his generation), of the Europe that Story had known; they also had established the conditions that now were robbing the elder memoirist of the Europe that *he* had known—the Europe that preexisted, for example, England's loss of Victoria and America's victory in the Spanish-American War. And he would find the consequences of the demise of that Europe, one might add, horribly confirmed in August 1914, when he found his own faith betrayed and when he expressed gratitude that *he* had not kenned the history that had swept him along.[73]

Though apparently unreluctant to expose those views, James seemed more cautious about exposing others. He not only intimates, in a common debunking tactic, that his subjects' views on progressive political causes often conflicted with their personal behavior; but he also insinuates that Story and his friends, Brahmins all, were enmeshed *as agents and as objects* in multiple acts of delusion and betrayal. In his depiction, they were aristocrats who professed liberal democratic values, and who, in the delusion of their belief, betrayed simultaneously their own class interests and those of the lower classes; they were men of letters who believed that art could be useful in advancing progressive political causes, and who, as a result, betrayed simultaneously art and those causes. They did all this, moreover, with a "good faith" in the world to come, one at whose birth they would assist; but when it did come, it betrayed them in two paradoxical ways: to the extent that it became less emancipatory, more imperial, it betrayed their professed values; but to the extent that it became more democratic, less aristocratic, it rendered them anachronistic, made them a "vanished" society. History, ultimately, betrayed Story, Lowell, and Sumner, their good faith in the Union and in the Risorgimento notwithstanding.

In the opening sentence of *Story*, James had figured those precursors as "the light skirmishers, the *éclaireurs*, who have gone before" (1:3), as a military vanguard.[74] Later in the opening chapter, he gave the metaphor specifically political coloration: Story's rejection of New England and the Law for Europe and Art was a "revolution without a betrayal" (1:14). That it is the *only* revolution without a betrayal proves key to James's disillusioned allegory of history. Founded in revolution, the American Republic suffered a rebellion, reconsolidated itself as Union, and marched toward empire; likewise founded in revolution, the French Republic repeated the cycle of revolution, counterrevolution, and empire, twice in the space of a century. Both republics, however, were merely reenacting the vaster history of the ancient Roman Republic and Empire, itself founded in rebellion, and of the modern state later built, through revolution, upon its ruins (from its "quarry"?), the Italian Republic with its modern capital, Rome. Though James may have been warning *fin de siècle* states to beware their own betrayals of their pasts in their imperial designs, he seems more obviously, if more regrettably, to have been pressing the simple moral, *plus ça change, plus c'est la même chose*.[75]

Ultimately, however, James's allegory reads out even more generally. Beguiled and betrayed by Rome and his vision of the artist-life, that is, the romantic Story paid with exile and with mediocre art; beguiled and betrayed by visions of equality and promises of liberty, the romantic generation paid with naivete and ultimate disillusion; and beguiled and betrayed by history, finally, the romantic epoch paid with blood and with a wrenched social order. As he had done in *Hawthorne*, James essentially was arguing that experiments in art betray, that revolutions in affairs betray, and that history itself betrays.[76] He went a step further here, however, to add that one's desire to read any such meaning out from history may reflect one's need to read some such meaning into history; he went on to add, in other words, that *historiography* also beguiles and betrays. And if historiography is so compromised and so compromising, then James can no more know nor accurately represent Story's life and times than Story could know or accurately represent the insurrection that ended Nero's reign and the line of the Caesars, that drove the emperor to suicide and thus spawned legends of his subsequent haunting of Rome. Like his biographical subject, James can only tell a romance of sensuality and perfidy, a ghost story that allows him to indulge his nostalgia for a vanished *society*—in every sense of the word—while concealing the less pleasant aspects of that nostalgia.[77]

James had warned that his imagination "must betray at the outset an inclination to lose itself" in the precursors' period (1:4); and he might have warned that he, moreover, would betray his deep investments in their circumstances and, ultimately, in his recovery of their perceptions.[78] He had remarked glibly to Frank Boott, in 1895, that the late Story's statues would be "loose upon the world" (*HJL* 4:24); but he seemed not to have anticipated, in even the rest of that morbid letter, the force with which his own memory would loose Story's friends, specters all, upon himself.[79] Looking back in *Story* to "live over" their perceptions, he found that he had to live over his own as well; he found himself, moreover, confronting the specter of his past self advancing to meet him, saw himself as his own precursor. He suggested that "one of the main effects of such a retrospect as this" would be union, or fusion (2:86), and he meant, in part, the kind of union that he would depict with poignancy in *A Small Boy and Others*: "To look back at all is to meet the apparitional and to find in its ghostly face the silent stare of an appeal. When I fix it, the hovering shade, whether of person or place, it fixes me back and seems the less lost—not to my consciousness, for that is nothing, but to its own—by my stopping however idly for it" (*SB* 92). He extended that union to others in *Story*, as he again would, in fact, in his "Family Book," *A Small Boy* and *Notes of a Son and Brother*.

Soon after James sent Henry Adams a copy of *Notes of a Son and Brother*, in 1914, Adams wrote a mutual friend, "Poor Henry James thinks it all real, I believe, and actually still lives in that dreamy, stuffy Newport and Cambridge.... Yet, why!"[80] What Adams wrote James has not survived, but James scolded Adams, in a return letter, for the "unmitigated blackness" of his response to the book. "*Of course* we are lone survivors," James lectured, "of course the past that was our lives is at the bottom of an abyss—if the abyss *has* any bottom; of course too there's no use talking unless one particularly *wants* to." But, he continued, he had written *Notes* to show "that one *can*, strange to say, still want to—or at least can behave as if one did. Behold me therefore so behaving.... It's, I suppose, because I am that queer monster the artist, an obstinate finality, an inexhaustible sensibility.... It all takes doing—and I *do*" (*HJL* 4:705-6). Adams had understood the pathos of James's nostalgia, but not, really, the power of his will. Though also a disillusioned Victorian, like Adams, James nonetheless saved himself from cynicism through his own good faith—a *romantic* faith not in the artist-life, but in artistry as the power that confirmed life and, perhaps, even conferred it. With that vision of the artist and art, the successor of Hawthorne and of Story became the precursor of Gertrude Stein.

Alvin Langdon Coburn, portrait of Henry James, 1906. National Portrait Gallery, Smithsonian Institution/Art Resource, New York.

Alvin Langdon Coburn, portrait of Gertrude Stein, 1913. Yale Collection of American Literature, Beinecke Rare Book and Manuscript Library, Yale University.

Alexander Gardner for Mathew Brady, portrait of Nathaniel Hawthorne, 1862.

Photograph of Nathaniel and Sophia Hawthorne at their Concord home, the Wayside, 1861. First published by Julian Hawthorne in *Hawthorne and His Circle* (1903).

Portrait of William Wetmore Story. From *Reminiscences of William Wetmore Story* (1897).

Photograph of William Wetmore Story and Tommaso Salvini. From *Reminiscences of William Wetmore Story* (1897).

William Wetmore Story, *Cleopatra*, 1858. The Metropolitan Museum of Art, gift of John Taylor Johnson, 1988 (88.5a-d). All rights reserved, the Metropolitan Museum of Art.

William Wetmore Story, *The Libyan Sibyl*, 1861. The Metropolitan Museum of Art, gift of the Erving Wolf Foundation, 1979 (79.266). All rights reserved, the Metropolitan Museum of Art.

Henry James in Rome. From a photograph by Count Giuseppe Primoli, 1899. By permission of the Houghton Library, Harvard University (PfMs Am1094).

"Alice B. Toklas at the Door, photograph by Man Ray," ca. 1922. From *The Autobiography of Alice B. Toklas* (1933). Uncropped version. © 1966 Artists Rights Society (ARS), New York/ADAGP/Man Ray Trust, Paris.

Photograph of Gertrude Stein and Alice B. Toklas with "Auntie," in service, ca. 1917. Yale Collection of American Literature, Beinecke Rare Book and Manuscript Library, Yale University.

"Room with Gas (Femme au chapeau and Picasso Portrait)." From *The Autobiography of Alice B. Toklas* (1933). Uncropped version. Yale Collection of American Literature, Beinecke Rare Book and Manuscript Library, Yale University.

Pablo Picasso, "Portrait of Miss Gertrude Stein," 1905–6. The Metropolitan Museum of Art, bequest of Gertrude Stein, 1946 (47.106). All rights reserved, the Metropolitan Museum of Art. © 1996 Artists Rights Society (ARS), New York/SPADEM, Paris.

Man Ray, "Gertrude Stein and Picasso Portrait," 1922. Yale Collection of American Literature, Beinecke Rare Book and Manuscript Library, Yale University. © 1996 Artist Rights Society (ARS), New York/ADAGP/Man Ray Trust, Paris.

Henry and William James, probably 1901. By permission of the Houghton Library, Harvard University (PfMs Am1094).

Alice B. Toklas and Gertrude Stein on their first airplane trip, 1934. Photograph by Carl Van Vechten. Yale Collection of American Literature, Beinecke Rare Book and Manuscript Library, Yale University. By permission of the Estate of Carl Van Vechten, Joseph Solomon Executor.

Four

IN THE HEROIC AGE OF CUBISM

The Autobiography of Alice B. Toklas

> This was the year 1907.... It was the moment Max Jacob has since called the heroic age of cubism.
>
> —THE AUTOBIOGRAPHY OF ALICE B. TOKLAS

Exactly thirty years after James banged out *William Wetmore Story and His Friends*, Stein apparently dashed off *The Autobiography of Alice B. Toklas* (1933), her anonymous representation of Toklas's memoir of her twenty-five years with Stein. In its sequel, *Everybody's Autobiography* (1937), Stein played down both the origins of the book and the duration of its composition, the first a typical Jamesian gesture, the second a habitual Steinian one. She casually noted that Bertie Abdy, a wealthy British collector and dealer, had instigated the *Autobiography*, something Toklas confirmed when she reported, years later, that Abdy "had said to Gertrude, You should write the history of your friends and time."[1] She also claimed twice that she had written the *Autobiography* in just six weeks, in October and early November of 1932 (*EA* 9, 40). Whether she "actually began [it] in early summer," as Edward Burns maintains, or in October, as she claimed and as Richard Bridgman and James R. Mellow accept, we do know that she finished it in November.[2] Within two years, Stein saw the *Autobiography* abridged and serialized in the *Atlantic Monthly*; saw it disseminated widely in trade and book club editions in the United States and in England; and saw it translated and published in her "home town," Paris.[3] She saw the book praised for its charm and attacked for its vanity, and she saw it turn her, in short order, from a coterie writer into a literary lion.

The public success of the *Autobiography* blocked Stein's writing for months, but it otherwise pleased her and her circle and encouraged her ambitions. In 1933, the lion proposed to Bennett Cerf that Random House "do a volume of reprints, all the things mentioned in the Auto[biography]" (*LGS/CVV* 284). In 1934–35, she made a lecture tour of America, and discussed the *Autobiography* in relation to that tour in *Everybody's Autobiography*.[4] By 1940, she was pressing Samuel Stewart and Carl Van Vechten to interest Hollywood in making a movie of the *Autobiography*, one in which the actual persons mentioned might play themselves; it would make a "swell film," she burbled, adding in a shrewder tone that such a film also might subsidize a second lecture tour.[5] In 1946, Stein, Cerf, and Van Vechten all agreed that the *Autobiography* should appear not only in its entirety, but also as the opening selection, in *The Selected Writings of Gertrude Stein* (1946), which Cerf published and Van Vechten edited.[6] And by 1950, finally, pleased but surprised by Yale University Press's announcement that it would publish posthumously all of Stein's "*inédits*," Toklas allowed to Stewart that publishers previously had "accepted enthusiastically" only three of Stein's books, the *Autobiography* and two that they had commissioned.[7]

If Stein and her intimates, publishers and the public, were all pleased, many persons mentioned in the *Autobiography* were not. Marie Laurencin and Arnold Rönnebeck, two of the less famous, complained privately.[8] George Braque, Henri Matisse, André Salmon, and Tristan Tzara, somewhat more famous, joined Eugene and Maria Jolas in a collective public complaint. In a special supplement to *transition*, titled *Testimony Against Gertrude Stein* (1935), the six collaborators took turns disputing Stein's facts and dismissing her "history" (to recall the term imputed to Abdy) as pernicious fancy.[9] Stein pronounced the pamphlet "a scream" and identified as its motive her detractors' envy of Picasso coupled with their resentment over her tribute to him (*LGS/CVV* 404). Pointedly unnamed in the *Autobiography*, Stein's estranged brother Leo held fire for years. Though he wrote coolly enough, in his *Appreciation* (1947), that the *Autobiography* "was so very romantic and so little related to the facts that what follows will make a quite different narrative," he also was savaging the book, in correspondence posthumously published in *Journey into the Self* (1950), as a "farrago of rather clever anecdote, stupid brag and general bosh, ... a rather clever superstructure on a basis of impenetrable stupidity."[10] Pointedly named in the *Autobiography*, finally, Stein's estranged protégé Hemingway waited even longer before getting even in the homophobic account of the Stein-Toklas ménage that blots his *Moveable Feast* (1964).[11]

Personally involved enthusiasts and antagonists, however, have not been the only ones making a great deal of an apparent *jeu d'esprit*. After years of neglecting the *Autobiography*, scholars recently have turned to it in numbers, giving it far more attention, if not always closer attention, than they have given Stein's other works. Scholars specializing not in Stein but in autobiography, modernist women's writing, or autobiography by women, for example, all have found it a challenging, almost obligatory text. They have tended to be advancing much broader historical, theoretical, or generic arguments, however, so they have tended to use the *Autobiography* primarily as illustration and, accordingly, have tended to find close scrutiny beside the point. Scholars specializing in Stein, meanwhile, have tended to judge her works of the 1930s *either* admirably experimental *or* less admirably designed for public consumption, they have tended to consign the *Autobiography* to the latter category, and, accordingly, they have tended to relax the closeness of scrutiny they accord such contemporaneous Steinian texts as *Stanzas in Meditation*.[12]

We need to resist both tendencies if we wish to examine closely the relation of genre to gender in the *Autobiography*. Professional viewers probably would not call Mary Cassatt's *Woman Reading* (1878), by way of analogy, a genre-study in reading, rather than a figure-study of a woman reading; yet professional readers usually treat the *Autobiography* as a genre-study in autobiography rather than as a figure-study—or, more precisely, a portrait—of a specifically identified woman telling her story.[13] Placing genre before gender, such readers also tend to frame generic issues within the dichotomies autobiography/novel or, more abstractly, fact/fancy, and they tend to regard veracity as the primary issue. Professional readers of Stein, moreover, as I stated above, tend to focus issues of genre and gender alike within such dichotomies as experimental/conventional or, less theoretically, hard/easy, and they tend to take such dichotomies as *données*. In my reading, by contrast, Stein wrote the *Autobiography* as *an imaginative construction of Alice B. Toklas's narration* about Stein, Toklas, and their relationship to each other and to their circle; and she essayed in it, moreover, a genre-inflected study in gender (not vice versa), a study that portrays a spouse portraying a spouse and that construes veracity or its lack to be an effect of desire. In so doing, she confuted such facile oppositions as experimental/conventional or hard/easy.

Whatever the case, the *Autobiography* confronts its reader immediately with its paradoxical premises as narrative act—premises that Stein later, in *Narration*, linked to Defoe's *Robinson Crusoe*, Boswell's *Life of Johnson*, and "Mark Twain in A Yankee at King Arthur's Court" [*sic*], premises that she even later encapsulated in the phrase "portrait narration."[14] She composed a self-contesting hybrid of autobiographical memoir, biographical memoir, and romantic historical novel (or pastiche of a parody of one), a hybrid, at the same time, of portraiture, autoportraiture, and narration. Through this mixing, she guaranteed not only that fact and fiction would remain undecidable, but also that voices and perspectives would remain unsortable, the exact agency of speech and sight, at any moment, indeterminable.[15] As I shall argue, however, Stein not only appropriated the conventions of domestic romance in order to "normalize" lesbian marriage, but she also experimented with genre in order to effect a textual marriage of perspectives and voices; she designed her narrative to convey and to enact Toklas's and her marriage while it conveys and enacts her unacknowledged literary genius.

If Stein indeed composed the *Autobiography* as an imaginative construction, as an interplay of imitation and invention, then she arguably cared less about historical accuracy than about textual efficacy—a possibility with significant implications. Many commentators, for example, argue that Stein and Toklas enacted patriarchal, heterosexual marriage in their relationship, with Stein as husband controlling the public sphere, Toklas as wife controlling the private, and that Stein, in turn, reinscribed that relationship in the form and content of her text. Whatever the actual conditions of their relationship, however, Stein could have imagined something different in the freer space of writing; and I shall argue, indeed, that she used the *Autobiography* to deconstruct patriarchal, heterosexual marriage and to posit lesbian marriage as a legitimate, possibly superior, alternative. Likewise, Stein obviously esteemed Picasso and obviously valued his celebrated portrait of her; nonetheless, she could have imagined a darker picture of Picasso for purposes of advancing a theme, using Toklas as her surrogate; and I shall argue, indeed, that her regard for Picasso as a person matters less than her mediated construction of him as a persona, her respect for his portrait of her less than her construction of the *Autobiography* as her counterportrait to it.

In the *Autobiography*, in sum, Stein neither simply constructed a book about Toklas and herself nor needlessly complicated an act of portrait narration. Rather, she began with a simple composition that she complicated by imitating a real person's voice and by assuming that person's point of view, and that she complicated further by having that created persona parody conventional forms of biographical and autobiographical writing. She had that narrating persona, moreover, not only describe her author's methods at length, abstractly and concretely, but also suggest, more indirectly, how they pertained to her narration and to her author's portrayal of it. And Stein did all of this, I shall argue, not just to raise narrow issues about aesthetics, but also to investigate broad questions about exemplary lives, whether artistic or domestic—how they are written, how published. Ultimately, she was exploring patriarchal representations of women and of women's lives, especially modern representations in art and in literature, and she was proffering the *Autobiography* as a better representation, one that joins the artistic and the domestic in a different vision of women and of their relations.

Stein was practicing what she later preached in the open letter "To Americans" appended to her *Brewsie and Willie* (1946) and in her subsequent "Transatlantic Interview." In the former, she enjoined her countrymen "to really learn to express complication," and, in the latter, she added that her "only thought [was] a complicated simplicity," that she always had liked things to "be simple through complication."[16] Among many other things, she seemed to be warning, on the one hand, that patriarchy often conceals complicated social realities beneath simple literary conventions, and that one should learn to express those complications; but also, on the other hand, that patriarchy just as often conceals simple acts of injustice and cruelty beneath complicated cultural conventions, and that one must use complication, in turn, to expose those simplicities. In order to see how Stein followed those prescriptions in the *Autobiography*, we might consider first its basic premises, next its explorations of type and technique, and finally its own technique for countering types while creating countertypes.

Stein had Toklas narrate the *Autobiography* as a memoir whose seven chapters form two distinct cycles, the first cycle, a kind of extended prologue, half the length of the second. In the first, Toklas tells of herself and Stein before and during their meeting in 1907: (1) her early years before she came to Paris, (2) her arrival in Paris in 1907 and meeting with Stein, (3) Stein in Paris from 1903 to 1907, and (4) Stein before she came to Paris. In the second, she chronicles her twenty-five years with Stein in three phases: (5) 1907–14, (6) the war, 1914–18, and (7) the postwar period, 1919–32. Toklas does not tell a biography proper of Stein, some commentators notwithstanding, in that she gives neither a chronological history of Stein's life nor, for that matter, *any* kind of systematic or comprehensive story of Stein's life. Nor does she tell an autobiography proper, title notwithstanding, for precisely parallel reasons. Rather, she melds the conventions of biographical memoir with those of autobiographical memoir. She relates the early histories of two individuals who became a couple so she then can recollect, systematically and comprehensively, the history of that *couple* as it moved on the cultural stage—a history that concludes with the couple's production of the *Autobiography* itself.

The discontinuity in the chronology of the first cycle serves not only to emphasize the memorial nature of Toklas's account, but also to convert a linearity culminating in the Stein-Toklas meeting in 1907 into a circularity revolving around that meeting as its epicenter.[17] The same discontinuity, moreover, produces another discontinuity between the first cycle and the second, which opens again, or still, in 1907. Though more obviously a classical story with beginning, middle, and end, this second cycle also forms a circularity, one revolving around the epicenter of the 1914–18 war.[18] Through her overall schematics, then, Toklas manages to accent and to link three key dates: 1907, 1914–18, and 1932. Without specifying any causal relation, she portrays Stein's and her meeting in 1907 as coincidental with the initial struggles and breakthroughs to Cubism—the struggles validated by the 1914–18 war, according to Stein's theories, the struggles that even now, in 1932, enable and inform the writing of the *Autobiography*. She joins the Stein-Toklas meeting to the development of Cubist portraiture and both, via the war, to the reenactment of that meeting in the composition of the *Autobiography* as portrait narration. Put differently, she joins the origins of Stein's methods, to their historical validation, to their current, and, indeed, *present*, application.

Those three moments also happen to coincide with Toklas's main themes: art, war, and marriage.[19] And she develops those themes, in turn, by simultaneously employing and parodying corresponding genres of biographical writing: biographically, the life of the artist, general, or saint; autobiographically, the conversion narrative; auto/biographically, the sentimental or domestic romance. To the extent that Toklas tells Stein's story, that is, she conflates a wide range of biographical types. She portrays Stein as pioneer and as inventor, and, above all, portrays her as artist and warrior-saint protecting holy mysteries and the holy site from infidel invaders, the interesting deviation being that vanguard art is the sect, Paris the site. To the extent that Toklas tells her own story, similarly, she patterns it on the spiritual autobiography as secularized by Defoe and by Benjamin Franklin. She portrays herself as having grown from a wonderstruck naif into an increasingly autonomous and influential presence in the social and literary spheres, the interesting deviation here being that she has done so as a woman. To the more important extent that Toklas tells the story of Stein and herself as a couple, finally, she shapes it with the terms of the domestic romance. She proffers the memoirs of a young woman who apparently has ascended to bourgeois uxorial status, with the interesting deviation here being that the young heroine marries another young heroine and that neither brooks domestic confinement.[20]

Toklas appears to be parodying, in general, patriarchal conventions that, first, appose the artistic and martial and, on that basis, assign artistry to men, and that, second, oppose the martial and the marital and, on that basis, assign domesticity to women. Breaking down and then reconstructing those conventions, she converts that which allows others to deny the rank of artist to Stein into the very basis for assigning it to her. She places Stein's development of Cubism in writing *between* the Stein-Toklas union in 1907 and their warwork in 1914–18, for example, and thereby suggests that the erotic and domestic aspects of Stein's life informed her art—that is, true modern art—more than did the combative or martial aspects, which served retrospectively to confirm it as truly modern. As we shall see, however, Toklas does none of this too simply. She defines and assigns the role of artistic warrior-saint with a good deal of ambiguity, and she at once seems to affirm the virtue of combat and struggle while questioning the ends that combat and struggle often serve. Similarly, she defines and assigns the role of spouse with even more ambiguity, and she again at once seems to affirm the virtue of marriage as a private arrangement while questioning the value of marriage as a public institution.

The historical Toklas, of course, did none of this; Stein portrayed her, rather, in the process of doing so.[21] And she portrayed her, moreover, as intensely interested in Stein as a portraitist. Emphasizing the interplay of description and construction at the heart of Stein's aesthetics of portraiture, and stressing Stein's exactitude—particularly as a crafter of precise sentences—in representing inner and outer realities, Stein's Toklas discusses Stein's artistic principles at length, often—at times incessantly—quoting Stein herself. Though it does not follow from Stein's artistic principles that Toklas must use them in constructing her portrait of Stein and herself, it does follow from them that Stein must use them to construct her portrait of Toklas's portrayal. Stein has Toklas, in fact, allegorize those principles in two related anecdotes about photography together with a series of references to memoration. And she also has Toklas point to the post-Impressionist and Cubist technique of *passage*, "the running together of planes otherwise separated in space," the technique that works locally and globally in the *Autobiography* and that, ultimately, makes the *Autobiography* the oxymoronic blend of fact and fiction that it is.[22]

While Toklas describes Stein's principles, and Stein uses those principles to portray Toklas, moreover, our narrator also gives a history of our author's portraiture and narrative fiction and gives that author's views of others working in those genres, with particular reference to Picasso and Francis Picabia as portraitists, Defoe and Henry James as writers of narrative. In fact, Stein has Toklas pack the *Autobiography* with references to other pictorial and verbal representations of people, often mentioning portraits and figure-studies, usually by men of women, and "lives" of artists, generals, or saints, usually by men of men. In the foreground, then, Toklas places Stein's *oeuvre* and the aesthetics governing it, paying special attention to Stein's portraits, plays, and later "landscapes" about artists, generals, and saints; to such narrative lives as *Three Lives* and the autobiographical *Making of Americans*; and, allegorically, to the *Autobiography* itself. In the middle ground, she places the modernist tradition and the aesthetics governing it, paying special attention to portraits and figure-studies by the Cubists—particularly Picasso's portrait of Stein—and to writings, autobiographical and otherwise, by Joyce, Hemingway, and Sherwood Anderson. And in the background, she places the longer Western traditions of portraiture and biography and the aesthetics governing them.

By a woman about a woman telling of the two women together, the *Auto-*

biography differs in subject and in treatment from most works in those traditions; and this difference gives the book its social and political color. Through repeated references to post-Impressionist and Cubist pictures, Toklas intimates a drift in modernism from portraiture to figure-study and, therefore, from particular to general, instance to type; rather than particularize women's identities, the Cubists had continued to generalize women's bodies, the complexities of their motives notwithstanding. By way of contrast, Stein and she paint a portrait of *one particularized* woman telling about *one* other *particularized* woman, and both portrait and narrative, moreover, are extremely decorous in their details—facts that matter a great deal. As we shall see, Stein considered generalizing to be a form of abstracting, and abstracting a form of pornography; and Toklas pays special attention in her account to figure-studies of nudes. As I shall argue, Stein and Toklas seem to use the event of the Armory Show in 1913 to suggest that the "heroic age of cubism," in Max Jacob's phrase (7), was less than heroic, or, at the least, to suggest that the conventions of heroism informing Jacob's phrase were narrowly patriarchal and aggressively misogynist—as evidenced by the pictures bracketing that age, Picasso's *Demoiselles d'Avignon* and Duchamp's *Nude Descending a Staircase*.

Toklas makes clear, furthermore, that the men whose portraits, figure-studies, and landscapes had approached the "pornographic" had become themselves wealthy and famous—exemplars of modern art; Stein had not. She offers two reasons, and she implicitly proffers the *Autobiography* in response to them. First, one must particularize a life before one can generalize it as exemplary, but Cubists already had generalized women, including Picasso and especially in his portrait of Stein; second, one must publish a "life" in order to broadcast its subject as exemplary, but journals and publishing houses, dominated by men, control which "lives" get published and, therefore, who and what come to be regarded as exemplary. Whether by gentleman's agreement or not, gallery directors and publishers succeeded in showing, publicizing, celebrating, *making exemplary* Picasso, Joyce, even Hemingway, while making Stein highly visible as icon but invisible as artist. Toklas tells this story, and, in the same act, Stein and Toklas change its *dénouement*. Stein has mastered the métier of writing, and Toklas has mastered the trade of publishing; so together they have reappropriated the means of representation and now can use them to particularize their own identities and to advertise themselves as exemplary.

As an essential part of this theme, Toklas emphasizes throughout her narrative the need not only to escape men in the domestic and public spheres but also to replace them with women. Immediately telling us, for example, that she had been writing to Henry James and "living with my father and brother" (3–4) when she was called to her "new full life" in Paris (6), she goes on to identify women as her guides in that *vita nuova*: Stein (French painting), Hélène (French cooking and housekeeping), Fernande (French language).[23] In a more detailed parallel account, she then indicates that men had dominated Stein's early life, from her father and brothers to her professors at Johns Hopkins, from Henry and William James as looming intellectual fathers (96–97) to Matisse and Picasso as pushy artistic brothers. Toklas had to escape her father and brother, in short, to "begin my apprenticeship of standing" and, eventually, to stand on her own (25, and see 27); and Stein had to escape her fathers and brothers, familial and intellectual, so she could take her rightful place beside Matisse and Picasso in 1907.[24] Since Stein subtly eroticizes Toklas's narrative, moreover, and since Toklas associates her own arrival in Paris in 1907 with Stein's artistic breakthrough, they not only trace their histories from daughters to spouses, but they also identify their having become spouses with their subsequent successes; they portray, in a word, a brilliant marriage.

It is through *this* portrayal, finally, that Stein offers the *Autobiography* itself as exemplary, as a sapphic Cubist text describing modern love and modern art and enacting them both. On one plane, as it were, Stein has Toklas portray their domestic union, having her first narrate the parallel initiations of the two young women and then narrate their quarter-century together as companions and, more covertly, lovers. On an intersecting plane, she has Toklas portray their professional union, having the latter narrate her own growth from "gently bred" young woman (3), to invaluable secretarial and editorial assistant, to founder and director of the Plain Edition, while having her narrate Stein's growth from bookish child, to rigorously vanguard collector and artist, to author (published by Toklas) of increasing influence and reputation. Focusing on Toklas focusing on Stein, the latter creates *passage*: she describes a narrator who emerges as ideal mate and editor-publisher and who, in turn, describes Stein as ideal mate and author; she thus enacts her love for Toklas as ideal woman while also enacting her desire to have Toklas see her as ideal woman. She proffers that double enactment, finally, that textual *tour de force*, as precisely the evidence for her ideality: she constructs an exemplary modernist portrait, a double portrait, that answers Picasso's *Portrait of Miss Gertrude Stein* with Toklas's portrait of her, and that succeeds James's *Portrait of a Lady* with her portrait of Toklas.

⁓

As the narrator of that *tour de force*, Toklas develops the three themes of art, war, and marriage, themes that span the whole text but that find their centers of gravity, respectively, in chapters 5, 6, and 7. In each case, she employs and parodies specific cultural stereotypes and generic conventions, and in each she advances not only a central point about Stein as artist, but also a central feminist point about Stein and herself as partners. In the first case, for example, she portrays Stein as a pioneer and, more extensively, uses Stein's love of automobiles and her skill as a driver to portray her, through analogy, as more vanguard than her contemporaries; at the same time, Toklas implies that *she* too pioneered and that she, indeed, introduced Stein to the automobile. In the second, more vexing case, Toklas portrays Stein as an artistic warrior-saint, but she complicates the art-war analogy by suggesting, among other things, that some male artists were warriors merely by analogy, Stein, she, and their women friends warriors in fact. In the third case, finally, she subverts apparent portrayals of herself simply as a wife, of lesbian marriage simply as "abnormal," and of Stein simply as uninterested in "the cause of women"; and she gives us, instead, a joint portrait of Stein and herself as equal partners in marriage and, as we later shall see, as successful partners in the production of books that *serve* the cause of women.

This all begins with Toklas linking art to expatriation. She tells us in her opening sentence that she was born in California and, immediately after, that her maternal grandfather was a "pioneer" (3); she later tells us, in a parallel formulation, that Stein was born in Pennsylvania—and that she *remains* born there despite Toklas's wanting her to be born in California (85). Though she apparently wants to indicate Stein's fidelity to fact even when fancy might prove more interesting, her quip more importantly establishes Stein as a true American pioneer who *first* went transcontinentally east to west, and only *then* went transoceanically west to east. She goes on to suggest, then, that Stein and she *pioneered* Paris: they established an outpost at 27, rue de Fleurus, to which other prewar American pioneers could come; they anticipated the happily named American Expeditionary Force; and they made Paris "home" long before the armistice, after which "everybody came over" (234).[25] On the one hand, Toklas thus establishes a genealogy: as Story had been to James, in effect, James had been to Stein, Stein to Toklas, Stein and Toklas to everybody else—*precursors*. On the other hand, Toklas alludes to Stein's quirky idea that America was the oldest country in the world because the first to enter the twentieth century, and she employs it to suggest that Stein and she had come to Europe not as pilgrims or as *éclaireurs* from the new world to the old, but, precisely, as pioneers from the old world to the new.[26] If Stein needed a Jamesian initiation into Europe for her art, the trope suggests, modern art needed this American in Europe for its existence.

Toklas complements the trope of travel, soon after, with one of domestic technology, and suggests that our pioneers, once settled, established a stable home as milieu for life and art. She tells us that Stein's "extremely conservative" old landlady had not allowed electricity in her house, and that it was not until 1914 (a crucial moment, of course) that Stein and Toklas installed electric lighting (11–12). Much later, she adds that, just recently, "We had installed electric radiators in the studio, we were as our finnish servant would say getting modern. She finds it difficult to understand why we are not more modern. Gertrude Stein says that if you are way ahead with your head you naturally are old fashioned and regular in your daily life. And Picasso adds, do you suppose Michael Angelo would have been grateful for a gift of a piece of renaissance furniture, no he wanted a greek coin" (303; and see *P* 31). At one level, Stein was following not only Flaubert's advice that to write like an original one should live like a bourgeois, but also Michelangelo's example: foreshadowing and paralleling Picasso's comment, suggesting the replay of Antiquity in the Renaissance and of the Renaissance in Modernity, Toklas had told us that Stein's home was filled with Italian Renaissance furniture (10, 11). At a second level, however, Toklas is intimating that *she*, the "gently bred" young woman (3), embraced modern domestic technology before Stein and, perhaps, by metaphoric extension, embraced the unnamed but modern domestic arrangement before her as well.

Toklas's central trope for art, in any case, combines travel and technology: she suggests that if Stein was no Edison in the home, she may have been a Henry Ford on the road. She recalls that Stein, in the prewar summer of 1914, had harangued Alfred Whitehead and Bertrand Russell "on the disembodied abstract quality of the american character and cited examples, mingling automobiles with Emerson" (187)—an apparent reference to Ford's equally known manufacture of the one and affection for the other.[27] Toklas herself mingles automobiles with Stein in the *Autobiography* in a ubiquitous and variegated motif. Apparently construing line assembly of automobiles together with automotive technology as quintessentially American and modern, she develops two distinct but related themes: one, she implicitly portrays the American Civil War as antecedent to the 1914–18 war, and she uses Stein's idea that warfare reflects and reveals cultural composition in order to suggest that seriality was central to the production of automobiles and of modern art and that the dynamic perspectivalism enabled by the automobile was central to the composition of that art; two, she identifies automobiles as an influence on Stein's art, the repair of automobiles as inspiration to Stein's understanding her art, and automotive technology as analogous to Stein's artistic technique.

Stein knows that the American Civil War, that is, inaugurated a specific mode of production—roughly speaking, uniform standards of measurement enabled interchangeable parts enabled line assembly enabled serial production—and that Henry Ford adapted that mode for the mass production of automobiles; she also makes the link between wars and cars by having Toklas dwell on the famous deployment of taxis at the battle of the Marne (184–85) and on the deployment of American Ford cars and drivers such as Stein and herself by the American Fund for French Wounded and its auxiliary, the Volunteer Motor-Ambulance Corps. Having told us out of sequence that William Cook taught Stein to drive "on one of the old battle of the Marne taxis" (200),

Toklas sets up the key passage in which she reveals the motive for Stein's wanting to have been taught: while walking one day, Stein and she had seen "a ford car being backed up the street by an american girl and on the car it said, American Fund for French Wounded. There, said I, that is what we are going to do. At least, said I to Gertrude Stein, you will drive the car and I will do the rest" (207; and see 218, 233). And Stein eventually did drive cars, Toklas later implies, in the same way that she created art: "she still does not back a car very well. She goes forward admirably, she does not go backwards successfully" (214).

In the second aspect of this motif, in fact, Toklas develops technical specifics of the analogy between Stein's driving and her art and, by implication, between automotive technology and aesthetic technique. She observes that no one should be surprised that Stein is such a good driver and "at the same time a well known author," since she was influenced, after all, "by the sound of the streets and the movement of the automobiles" (253–54). She then sketches a very funny, parodic scene that conflates the inspirational moment in the life of the artist with the revelatory moment in the life of the saint, a scene in which Stein, while watching a mechanic take apart and reassemble a Ford, understood how to analyze and synthesize her aesthetics and wrote "Composition as Explanation" on the spot (see 286). Finally, while Toklas may or may not be using the automobile, self-propelled by self-generating horsepower, to figure an autonomous and autotelic modern art, she does seem to be anticipating an analogy that Stein employs elsewhere, an analogy that likens, on the one hand, the movement within the engine of an automobile as generating but also as differing from the movement of the automobile across the landscape and, on the other hand, the internal dynamics of artistic composition as affecting and reflecting but also as differing from the dynamics of the composition of living (see *LIA* 170, 195).

That possible degree of specificity notwithstanding, Toklas also seems to be after something broader, something that links the war closely to the art-automobile analogy. She is suggesting that the technological conditions of modern life informed Stein's work, but that Stein did not err like the egregious worshipers of the automobile, the Futurists, in accepting uncritically either modern technological conditions or the artistic techniques they generated. Contrasting Stein with the Futurists, she contrasts an American woman who served the war effort by using automobiles behind the lines, and who now writes neutrally about automobiles and the war, with the European men who actively promoted the war and fought in it, and who used an aesthetics informed by automotive technology to glorify the war as a clean, mechanical cleansing of Europe. Overall, then, Toklas may be using this motif to dissociate Stein not only from pacifists in the Whitehead/Russell mold, but also, especially, from militarists in the Marinetti/Severini mold. Stein might be driving the automotive *Autobiography*, in a manner of speaking, but Toklas is doing all the rest here: *she* is distancing Stein from the Futurists whom, she remarks, "everybody found . . . very dull" (153), but with whom the public, in 1932, still closely associated Stein.[28]

Identifying Stein with Henry Ford as opposed to the Futurists, moreover, Toklas adds another stroke to her picture of Stein as "completely and entirely american" (19) and, *as a consequence*, as ahead of other vanguardists. In creating a usable past for Stein as pioneer and technical innovator, as creator rather than follower, however, she also must encounter the aporia of "originality." Stein believed more strongly than did James that *race, moment*, and *milieu* determined art—that national, regional, and even local forces, particularly with respect to geography, make styles of art "inevitable" (123, 231), make "traditions" likely (see 268), make something as unique as Picasso's vision intelligible. And she also believed that great artists influence their successors, as do types of art and even individual artworks, as repeated references to Cézanne, for example, and to African art make clear.[29] Her sense of determinism, however, conflicts somewhat with her sense of original genius in general, her own genius in particular, so she has Toklas fudge the issue. Toklas later enumerates all such determinants at work on Stein, and all such influences; her trick, however, is to name so many places in Stein's background that no one place could have made her art "inevitable," while naming a number of precursors but identifying none of them as, specifically, "influences."[30]

As an original artist, producing original art, however, Stein also faced all attendant problems. In a key passage, Toklas recalls Stein as having said, "as Pablo once remarked, when you make a thing, it is so complicated making it that it is bound to be ugly, but those that do it after you they don't have to worry about making it and they can make it pretty, and so everybody can like it when the others make it" (28; and see CAE 26–29; *P* 9). Picasso, Stein, and Toklas are all suggesting that the true creator "struggles" to express himself or herself, struggles to compose recalcitrant materials, above all struggles to represent reality with accuracy and with contemporaneity; that the imitator, by contrast, expresses emotions or ideas derived from others, composes with forms already developed by others, and represents previous mediations of reality *uncritically* and from viewpoints, moreover, themselves archaic. The true creator suffers rejection in his or her time; the imitator, by contrast, adverts only to convention, to the comfortably familiar, and "everybody" therefore "likes" the result. With this point about artistry *and* audience, portraiture *and* reception, Toklas is suggesting not only that an original work inevitably shows signs of the "struggle" behind it, while imitative work, having taken no struggle, shows none, but also that an audience apprehends an original work as ugly because it has yet to learn the conventions that naturalize the work, familiarize it, and make it easily readable.³¹ Followers teach those conventions by "translating" such work, and they translate it, in Stein's repeated etymological wordplay on "vulgarise," into the language of the rabble.³²

Stein uses Toklas's testimony, in sum, to portray herself as an American and a vanguardist original. Toklas devotes much of the first cycle of the *Autobiography* to establishing Matisse, Picasso, and Stein as the creators who broke through to the truly modern idiom circa 1907.³³ The two painters attracted followers quickly, spawned partisan Matisseites and Picassoites (79), but Stein had no Steinites, as it were, until well after the war.³⁴ These painters had "translators": those followers who "vulgarised" their work immediately, who made Matisse's and Picasso's work seem "natural," eventually, by providing the conventions for reading it. And they had "publishers" of sorts: gallery owners like Vollard, who had no imagination, and Kahnweiler, who had, both of them publicists who could withstand even pointed attempts to "kill cubism" (133, 196). But Stein would gain no "translator," figuratively, until the wave of postwar American expatriates like Hemingway and, literally, until the current effort to translate into French her "big book," *The Making of Americans* (307); and Stein would gain no fully committed publisher, no publisher with the vision and daring of Kahnweiler, until Toklas "began to think about publishing [her] work" (298). Stein not only struggled heroically, in a word, to make her art; she also had to struggle to make it known.

Like everyone else in Western Europe, however, Stein and Toklas faced an even greater struggle in 1914–18, one that Toklas develops, as.I earlier mentioned, through a witty motif of holy war. In the first cycle of chapters, in essence, Toklas first related how she was called to Paris by "three little Matisse paintings" (5) and, once at the site of the mystery cult, was initiated into modernism by her spiritual guide Stein and began her "new full life" (6); she then returned through time to show us the guide at the moment of the latter's initiation, and even further back to reveal the circumstances that brought the guide to the site.³⁵ In the second cycle, Toklas traces the period from when "life in Paris began" (105) to the "spring and early summer of nineteen fourteen [when] the old life was over" (175); she recalls the war, including the German advance upon Paris, the dispersal of the Parisian crowd, the arrival of the American Expeditionary Force, the tenure of Stein and Toklas in the Volunteer Motor-Ambulance Corps; and she finally recounts Stein's theory that painting had become a "minor art" again and tells "the story" of Stein's postwar quest for "who was to be the leader of this art" (277).³⁶ Put differently, Toklas details the growth of a religion and relates marvelous tales of its founders; she then tells of the sacred site threatened by barbarians from the east, abandoned by many native religionists, defended by noble warriors from the west and by our heroines, also from the west; and she finally tells of the restoration of the sacred site to safety and of our heroines' guiding a new generation of initiates into the next phase of the religion.

Though one almost can hear "Onward Christian Soldiers" playing ironically in the background, Toklas is using religion to make a serious thematic link between art and war. She takes pains to establish that Stein's and her generation believed in patriotism and in religion and, as a result, *could* believe in the idea of defending places and principles at great cost. By analogy, they *could* believe in defending places conducive to art (27, rue de Fleurus; Paris) and in defending the principles of modern art itself. They remained, as it were, a generation still under the Arnoldian influence. In the course of recounting Stein's postwar quest for a new artistic leader, an equivalent of prewar Picasso, Toklas observes that the war destroyed for the younger generation "both patriotism and religion as a passion" and left at least one typical young man turning to Surrealism to justify the "confused negation" in which he lived and which, perhaps, he actually loved (278–79). Without patriotism and religion, in other words, his generation became "lost" in the second sense of the phrase that Hemingway already had enshrined as Stein's in the epigraph to *The Sun Also Rises* (1926); "lost" to the extent that art no longer served as system of belief and that Surrealism, the cult of the unconscious, took its place; lost to the extent that Stein had to try, but could not succeed, in finding and identifying the new "leader" among them.[37]

Stein could not find such a leader, in part, because the war had made painting "minor," and it had done so, Toklas suggests, by destroying two central subjects: humans and landscapes. Toklas tells us that she had been amazed at the "quantity" of men in the streets of Barcelona in 1915, because "one's eyes had become so habituated to menless streets [in Paris], the few men one saw being in uniform and therefore not being men but soldiers" (199). Developing a parallel idea, she quotes Stein as saying that "a landscape is such a natural arrangement for a battle-field or a play that one must write plays" (163, and see 202); she points out that the landscape of the Rhône Valley, spared by the war, had "stimulated" Stein to begin "writing a great deal again" (228); and she recalls that Stein and she had visited the front after the war and had found its landscape "strange. We were used to ruined houses and even ruined towns but this was different. It was a landscape. And it belonged to no country" (230).

In essence, Toklas is complementing Stein's theory about the effects of painting on war with a theory about the effects of war on painting—a theory rooted in the idea of difference. Approving difference in general, national differences in particular, Toklas points out that "the three really great dancers" she has seen, like "the three geniuses" she has known, represent three different nationalities (167); and she also points out that the different nations had different styles of camouflage (231) and of marching (236)—the former of which she expressly identifies with modern art (110). She also implies, however, that precisely such national differences led to a war that had the effect, paradoxically, of eradicating difference: *conscripted, men become uniform; laid waste, landscape becomes universal*. And in eradicating difference, the war virtually precluded portraiture of individuals and landscape painting of specific locations; it allowed, instead, only generalized figure-study and genre-study—in a word, *type*. Even redirected into camouflaging or marching, then, art produces differentiation, while war produces standardization; but if wars, as Stein often argued, confirm *prior* artistic practices—the Great War cubistic practice—then Cubism, therefore modernism, complied in the very effects Toklas is describing, and Stein and Toklas, perhaps, are not advocating Cubism or modernism quite so unconditionally as they appear to be doing. After all, they now are in the Rhône Valley attempting to differentiate the individuals who had seemed interchangeable in prewar rue de Fleurus (228, 274).[38]

Whatever her precise point is, Toklas puts it in a broader context, paradoxically, of national types. Often citing Stein as authority, for example, Toklas identifies Americans with Spaniards on aesthetic grounds, and Americans with French on political grounds, while she distinguishes Americans from Germans on both aesthetic and political grounds. Having elaborated at length that Americans and Spaniards share a fundamental penchant for artistic "struggle," she goes on to suggest that Americans and French share a fundamental commitment to liberal political struggle: both nations are republics (188), formed in revolution (193), and committed to egalitarian and democratic principles (215).[39] By contrast, Americans and Germans differ fundamentally in aesthetics and politics, and Stein, Toklas dutifully reports, doesn't "like" Germans (125). As Stein had said in 1914, the Germans have method but lack organization, and they are consequently a "backward" people who are not "modern" and "cannot therefore possibly win this war"; as republicans, Americans are naturally sympathetic to England and France, fundamentally antipathetic to "a mediaeval country like Germany" (187–88). Wanting to correlate culture and politics, she accused Germans of preferring metaphysics over pragmatics (method over organization) and autocracy over democracy; she imputed to Germany the same medievalism, in fact, that the Futurists had imputed to it in 1914, and neither she nor Toklas withdrew the imputation in 1932.[40]

Though such egregious national typing was then common, one cannot easily determine the degree to which Stein, Toklas, or both take their own typing seriously. They have figured American and Spanish abstractionism as the salvation of writing and painting in France; and they have figured American technology, money, and personnel (via, respectively, the Ford car, the American Fund for French Wounded, and the American Expeditionary Force) as the salvation of society in France. They have suggested that being a good American predisposes one to being not only a good Cubist, but also a good soldier in the war that confirmed the historical legitimacy of Cubism by being, itself, cubistic. And, needless to add, they have figured themselves not only as *good* Americans but as *better* Americans than natives, as *more American*, by virtue of their exile: "Gertrude Stein always said the war was so much better than just going to America. Here you were with America in a kind of way that if you only went to America you could not possibly be" (227).[41] In short, they have figured America in advance of Europe and themselves in advance of America; and they have linked Stein the avant-garde artist with Stein the avant-garde expatriate war worker—the woman who joined the battle of modern art before other Americans with the woman who joined the 1914–18 war before America itself (207, 220), the woman who was in France before "the first piece of the American army" (221), who was, then, avant the avant-garde.[42]

Toklas highly ambiguates the martial theme, however, when she inflects it with gender, when she distinguishes, or appears to distinguish, not only male artists elsewhere from those at the front, but also male artists in general from the many women—including Stein and herself—who served tirelessly and, again, bravely. Toklas seems to be suggesting that patriarchy associates art and war and makes both the province of men while, simultaneously and paradoxically, it dissociates art from war and makes the former the arena of the womanly, the latter that of the manly; in one case, art as "struggle" with the world, in the other, art as "retreat" from the world. At the same time, however, she reenacts that cultural ambivalence, *multiplies* it, indeed, to a point of apparent confusion. On the one hand, that is, *she* associates art and war; on the other, *she* dissociates art from war. On the one hand, she suggests that the greater male artists were the lesser warriors (Picasso, Matisse) and vice versa (Apollinaire, Braque), while she contradictorily suggests that the greatest female artist (Stein) also might have been the greatest warrior had she been permitted at the front. On the other hand, she suggests that *both* artistic exemplars, both creative geniuses, "struggled" in what was the moral equivalent of war (Picasso, Stein), while she again contradictorily suggests that the former retreated from the war into art (Picasso in Rome with Cocteau) but that the latter abandoned art to serve bravely in the war effort (Stein behind the lines with Toklas).[43]

The ambiguity crystallizes in a deceptively offhand anecdote about Duncan, a southern doughboy befriended by Toklas and Stein during the war.[44] "Poor Duncan," a supply sergeant, "was miserable because he was not at the front. He had enlisted as far back as the expedition to Mexico and here he was well in the rear and no hope of getting away because he was one of the few who understood the complicated system of army book-keeping and his officers would not recommend him to the front." Poor Duncan (the repeated epithet) becomes so miserable that he threatens to go AWOL and becomes "drunk and bitter" from the shame of having to "face his family never having been to the front" (225). Toklas apparently uses this story—one of the many "doughboy stories" she claims to like (226)—to figure the plight of the artist or of the woman, or, perhaps, of both. With respect to art, that is, she seems to be employing a Steinian metonymy that uses etymology to link *counting* to *telling* to *narrating* and, thus, complicated systems of bookkeeping to comparable systems of bookmaking.[45] Insulated from the dangers of the front, and ashamed of his own insulation, Duncan perhaps figures the artist insulated by letters from action—"poor Duncan" as the descendent, as it were, of "poor Dencombe" in James's "The Middle Years." With respect to gender, moreover, she seems to associate Duncan with Stein and herself, two women also denied access to the front until after the war. These two women, however, had chosen to relinquish art for active service, and they had not, when denied the front, become drunk, bitter, or ashamed.

As I have been suggesting, however, none of this adds up to an obvious or even obviously clear point: Toklas's story of art as told in chapter 5 becomes far more ambiguous when extended to art and war—to some extent, art *as* war and war *as* art—in chapter 6, and to the effects of art on war, and war on art, in chapter 7. She clearly seems to juxtapose prewar rue de Fleurus as the site of the religion of modernism to postwar rue de Fleurus as the site of its disarray; the already ambiguated "leader" in the first moment (Picasso) succeeded by no one in the second, the less ambiguated interpreter of painting and creator of writing in the first moment (Stein) left with her own writing to be interpreted and recreated (translated, abridged, set to music, and so on) in the second. In between, she places the war, specifically, the military institution that keeps *some* men from the front and, doing so, feminizes and shames them, while it keeps *all* women from the front and, doing so, offers the rear as their proper place—a military institution, a metonymy of its culture, that masculinizes any woman who insists on *driving forward*, on heading toward the "front" as place and as trope, but that, doing so, also converts the type masculine into the stereotype "mannish," that is, a pejorative "butch." However unclear the allegory finally may be, then, it clearly points to the conclusion that one can use modernism to fight the kind of medievalism that even the modern Allies practiced, the medievalism of misogyny and homophobia, and that Stein and Toklas are using modernism to fight precisely that battle.

Not everyone would agree. Many professional readers of Stein, in fact, devalue the *Autobiography* for an alleged complicity in misogyny—if not precisely homophobia—on grounds that Stein merely portrays Toklas as wife (or portrays her as mere wife?) and that she veils their lesbianism (particularly in its sexual aspect). Since a goal of this chapter is to revalue the *Autobiography* as a pointed lesbian-feminist critique of patriarchal institutions, one that neither "reduces" Toklas to the status of heterosexual wife nor veils the true, and truly sexual, nature of their relationship to anyone with eyes to see, I want to take up here issues of uxoriality and of lesbianism that not only focus the *Autobiography* but that also, as I read the book, constitute its central theme. Specifically, I want to note briefly how Stein has Toklas tell the story of her "twenty-five years with Gertrude Stein" (17) as a parody of the conventions of the domestic romance and of the norms those conventions legitimate, a parody that also generates serious thematics of family, friendship, and marriage. And Stein has Toklas turn these thematics, I shall argue, on crucial passages about "normality," passages related directly to a passage about "the cause of women" that detractors of the *Autobiography* find especially troubling.[46]

Parodying the genre that is predicated on the sanctity of heterosexual marriage and the nuclear family, Toklas can redefine the norms for a good marriage and can propose homosexual marriage as closer to them. As I noted earlier, she not only talks about Stein's and her families, but she also uses familial relations as tropes for Stein's relations with artistic predecessors, contemporaries, and successors.[47] When she reaches 1907, however, she shifts narrative emphasis from family to friends, and, if she pays considerable attention to male friends, particularly the celebrated artists and writers, as commentators emphasize, she also pays a great deal of attention to women; in fact, the men represent less durable and less stable friendships than do the women.[48] In parallel fashion, Toklas mentions many heterosexual marriages in passing, usually without comment, and she cites rather cynical and glib remarks about marriage from Max Jacob and Picasso—the namer and the embodier of "the heroic age of cubism"—also without comment. Apparently acknowledging that marriage, as culturally and legally defined, means heterosexual marriage, she also suggests that, as such, it fails as social institution, as type, and, perhaps, often fails as personal relationship, as instance. Specifically, she silently contrasts to Jacob's "famous remark" about marriage as male "possession," and to Picasso's about the inevitability of divorce, the cooperative and the obviously durable marriage of Stein and herself. She can name this marriage, however, only in negative space, only by parodying the genre whose glorification of heterosexual marriage has left, precisely, no discursive space for homosexuality.[49]

She appears to find an analogy for her marriage, though, and finds it, tellingly, in the marriage of a figure neither the namer nor the embodier of Cubism: Matisse. One again must be careful, however, for her frequent comments on the Matisse ménage employ reasonably attractive terms in rather troubling oppositions. She sets Matisse's "virility" (a repeated term), that is, against Madame Matisse's *vitality* (a term implied by the repeated phrase, "feeling of life" [e.g., 44], its use, in turn, an allusion to Matisse's *Bonheur de Vivre*); she sets Matisse's artistry against Madame Matisse's domesticity (115); but she also notes that Matisse could and did distinguish between Madame Matisse as a "wife" and as a "picture," no mean achievement in a book that generally thematizes pictorial representation as masculine appropriation (e.g.,

184), and that specifically features, as a central example, Picasso's proudly boasting that Stein would *become* in the public's imagination *his* portrait of her (14). At first sight, it appears that Toklas also is imputing "virility" to Stein, by identifying her with famous men, and is setting it against her own vitality, and that she is setting Stein's artistry against her own domesticity. She appears to be ratifying a heterosexist conception of marriage, moreover, with her repeated identification of herself as someone who "sits with the wives of geniuses," with her initial plan to write "the wives of geniuses I have sat with" (17), and with her suggestion that the *Autobiography* is that book (309; and see 105–6, 143).

Though virtually all of Stein's commentators argue that Toklas (therefore Stein) has done so, I offer three counterpoints. First, if Stein, indeed, does present Toklas as her "wife," then, at the least, she has written women's history with respect not only to herself but also to Toklas, has countered doubly the construction of history as comprising the lives of male geniuses. Second, Stein (through Toklas) makes two explicit and extended references to Toklas as a "sitter with wives" in chapter 5 (105–6, 143), and two implicit references in chapter 6 (182–83, 194), and then begins to shift Toklas's role from that of putative "wife" to that of mother: godmother to soldiers (214–16) and, in chapter 7, godmother to Hemingway's son (263). She may be depicting Toklas as maturing from young wife of a genius to surrogate mother of sons, but just as Matisse knew the difference between his wife and a picture of her, so does Stein know the difference between Toklas and this essentially parodic picture of her *as* conventional wife and mother. Third, and most subtly, Stein has set her reader a syllogistic lure. Toklas identifies Picasso, Whitehead, and Stein as the "three first-class geniuses" she would know (6), identifies Picasso's and Whitehead's wives as wives of geniuses, and she observes that she sits with the wives of geniuses; therefore, we conclude, Toklas *is* the wife of a genius—*an inference that proper logic disallows.* Rather than assign Toklas uxorial status, Stein in fact sets up her reader first to make a flawed inference rooted in heterosexist assumptions, and, presumably, then to recognize the error.

Performing a similar but more complex set of maneuvers with respect to norms and lesbian sexuality, Stein has Toklas describe Stein's participation, while at Radcliffe, in an experiment on "suggestions to the subconscious." Toklas reports that Stein gave no response: "Ah, said [William] James, if Miss Stein gave no response I should say that it was as normal not to give a response as to give one" (97). A few pages later, she reports Stein's having told a medical school professor at Johns Hopkins "how little I like pathological psychology, and how all medicine bores me." Toklas adds: "She always says she dislikes the abnormal, it is so obvious. She says the normal is so much more simply complicated and interesting" (102). At the more apparent level, Stein is having Toklas suggest that she, Stein, always wrote consciously and is doing so in the *Autobiography*—that just as she was no Futurist, so is she no Surrealist. At the less apparent but more important level, Stein is commenting on normative valuations of sexuality. Though she seems to be making a judgment about normality that her detractors can read as an expression of discomfort with her lesbianism, she actually is doing something different.

For one thing, Toklas does not show Stein accommodating herself to William James's view of the normal, but, conversely, shows James using Stein as his measure for normality. For another, Toklas is being semantically and etymologically exact: Stein dislikes the abnormal not as a substance (which it cannot be) but as a category (which it always is); as Toklas exactly reports, Stein dislikes not pathological psyches, but pathological psychology—dislikes, that is, a scientific descriptiveness based on norms, on statistical types rather than on actual instances, a descriptiveness that becomes social prescriptiveness and proscriptiveness. The patriarchal institution of medicine, therefore, not only "bores" her, fails to interest her, because it traffics in pernicious types, but it also "bores" her, crudely but pertinently put, *screws her*, condemns her as abnormal. As a result, the *normal* (that which is legislated as acceptable) is *complicated* (its meanings and implications hidden in folds) and "interests" Stein because the scientific and social construction of normality directly and negatively affects her. The *abnormal* (away from the rule or norm), by contrast, is *obvious* (against the way); a tautology uninteresting in itself, the abnormal is interesting only as the category defined in opposition to a false normality. Representations of the normal being not only more complicated (that is, more hidden) but also more coercive (as a direct consequence), Stein herself will choose to practice "simplification" (259), and will do so, indeed, even if it means sounding "commonplace" (276).[50]

Stein does precisely that, in fact, in Toklas's infamous anecdote about Stein's lack of interest in "the cause of women." Following Toklas's reference to William James and to Stein as his measure of normality, and bracketing the two-paragraph passage in which Toklas cites Stein's dislike of abnormal psychology and her interest in the normal, Toklas reports (first) an incident in which Margaret Walker pressed Stein to stay in medical school by urging her to "remember the cause of women" and (second) a much later incident in which, still disagreeing "violently about the cause of women," Stein explained that she did not mind it "but it does not happen to be her business" (101–2). Toklas presents Stein's business, her métier, as writing (94), and she presents her own business, in the broadest sense, as the cause of women—the cause of women in general, of Gertrude Stein and of herself in particular. She presents these businesses, however, as interdependent: Stein is pursuing her métier by representing Toklas in pursuit of hers; and Toklas's pursuing hers, of course, will ultimately enable Stein—through publication and publicity—to pursue hers. But if Toklas is the helpmeet of Stein the writer, then Stein is the helpmeet of Toklas the feminist.[51]

That circularity gives special meaning to certain internal representations of Stein's texts. Toklas deceptively associates Stein's composition of *Three Lives*, for example, with the year 1907, and, more pointedly, she ends chapter 3 with its publication. "But this last was after I came to Paris" (84), she says, in a phrase whose vocal stress on "after" or on "I" remains undecidable, a phrase whose surface stress on subsequence, put differently, conceals a deeper stress on consequence. More important, Toklas follows Stein in claiming that the latter wrote *The Making of Americans* between 1906 and 1908 (275).[52] The claim not only makes Stein seem a more prodigious worker than she was, not only plants *The Making of Americans* in the crucial year of artistic revolution, but also plants it in the crucial year of erotic fulfillment—the year of the Stein-Toklas union. My point is not that Toklas is claiming credit for the publication of *Three Lives* or for the composition of *The Making of Americans*, since Stein, after all, is writing this; *my point, precisely, is that the surface of the* Autobiography *indeed may have Toklas telling the story of her life with Stein and therefore implying that her meeting with Stein was the formative event of her early years, but that its depths have Stein telling us of her life with Toklas and therefore implying that her meeting with Toklas was the decisive event not only in her private life, but also in the development, in 1907, of her revolutionary art.*[53]

It is significant, then, that Stein has Toklas subtly shift the referent of the phrase, "two Americans ... in the heart of an art movement," from Leo and Gertrude Stein in the first cycle of chapters to Toklas and Stein in the second cycle (see 34). In essence, Stein shifts representational emphasis from Leo and herself as collectors, specifically, collectors of portraits by others, to Toklas and herself as creators, ultimately, creators of the double self-portrait we are reading. The shift had begun in 1907, when Toklas and Stein married; it had climaxed circa 1914, after Leo had left rue de Fleurus, and Alice and Gertrude, joining the domestic and the artistic, had "a little passage-way made between the studio and the little house" (172); and it now culminates in 1932 in the joint venture of the *Autobiography*. In a subtext to this story, Stein encodes another story, that of "a short novel" that she completely "forgot" for many years and whose resurfacing she places at the conclusion of chapter 4 and, therefore, of the first cycle of chapters. Concerning her affair with May Bookstaver thirty years earlier, the novel resurfaced "this spring just two days before our leaving for the country" where, of course, Stein is writing the *Autobiography*, her celebration of her marriage with Toklas (104).[54]

༶

Stein produced such thematic complication, of course, through her techniques; and she fused the theme of marriage in the *Autobiography* with the book's techniques. Given that Stein is portraying Toklas portraying Stein as creative genius as well as spouse, however, and given Stein's commitment to Cubist autoreference, it follows that Stein would have Toklas address Stein's techniques—explicitly and implicitly. She has Toklas say, in a key line on those techniques: "Observation and construction make imagination, that is granting the possession of imagination, is what she has taught many young writers" (94). In what only appears a circular formulation, Stein is teaching fundamental Cubist principles: the writer must observe visual reality but can describe it only in a constructed representation; the writer must observe the terms of that representation and analyze it as a construction; and the writer must observe the other texts that impinge upon that construction and that create with it a larger intertext. As we shall see in the following pages, Stein has Toklas explain Stein's basic principles and how they informed the composition of *The Making of Americans* and the *Autobiography*; she has Toklas allegorize how those same principles govern the *Autobiography* as a composition in portrait narration; and she has Toklas place those principles and the *Autobiography* in the context of portraits and narratives produced by Stein and by others.

Given those principles, it makes sense that Toklas first characterizes Stein as a descriptive writer. She tells us in her opening paragraphs that in "Ada" (1913) Stein gave "a very good description of me" as a young woman (4), and she later constructs chapter 4, which requires her to narrate events from Stein's childhood, on the premise that Stein had "described" her family—the word is used repeatedly—in *The Making of Americans* (see 87, 89, 91, 92). At that time, Toklas reports, Stein described what was inside people—in essence, those psychological traits that she was calling "bottom nature."[55] As Toklas goes on to explain, however, Stein had shifted her interest from "inside" to "outside" during her trip to Spain in the summer of 1912, when she began the very cubistic *Tender Buttons* (1914): "She says hitherto she had been interested only in the insides of people, their character and what went on inside them, it was during that summer that she first felt a desire to express the rhythm of the visible world" (145). Toklas adds, finally, that these writings about Objects, Food, and Rooms "were the beginning, as Gertrude Stein would say, of mixing the outside with the inside. Hitherto she had been concerned with seriousness and the inside of things, in these studies she began to describe the inside as seen from the outside" (192). Toklas is tracing, to put this differently, Stein's increased awareness of perspective—her evolution as an artist who thought of subject matter as being either interior or exterior into an artist who thought that any subject matter could be described only from an external point of view.

The evolution has several implications. It suggests, for example, what drove Stein to the theory and practice of portraiture—a genre whose first principles hold that one observes the subject by inferring inner nature from outward appearance, and that one represents the subject by using outward appearance to imply inner nature; it suggests, more specifically, what drove Stein from an essentially Jamesian representation of consciousness to an essentially Cézannean and, later, Picassian representation of figure. The evolution suggests, moreover, how William James's theory of the stream of consciousness drove Stein to see both other people and herself as subjects whose inner reality could be approached only from external perspectives, and could be represented most accurately and adequately, like the inanimate objects in *Tender Buttons*, from multiple perspectives.[56] And the evolution suggests, finally, how these principles, together with an obsessive privacy, drove Stein to argue that the emotions of others, whether fictional or real, are not directly available as subject matter, and that her own emotions, likewise only indirectly available, form neither the subject matter nor the motivation of her work. In the *Autobiography* as elsewhere, indeed, Stein emphasizes not only that she intends not to express her emotions or feelings, but also that she intends not to reveal any aspects of her psychic life except what she already has processed through consciousness and elected to reveal.

Thus we find Toklas specifically dissociating Stein's work from the unconscious in general, and from automatic writing in particular, and we find her associating it, on several occasions, with Bach's Fugue and with mathematics (see 62, 97, 258–59, 306–7). Depicting Stein not as just an accurate observer and describer, but also as a cool, unemotional, composer, Toklas makes her key point: "Gertrude Stein, in her work, has always been possessed by the intellectual passion for exactitude in the description of inner and outer reality. She has produced a simplification by this concentration, and as a result the destruction of associational emotion in poetry and prose. . . . [Poetry and prose] should consist of an exact reproduction of either an outer or an inner reality" (259). In this mediated self-depiction, Stein presents her passion, intellectual rather than emotional, as being for the kind of exact description demanded by the Realists; but she also signals her drift from Realist description toward Cubist construction with her concept of "reproduction." Her descriptions need not, and indeed cannot, imitate a reality; they must reproduce a reality, must replicate either in paint on canvas and in visual language, or in type on the page and in verbal language, the nature of that reality and the process of its apprehension. To accomplish this, Stein informs us, she had to remove emotion and replace it, apparently, with precision—a process she discusses with respect to words, sentences, and paragraphs.[57]

Toklas tells us early on that Stein "experimented with everything" in her struggles to describe accurately and adequately, including a period of "inventing words," but that "the english language was her medium," and "the use of fabricated words offended her, it was an escape into imitative emotionalism" (146). Stein previously had argued in *How To Write* (1931), moreover, that "a sentence is not emotional a paragraph is," and she now has Toklas not only emphasize her marked predilection for sentences and discuss their specific qualities, but also carry forward from *How To Write* the idea that both sentences and paragraphs have the internal *motion* of syntactical elements, but that only paragraphs depend for their construction upon associations produced by, broadly speaking, *emotion*.[58] Stein and Toklas are making a technical analogy: words employ etymology as passionlessly as sentences employ syntax, and neologisms share with paragraphs a dependence on imitative or associational emotionalism. They perhaps are using the analogy, moreover, to dissociate Stein from her chief rival Joyce, a master of neologism, and her chief predecessor James, a master of the paragraph, while simultaneously associating her with the Cubists, themselves devoted to elemental shapes and to rigorous and unemotional visual syntax.

None of this means that Stein was rejecting expressionism, in the broadest sense, for formalism, for composition as such, since she was putting her precise sentences, comprising basic English words, in the service of "exact reproduction." Toklas raises the problem, however, when she first tells us that Stein based *Three Lives* on what she heard in the Paris streets while walking home from her sittings to Picasso's portrait of her (60), and then later tells us that "it was at that time [Stein's period at Johns Hopkins] that she noticed the negroes and the places that she afterwards used in the second of the Three Lives stories, Melanctha Herbert" (100). Toklas apparently wants to show how Stein first observed an urban reality from an external perspective; how she later derived rhythms (or principles of organization) from a similar but unrelated urban reality; and how she then used the former observations as the basic elements in a composition organized according to the latter principles—emotional associations, as it were, disappearing in the gap—in order to produce not an imitation of the original reality but a "reproduction" of its elements and the dynamics holding them together. In suggesting all this, moreover, Toklas brings the term "story" into line with words, sentences, and paragraphs as belonging neither wholly to description nor wholly to construction—a motif that she extends from her initial characterization of the descriptive "Ada" as a "story" (4) to her closing passage with its six variations on the oxymoronic formulation that Stein "wrote my autobiography" (309–10), that Stein told the inside of Toklas's story, that is, from an outside perspective.[59]

Stein has Toklas acknowledge, in effect, that the same inherent traits of writing that compromise "Ada" and *Three Lives* as Realist description likewise compromise *The Making of Americans* and the *Autobiography* itself. Thus, Toklas may appear to adduce *The Making of Americans* as evidence for facts in Stein's early life, particularly in chapter 4, but she never actually makes that confusion of autobiographical fiction with fact; rather, she presumably has learned of Stein's past from Stein herself, and simply points out to the reader that Stein had used her experience as a *basis* for her early fiction. At the same time, however, Toklas justifiably can say that one of Stein's remarks to Pound "was literally true, *like all of [her] literature*" (248, emphasis added)—literally true *to itself* as a particular kind of representation. Toklas is warning us that just as we should not confuse autobiographical fiction with fact, Stein's representation of her family with her family, so should we not confuse autobiography with fact, Stein's representation of the Parisian circle with the historical Alice B. Toklas and other real people. But she also is inviting us to read the *Autobiography* as "literally true," as consistent with its own *données*; and, in fact, she elaborates those *données* at length through metaphor and through direct reference.

Stein is describing the inside from the outside in the *Autobiography*, reproducing Toklas's perspective and voice in order to describe Toklas remembering the past, representing someone else's continuously present moment of remembrance rather than herself remembering past events; her representation, in short, is a construction, less a description of the real Toklas as an observer and a narrator than a construction of the textual Toklas as one, a composition in which Stein uses her portraiture to frame Toklas's autobiographical narration. In Cubist fashion, however, she also has designed Toklas's representation of Stein and of Toklas herself as likewise less a description of real persons than Toklas's construction of textual personae, a composition in which Toklas uses her autobiographical narration to frame her own autoportraiture and portraiture. Moreover, Stein has Toklas imply how Stein's aesthetic principles are governing Stein's portrait of Toklas as a memoirist, while perhaps also governing Toklas's autobiographical memoir. More specifically, as I see it, Stein has Toklas imply how Stein's principles would apply to Toklas were she the real author of the text *as a means of implying* how they do apply to Stein as the real author of the text. She does the former, I believe, through references, not unlike those in *Story*, to photography and memoration; and she does the latter through allusions to the interpenetration, in the *Autobiography*, of background and foreground, outside and inside, fact and fiction.

In the course of her first description of Stein's home, for example, Toklas says that she has "refreshed my memory by looking at some snap shots taken inside the atelier at that time" (11), that, put simply, she has used photographically recorded observations to reconstruct the past.[60] Choosing the term "snap shot," she invokes not only photographs taken quickly and casually, but also photographs taken of something personal in order to aid later recollection; she invokes, in other words, not only the promise of instantaneous and unmediated representation, but also the promise of enhanced memoration. Whatever Toklas means to say, Stein surely knows that a snapshot records, precisely, an *observation* of a subject, a perspective rendered not only partial by its taker's spatiotemporal positioning but also, perhaps, interested by its taker's emotional and ideological investments; just as she knows that a snapshot enables recovery of a subject *for* memory only because memory enables recognition *of* the photographed subject. With Toklas's apparently innocuous remark, then, Stein alludes to problems of representation that reflect both William James's theory of the stream of consciousness and Henry James's theory of the proper relations between picture and story; and she alludes to the historical evolution from Realism, which aspired to objective documentation, through Impressionism, which admitted partial perspectives, to Cubism, which asserted the already mediated nature of all observation. With Toklas's references here and elsewhere to snapshots of paintings and sculptures, in sum, Stein alludes to recorded observations of constructed representations of previously mediated observations.[61]

With Toklas's subsequent references to photography and to memory, Stein seems to elaborate those problems as they pertain, implicitly, to Toklas's memoiristic representation. In the first relevant anecdote, Toklas recalls Picasso's first Cubist landscapes and the fact that he also had photographed the Spanish villages he had painted; she reports that critics had dismissed the landscapes as looking like nothing but cubes; and she adds that Stein, to prove the landscapes, on the contrary, "too photographic a copy of nature," later had asked Elliot Paul to "reproduce" on the same page in *transition* "a photograph of the painting by Picasso and the photographs of the village" (110; and see *P* 9). In a related and parallel second anecdote, Toklas recalls that the sculptor Arnold Rönnebeck had appeared in the winter of 1913–14 with "lots of photographs... of the german navy" and of himself with German nobility; she reports that he then took a trip to the French cathedral towns and "brought us a series of photographs of all these northern towns seen from above," views taken from the steeple that "look[ed] exactly like the pictures of the followers of Delaunay, what you [Rönnebeck said to Toklas] call the earthquake school"; and she adds, finally, that "later when during the war I found them, I tore them up in a rage" (125).

Stein uses these anecdotes to shape a nice allegory in the interpretation of pictorial documents. In the first, she figures her belief that Cubism was "a new kind of realism," to echo William James on *Three Lives*, that the mistaken cubes were functioning descriptively as well as compositionally; while she simultaneously figures her only apparently contradictory belief that Cubist representations, indeed all representations, inevitably *re*present unavailable natural realities through unavoidable cultural mediations. In the second anecdote, Stein shows us Toklas (and herself) perhaps having made the same error that the critics had done. Viewing Rönnebeck's aerial photographs through the lens of aesthetics and seeing them as interesting approximations of what she elsewhere calls Delaunay's "vulgarisation of Picasso" (258), Toklas apparently had failed to see their true content and real intent; she had become a dupe in Rönnebeck's scheme to pass off as art photographs what were in fact reconnaissance photographs, and only later had recognized that she had been had. With ironic subtlety, however, Stein intimates that Toklas again may have made the same error (and still may be making it)—namely, she viewed Rönnebeck's photographs of Germans through the lens of politics and saw them as signs of perfidy, and then viewed his aerial photographs, on that basis, as naturally being reconnaissance photographs. In a word, Stein is exploring both the aesthetic and political implications of mistaking descriptions for constructions, or vice versa, something the critics and Toklas did, something Toklas as narrator of the *Autobiography* and we as its readers must avoid doing.

With references more frequent but less elaborated, Stein also develops related themes of memoration that owe much to William James and to Henri Bergson. Echoing James's distinction between instantaneity and duration, for example, she suggests that if one tries only to observe and record, to eliminate memory, then one has only discrete data that literally make no sense; but that if one tries, conversely, to frame every observation within the already constructed, to "remember" at all times the already known, then one makes sense that is only conventional.[62] Arguing that one must negotiate those extremes, Stein nonetheless advocates confronting the new with as little mediation as possible, letting the new disrupt the known rather than the known constrain the new; for if one does the latter, one becomes a follower rather than a creator, and one also becomes a potential victim. Echoing Bergson's distinction between voluntary and involuntary memory, however, she also shows, in any case, that one can neither rely on memory nor wholly control it (see, e.g., 55, 104, 108, 198). And she suggests, indeed, that one can cause real damage as a result—by failing, for example, as Toklas once had done, to keep personal histories straight.[63]

Many of Stein's references to memory, in fact, point directly to Toklas as memoirist. Toklas, for example, explicitly confesses to difficulties in remembering the events of her narrative and in remembering the sequence of events, and she also admits to other lapses in memory (see 182, 237, 244). Even more extremely, she allows that she cannot always remember the difference between realities and representations—when, for example, she tells us that Jo Davidson was sculpting Stein, but that she "cannot remember who came in and out, whether they were real or whether they were sculptured [*sic*]." She remembers, however, that Lincoln Steffens was one of these and was "in some queer way . . . associated with the beginning of our seeing a good deal of Janet Scudder"; she does "not well remember just what happened," but does "however remember very well the first time I ever heard Janet Scudder's voice" (251). She may not remember facts, that is, may not remember what was actual, but she does remember those things that reach her, to use Henry James's nice phrase, through "the beautiful circuit and subterfuge of our thought and our desire" (*AN* 32). To the shaping power of aesthetics and of politics, Stein is adding that of erotics; she is suggesting the complicity of memory and desire, for Toklas characteristically, perhaps "queerly," remembers such details as Stein's voice and her brooch, Janet Scudder's voice, and Edith Sitwell's distinguished nose (5, 251, 285).

Showing such problems of description and construction at work in Toklas's narration, in any case, Stein points to the even more complicated variants in *her* portrait of that narration. In one of many instances of *passage*, for example, Toklas opens chapter 5, beginning her twenty-five years with Stein, thus: "And so life in Paris began and as all roads lead to Paris, all of us are *now there*, and I can begin to tell what happened when I was of it" (105, emphasis added). Overtly, Toklas is suggesting, with respect to theme, that her initiation led to a new life, and, with respect to form, that her secondhand reportage of Stein's early life in chapter 4 now will give way to direct recollection of events. Covertly, Stein has elided the antecedent of the pronoun "us" and has transposed temporal and spatial indicators, apparently to point to Toklas's narration and to her own portrait as constructions. Persons introduced in chapters 1–4 (one possible antecedent) *were* then *there*, but the narrator and reader (the other possible antecedent) *are now here*. "There" can refer only to a *time* finally unrecoverable by either memoration or narration, and "now" can refer only to the conceptual "space" of memoration as realized in narration. Toklas purports to recollect events, to tell what happened—and "a great deal happened" in those years (109); but Stein has compromised the possibility of her having done so by displacing in that sentence "there" to here, by bringing the illusory narrative depths to a real textual surface, by drawing attention to the written text, to the text as writing.[64]

Stein uses that very local instance to suggest the more global use of *passage* in the *Autobiography*. Toklas could have observed Stein, that is, only from the outside, could not have had direct access to Stein's consciousness; Stein can observe Toklas only from the outside, only can *infer* what Toklas might have been thinking about Stein and the others and how she now might choose to represent what she is remembering and what she is thinking of it; and Stein, as a result, must portray *within those sets of limitations* Toklas's representing her.[65] Stein constructs the *Autobiography*, that is, as a text of exteriorities: a first-person narration whose narrator lacks direct access to the consciousness of her central figure, executed as a portrait by an author who lacks direct access to the narratorial consciousness. Stein places those exteriorities, moreover, in a circulation in which Stein the author portrays Toklas the narrator who describes Stein the character who is Stein the author. Taking as her subject Toklas taking as her subject the Stein who already has elaborated the principles she now uses to write the *Autobiography*, Stein makes clear that circulation does not resolve itself as simple circularity, but rather plays itself out in complicated *passage*.

Using *passage*, Stein moots not only distinctions between background and foreground and between outside and inside, but also, and more famously, between fact and fiction. Specifically, she moots the assumption that she is recording her observations of a real person by placing that person in an oxymoronic discourse. A literary persona named Toklas, that is to say, cannot stand *autobiographically* either for a factual Toklas who did not author her or for a factual person who is other than herself and who is named Stein; nor, however, can she stand *fictionally* for that factual person named Stein, for that person already has another fictional persona, named Stein, in the text. As one result, the factual Stein can present only *an* interpretation of the factual Toklas, but she also can present *any* rendition she chooses of her textual Toklas. As another result, the factual Stein cannot purport that her textual Toklas is reporting accurately the behavior of Stein and her friends or, for that matter, is even quoting them accurately. And as a third result, finally, the factual Stein cannot attribute thoughts to her textual Toklas with any authority, the textual Toklas cannot attribute thoughts to her textual Stein with any authority, and, it follows, the textual Toklas cannot express or represent the factual Toklas's thoughts with any authority. Stein's Toklas is a construction, and so is Toklas's Stein; neither is necessarily true to her model, though each is true to the requirements of the composition.[66]

Toklas not only discusses Stein's aesthetics and allegorizes their specific application in the *Autobiography*, but she also addresses the portraiture and biographical writing that provided the immediate context for the *Autobiography* as portrait narration. She packs the *Autobiography*, for example, with references to portraits, usually but not exclusively by men of women, with Cézanne's *Portrait d'une Femme*, Matisse's *La Femme au Chapeau*, and, especially, Picasso's *Portrait of Miss Gertrude Stein* as the key pictures and with later portraits of Stein figuring in the book's second half. And she packs it with references to Stein as a portraitist and to the development of her portraiture from "Ada" to the *Autobiography* itself. Toklas tells how the "portrait writing began" with "Ada" while Stein was writing *The Making of Americans*, and how Stein since "has written portraits of practically everybody she has known" (139–41). She tells how Stein has been "tormented by the problem of the external and the internal," the problem that drives painters to still lives, the problem "that after all the human being essentially is not paintable"; but adds that Stein, nonetheless, "always however made her chief study people and therefore the never ending series of portraits" (146).[67] And she tells, finally, how Mabel Dodge was so "pleased" with Stein's *Portrait of Mabel Dodge at the Villa Curonia* that she "immediately conceived the idea that Gertrude Stein should be invited from one country house to another and do portraits and then end up doing portraits of american millionaires which would be a very exciting and lucrative career" (162)—Stein as a society portraitist, a successor of Sargent, as it were, and a precursor of Warhol.[68]

Those references to the problems of portraiture and to Stein's work in the genre are all from chapter 5, and Stein carefully links them, through Toklas, to references to a possible solution and to her continuing work that appear in chapter 7. When Toklas cited Stein's first considering the problem of painting the human being, for example, she also cited her recent interest in Picabia "because he at least knows that if you do not solve your painting problem in painting human beings you do not solve it at all" (146). When Toklas later returns to Stein's sense of a "solution" to the problem, she cites in some detail her view of Picabia's quest for the "vibrant line," "his way of achieving the disembodied," and her view that "perhaps he is now approaching the solution of his problem." As Toklas reports, however, Stein thinks that whoever does "create" the vibrant line will know it to "be dependent upon the emotion of the object which compels the vibration," and she moves immediately in the next paragraph to the key point about Stein's "destruction of associational emotion" (258–59).[69] It thus appears that Stein rules out Picabia and his followers as the creators of the new art, and, interestingly, as Toklas says, Stein "had come back to portrait writing with renewed vigour and she, to clarify her mind . . . did portraits of the russian and of the frenchman" (280). In order to find the creator of the new portraiture, that is, Stein did portraits of leading contenders. Before turning to whom she finds, we must turn to related comments on biographical writing.

Toklas includes fewer references to such writing, but they are no less calculated. She depicts Stein as a lifelong reader in the genre: when a young woman in London, she bought and read "a quantity of eighteenth century memoirs" (103); when in Florence with Leo, a few years later, there was "a most excellent english lending library with all sorts of strange biographies which were to Gertrude Stein a source of endless pleasure" (68); and when in Spain with Toklas, some years after that, Stein "read aloud to [Toklas] all of Queen Victoria's letters and she herself became interested in missionary autobiographies and diaries" (202). Toklas also depicts her as a lifelong writer in the genre: Stein first published *Three Lives*; in the summer of "strange biographies," she began *The Making of Americans*, "a history of a family" that became "a history of all human beings, all who ever were or are or could be living" (68–69)—a description she later repeats with variations (138); recently, she and Sherwood Anderson "planned collaborating on a life of Grant," and she "still likes to think about this possibility" (304).[70] Finally, Toklas distributes three explicit references to the *Autobiography* itself across its length: she first speaks of "this book my twenty-five years with Gertrude Stein" (17); she later allows that she "began [to read "Ada"] and I thought [Stein] was making fun of me and I protested, she says I protest now about my autobiography" (139–40); and she concludes the book with the six-paragraph discussion whose famous closing line attributes the *Autobiography* to Stein's hand (309–10).

As the reader will have noted, the comments on portraiture and those on biographical writing converge on a passage that expressly links "Ada," *The Making of Americans*, the *Autobiography*, and Stein's "long series of portraits" (138–41), and that precedes by a few pages the passage in which Stein finds the human being essentially unpaintable but the painting of human beings the only way to solve one's painting problem (146). Put differently, the passage that links Stein's first portrait of Toklas, her "history of every kind and of every individual human being" (138), her current portrait narration of Toklas, and her recurrent portraiture, sets up the closely following passage that specifies the problem with which Stein has "struggled" in moving toward the *Autobiography*. Though her formulation of that problem might seem to confuse a matter of representation with one of composition, it does not do so. Actually, Stein's formulation that "the human being essentially is not paintable" relies on a repeated slippage between singular "human being" and plural "human beings" (69/138, 146), and it then exploits a very precise slippage between the nominal and the participial. One must paint *human beings* as individuals before (and perhaps after) one tells histories of human types ("kinds"); but one cannot paint the *human* (in the process of) *being*, in any case, because the process of sitting to a portrait may be temporal, but its product, portraiture, is not. If Picabia has "added something to the solution of the problem," then, a compositional line that corresponds to an emotion, he still has not *solved* the problem. To do that, someone must find how to make modern painting narrative without making it emotional and romantic.

Rather than pursue that problem, however, Stein and Toklas instead show how someone—Stein—is making *literary* portraiture narrative without making it emotional and romantic. They give the first clue in the opening allusion to James that scholars tend to overlook in favor of its counterpart, the closing reference to Defoe; but in that opening allusion, Stein has Toklas point to the central narrative principles behind her text. Toklas had written to James, we recall, to propose that she "dramatise" his novel *The Awkward Age* (3–4), a telling choice because James had used its preface in the New York Edition—to which Stein and Toklas had subscribed—to theorize novelistic narrative *as* drama. Stein, in turn, not only is adapting Jamesian novelistic principles to autobiography, but she also, again more important, is following James's injunction, "Dramatise it, dramatise it!" (*AN* 236).[71] By following the Jamesian allusion with Toklas's comment that Stein already "described" her in "Ada" (4), Stein may be implying that she now, by contrast, is "dramatizing" Toklas in the

Autobiography. Stein resembles the James of *The Portrait of a Lady*, indeed, in presenting her own portrait of Toklas, but she differs from him in portraying Toklas as a first-person narrator; and she simultaneously resembles the James of *William Wetmore Story* by presenting a panoramic group portrait of an artistic American colony expatriated in Europe, but, again, she differs from him in portraying it from Toklas's perspective, and not from her own.

Stein actually glosses that resemblance and, especially, that difference in the closing reference in which Toklas quotes her saying she would write Toklas's autobiography "as simply as Defoe did the autobiography of Robinson Crusoe" (310).[72] In the opening allusion to James, that is, Stein picks up on James's titular ambiguity and suggests that Toklas will chronicle her personal "awkward age" of maturation *in* the epochal "awkward age" in which Victorian society stumbled into modernism; and that she, Stein, will renovate Jamesian protomodernist technique. In the closing reference to Defoe, however, Stein also suggests that Toklas will chronicle the couple's domestic and vocational histories as diligent, pragmatic women; and that Stein will look beyond Jamesian complications to prior and perhaps simpler principles of realism—will look beyond James's "disembodied" American technique, as she soon would call it (*LIA* 53), to Defoe's more descriptive and empirical English technique.[73] With each comment, then, Stein makes a thematic point about the origin and the context of a technique which she employs in the *Autobiography*; and with the two comments together, she suggests *not* that she is shifting backward to simplicity—engaging in nostalgia, refusing to be modern—but rather that she is shifting forward in a way that gathers up the past implicit in the present in order to advance that present into the future. She is suggesting not only how her portrait narration works but also why it makes *her* the creator she in fact has been seeking.

Stein intends to *re-embody* her narrative line, as it were, to succeed where Picabia and James failed. She sees the difficulty, however, and figures it in two related anecdotes. In one, Toklas recalls a German artist who sculpted Roger, the concierge's boy, and sold the sculpture "to the royal museum at Potsdam. The concierge during the war often wept at the thought of her Roger being there, sculptured [*sic*], in the museum at Potsdam" (59). In the other, she had recalled that Matisse had spent a "winter painting a very large picture of a woman setting a table and on the table was a magnificent dish of fruit. It had strained the resources of the Matisse family to buy this fruit" (45–46). Through Toklas, Stein apparently means to find the concierge's confusion of realms amusing, just as she apparently means us to see that Matisse still was tied to models in a way that Cubists in general and Picasso in particular were not (55; and see *EA* 29; *P* 1, 7–8, 10); and she perhaps also means us to see how Matisse, too, was struggling with the problem of painting the human being.

And yet, Stein has Toklas describe the German sculptress's instructor as looking "exactly like the pictures of Huckleberry Finn's father," she concludes the passage with an oblique allusion to James's "The Real Thing" (59), and, in fact, she gives us in the *Autobiography* almost as many examples of life imitating art as of art imitating life (see 22, 44, 103, 194). It is *her* syntax, moreover, that mimics Matisse's style and conflates his red table and fruit with his representation of them.

Stein wants to negotiate the distance between naive confusion and sophisticated fusion in both portraiture and narrative. Her concierge subscribes to a naturalistic mimesis and naively confuses represented and representation; Matisse abandons naturalistic mimesis but continues to connect represented and representation; the Cubists as *antinaturalists* stress the complete separation of the two but as *abstractionists*, simultaneously, reassert the relationship at a different level. Stein wants to separate the real Toklas she observes from the textual Toklas she constructs while showing the relationship between the two, just as she wants to separate Toklas's construction of her from the real author she is while showing the relationship between those two. Since Stein portrays Toklas's narration, moreover, her portrait of Toklas also comprises a Jamesian metanarrative (Stein's) containing a Defoesque narration and narrative (Toklas's); Stein's abstract metanarrative contains Toklas's concrete narrative, just as Stein's abstract portrait of Toklas contains Toklas's concrete portrait of Stein. But Stein knows, of course, that "abstract" and "concrete" lose both fixed location and fixed meaning in this circulation, and that Stein's Toklas, Toklas's Stein, and *Stein's Toklas's Stein* are all mediated by conventions informing observation and construction.

Stein apparently had considered ending the *Autobiography*, "Sincerely Yours, Alice B. Toklas"; though she would have sacrificed the elegance of the James-Defoe symmetry with this allusion to Clemens and *Huckleberry Finn*, she would have made two things clearer.[74] First, she would have implied the analogies Stein/Tom Sawyer and Toklas/Huck Finn and might have recalled the debate between romance and realism that, encoded in those two characters, *Huckleberry Finn* conducts. She would have given us the romantic author (Stein) creating the realist narrator (Toklas) who creates her author as a realist (internal Stein), a nice contradiction reminding us that the *Autobiography* does not loop back to an easy repetition of its beginning but comprises, rather, a fundamentally cubistic set of unresolvable images. In fact, she would have signaled the debate between realism and Cubism encoded in the *Autobiography*. Second, she would have implied, in a different schematic, the analogies Stein/Clemens and Toklas/Huck Finn and therefore would have suggested her sense of her literary genealogy. Given that the *Autobiography* contains only one very slight reference to Hawthorne (163), indeed, Stein seems to construct not the lineage Hawthorne-James-Stein / romance-realism-Cubism, but rather the lineage Defoe-James-Stein / social realism–psychological realism–Cubism, a lineage that accommodates not only Clemens, but also George Eliot and Joyce.

☞

With the shifting perspectives of the *Autobiography*, Stein embodies the political theme that Toklas's narrative conveys. By making foreground and background fluid sites, that is, she makes it impossible to identify either Toklas or herself as "behind" the other and, thus, moots the disingenuous patriarchal contrivance that posits a great woman behind every good man: equalizing Toklas and herself in the *Autobiography* as composition, Stein virtually equalizes the couple as producers of the *Autobiography*. She does this, however, with considerable complication, for she not only uses vanguard techniques to embody and to convey her point and not only incorporates a metadiscourse, as we just have seen, on her theory and practice of those techniques; she also incorporates a metadiscourse about the social and political implications of her practicing of them in the *Autobiography* itself. Though she makes it clear, finally, that her text works within multiple contexts, she makes it equally clear that it does not do so as a closed artifact framed by them. Embedded in artistic and social intertexts, rather, the *Autobiography* both derives from and comments on Cubism, both depends upon and deconstructs cubistic and other representations of women in general, and of Stein in particular.

Stein "has a weakness for breakable objects," Toklas tells us early on; "she has a horror of people who collect only the unbreakable" (16). Picking up the theme when first discussing "the heroic age of cubism," Toklas recalls a servant's pretending to break a "black renaissance plate," and Stein's fairly temperate response: "Gertrude Stein is awfully patient over the breaking of even her most cherished objects," she notes, and "loves objects that are breakable" (106–7). At one level, she is offering a domestic metaphor for the Cubist breakage of Renaissance perspective, the shattering of the platelike surface with its illusion of depth, before she traces the development of that breakage as an aesthetics. As she does the latter, she also traces the increasing visibility and reputation of its practitioners, and she eventually reaches the critical moment of their publicity and its relation to Stein: she mentions the important show of Italian Futurism in Paris (153), expressing vague disapproval, then mentions Stein's *Portrait of Mabel Dodge at the Villa Curonia*, and adds that soon after "Mabel Dodge went to America and it was the winter of the armoury show which was the first time the general public had a chance to see any of these pictures. It was there that Marcel Duchamp's Nude Descending the Staircase was shown" (163–64).

In this utterly compact moment, Stein uses the *objet trouvé* of the venue of the Armory Show (which she spells "armoury") to connect Toklas's central themes of art, war, and love. Discussing in the preceding pages such women friends as Mildred Aldrich and Mabel Dodge, Toklas anticipates here her much later depiction of Aldrich as an American expatriate who remained in her house on the Marne throughout the war, who served the French cause, who wrote a famous memoir about her service, and who was decorated through the help of Stein and Toklas (252–53). She thus seems to use Aldrich here to foreshadow Stein and herself as American expatriates who would be caught in London by the outbreak of the war, who would return to Paris rather than remain safely in England or embark for America, and who would serve the effort, would write about it, and would be decorated (221). The reference to Dodge notwithstanding, she is contrasting Aldrich to Duchamp, who went to America during the war (164); she is contrasting an American expatriate in Europe with a European expatriate in America, toward the end of contrasting defenders of Paris (like Stein and herself) with abandoners of Paris—as she later will contrast the Apollinaire who served in the military with the Picasso who decamped for Rome.[75]

Toklas uses the reference to Dodge, however, to underscore her connected themes. She had mentioned earlier how Stein came to prove central to "an art movement of which the outside world at that time knew nothing" (34); and she dwells in the "heroic age" chapter on the increasing celebrity and financial success of Picasso and the others largely as a result of Kahnweiler's "taking on commercially the cause of the cubists" (135). She also tells here of friends who devoted themselves to promoting Stein's reputation—Henry McBride (149), Myra Edgerly (154–55), Carl Van Vechten (169)—and she mentions Alvin Langdon Coburn, who "had just finished a series of photographs that he had done for Henry James," and who "was the first photographer to come and photograph her as a celebrity and she was nicely gratified" (171–72).[76] She alludes to the fact, finally, that the first major, sympathetic treatment of Stein's work, Mabel Dodge's "Speculations, or Post-Impressionism in Prose," was reprinted in the June 1913 issue of Stieglitz's *Camera Work* along with Stein's most celebrated Cubist literary portrait, *Portrait of Mabel Dodge at the Villa Curonia*. And Stieglitz had published the issue, we might recall, in conjunction with the Armory Show, "the first time," to repeat a citation, "the general public had a chance to see any of these pictures."[77]

Stein can assume, in 1932, that her reader will know that the public began to associate her with Cubism at the time of the Armory Show, and she exploits that fact.[78] In the early chapters of the *Autobiography*, she had Toklas associate *Three Lives* and *The Making of Americans* with Picasso's *Demoiselles d'Avignon* and *Three Women*—the former arguably *the* most important Cubist painting; she now has Toklas associate the *Portrait of Mabel Dodge* with Duchamp's *Nude Descending a Staircase*—"an explosion in a shingle factory," as one critic derisively called it, *un succès du scandale*, the equivalent of *Le Sacre du Printemps*, which Toklas has not failed to mention in this context (166–67).[79] Toklas is locating *Stein's* acts of portraiture in the explosive moment that began Cubism in 1907 and in the moment that marked its public appearance in America (and, in some sense, the end of its heroic period) in 1913; and she is associating Stein's portraits with paintings that seem from the retrospect of 1932 to exemplify the Cubist program. Such associations notwithstanding, and Stein's use of analogous techniques in the *Autobiography* notwithstanding, Toklas is not simply paralleling Stein's work with Picasso's and Duchamp's; the more overtly feminist persona, Toklas is also contrasting Stein's work with theirs in a way that suggests the deeper, and more deeply radical, point of the *Autobiography*.

From the beginning, Stein has Toklas anticipate the Armory Show passage by developing a careful sequence of paintings: Matisse's *Femme au Chapeau*, Picasso's *Portrait of Miss Gertrude Stein*, Picasso's *Demoiselles*, and Duchamp's *Nude*. The first two are essentially illusionistic, or at least noncubistic; the second two are cubistic with a vengeance, indeed, mark the beginning and the ending of the "heroic age of cubism." The first two are essentially portraits, with particular referents: Madame Matisse and Stein; the second two are figure-studies, with general referents: nude women (though they are also, of course, highly metadiscursive pictures whose subjects, or referents, are the genre of the female nude). The first picture carries a hint of intimacy, though not exactly eroticism, insofar as *femme* signifies "married woman" in particular as well as "woman" in general, while the third picture carries a sense of eroticism without intimacy, insofar as *demoiselle* signifies "whore" in particular as well as "unmarried woman" in general; the second picture emphasizes, in its title, the unmarried status of its subject, while the fourth emphasizes, in title and content, figural type and genre. If Stein is suggesting that linguistic practice equates "woman" and "wife," on the one hand, and "unmarried woman" and "whore," on the other, then she is indicting social and linguistic practices that consign her (Miss Gertrude Stein) to the latter category; at the least, she seems to be indicting Picasso for making her another *demoiselle*.[80]

As pictures, moreover, as visual language, these paintings progress toward abstraction. Matisse, after all, did abstract Madame Matisse's specific identity into the general figure of a woman with a hat; and Picasso, more blatantly, had erased Stein's specific visage to replace it with a masklike face.[81] Continuing the pattern in *Les Demoiselles*, Picasso began with a type rather than with individuals, and further abstracted the female face into pure mask, the female body into pure form; and Duchamp, more blatantly still, exploded the female face and body. They all may have set out, indeed, to employ and (progressively) to deconstruct the conventions of highly traditional genres and subjects, but that only suggests the legitimacy of Stein's apparent point: patriarchal painting has been a history of abstracting in general and of abstracting women in particular, a history of converting individuals into types and of converting figures, particularly female figures, into form. Seen from this point of view, Picassian Cubism seems less a solution than a worse problem, seems itself to exacerbate that abstraction and that misogyny by its extreme deformation of the female body. Stein seems to counter the problem, then, by *returning* specific reference to Matisse's picture of his wife and to Picasso's portrait of Stein, as well as by *revealing* the pernicious implications of *Les Demoiselles* and of the *Nude*. To accomplish the latter, Stein and Toklas need to remove those pictures from the concealing discourse of aesthetics, just as they needed to do with Rönnebeck's reconnaissance photos.[82]

In fact, Stein does this with a pertinent anecdote. Toklas recalls a five-year-old boy, the janitor's son, who saw a Matisse at the rue de Fleurus and "cried out in rapture, oh là là what a beautiful body of a woman." Toklas cites this incident as Stein's retort whenever a guest aggressively asked of a picture, "what is that supposed to represent" (21); and we are to see, presumably, that a child with a fresh eye can "read" modern art while an adult with a habituated eye cannot. Surely, however, Stein also wants us to see a boy already acculturated to seeing women as bodies and to seeing those bodies as well as their representations (specifically, their iconic representations) as things to own—a form of commodification that makes sense of Vollard's otherwise cryptic remark that "ordinarily a portrait of a woman always is more expensive than a portrait of a man" (40). Stein presses the point with Toklas's repeated attention to *Les Demoiselles*, suggesting not only that Picasso acts figuratively as a panderer but also that he acts literally as a pornographer, since "pornography" means, etymologically, "writing about whores." Stein would comment in *Everybody's Autobiography* that "the minute painting gets abstract it gets pornographic" (*EA* 127), and, read back into the *Autobiography*, the remark takes on a twofold logic: first, *when* painting *became* abstract (Cubism), it became pornographic (*Les Demoiselles*); second, *whenever* painting *becomes* abstract (type rather than instance), it becomes pornographic (fantasy over reality). That Stein strives for an "elemental abstraction" in her own work (78) does not contravene this reading, but rather thickens its implications.[83]

We can see why, perhaps, if we begin with the premise that Matisse's *Femme au Chapeau* was of Madame Matisse but that Picasso's *Portrait of Miss Gertrude Stein* had been of her until he changed it and tried to make *her* his painting's image; and if we place Picasso's portrait of Stein in a sequence of portraits (Cézanne's *Portrait d'une Femme*, Matisse's *Femme au Chapeau*, Picasso's *Portrait of Miss Gertrude Stein*) related to a sequence of nudes (Matisse's *Bonheur de Vivre*, Picasso's *Nude Girl with Basket of Flowers* and his *Demoiselles*, Duchamp's *Nude Descending a Staircase*). Toklas apparently juxtaposes Matisse's *Bonheur de Vivre* and Picasso's *Demoiselles*, in 1907, to Stein's *Three Lives* and *Making of Americans*; and she apparently juxtaposes Stein's *Portrait of Mabel*

Dodge, in 1913, to Duchamp's *Nude*—juxtaposes nudes of women done by men, in short, to portraits of women by a woman.[84] Moreover, she juxtaposes Picasso's *Portrait of Miss Gertrude Stein* to *The Autobiography of Alice B. Toklas*. Insofar as the *Autobiography* resists abstraction, remains concrete, it remains a decent and dignified portrait: Stein portrays Toklas as a woman and as a spouse, if not a wife, one who is neither a madonna nor a whore. Insofar as the *Autobiography* becomes abstract, however, it too may approach the "pornographic," though perhaps only ironically: Toklas tells, and Stein writes, a story of artists who first struggled with great integrity but who then became famous and wealthy, and who, perhaps, whored themselves and others to do so; if Toklas and Stein are depicting Picasso as an offender, they also may be implicating Stein.

In the *Autobiography*, that is, Stein not only portrays Toklas and herself, thematizes and theorizes that double portraiture, and places it in the context of comparable artistic acts; she also presents artistic (and literary) portraiture as simply one mode of representation among others, as cultural production occurring within a larger artistic and political economy of social productions. She includes, and thematizes, a good deal of hearsay, for example, and even more of the organized hearsay we call gossip.[85] And she suggests that, through these media, persons and things come to be "known" as something or for something: Picasso heads a movement "known as" Cubism (77), Stein is "well known for saying things" (249–50), Hemingway is "getting to be known" (267), and so on. At one level, Stein is advancing her argument that we should strive for direct, unmediated knowledge, however impossible the quest, that we know a person or thing well in inverse proportion to the degree of mediation—that, in short, the "known" quantities that she enumerates actually remained *unknown*. At a clearly related second level, she is drawing a parallel between increasingly modern and technologically accelerated means of locomotion (standing, walking, driving, and, in *Everybody's Autobiography*, flying) and equivalent means of producing and disseminating representations (gossiping, writing/painting, broadcasting on radio, and, in *Everybody's Autobiography*, filming). In a word, she is extending the theme of portraiture to that of reputation, and reputation to the machinery of publicity—to *publishing* in the broadest sense.

As an autobiographer tracing her rise from apprentice to publisher, Toklas closely resembles Benjamin Franklin; "completely and entirely American," Stein, too, resembles the paragon who announced his theme, in the opening paragraph of his autobiography, as being his rise from Poverty and Obscurity to Affluence and Reputation.[86] Stein introduces the same theme almost as quickly, when Toklas recalls Hélène, just returned in 1932, saying, surprised, "all those people whom I knew when they were nobody are now always mentioned in the newspapers, and the other night over the radio they mentioned the name of Monsieur Picasso" (9). Though Toklas speaks here of Hélène's current "legend" among all of Paris (10) and, much later, of Picasso's friend Manolo as "a legendary figure in Paris" (117), Hélène is still a servant and Manolo not mentioned on the radio. Similarly, though Toklas points out that, in those days, the modern pictures "had no value," in terms of money or fame (10, 15), she indicates that not long afterwards Matisse became prosperous and Picasso was approaching prosperity (118) and that, indeed, Matisse began investing in the paintings of others to increase his holdings and his patrimony, but Picasso began hoarding his own paintings for precisely the same purposes. Stein suggests that painters' reputations convert into money more easily than do writers' reputations (278), because paintings are more easily commodified than are books, and that, as both cause and effect, picture-dealers are more adventurous than are publishers. She is also suggesting that men and painters, and especially men painters, remain in control of one system of production and distribution, while women and writers, and especially women writers, are locked into another. And she is suggesting, finally, that those who control the means of representation also control the content, and the content specifies, not surprisingly, who should remain in control of the means.

That is the context, now familiar, in which we should view the initially offputting obsession in the *Autobiography* with Stein's reputation. Toklas gives us a near litany of "firsts," for example, that together suggest the gap between Stein's efforts and public recognition of them.[87] She also tells of the friends who kept Stein's name before the public in previous years, and, particularly, of the friends who did so after the war. Mildred Aldrich, for example, wanted the *Atlantic Monthly* to publish Stein, became angry when Stein was not in *Who's Who in America*, and now wishes Stein were not "outlawed" so is pleased that *Who's Who* added her just this year (238–39). Edith Sitwell reviewed *Geography and Plays*, then wrote an article on Stein (284–85); Elliot Paul tried to open "the eyes of the public" to her in *transition* (296); and, Toklas observes, Stein's "reputation among the french writers and readers [has been] steadily growing" (306). In the closing pages of the *Autobiography*, indeed, Toklas reports that Madame de Clermont-Tonnerre says that the time has come when Stein "must be made known to a larger public" in France, that Stein agrees that she "too believes in a larger public," and that they decide that the previously "barred" way can be opened by the translation of Stein's abridgment of *The Making of Americans* (307).

This all would seem quite positive. Toklas reports that Stein always has been confident of coming fame, realizing while writing *Three Lives* that she eventually would have a biography (54), never throwing out any paper on which she has written (64), and knowing that she is the only one in English literature and now saying it (94). And, sure enough, we learn that an English Bishop's wife in 1914 understood that Stein was "an important person in Paris" (187), that a senator's secretary after the war thought she was a well-known author (253), that Stein herself discovered that she had an Oxford following in 1920 (241) and felt "like a prima donna" when she lectured at Oxford and Cambridge in 1925 (288–89). Stein has become so well known, in fact, that newspapers lampoon her, though they also ridicule her (192, 210). The fact that they also *quote* her sentences when lampooning her, however, shows that she is "under their skin" (86–87), a remark sufficiently important to Toklas (and to Stein) that she repeats it in her closing pages (300). With her name finally listed in *Who's Who in America*, with her lectures heckled but otherwise well received at Oxford and Cambridge, with her reputation steadily growing in France, Stein's early confidence seems justified, her fame secured in America, England, and France.

If Stein craves this "glory," however, as she admits (289), she also recognizes its problems. She has Toklas enumerate portraits of her and translations of her work, mediations, however necessary, that keep her and her work from truly being "known."[88] And she has Toklas echo her concerns about having celebrity but lacking a readership: Stein says, for example, that if people "bring themselves to read [her work] they will be interested" (63), that her status as a coterie writer is "ridiculous" (86), and, implicitly, that "her childish delight amounting almost to ecstasy" at seeing her books in a bookstore window (299) has its basis not in vanity but in her wish to have her work widely circulated, to have readers rather than collectors (301). Acknowledging the aporia of modern mass culture, Stein sees, on the one hand, that her wish to publish her person might conflict with her wish to publish her work, since her celebrity as a vanguard figure and the portraits of her as a vanguard icon, especially Picasso's, might have impeded her reputation as a vanguard artist; but she also sees, on the other hand, that she might have to publish her person in order to publish her work, since her celebrity status, for better or for worse, can be used to provoke interest in her as an artist. Stein must publish an image of herself as a vanguard writer, then, to attract a readership, while simultaneously publishing her work to justify that image and satisfy that attraction. She thus makes publication both the subject and the function of her book's conclusion.

Throughout the *Autobiography*, Stein has inflected publication with gender and has linked it closely to the central marital theme. As Toklas tells the story, men had intervened throughout Stein's career to help her into print.[89] She also intimates, however, three things: one, men have had the power to intervene because they retain control over publishing; two, the men who have helped Stein into print have done less than a spectacular job; and three, women such as Mildred Aldrich, Mabel Dodge, and Edith Sitwell have made the more serious efforts to interest a readership directly in Stein's work (rather than in her person) and thus to spur a demand for its publication. Toklas herself, though, becomes the key figure. From the beginning, she has identified her role in the production of Stein's manuscripts as typist and proofreader, from *Three Lives* (83, 105, 137), through *The Making of Americans* (105, 138, 275), to her now, in 1932, typing *Stanzas in Meditation* (276). She explicitly compares such work to cleaning and dusting (138–39), to domestic labor, and Stein, behind the scenes, implicitly develops the comparison toward a key point. At the end of chapter 5, the "heroic age" chapter, Toklas notes in succession Stein's finding a publisher (John Lane, whom Aldrich warns is "a fox"), Hélène's leaving Stein's household, and the old life's being over (174–75). In effect, Stein first had a domestic but lacked a publisher, then had a publisher but lacked a domestic. Without becoming either a domestic or a publisher, Toklas joined domestic and editorial duties in her preparation of Stein's work for publication, a junction of art and life like the couple's joining the atelier and the pavilion. As Toklas tells us, however, these edited manuscripts continued to remain largely unpublished (238–41), so Toklas, child of pioneers, must become the "adventurous" publisher that Stein needs (297).[90]

We learn of this, as of so many other things, in advance of the proper chronology. Toklas lets drop, twice, in chapter 6 that she just has published Stein's *Operas and Plays* in Plain Edition (200, 236), a telling point in juxtaposition to Robert McAlmon's unsatisfactory handling of the book publication of *The Making of Americans* and Hemingway's dubious intervention in its serial publication in *Transatlantic*. The foreshadowing continues when Mildred Aldrich says that when Stein and Toklas set out to do something it will be done (253), when Harry Gibb says that Stein must publish "a big book" in a large printing and encourages Toklas to handle it (254), and when Toklas says that Stein has written *How To Write*, which she, Toklas, just has published (257). The foreshadowing allows Stein to juxtapose her other, male, publishers with Toklas, and to suggest, indeed, that the poor handling of Stein's major work, *The Making of Americans*, again by men, necessitated Toklas's taking over, adding to her role as editor that of publisher. Toklas decides that *she* will publish Stein, founds Plain Edition, learns "my new business," and insists that "one must learn one's trade" (298–99)—one's métier. She tells us that Stein had picked *Lucy Church Amiably* as the first book to be produced, but that she, Toklas, chose *How To Write* as "my next book." Blurring the lines of proprietorship with a second such pronominal usage, she goes on to detail her problems as a publisher—from getting money to "print my books," to arranging for bindings and slipcases—and to suggest her increasing ambitiousness as a publisher (298–302).

Toklas thus sets up the concluding passage in which she introduces three subsidiary themes—Stein's and Sherwood Anderson's warm relations, Stein's having her hair cut short and Picasso's response, and Stein's involvement in the translation of *The Making of Americans*—and interweaves them with the principal autoreferential theme of Stein's authorship of Toklas's autobiography. Toklas has documented her transition from the domestic space to the professional, from the private sphere to the public, and, in collaboration with Stein, has reappropriated the production and distribution of books that either woman legitimately can call "mine." In contrast to the last man mentioned, Ford Madox Ford, who complains of having to juggle three roles, Toklas allows that her work as "housekeeper ... gardener ... needlewoman ... secretary ... editor ... vet for dogs" and, of course, publisher, has made it difficult for her to be an "author" as well. As a result, Stein has agreed to write her autobiography for her, "and she has and this is it" (309–10).[91] In sum, Toklas has published Stein's work, and Stein is now publishing Toklas's persona; furthermore, this narrating persona portrays Stein biographically, while she also portrays herself autobiographically. Though Stein and Toklas have not regained either the kind or the degree of control they sought, as we shall see, they have regained some control of their reputations by taking control of their representations.

To see how, we might begin by noting that Stein has Toklas not only covertly critique Picasso, the genius who looms as large as Stein in the chapter on the "heroic age," but also overtly attack Hemingway, the follower who fails to loom large in the chapter on Stein's postwar search for the new creator.[92] As part of the negative assessment, Toklas quotes Stein on Picasso's and Hemingway's rivalrous personalities. Accusing Picasso of needing to "wish away" Juan Gris (260) and Hemingway of "having killed a great many of his rivals and put them under the sod" (270–71), Stein and Toklas imply, in effect, that these two men were more bellicose in the aesthetic wars than they had been in the Great War. And if Stein and Toklas also are implying that Picasso, a powerful creator, needed to wish away Stein, they seem to be expecting that Hemingway, a weak follower, will attempt a symbolic matricide.[93] Their making such accusations, of course, is ironic, perhaps by intention, since Stein regarded as rivals not only Picasso and, differently, Hemingway, but especially Joyce, and since she regarded James as a precursor that she needed to put under the sod, as we shall see in our discussion of *Four in America*. Whatever the biographical facts might have been, however, we need to consider here how Stein incorporated the theme of rivalry into her double portrait of Toklas and herself.

Obviously, Stein wants Toklas to concoct a family romance that represents Stein as competing with male siblings and as succeeding fathers; she allows Toklas, in effect, to show Stein as preoccupied with rivals, as competitive toward Picasso as an artist, and as resentful toward Picasso and Hemingway as men who had attained, by 1932, the wealth and celebrity that Stein lacked. She also allows Toklas, moreover, to parallel that concession of Stein's professional rivalry with a hint of Toklas's more personal rivalry, her competing first with Picasso and then with Hemingway for Stein's attention, and her treating James as a father.⁹⁴ Stein and Toklas make familial dynamics secondary, however, to the larger social formations modeled on them, and they inflect their understanding of those formations, as I have suggested throughout, with feminism.⁹⁵ Toklas makes it clear, for example, that Picasso served the patriarchal institution of art that, in turn, rewarded him, and Stein, as we shall see, makes a related point about James in *Four in America*. Stein presents Picasso and James, then, as figures she not only must confront, but also must confront on battlefields that favor them. In the *Autobiography*, the battlefield is portraiture: not just a rival who must be wished away, Picasso specifically created the principal contemporary portrait, his *Portrait of Miss Gertrude Stein*, to which Stein responds; not just a precursor who must be "put under the sod," James specifically created the principal antecedent portrait, *The Portrait of a Lady*, to which she reacts.

It was Neil Schmitz who first kenned the thematic significance of Picasso's *Portrait of Miss Gertrude Stein*.⁹⁶ Toklas carries the motif from the beginning to the very end of the *Autobiography*, first noting Picasso's claim that Stein would come to resemble his picture; later describing how he had painted out Stein's head and replaced it with another and adding that no one remembered the original; and finally rehearsing an anecdote, already told once, about his response to Stein's subsequently having her hair cut short.⁹⁷ In essence, Stein has Toklas suggest that Picasso first described Stein, then erased the description, then constructed Stein, and then asserted that his construction would replace her; and Toklas suggests, moreover, that Picasso did all this to erase Stein's importance as a *creative agent* in the initial formulation of Cubism by making her a *created icon* of that formulation. He painted out her "head," we might recall, just before he became the "head" of Cubism (77), and he succeeded in his erasure of Stein, after all, to the extent that neither memorial nor photographic records exist of this transitional portrait (in contrast to the first Cubist landscapes) (see 57, 70, 110); and, more important, to the extent that his "famous" (7) portrait of Stein might be more "widely known" (55), in 1932, than is Stein herself—or, more precisely, to the extent that Stein is known, in 1932, as the icon Picasso made.⁹⁸

As with so much of the *Autobiography*, however, Stein ambiguates this theme. At one level, for instance, she clearly is paralleling Picasso's visual beatification of her with Toklas's (and thus her own) verbal beatification.⁹⁹ At a second level, she is presenting Picasso's portrait of her, and her portraits of him, not only as tokens of the affection and the respect that the real Picasso and Stein obviously shared, but also as examples of the Cubism they were struggling, in different media, to create.¹⁰⁰ At another, closely related level, she is ascribing to Picasso and to his *Portrait* the same aesthetic principles that Toklas ascribes to Stein and to her *Autobiography*: Picasso had not painted from a model for years (55), and when he later "painted out the whole head," it was because, he claimed, "I can't see you any longer when I look" (64–65).[101] In effect, his eye had become so habituated through repeated sittings that he was not seeing Stein (*there*, immediate), but rather *his* cumulative, mental, and thus abstract picture of her; so he erased this corrupted description and replaced it with an imaginative construction that, in a shrewd assessment of mass media, he further understood would *become* Stein to the mass audience. Simultaneously undermining that level, however, Stein also is working a variation on Hawthorne's theme in *The Marble Faun* that art executes the model. She seems to be suggesting, that is, that if one eliminates the model either before or after the fact, and paints the subject from one's imagination, then one may escape Hawthorne's alleged criminality, but only, as it were, because one is, or can claim to have been, innocent by virtue of insanity: in her nicely ambiguous phrasing, Picasso "sat down and *out of his head* painted the head in without having seen Gertrude Stein again" (70, emphasis added).

Stein encodes this crucial ambiguity in the photographic illustration titled "Room with Gas (Femme au chapeau and Picasso Portrait)" (56). On the one hand, she uses the photograph simply to show the Picasso portrait occupying a place of honor in her home (and we know from similar photographs and from additional information that the historical Stein valued it highly); on the other hand, however, she uses it to make a complicated comparison.[102] If I was correct in arguing that Stein uses *Femme au Chapeau* to show not only that Matisse did not confuse models with pictures, women with paintings, but also that Stein (and arguably Toklas) does not either, then her illustrative pairing of the Matisse study and the Picasso portrait would suggest that she either is comparing them or is contrasting them with respect to that kind of confusion. More precisely, she might be comparing them as similar masculine appropriations of the female model, while simultaneously contrasting them as differing in egregiousness: Matisse executed his model by abstracting her, but at least he distinguished the reality from the abstraction; Picasso executed his model by imagining a substitute face for her, and then by insisting that his image of her, his painting, would take her place in the public imagination. However ironically, she may be comparing Matisse as criminal to Picasso as lunatic.[103]

Actually, Stein seems to be creating an even broader allegory. She tells us, through Toklas, that when Leo Stein left rue de Fleurus to the women, he and she split the collection they together had acquired, with Leo keeping the Renoirs and Matisses, Gertrude the Cézannes and Picassos, the one exception being their original Matisse acquisition, *Femme au Chapeau* (172). Stein thus depicts herself as having taken her stand not only with Picasso and Cubism but also, since she carefully associates Toklas with hats (17, 31, 126, 195), with Toklas and marriage. She seems to use "Room with Gas," then, a cropped version of a photograph taken circa 1907, not only to criticize the two masculine representations of women, but also to appropriate them for an encoded representation of Toklas, herself, and their lesbianism.[104] Repeating the foregrounding and the backgrounding of the picture itself, moreover, she places domestic space and illuminating agent in the foreground of her title and relegates the paintings to a parenthetical background, a gesture that recalls the photographic frontispiece to which we shall turn momentarily, and that also serves as metonymy for the *Autobiography* and its many appropriations. In a word, then, Stein opposes the *Autobiography* as Toklas's portrait of her to Picasso's *Portrait of Miss Gertrude Stein* and to Cubist abstraction; and though she similarly opposes it as her portrait of Toklas to Matisse's *Femme au Chapeau*, she more importantly opposes it as such to James's *Portrait of a Lady*.

Though Martha Banta has pointed out the continuity of representational styles between *The Portrait of a Lady* and the *Autobiography*, no one has noticed the centrality of James's text to Stein's—indeed, the degree to which Stein rewrote James's portrait of Isabel Archer in her own portrait of Toklas.[105] It is only a short step, however, from the Isabel Archer who would have "mild adventures" convertible by herself and her author "into the stuff of drama," who would lead "an 'exciting' inward life" but a "perfectly normal" outer one (*AN* 55–57), to the Alice B. Toklas who had "intellectual adventures ... but very quiet ones" before the "complete change" to her "new full life" of ardor (3–6), who would lead an exciting private life as a lesbian that she and her spouse would define as "normal." It is a short step from the Jamesian composition whose central and exemplary chapter was "designed to have all the vivacity of incident and all the economy of picture," was designed to be "a representation simply of [Isabel's] motionlessly *seeing*," to the Steinian composition designed as a portrait narration, designed as a picture of the Toklas who was "constantly seeing" (57) and who now constantly tells what she saw. And it is a short step, finally, from the realistic novel written immediately after *Hawthorne*, the novel that enacts and thematizes the need to move from Hawthornian Romance to Realism even as it declares some allegiance to the former, to the novelistic autobiography written immediately before the portrait, "Henry James," the cubistic autobiography that enacts and thematizes the need to move from Jamesian Realism to Cubism even as it declares some allegiance to the former and some reservations about the latter.[106]

That Stein regarded James as a precursor means, by definition, that she regarded him as having anticipated her, as having done something similar to what she was doing. She signals through a parallel symmetry in titles, in fact, even before she mentions *The Awkward Age*, the precise nature of the similarity and differences: James gave us the *portrait* of a *lady*, but she will give us the *autobiography* of *Toklas*. James had fashioned a portrait of Isabel Archer not only as seen by her satellites and, at a different level, by James and his reader, but also, centrally, as seen by herself; he had elaborated a portrait not only of an institutional and collectively fashioned type, that of *lady*, but also of an individual woman who plays only partly to type; and he had built into this act of portraiture a metadiscourse not only on the aesthetics of portraying ladies, but also on the social and political implications of such portrayals. Extending James's work with critical differences, Stein shifts in perspective from principal woman primarily as object to principal woman primarily as subject; she shifts in figuration primarily from type as embodied in instance to instance as embodied in countertype; and she shifts metadiscourse even more overtly from the aesthetics of representing women to the politics of women representing themselves.

We find these critical differences played out in composition. We recall that James said, in the preface to the *Portrait*, that chapter 42 of the novel, Isabel's "vigil of searching criticism," was "only a supreme illustration of the general plan" (*AN* 57). Motionlessly sitting and seeing, Isabel not only looks inward but also, paradoxically, in so doing, looks outward to what others see in her. From the center of the novel, to put this in compositional terms, she looks out to the frame of the novel, to the opening scene in Gardencourt, where Warburton and Ralph Touchett portray her prior to her entrance, and to the closing scene in Wimpole Street, where Goodwood and Henrietta Stackpole portray her after her exit. Simultaneously compositional and ideological, that interplay of center and frame shapes James's novel even as it seems to hold in equipoise type and countertype, coercive representations of Isabel and Isabel's resistant self-representation. When Stein says in her "Transatlantic Interview" that "Cézanne conceived the idea that in composition one thing was as important as another thing. Each part is as important as the whole," that in *Three Lives* she "tried to convey the idea of each part of a composition being as important as the whole," that no one before her had tried "that idea of composition in literature," but that James had had a "slight inkling" of it, she also tells us, in effect, how *The Portrait of a Lady* decentered, filtered through the aesthetics of Cézanne's *Portrait d'une Femme*, becomes *The Autobiography of Alice B. Toklas*. Toklas, too, looks inward as well as outward, but she occupies the subject position throughout; not relegated to a central chapter, her vigil of searching criticism, ubiquitous, is coextensive with the frame of her autobiography. Even more important, however, this book *without a center* (the critical moment of 1907 repeatedly displaced and dispersed) also *has no frame*: Toklas looks out to see Stein, but Stein, ubiquitous, is already inside.

If Stein first signals this Jamesian connection with her title and then underscores it with Toklas's reference to *The Awkward Age*, she also encodes it in the intervening photographic frontispiece, "Alice B. Toklas at the door, photograph by Man Ray." Generally read as Stein informing us pictorially, immediately opposite the anonymous title page, that she is the author, the photograph represents Stein, large in the foreground, at her worktable, her face in the shadows but her writing implements highly illuminated from the side and back, and Toklas, smaller in a doorway in the background, apparently entering the room with her hand on the latch, her face and figure highly illuminated from back and front.[107] Wholly intertextual with James's *Portrait*, the photograph directs us to three critical, pictorially linked moments in his narrative. When James's "American girl" first enters the text, Ralph Touchett has left the garden for the house, "but his eyes were bent musingly on the lawn; so that he had been an object of observation to a person who had just made her appearance in the ample doorway for some moments before he perceived her" (*PL* 25). When this American girl first reenters the text, much later, as a married woman, Ned Rosier, approaching an "adjoining room," meets "Mrs. Osmond coming out of the deep doorway. . . . Now, . . . framed in the gilded doorway, she struck our young man as the picture of a gracious lady" (*PL* 309–10). And when Mrs. Osmond exits the text, finally, she also has just left Goodwood's embrace: "There were lights in the windows of the house; they shone far across the lawn. In an extraordinarily short time . . . she had moved through the darkness (for she saw nothing) and reached the door. Here only she paused. She looked all about her; she listened a little; then she put her hand on the latch. She had not known where to turn; but she knew now. There was a very straight path" (*PL* 489–90). The path takes her, Henrietta Stackpole informs Goodwood and us, to Rome and to Osmond.

No mean pictorialist, James first introduced Isabel Archer as the subject of perception before she became, in the blink of a clause, the object of perception; she already had been, however, the object of Warburton and Ralph's conversation about "American girls" and the latters' marital expectations (*PL* 25). When James comes to her reentrance as a married woman, he presents her, through the eyes of a young aesthete and suitor of her stepdaughter, as a "picture" of a "lady"; and the young aesthete approaches her from a room where he has been conversing briefly with her villainous husband Osmond. And James immediately precedes her exit, finally, indeed prompts it, with Goodwood's passionate embrace: Goodwood has "glared" at Isabel and she has "felt his arms about her," he has kissed her with the effect of "white lightening," and she has "felt each thing in his hard manhood that had least pleased her" in "this act of possession" (*PL* 490). Three scenes, three suitors; and following Isabel's final exit, in perfect symmetry, she again becomes the object of conversation: Goodwood of the phallic surname discusses her with Henrietta Stackpole, the "new woman" of whom James may or may not approve but to whom he assigns the closing words and closing action, the "new woman" who bears not only the novel's other phallic surname but also the feminine form of the author's first name. If Henrietta/Henry condemns Isabel Archer to the straight path of heterosexual marriage in that conversation, however, Henry has left her poised, motionless, her hand on the latch, in *his* picture of a gracious lady.[108]

Stein rescues her. In a *tour de force* of intertextuality, she has Isabel Archer walk out the door of James's novel and, the reader's perspective reversed, walk as Toklas into this novelistic autobiography.[109] She proffers a photographic frontispiece in which Isabel/Toklas approaches counter-James/Stein, while, at another closely related level, Isabel/Toklas also approaches counter-Osmond/ Stein. Though James may have found heterosexual marriage coercive to women, or so I infer Stein's point, he failed to imagine a future for Isabel Archer other than martyrdom, a martyrdom rooted in a romantic and ultimately masochistic conception of sainthood; despite his own sexuality, he wound up virtually colluding with Osmond, with *le monde*. Stein did find heterosexual marriage coercive to women, and she succeeded in imagining an alternative future for Isabel Archer in the continuous present of the *Autobiography*, in the narrated life of the Alice B. Toklas who did not marry an expatriated male dilettante, bitter and cruel, but an expatriated female genius, content and generous, the Toklas who did not suffer martyrdom, but who instead found freedom.

James not only had framed Isabel Archer in doorways, he also had made his portrait of her dependent upon his reader's ability to play her central "vigil" against its framing conversations. Pressing the image and the related technique for all it was worth in his later novels, he linked them again to marriage in *The Golden Bowl* and described them so linked in his preface to that novel: "It is the Prince who opens the door to half our light upon Maggie, just as it is she who opens it to half our light upon himself; the rest of our impression, in either case, coming straight from the very motion with which that act is performed. . . . We see very few persons in 'The Golden Bowl,' but the scheme of the book, to make up for that, is that we shall really see about as much of them as a coherent literary form permits" (*AN* 330). When Toklas tells us, in her final line, that Stein has written the autobiography "and this is it" (310), she refers with the demonstrative pronoun simultaneously to the book we just have finished reading and to the photographic illustration on the facing page, "First page of manuscript of this book"; and she returns us with this illustration, of course, to the frontispiece photograph of Stein preparing manuscript while Toklas enters the room, each woman casting light on the other. Toklas has thematized frames in the *Autobiography* (13, 40), moreover, and Stein would claim in *Everybody's Autobiography* that she wanted to free pictures from "the prison of framing," and that "for many years I have taken all pictures out of their frames" (*EA* 312; see also *LIA* 87 and *P* 12). Combining Jamesian with Cézannean-Picassian techniques in the *Autobiography*, she ultimately freed Toklas's narration from even her, Stein's, portraiture by making that portraiture an effect of Toklas's narration. She had let us see about as much of these two women as her differently coherent cubistic literary form permits.

Stein constructed these images of Toklas and herself, I have argued, so that the couple could regain control of their representations and, thus, reputations. Even she could not control, however, precisely *how* her picture would escape its frame, figuratively or literally, and the historical ironies abound. Toklas may have founded Plain Edition to publish Stein's books, but she could finance the venture only by selling a Picasso.[110] Stein may have written the *Autobiography* to publish Toklas's name, but Toklas, ultimately, did not publish the *Autobiography*; Harcourt did. And Mildred Aldrich, finally, may have despaired of Stein's ever appearing in the *Atlantic Monthly*, but her persona, at least, surely would have been horrified to find that when Stein did appear there, when the *Atlantic* serialized the *Autobiography* in 1933, its editors represented Stein as the memorialist of Picasso and Hemingway.[111] Long after Stein's death, though, Toklas may have had the last laugh. In April 1958, Toklas wrote Edward Weeks, at the *Atlantic*, to acknowledge acceptance of her article on "Fifty Years of French Fashion": "It is a great pleasure and honor for anything of mine to appear in *The Atlantic Monthly*—which published Henry James and Gertrude Stein. Who am I who should find myself—however distantly—in such overwhelming company."[112] Years earlier, Stein had shown the world not only who Toklas was, but also how Toklas had found herself in the company of James and Stein.

Five

GENERALS JAMES AND STEIN

Four in America

> I have just been writing about four Americans and one of them Henry James has cleared up a lot of things for me that is in trying to put him down.
>
> —GERTRUDE STEIN TO SHERWOOD ANDERSON, 1934

It is commonly known that William James taught Stein and influenced her work; less commonly known that Stein portrayed his brother Henry as having exerted an equal, if not greater, influence. Henry James and Stein never met nor, apparently, corresponded, though Stein did attempt to arrange a meeting, in 1914, through Alvin Langdon Coburn.[1] In subsequent years, Stein wrote two cryptic pieces apparently about James—"Henry and I" (1916) and "James Is Nervous" (1918); and she mentioned him by name in each of two longer, though no less cryptic, compositions written in 1920.[2] When Stein turned to the narratives and lectures of her later phase, however, she also began to refer repeatedly and substantively to James as an influence.

In *The Autobiography of Alice B. Toklas*, in effect, Stein opened a narrative of her relation to James that she would continue in subsequent works. As we saw, she has Toklas introduce James into the *Autobiography* in the fourth paragraph, as one whom Toklas early admired, and then has Toklas immediately introduce Stein in the fifth paragraph (3–4). Toklas later quotes Stein saying that she, Stein, had not had an early interest in James but now admires him greatly and considers him "quite definitely as her forerunner, he being the only nineteenth century writer who being an american felt the method of the twentieth century"; and, again, that she now thinks James "the first person in literature to find the way to the literary methods of the twentieth century" but did not read him during her "formative period" probably because "one is always naturally antagonistic to one's parents" (96–97).[3] In this first work of her later narrative phase, then, in the work that was clearly her bid for a wide audience, Stein not only enacted James's priority in her opening passages but also expressly identified him as her precursor.

Stein continued this intertextual narrative in her theoretical writings of the mid-1930s, where she elaborated the technical aspects of James's influence upon her. In *Lectures in America* (1935), she named James as the "culmination" of a shift from writing by phrases to writing by paragraphs that she claimed James and his English contemporaries together effected at the end of the nineteenth century. But while the others, Stein adds, "all stayed where they were," James "knew he was on his way" because he was an American, because "this did connect with the American way. And so although they did in a way the same thing, his had a future feeling and theirs an ending." Unlike their paragraphs, Stein judges, James's "whole paragraph was detached what it said from what it did, what it was from what it held, and over it all something floated." This "disembodied way of disconnecting something from anything and anything from something" resulted in "the paragraph having been completely become," which, Stein concludes the discussion, left her "to do more with the paragraph than ever had been done" (47–54).[4] Some pages later, while discussing the construction of sentences by internal balance and movement that she had practiced in *The Making of Americans* (1925), she again points to the example of James. Indeed, she speculates that "Henry James in his later writing had had a dim feeling that this was what he knew he should do" (225).[5] In *Narration* (1935), Stein went on to argue that words "in the American writing," as opposed to the English, "began to have within themselves the consciousness of completely moving, they began to detach themselves from the solidity of anything, they began to excitedly feel themselves as if they were anywhere or anything." She cites as exemplars of such writing eight American authors since Emerson, with herself immediately preceding Sherwood Anderson and succeeding James (10).

Stein concluded this narrative of James's priority in the "Transatlantic Interview" she granted shortly before her death in 1946. As I have noted, the interview opens with a crucial discussion of the Cézannean and Flaubertian influences on "decenterment" in Stein's composition. Although Stein claims that no one previously had "used that idea of composition in literature," she allows that "Henry James had a slight inkling of it and was in some senses a forerunner." The difference, she continues, was that she "made it stay on the page quite composed," while James "made it sort of like an atmosphere" (15). And, later in this interview, she proposes that James's characters "do not live very much. The ensemble lives, but nobody gets excited about the characters" (21). She thus implicitly credits James with having anticipated her own strategy of not "making the people real" in the manner of nineteenth-century realism but of locating "the essence or, as a painter would call it, value" (16).[6]

Even shorn of context, these selected citations reveal three aspects of Stein's portrayal of James and herself. First, Stein did not specify exactly when she had begun to read James with "interest"—a highly charged word in her vocabulary—but she chose to proclaim this interest in the period when she turned from portraiture to "portrait narration," and she thus implicitly linked her reading of James with the work of her later phase. Second, Stein discussed James over a period of years with specific reference not only to paragraphs, sentences, and words, but also to composition and characterization, with specific reference, that is, to the verbal elements of narrative literature in general and of portrait narration in particular.[7] Stein credited James with having brought to fruition the nineteenth-century use of each element and with having thereby pointed the way to a twentieth-century writing. Third, Stein coolly transformed this tribute to James's prescience into an aggrandizement of James as specifically *her* "forerunner." James "felt the method of," or "found the way to," or "had an inkling of" the twentieth century writing, but he could not arrive there; Stein, we are to see, could and did.

Less arrogant than it appears, Stein's claiming this succession reflects two of her basic ideas about creativity and about progress in art. First, she clearly believed that the composition of a generation's way of living (in effect, its *milieu* and *moment*) determines the composition of its writing and painting. She would argue in *Picasso* (1938) that, as a result, "a creator is not in advance of his generation but he is the first of his contemporaries to be conscious of what is happening to his generation" (30). James had been among the first to recognize the superannuation of the Hawthornian romance as one of the things happening to his generation, for example; and Stein, so she implies, had been the first to recognize the superannuation of the Jamesian novel as one of the things happening to hers. Second, Stein apparently believed that the composition of an artist's way of living can determine a predisposition to consciousness of contemporaneity and does determine the composition of the artist's writing or painting. Stein would imply that James and she shared unconventional sexuality, nationality, and expatriation, but she also would imply that they differed in gender and in specific sexuality, and in place of expatriation. She would claim for James and for herself the consciousness of contemporaneity that marks the true creative genius, but she would stake her claim to succession on the aesthetic consequences of their generational and personal differences. Given all this, Stein not surprisingly reserved her fullest treatment of James for her study of creativity in Americans, *Four in America*.

❦

Apparently composed between 1933 and 1934, *Four in America* first appeared, posthumously, in 1947.[8] Stein twice noted in *Everybody's Autobiography* (1937) that she had badly wanted it printed but explained that it "was very difficult reading so they said" (91, 107).[9] Ten years later, a no longer anonymous "they" would say that with a vengeance. Whatever their degrees of acuity or sympathy, all the book's reviewers remarked upon its difficulty or, more often, its unreadability. Doubtless responding to Stein's celebrity, the reviewers for *Time* and *Library Journal*, for example, each conceded the significance of *Four in America*; yet the former pronounced it "written in Stein style at its Steiniest, and reading it takes more than most readers want to give," and the latter more succinctly allowed that it might "seem like prattle to the general reader."[10] The extreme demands to which these reviewers were responding have an immediately apparent source. *Four in America* combines the very close, abstracted style of Stein's earlier, brief, and narrowly focused portraits with the broad, vernacular content of her later, lengthy, and panoramic narratives. This particular combination, however, reflects a less apparent and even more complex mixing of genres and multiplying of subjects to which Stein alluded in various commentaries.

With respect to genre, Stein first spoke in *Lectures in America* of "the portraits" of *Four in America* (206); some pages later, however, she says that she has been wondering about "a new way to write a novel" and adds, immediately, that "I have just tried to begin in writing Four In America because I am certain that what makes American success is American failure" (172); and, some pages after that, she distinguishes "newspaper narrative" from "real narrative," claims to have begun the latter in *Four in America*, and further claims that such narrative "must of necessity be told by any one having come to the realization that the noun must be replaced not by inner balance but by the thing in itself" (245–56; and see *NAR* 30–45). In *Narration*, she first defines narrative as "the telling of how anybody how everybody does anything and everything" (2); she specifies its uses as being "to make a story to tell a life to express a thing to say" (7); and she later speaks in this general context of "autobiography I have already done, biography I have already done," the former probably being *The Autobiography of Alice B. Toklas*, and the latter *Four in America* (45). In *Everybody's Autobiography*, she reports having told Thornton Wilder "that what worried me was narration, no one in our time had really been able to tell anything without anything but just telling that thing and that I was going to try once more to try to simply tell something" (107). Although the remark refers directly to *Everybody's Autobiography*, the context also refers it indirectly to *Four in America*. Finally, of course, Stein says in her "Transatlantic Interview" that "after the *Four Saints* [1927] the portrait narration began, and I went back to the form of narration" (19).

With respect to subject, Stein told a *New York Times Magazine* interviewer in 1934 that *Four in America* would treat "many of her ideas about government and American democracy," and she "promise[d] that the new book [would] not be difficult to read."[11] In *Lectures in America*, she claims to have "told what happened as it had happened" in *The Autobiography of Alice B. Toklas*; observes that "there is something much more exciting than anything that happens and now and always I am writing the portrait of that"; and adds that she has "been writing the portraits of Four In America, trying to write Grant, and Wilbur Wright and Henry James and Washington do other things than they did do so as to try to find out just what it is that what happens has to do with what is" (205–6). In *Narration*, she says that she has "just been trying to write the history of some one if his name had not been the name he had and I have called it Four In America" (29); and, in *Everybody's Autobiography*, she adds that she "took four Americans, Washington, Henry James, Wilbur Wright and General Grant, and I wanted them to be what their names would be." She also explains in the latter that she "wanted to find out why war was and campmeetings"; and she concludes her discussion: "That is what war is and dancing it is forward and back, when one is out walking one wants not to go back the way they came but in dancing and in war it is forward and back. / That is what I tried to say in Four In America" (106–7).

Given Stein's indications, however contrarious or unreliable they may be, I cannot agree with Wendy Steiner's judgment that *Four in America* only "perhaps" qualifies as a "new experiment" in Stein's development of portraiture and that it "added little to the progression of [her] ideas about portraiture"; I do agree, however, with Steiner's judgment that the book comes "near to being" biography but has "interests other than the presentation of the chronological space of a life."[12] Stein may have wanted "to simply tell something," but, as we have heard her later say, "my only thought is a complicated simplicity. I like a thing simple, but it must be simple through complication" (TI 34). In this later phase of her work, she had moved from the poetry and portraiture in which she had sought to apprehend a subject directly and to enact in the movement and inner balance of language the movement of that subject; she had moved to the portrait narration in which she would continue such a representing of a subject while simultaneously writing a "real narrative" about the process of doing so. She complicated autobiography and biography, genres that would seem to include "story," by conjoining them to her practice of portraiture, from which she expressly had excluded "story" (*LIA* 121, 184–85);

and she further complicated this conjunction by pursuing its potential for autoreference. This was, in fact, a new experiment, a natural step in the evolution of Stein's program, a necessary step for a writer who would claim that "the three novels written in [my] generation that are the important things written in this generation"—namely, *A la recherche du temps perdu*, *Ulysses*, and *The Making of Americans*—"do not tell a story" (*LIA* 184–85); but who by the 1930s virtually had abandoned "the novel scheme" as "quite out of the question" in the twentieth century in order to explore generically hybrid and radically autoreferential narrative forms (TI 22).[13]

As a primary example of such hybridity and autoreferentiality, *Four in America* certainly does deviate from the accepted norms of biography. Stein advances in it four counterfactual hypotheses: she envisions Grant as a religious leader, Wilbur Wright as a painter, Henry James as a general, and Washington as a novelist. And she develops these hypotheses with reference to subjects we saw her elsewhere indicate: government and American democracy; success and failure, or, winning and losing; the relationship between what happens and what is, or the relationship between event and consequence; the relationship of war to religion, and of war and religion to aesthetics. Attending to this referential level, one contemporary reviewer noted that Stein meant "to show how each of her representative Americans would have expressed his genius if he had been in some very different relation to the problems of human experience."[14] Another noted that *Four in America* reflects the American principles of the "democratic" and the "pragmatic," and concluded that the "ultimate symbol of creativity" in the book is the novel.[15] That conclusion not only obscures Stein's apparent motive for mixing genres and multiplying subjects in *Four In America*; it also occludes the meaning of the book.

If we want to approach that meaning, we must understand that Stein chose as subjects four historical figures who could serve an autoreferential analysis of artistic practice. First, these four figures performed imaginative or creative acts either in the arts or in fields analogous to the arts. Second, they have attained an iconic status in the American imagination that confers an easy familiarity upon them. Comparable, in this sense, to the common objects favored by Cubist painters and by Stein herself in *Tender Buttons* (1914), they attract attention as compositional elements and thereby direct attention to their treatment in the composition. But third, paradoxically, their iconicity makes them precisely *un*available for immediate apprehension. Indeed, these figures exist only within a complex mesh of self-representations and of cultural representations that all entail the mediation of memory. And these representations include four to which Stein explicitly or implicitly alludes in her compositions: Grant's *Personal Memoirs*; the Wilbur Wright memorial at Le Mans; James's memoirs, *A Small Boy and Others*, *Notes of a Son and Brother*, and *The Middle Years*; and Henry Lee's *Funeral Oration on the Death of General Washington*, also published as *A Funeral Oration, in Honour of the Memory of George Washington*.[16] Stein's four figures, then, pose questions about the processes of self-representation and of cultural representation to which she responds in her representations of them and in the self-representation that those serve.

As a consequence of this autoreferentiality, we also must understand that the subject matter we have seen Stein elsewhere indicate refers not only to the living composition of American society but also to the written composition of this book; and that the "four" of *Four in America* designates not only the book's human subjects but also its constituent parts. That Stein repeatedly referred elsewhere to a book that was not, much to her chagrin, in the public domain suggests something further about its inclusion of James as a subject and about its autoreference. *Four in America* exemplifies a major development in Stein's evolving theory of aesthetics, and it advances as its covert thesis Stein's centrality in twentieth-century art and aesthetics—*her* true artistry. *Four in America*, that is, shows how Gertrude Stein is expressing *her* genius in writing; and it offers as its symbol of creativity *not* the novel—not even the Jamesian novel—but itself as portrait narration.

⤻

Stein introduces *Four in America* with four hypothetical questions, the third of which reads: "If Henry James had been a general what would he have had to do." I would propose three sources for the conceit. Stein is alluding to James's three volumes of memoirs, in which the novelist revealed a distinct fondness for generals from Napoleon to Winfield Scott to U. S. Grant, and in which he tortuously sought the meaning of his own role as a "wounded" noncombatant during the Civil War.[17] She is also applying to James a common analogy between warfare and writing: James planned his works with the care of a strategist and devised literary tactics to assure the success of his strategy, but could improvise tactics when faced in the heat of composition with unforeseen contingencies.[18] Finally, she is employing an etymological pun that José Ortega y Gasset had elaborated before her: "The poet begins where the man ends. The man's lot is to live his human life, the poet's to invent what is nonexistent. Herein lies the justification of the poetical profession. The poet aggrandizes the world by adding to reality, which is there by itself, the continents of his imagination. Author derives from *auctor*, he who augments. It was the title Rome bestowed upon her generals when they had conquered new territory for the City."[19] Stein, then, is moving from a specific allusion to James's memoirs, through a common analogy implicit in the allusion, to an etymological pun inherent in the terms of the analogy.

Stein's basic conceit thus not only refers to James but also forms an autoreferential wordplay: it names its own movement from the specific to the general. In so doing, moreover, it suggests the systemic wordplay of Stein's composition. The key to this wordplay lies in Stein's brief poem, "James Is Nervous," composed over a decade earlier. There she had written: "James is not nervous. / Any more. / Indeed he is general."[20] Now James is both *a* general and *general*. James is a general because he identifies himself with generals, because he composes his works in the way that generals conduct battles, and because he is an *auctor*. And James is general because he comprises, in two related senses, both a particularity and a generality of selfhood. First, the psychological being called James comprises a discontinuous "Empirical Self" and a continuous "Pure Ego"; and each of these, as William James taught in his *Principles of Psychology*, transforms in time and through memory.[21] Second, the iconic being called James comprises a discontinuous multiplicity of images generated by his individual readers and a continuous image constructed by his collective readership; and each of these, similarly, transforms in time and through memory. In her James composition, Stein coordinates James's being a general with his being general; put less figuratively, she explores how his method of composition reflects psychological and social pressures on creation and produces psychological and social pressures on reception.

Stein also explores, simultaneously, her own method of composition, a method she presents as a variation of James's method and as a legitimation for her regarding herself as a successful general in the aesthetic wars of the twentieth century. Indeed, she explores James's memorial writing in relation to her reading of it and suggests that James the memoirist came to represent for her a type of autobiographical writer. Her constructing James as a general and as general thus suggests, in a further wordplay, that she has derived from her particular reading of James's memoirs general principles about writing that she will exemplify in her composition. Stein, then, represents the autobiographically and culturally mediated James who acted in deed *like* a general, she presents a textual James who *is* a general precisely because she constructs him according to that analogy, and she composes her text as an *exemplification* of general principles formulated by James and developed with appropriate variations by Stein, herself an *auctor*.

Stein, however, actually opens her "Henry James," her forty-one-page treatment of James in *Four in America*, with seemingly irrelevant propositions about "the difference between Shakespeare's plays and Shakespeare's sonnets" and about her having "found out the difference" either by "accident" or by "coincidence." She then differentiates accident and coincidence: "An accident is when a thing happens. A coincidence is when a thing is going to happen and does" (119). In the twenty-one-page "Duet" that follows, Stein elucidates those differences in a prose so finely parsed and so cunningly wrought with wordplay that it defies paraphrase. In the opening passage of this "Duet," in any case, she quickly establishes the connection between Shakespeare and herself: "it is not an accident but a coincidence that there is a difference between Shakespeare's sonnets and Shakespeare's plays"; "the coincidence is with Before the Flowers of Friendship Faded Friendship Faded," that is, with Stein's translation, published under that title in 1931, of Georges Hugnet's poem "*Enfances*"; Shakespeare's sonnets and her *Before the Flowers* "were not as if they were being written but as if they were going to be written," whereas Shakespeare's "plays were written as they were written" (119–20).

In the process of establishing that connection as it bears upon her understanding of the difference between accident and coincidence, Stein also proposes that "I am I not any longer [that is, am no longer I] when I see" and identifies this "sentence [as being] at the bottom of all creative activity" (119). When she reformulates it to read, "I am I, not any longer [that is, am no longer than I] when I see" (125), she points to the difference between, respectively, the discontinuous creating self forming at each instant of perception and the continuous creating self reforming itself as the self-perceived sum of those instants. Implicitly, then, Stein raises the question of memory, one she expresses here as a question of why "anybody writing writes" in relation to "the question of audience of an audience" (121). Stein then establishes the principle, partially derived from her writing of *Before the Flowers* and her remembering of Shakespeare, that serves as basis for her analysis of James: there are two ways of writing, "writing what you are writing" and "writing what you are going to be writing" (122). This principle about the composing of texts entails corollary principles about texts as compositions and about the reception of such compositions.

James first appears on the tenth page of this "Duet," where Stein interjects that "nobody has forgotten Henry James," presents a set of permutations on James's being a general and winning an army in order to win a battle or a war, and charges herself and, apparently, her reader to "remember how Henry James was or was not a general" (128). Stein now connects Shakespeare and James through her principle about the two ways of writing. Shakespeare "wrote both ways"—that is, "as he wrote" and "as he was going to write" (132)—but did so, respectively, in the two distinct genres of plays and sonnets. James, by contrast, "saw he could write both ways at once" (133), and, in so seeing and in so doing, did what he would have had to do had he been a general. As Stein explains her trope, James "came not to begin but to have begun" (137), he "came to do this" (137), and, she concludes this "Duet," "you must remember that in a battle or a war everything has been prepared which is what has been called begun and then everything happens at once which is what is called done and then a battle or a war is either not or won" (139).

It turns out that Stein's opening propositions and her elucidating "Duet" together constitute only "Volume I" of her James composition; its remaining twenty pages comprise passages of varying lengths individually labeled Volumes II through XXXIV. As Stein's parodic mode of labeling suggests, these "volumes" present a "life" of Henry James; and they are, indeed, replete with such biographical facts as James "was not married in any way" (141), and James "did not prepare for flight" (151). At once perfectly literal and studiously figurative, such facts indicate the presence in this composition of more than one Henry James. Although Stein has said in the "Duet" that "it is not necessary to know the life history of a general" and that James was "not the same thing as a general but really one" (138), she says in Volume IX that she wishes "now to give the life history of Henry James who was a general" (146) and in Volume XXIV that she will "tell the history of Henry James simply tell the history of Henry James" (153). There is no contradiction. As is indicated by the precise slippage between the restrictive and the nonrestrictive in "Henry James who was a general," Stein is speaking of two Henry Jameses: the autobiographically and culturally mediated James who was *like* a general and her textual James who *is* a general. We readers need not know the life history of the former for Stein to construct the "life" of the latter; or for Stein to tell about James's telling his own history in his memoirs.

Stein, however, speaks at length in Volumes II–IV of "the *three* Jameses" (139–43, emphasis added). She arguably means to refer to the complex form of James's memoirs, a triad within a triad, in which (1) a boy, youth, and young man are apprehended through (2) a highly self-conscious persona being created by (3) an equally self-conscious elderly writer.[22] With such a reference, she would cause her reader to consider the process first of living a reflective life and then of writing an autobiographical "life" that reflects upon itself, a process exemplified in James's life and memoirs. She also would be pointing, by analogy, to the form of her own text, in which the double Jamesian triad occurs within a Steinian triad. The third James of *Stein's* text, that is to say, *is* Stein's text, whose name is simply "Henry James." It is the history of *this* "Henry James" that Stein is telling in detail, and, as she indicates in a purposeful pronominal slippage, "Henry James is a combination of the two ways of writing and that makes *him* a general a general who does something. Listen to *it*" (137, emphasis added).

The reader who listens closely to this third "James," to Stein's aural and visual composition, will find an argument parallel to one Stein subsequently elaborated in *Lectures in America*, where she distinguished between writing for mammon and writing for god. To serve mammon is to write "indirectly," to write what one "intends to have heard by somebody who is to hear"; to serve god, by contrast, is to write "directly," to effect a direct "relation between the thing done and the doer.... In this way there is completion and the essence of the completed thing is completion." Stein spoke the truth when she added in another purposeful slippage that she had "had a very great deal to say about this in the life of Henry James in my Four in America" (*LIA* 23–24). What Stein "had to say" there, in both senses of that phrase, applies to the life James lived, to the life Stein imagines for James in her composition, and to her composition as itself a "life." And what Stein had to say makes sense if understood within a matrix formed by the parallel oppositions accident/coincidence, writing as written/writing as going to be written, forgetting/remembrance—oppositions themselves parallel to the oppositions serving god/serving mammon, writing directly/writing indirectly.[23]

The second term in each oppositional pair describes Shakespeare's sonnets because, as Stein says elsewhere, the sonnets "were not written to express his own emotion [but] he put down what some one told him to do as their feeling" (*N* 52). She is suggesting not that another individual human being expressed his or her emotion through Shakespeare, but, rather, that two interrelated processes took place. First, Shakespeare the man relayed his emotion through Shakespeare the poet, while, conversely, Shakespeare the poet translated the emotion of Shakespeare the man. He thus represents the particular artistic case of the general psychological process of the "Empirical Self" relaying its emotion through the "Pure Ego" that, conversely, translates that emotion. Second, Shakespeare knew the generic conventions of the sonnet form and, as the plural "their" in Stein's formulation above might suggest, knew that his audience also would know them. These conventions, then, informed the expression of the emotion by Shakespeare the poet and, in fact, may have informed the emotion earlier felt by Shakespeare the man. He thus also represents the particular artistic case of the general process of cultural mediation intervening upon anyone's apprehension, and further represents the process by which audience and man conspire to construct the man as poet. Shakespeare apparently circumvented these two processes in his plays, those sublime inventions, in Ortega's phrase, of "what is nonexistent." In the sonnets, however, Shakespeare remembered his emotion, and he and his audience remembered generic conventions; and these recollections made the sonnets coincidental, made them happen as if they were going to happen, made them, in sum, written as if they were going to be written.[24]

The second term in each oppositional pair more obviously describes Stein's *Before the Flowers*, because she actually translated in that poem the already expressed emotion of another poet—even though, one must add, she played loose with the generic conventions of literary translation when she did so. Pondering this parallel that Stein was developing between Shakespeare's sonnets and her own *Before the Flowers*, Shirley Neuman has astutely observed that "by the mid-thirties, the relationships of the self to its audience, the writer to the translator, and the writer to his self as he observed his own writing had become analogous for Stein."[25] Stein was shaping her argument in the James composition and in *Four in America*, indeed, on that set of analogies. She was using them to argue that Shakespeare and she each completed something incomplete—inchoate felt life, generic conventions, or earlier texts—by doing something that was going to happen, by doing it in writing written as it was going to be written, and by writing it in this way precisely because remembering those things whose priority—inchoate felt life, generic conventions, or earlier texts—motivated the very act of writing.

Stein developed this argument about Shakespeare and herself, however, not with regard to the substance or form of their respective works of poetry but with regard to the "coincidental" relationship of those works. Literally coincidental, Shakespeare's sonnets and Stein's *Before the Flowers* are texts with only an accidental or noncausal relationship. Also coincidental in the sense of an etymological pun, however, they are texts that "happen together" in Stein's mind because writing *Before the Flowers* caused her to remember the sonnets and to see a relationship between them. Subsuming the first sense of coincidence into the second, Stein arrives at the real subject of her argument, namely, her knowledge of that relationship. And she could have achieved that knowledge only by having done *Before the Flowers*, for, as she says, "a coincidence is having done so" (130) and "the way to find this out all this out is to do likewise, not to do it alike but to do it likewise" (134).

Having done "likewise" in *Before the Flowers*, Stein completed her knowledge about the two ways of writing that she has written about in the James composition. But if writing about this knowledge entailed, on the one hand, remembering what she already knew and thus writing what she was going to be writing, it also should entail, on the other hand, gaining new knowledge in the process and thus writing what she is writing. And that is where James comes in. Shakespeare had done something in his sonnets, Stein had done likewise in *Before the Flowers*, Stein had kenned the similarity; Stein thereby had come, coincidentally, to her knowledge of the two ways of writing. In a second coincidence, I surmise, soon after Stein wrote *Before the Flowers* she *happened* to be reading James.[26] Her reading of James caused her not only to *reconsider* the two ways of writing but also to *consider* for the first time the process of writing both ways at once—the process of being an *auctor* and a general. Stein could complete her knowledge of this process, however, only by doing likewise, not only by writing about it in the James composition but also by "doing" it in the writing of the James composition. And if doing that completes her present knowledge, it should generate, in turn, new knowledge that would require additional writing, the writing, say, of a companion book: *The Geographical History of America* (1936).[27]

Stein thus moved from the initially proposed difference between Shakespeare and James and the subsequently elaborated relationship between Shakespeare and herself to the pivotal but covert connection between James and herself. She used the specific relationship between Shakespeare's sonnets and her *Before the Flowers* together with her present knowledge of that relationship to approach a general problem that continually vexed her, namely, the problem of tracing the development of one's present knowledge without reducing one's writing to a mere, distortive act of remembrance, to writing what you are going to be writing. If I have surmised correctly, she coordinated those analyses with her use of the relationship between James's memorial writing and her own writing of this period, including and especially the very writing in progress, "Henry James." She used the second relationship, that is, to conduct an *ongoing* analysis of her *currently evolving* present knowledge of that relationship, as the occasion for also writing what she is writing and, it follows, for writing both ways at once. She was exemplifying in this composition the seemingly banal thesis that any process of completing leads to its own incompletion, that the essence of the completed thing may be completion, as she said, but the existence of the completed thing entails incompletion. She also was suggesting, however, that she was succeeding James precisely by incompleting his two ways of writing, by making his two ways her own.

Portraiture, as Stein theorized and practiced it, was one way of writing. In *Lectures in America*, she stressed that she had tried in her portraits "to tell what each one is without telling stories" (121); that she "wanted not to write about any one doing or even saying anything" (174); that she did not intend her portraits to be "descriptions" of their subjects (166, 177); that "the making of a portrait of any one is as they are existing and as they are existing has nothing to do with remembering any one or anything" (175); and that she began this making because she "wondered is there any way of making what I know come out as I know it, come out not as remembering" (181). She designed her portraits "to find out what it was inside any one, and by any one I mean every one . . . not by what they said not by what they did not by how much or how little they resembled any other one [which includes, of course, one's resembling oneself] but I had to find it out by the intensity of movement that there was inside in any one of them" (183); she designed them, in sum, to enact in the compositional movement of paragraphs, sentences, and words the physical and psychological movements of her subjects. Only thus, Stein believed, might she avoid telling stories and writing descriptions, each of which entails distortions of remembrance.

Narration, as Stein theorized and practiced it, was the other way of writing. In *Narration*, she defined narrative simply as "one thing following any other thing" (26), but she also complicated this simplicity with a characteristic indeterminacy. She used "following" in a way that indicates both seriality and sequentiality, or unmotivated succession and motivated progression, while specifying neither; she had similarly used "coincidence" in the James composition to mean a noncausal relationship that becomes causal in the apprehension of a perceiver. In *Narration*, in fact, Stein attributed to narrative and to narration characteristics she had attributed in the James composition to Shakespeare's sonnets and to her *Before the Flowers*; and she did so with specific reference to those two works of poetry. Years later, in her "Transatlantic Interview," she again would refer to those two works of poetry to argue the same point; she would state bluntly that "the narrative in itself is not what is in your mind but what is in somebody else's" (19). If narrative requires events, even interior, psychological events, she seems to say, narration requires remembrance; the narrating perceiver reconstructs a serial succession of events as a meaningful and sequential progression of events. The compositional movement of portraiture that is based on direct apprehension of the subject, then, collides with the memorial movement of narration.

Yet Stein sought to effect the combination of the two ways of writing that she claimed for her "Henry James" precisely by joining in it portraiture and narration as she understood them. She negotiated the tension between the immediate observation and spatial representation she identified with portraiture *and* the mediated observation and temporal representation she identified with narration. She observed her subject, the already autobiographically and culturally mediated James, and enacted the "movements" of that subject as a series of instants; simultaneously, she not only observed herself observing that subject but also represented her observing and her representing as the processes that transformed those discreet instants into duration. Joining portraiture and narration, that is, she also joined reference to autoreference and, further, to a second-order autoreference. She had produced a "real narrative" that replaced the titular noun "Henry James" with "the thing in itself," with her exemplary demonstration of writing both ways at once *more than once*. Therein lay her incompletion.

Stein suggests, however, that even this achievement might leave her with a problem. In other texts, as we have seen, she presented James as her "forerunner" in matters of composition; in this text, she presents him as her forerunner not only because he joined character and incident, picture and story, but also because he joined autobiography and autoreferentiality in his memorial writing. The very priority of James's already having mediated his life in language, in his own highly autoreferential "life," initiates the chain of coincidences, of writings that were going to be written, and of remembrances, that all constitute completions again becoming incomplete: James's living, and his writing of his living; Stein's reading James's writing, and her writing of her reading; Stein's reader's reading her writing, and her reader's literal or figurative writing of his or her own reading. Neither Stein, nor her particular reader, nor the readership for whom James was and is iconic "has forgotten" James or, indeed, could forget him. Stein's imagined James may now comment to her—while she comments to herself, to her reader, and to such a readership—that "I understand you undertake to overthrow my undertaking" (*FIA* 150); and Stein, nonetheless, may "commence to cover the ground" (157). But in this Cubist conflation of exequial and martial metaphors, Stein acknowledges James simultaneously as one dead "parent" not easily interred and as one general not easily outmaneuvered, no matter how much ground she likewise takes for the City in her inventions of the nonexistent.

With this conflation, in short, Stein points precisely to her problem. On the one hand, she must forget James, must forget his methods of composition, if she is not only to achieve her own variation of writing both ways at once but also to reflect on her writing, as part of her variation, with the requisite immediacy of portraiture. On the other hand, however, she cannot fail to remember James, cannot fail to remember his methods of composition, if she is to practice in her portrait narration the requisite mediacy of narration. James saw that he could write both ways at once, and Stein saw that she had to do likewise, at two levels, in order to know his methods *and* her knowledge of them: first, she had to extend her portrait of James into a narrative in order to enact the durations of his life and memoirs; second, she had to extend her portrait of "Henry James" into a "real narrative" in order to enact through autoreference the durations of its own writing and reading. Obviously, though, she wanted not only to know James's methods and to repeat, however self-knowingly, his achievement; she also wanted to succeed him within the terms of her conception of literary development. She needed to be doing something different in her "Henry James," some maneuvers, as it were, that reflected forms of incompletion peculiar to herself and to her generation.

She gave us the clues to her achievement after the fact, and they concern *The Autobiography of Alice B. Toklas*. While discussing in *Lectures in America* her portraits, operas, and plays of the 1920s, Stein reports having gone on to do "an entirely different something" in the *Autobiography*, something that "came out of" her writing of *Before the Flowers* (204–5). Several years later, in her "Transatlantic Interview," she adds: "I did a tour de force with the *Autobiography of Alice Toklas*.... But still I had done what I saw, what you do in translation or in a narrative. I had recreated the point of view of somebody else" (19). Although Stein had only "told what happened as it had happened" in the *Autobiography*, she had begun in that portrait narration her later phase of experiments with voice and with perspective—as marked, for example, by her recreation of Toklas's autobiographical point of view. Such complexity, however, seems to mark no great technical advance upon James, the acknowledged master of such recreations, and especially not upon James's memoirs, in which he also "told what happened as it had happened," and in the second volume of which, *Notes of a Son and Brother*, he had recreated, by editing and arranging correspondence, the points of view of his father, his three male siblings, and his cousin, Minnie Temple. But Stein had begun something less obvious with her experiments, something that she developed fully in the particular form of writing both ways at once that she practiced in *Four in America*.

The two central personae of the Toklas-Stein *Autobiography* form a relationship whose relevant significance Stein elsewhere glossed. While speaking in *Lectures in America* about the relationship between *Before the Flowers* and the *Autobiography*, Stein says "that for the first time in writing, I felt something outside me while I was writing, hitherto I had always had nothing but what was inside me while I was writing" (205). This dichotomy of outside/inside encapsulates the analogous relationships of audience/writer, translator/writer, writer as self-observer/writer as self-observed. Though Stein was speaking in this passage specifically of "audience," her references to *Before the Flowers* and to the *Autobiography* suggest "outside" texts to be translated and "outside" points of view to be recreated and imply the process of self-observation in writing. In *Narration*, Stein proceeded to characterize similar writing, that in which "the outside and the inside flow together without interrupting," that which is "a diffusion but not a confusing," as "really a kind of an imitation of marrying of two being one, and yet being two and presumably two as much as anything" (55). Given her elaboration of the Toklas-Stein marriage in the *Autobiography*, we can infer three things about the composition of the book. First, Stein realized while writing *Before the Flowers* that she could translate a poem by another person, Hugnet, in a way that would produce two distinct voices, Hugnet's and her own, that would remain intimately related as a dyadic voicing of one poem. Second, she realized that she could recreate the point of view of another person, Toklas, in a way that would produce two distinct points of view, Toklas's and her own, that would remain intimately related within the one dyadic perspective of the *Autobiography*. Third, she realized that these compositional methods would be the linguistic equivalent of the emotional and erotic movement of the Toklas-Stein marital relationship as she experienced and directly observed it—outside and inside flowing together, voices and points of view becoming one while maintaining their duality.

Stein connected this relationship, as enacted in the composition of the *Autobiography*, to the dynamics of her James composition. Volume XXVII of "Henry James" begins: "A narrative of Henry James told by one who listened to some one else telling about some one entirely different from Henry James" (155). The first one mentioned appears to be Stein, who is telling a narrative about Henry James. The second one mentioned, "the one that tells any story that she tells about what happens to any one" (156), appears to be Toklas, who told "what happened" in the *Autobiography*. Stein identifies the third one mentioned as "a woman who might have killed somebody else"; who "was entirely a different kind of human being from Henry James"; who "lived alone and in the country" like James and shared physical and vocal traits with him; but who "was not at all at all at all resembling to Henry James and never knew him and never heard of him" (155). Although this third one might be, indeed, a third woman, she seems more obviously to be Stein herself at an earlier point. Stein tells us that the second one "had always admired Henry James" (156) and concludes the "volume" by specifying this datum as the "connection" (156). Since Stein had indicated in the *Autobiography* that Toklas admired James long before she did, we can infer that the first and third ones are Stein as the one who listened to the *Autobiography* and as the one about whom it was told.[28] Stein thus implies that she has expanded a doubly dyadic relationship into a doubly triadic one; and, as she explains in *Narration*, "That is what mysticism is, that is what the Trinity is, that is what marriage is, the absolute conviction that in spite of knowing anything about everything about how any one is never really feeling what any other one is really feeling that after all after all three are one and two are one" (57).

Mysticism notwithstanding, Stein is signaling an advance from the *Autobiography*, in which two interpenetrating voices present two intersecting points of view, to "Henry James" itself, in which "Duet" serves only as a procedural model for constructing a multivocal and multiperspectival Cubist composition. Volume XXVII exemplifies the complexity of this composition, for Stein confounds the kind of interpretation I just have proposed. She lures us with the possibility of autobiographical reference, invites us to refer the three ones of the passage to herself, Toklas, and another woman *or* to herself, Toklas, and herself at an earlier point in time. But she also prevents our reducing this passage to even that degree of ambiguous reference, for the constellation of three ones shifts and slides with an indeterminacy that permits several permutations of relationship between three persons or two persons and, in addition, does not prohibit the three ones from being, in turn, three aspects of any one of three persons. Stein employs the lure of autobiographical allegory, in sum, to bring into the foreground an allegory of reading and writing that she renders concrete in the text that presents it. She accommodates three vocal and perspectival sources in the James composition—James in his memoirs, Stein reading James, and Stein's reader reading Stein—and each of these participants enters a relationship not only with the others but with himself or herself *as other*. She thus multiplies possibilities of voice and perspective through a compositional method that differs from James's while remaining indebted to his, and she produces with it a text perpetually in the process of an impossible completion.

Stein acknowledges that James could write both ways at once in several senses: he could, like a good general, plan and improvise; he could tell "what happened [to him] as it had happened" and could tell the more "exciting" story of what did not happen but might have; he could represent an extratextual reality while reflecting upon his process of representation. In his memoirs, he translated the felt experience of his life, he recreated points of view of others and of himself as other, and he anticipated audience expectations and interventions; and he also told a metanarrative about his doing all three. Stein, herself, has reenacted James's achievement: she, too, plans and improvises; she tells what happened to James as he reports it and tells the more "exciting" hypothetical story of James as a general; she represents James's life and memoirs while reflecting upon her process of representation. In her "Henry James," she translates the felt experience of her reading of James, she recreates the points of view of James and of herself as the reading other who preceded the self now writing, and she anticipates audience expectations and interventions; and she also tells a metanarrative about her doing all three.

That James "was not married in any way," however, now assumes its considerable significance. Just as James never married in life, Stein seems to suggest, so did he never effect the marriage of voices and of points of view that she claims to have begun in *The Autobiography of Alice B. Toklas*. In the centerpiece of his memoirs, *Notes of a Son and Brother*, James details his filial relationship with his father, his fraternal relationship with his brothers, and his tenuous relationship with his cousin Minnie Temple, whom, significantly, he did not marry, though one gathers that he wishes he might have. Throughout these memoirs, moreover, James strives to retain control over voice and point of view, to keep his composition centered upon himself, and, with his endlessly qualifying periodic sentences, to contain and to order every possible nuance of meaning. Stein uses a metaphor of celibacy implied by bachelorhood to connect the content to the form of James's memoirs and to reject the model of autobiographical writing those memoirs suggest. She implicitly treats them as a narrative of celibate heteroerotic relations and vaguely incestuous and rival homoerotic relations—a narrative told within the essentially autoerotic narration of the elderly James creating a persona through whom to apprehend himself as a boy, youth, and young man. If my reading is correct, James's memoirs serve Stein as a model of repressed desire seeking an impossible completion—a closure—in the realm of remembrance.

Stein, however, offers a different model toward a different end. She conflates language and metalanguage in the Cubist structure of her composition. She constructs a portrait that enacts the movement of James's memoirs as being read by her; simultaneously, she constructs a real narrative that tells, *in precisely the same words*, a story about that portrait's being written by Stein and being read by her reader. She does so with a multivocalism and a multiperspectivalism that opens her text to James's and, more particularly, to her reader's expectations and interventions. She thus extends the compositional method of the *Autobiography* that she had analogized with marriage into a more radically open textual process. She relinquishes considerable control over voice and over point of view, decenters her composition with respect to content and form, and allows her indeterminate linguistic surface to proliferate a multiplicity of contesting meanings. Using a metaphor of sexuality implied by "marital relations" in the broadest acceptation, she projects a model of auto/biographical writing as necessarily—and joyfully—free from the closure of remembrance.[29] The model can be said to anticipate more recent manifestations of "feminine writing," and it accords with Stein's most famous pun: eros is eros is eros is eros.[30]

My reading of Stein's erotics of writing, however, requires us to regard her as attributing repression to James; and we must recall that she elsewhere specified James's "disembodied way of disconnecting something from anything and anything from something" *not* as "repression" but as "a lack of connection, of there being no connection with living and daily living because there is none, that makes American writing what it always has been and what it will continue to become" (*LIA* 53–54). In essence, she distances the problem not so much from sexuality as from Freudian analysis.[31] With respect to psychology, she portrays James as seeking to connect his various selves through memory, while he acknowledges, reluctantly, that he creates new selves as he does so; with respect to aesthetics, she portrays James as connecting the elements of his writing within an "atmosphere," while he effects, by virtue of that, an abstractionism that disconnects his writing from the concrete "living" to which it refers; with respect to social context, she portrays both these psychological and aesthetic tendencies as reflecting the effect upon James of the "lived composition" of his historical moment. Disapproving and fearing the discontinuities and disconnections he perceived in modern life, James sought to assert a continuous self against the forces that would fragment it and sought to do so in a literary style marked by compositional centers and attendant continuities of theme and form. As "the first of his contemporaries to be conscious of what was happening to his generation," James enacted not only what he approved in the composition of living but also what he disapproved in it. Hence discontinuity and decenterment encroached upon his work, willed by him or not.

As a fellow practitioner of the American writing, Stein shares this problem of disconnectedness—but with variations imposed by the composition of living in her generation. With respect to psychology, she freely acknowledges the disconnections between her multiple Empirical Selves but still argues for the continuity of her Pure Ego as a perpetually present, and present-tense, perceptual process; with respect to aesthetics, she keeps the elements of her writing "on the page quite composed" but does not succeed fully in escaping an abstractionism that, as we already have seen, she seemed to deplore; with respect to social context, she seems to recognize both tendencies as reflecting the effect upon her of her historical moment. Disapproving and fearing the radically escalated discontinuity and disconnectedness she perceived in post–World War I life, Stein asserts the continuous process of perception as a counterforce to fragmentation but does so in a literary style distinguished by decenterment and discontinuity. Claiming the same relation to her contemporaries in which she places James to his, Stein, too, enacts not only what she approves but what she disapproves in what she sees "happening." On the positive side, she proposes discontinuity and decenterment not as disconnection but precisely as its corrective in her time; she employs them to create art as process rather than as product—as a process of incompletion, moreover, in which multiple perceiving egos share. On the negative side, however, Stein seems to acknowledge that the decenterment and discontinuity in her work conspire with her emphasis on words as words, as signs autoreferential as well as referential, to generate an indeterminacy that threatens to disconnect her writing from the concrete living to which she intends it to refer. Stein believed that the geography of America predisposed Americans to abstraction, as it had predisposed James; a modern but still American abstractionism would encroach on her work, willed by her or not.

We can use Stein's erotics of writing, then, to differentiate her work from James's, but she apparently concluded that she could replace his negative disconnection with her positive decenterment only by succeeding him as a general, notwithstanding that rank's masculine and, perhaps, repressive associations. Thus Toklas and Stein reported in the *Autobiography* that "I [Toklas] often teased her [Stein], calling her a general, a civil war general of either or both sides" (19); and, many pages later, that "Gertrude Stein's elder brother once said of me [Toklas], if I were a general I would never lose a battle, I would only mislay it" (108). Stein would take her ground by being, with Toklas and after James, a winning general in the war of twentieth-century aesthetics. Later connecting the *Autobiography* to the James composition, she not only enabled that inference, but she also pointed to the substantive justification for her connecting a species of autobiography, James's memoirs, to a species of biography, her "life" of James. With "Henry James" and with the book of which it is part, with these examples of writing both ways at once within the demands of the twentieth century, Stein advanced her theoretical program and, as part and parcel of that program, her evolving self-portrait. Indeed, she employed her biographies of four Americans to construct *Four in America* as the autobiographical portrait narration of her own successful generalship.

Stein gave us the clues to its success also after the fact, this time in *Picasso*, her "life" of Picasso that tells the history of Cubism in painting as the history of her eponymous hero's struggles. Early in this book, Stein speaks of Picasso's "beginning" to "struggle" in 1909 with problems of Cubist portraiture (13), specifically, with the problem of trying to "express things seen not as one knows them but as they are when one sees them without remembering having looked at them" (15). Picasso had to avoid doing what "everybody" is "accustomed" to doing, namely, "complet[ing] the whole entirely from their knowledge"; instead, he had to do what true painters do, namely, look directly at his subject and thereby avoid "reconstruction from memory" (15). Stein adds that "I was alone at this time in understanding him, perhaps because I was expressing the same thing in literature, perhaps because I was an American and, as I say, Spaniards and Americans have a kind of understanding of things which is the same" (16). She then interjects that "we are now still in the history of the beginning of that struggle" (16), referring with this polysemous remark simultaneously to the events she is narrating, to the narration in *Picasso* of those events, and to the composing of *Picasso* and similar texts as an event occurring in the mid-1930s. Stein is speaking, in short, of the continuing history, begun in 1909, of Picasso's and her analogous struggles to express things directly in portraiture. Her struggle had led to the Cubist portrait narration of *Four in America*.[32]

At first glance, *Four in America* appears to be a serial polyptych comprising four panels of equal importance. Its two outer panels are clearly symmetrical. The left-hand panel treats a general, Grant, who lived wholly in the nineteenth century and who commanded the victorious army in the Civil War, the war that reunited the United States of America and that, so Stein believed, initiated America into the twentieth century.[33] The right-hand panel treats a general, Washington, who lived wholly in the eighteenth century and who commanded the victorious army in the Revolutionary War, the war that founded the United States of America, the nation that eventually would be the first to enter the twentieth century. For the import of these panels, we must recall Stein's theory that wars only confirm a new reality for "everybody," that "the entire change has been accomplished and the war is only something which forces everybody to recognize it." Wars, moreover, force the public to recognize the "creator who has seen the change which has been accomplished before a war and which has been expressed by the war," the creator, again, who is not in "advance" of his or her generation but who is the first to perceive the conditions of its composition of living and to practice successfully the artistic composition appropriate to them (*P* 30).

The asymmetrical central panels of *Four in America* treat two such creators in Wilbur Wright and Henry James, nineteenth-century figures who lived into the twentieth century and who saw before everybody the new movement that defined their generation's composition of living. More precisely, Wright was *not* such a creator, but he indirectly anticipated one by inventing a technology that anticipated, in a different realm, the technique of Cubism. Wright invented the controlled powered flight (of heavier-than-air machines) whose form of movement Stein saw as defining the twentieth century and as affording it the shifting perspectivalism that Picasso independently discovered in Cubism.[34] Had Wright been a painter, as Stein hypothesizes him, he might have been a direct precursor of Cubism, a Cézanne. James *was* such a creator, but the fact that he "did not prepare for flight" now assumes its considerable significance. James was not prepared to accept the consequences of controlled powered flight either for the conditions of the composition of living or for the artistic composition appropriate to them.[35] James, however, directly anticipated Stein and, with Cézanne, specifically prepared the way for her decenterment in composition, a decenterment that she felt the Civil War had initiated in the composition of living but that only World War I had brought to full expression.[36]

We can see now that Stein's serial polyptych comprising four panels of equal importance actually forms a decentered triptych. Two symmetrical outer panels thematically support a central panel "decentered" by *its* bifurcation into two asymmetrical subjects: Wright and James. And each half of this panel accrues meaning when we supply the associations and identifications we have derived intertextually. Stein associated Wright with the invention of controlled powered flight, Picasso with the invention of Cubism, controlled powered flight with Cubism, and thus Wright with Picasso; and, as we just have seen, she associated Picasso's struggles with Cubist portraiture with her own struggles. Similarly, Stein identified James as having culminated nineteenth-century narration and as having anticipated her forging of twentieth-century narration: and, as we just have seen at length, she identified James's ability to write both ways at once, his generalship, as having anticipated her own variation of doing so, her generalship. From this central panel, then, emerges dialectically the triptych's real subject: Stein's development of Cubist portrait narration.

The salient biographical "facts" detailed in the four "lives" flesh out this subject. Grant and Washington were married men who gained fame as military and political leaders and who performed their significant work in the United States; by contrast, Wright and James were bachelors who gained fame as inventors of aeronautic technology and "atmospheric" literary technique and who performed much of their significant work outside the United States. Although we again must derive the particulars intertextually, we can fit Picasso and Stein within these oppositions. Picasso had a series of heterosexual marriages and cohabitations (see, for example, *ABT* 17, 73, 109–10), and Stein had a lesbian marriage, so both were unconventionally married while being conventionally unmarried; Picasso likened himself to Lincoln (*ABT* 18–19), Stein had Toklas liken her to a Civil War general and to Washington (*ABT* 19, 276), and both were artistic revolutionaries and founding figures as well as inventors of new painterly and literary techniques; finally, Picasso and Stein expatriated themselves from countries whose geography, she argued, predisposed them to a similar abstractionism in their "understanding of things," both settled in Paris to work, but Picasso remained "Spanish" in his sensibility and Stein, as she insisted, fiercely "American" in hers. Stein thus implies how Picasso's and her similar ways of living within their generation's composition of living determined their specific contributions to the appropriate artistic composition.

Stein's triptych, then, reads as follows: Washington and Grant were the victorious generals in the political wars that first founded and then reunited the country that was the first to enter the twentieth century, the country of Stein's origin; Wright invented controlled powered flight and indirectly anticipated Picasso's invention of painting in the twentieth century, Cubism; James fully developed nineteenth-century narration and directly anticipated Stein's development of writing in the twentieth century, also Cubism. *Four in America* thus foreshadows Stein's *Picasso*, in which she argues that Spain and America "were the natural founders of the twentieth century" (12), and which she opens with the claim that "painting in the nineteenth century was only done in France and by Frenchmen," but "in the twentieth century it was done in France but by Spaniards" (1).[37] She implies, clearly, that writing in the twentieth century is done in France but by Americans, that is, by Gertrude Stein.[38] In a crucial sense, then, *Four in America* simultaneously looks backward to *The Autobiography of Alice B. Toklas* and forward to *Picasso*. Stein joins her marital relationship with Toklas to her sibling relationship with Picasso; and just as she used the former to suggest the lesbian-feminist aspect of her advance upon James, so does she use the latter to suggest the Cubist aspect of her advance upon this "parent" to whom she was "naturally antagonistic."[39]

Stein suggests, however, that even this achievement might have left a problem. Picasso and she had developed Cubism concurrently in painting and in writing in the first decade of the century, years before she wrote *Four in America*. World War I subsequently had revealed Cubism as the appropriate expression for the composition of prewar life; but the changed conditions of the postwar life required an artistic expression appropriate to them (see *P* 11). In the 1930s, Stein evidently believed that she needed to *correct* the former bifurcation of Cubism into the distinct genres of painting and writing, however metaphorically, in order to shape that expression: just as she had to practice a feminist "diffusion" of masculinist narration to assume her generalship and win her army, so she had to write the two Cubisms "both at once" to win her battle in the artistic war. It follows that Stein could not simply narrate the history of Cubist portrait narration as the history of her struggles; she had to *use* the form that her struggles had revealed to her to be the appropriate one—though, unfortunately, only a subsequent war could reveal it to everybody else as having been appropriate. Living in France, where Wilbur Wright pursued his program of flight and Picasso his program of Cubism, Stein used this form to point in *Four in America* to a "foreign America" whose exemplars of creativity, especially Henry James, she had not forgotten but had nonetheless succeeded—whether everybody recognized this or not.

Stein suggested as much, and much more, finally, with the multiple wordplays in her title and subtitle. With her title, she not only referred semantically to her four human subjects and to the four parts of her book—the book that depicts and enacts her succeeding those subjects; and she not only referred phonologically to the America that had become foreign to her, as she had become foreign to it. She also referred bilingually, through familiar French, to a mess (*un four*) in America and to committing a blunder (*faire un four*) in America, to failure (*un four*) in America and to being a failure (*faire four*) in America. Without exploring the many permutations of meaning contained in those wordplays, we might infer generally that America, perpetuating militarist and patriarchal values, committed blunders that made a mess of things, and that the nation, among its many blunders, judged at least two of Stein's human subjects as successes and herself as a failure and an alien. Printed as a superscription rather than as a subscription to the title, Stein's subtitle, "What They Thought and Bought," appears to support that inference. Either an unspecified "they" thought and bought her four subjects, or her four subjects thought and bought an unspecified direct object . . . or both. At risk of being egregiously reductive, we might infer, again generally, that America thought—or at least did what passed for thinking—and then bought two of Stein's subjects as geniuses, as heros and leaders, because those subjects, Grant and Washington, thought and bought into militarist, patriarchal ideology; the nation so thought and bought neither Wright nor, apparently, James—and certainly not Stein. And the nation, of course, had company in so doing.

☙

Most audiences, American and otherwise, have judged James and Stein extremely difficult writers. They often have charged James with an indifference toward the reader, or, alternatively, an excessive demand upon the reader, together with an indifference toward the portrayal of common human experience, or, alternatively, an excessive concern with literary technique. Even James's most ardent modernist admirers qualified their praise when speaking of his later phase. Pound, for whom James's was "great art as opposed to overelaborate or over-refined art," nonetheless recognized James's demon as the "cobwebby," a term Pound used ten times in his "Baedecker" to the "continent" of James's *oeuvre*;[40] Eliot, who commended James's focus on "a situation, a relation, an atmosphere," nonetheless ceded that such focus made "the reader, as well as the *personae*, uneasily the victim of a merciless clairvoyance";[41] and Forster and Leavis, with far stronger disapproval, protested that

James's fervor for "pattern" and "technique" muffled the human dimension of his material and sharply diminished his reader's ability to apprehend that material.[42] James's detractors, meanwhile, had reached the consensus that enabled Stephen Spender flatly to declare in *The Destructive Element* that "most criticism of James boils down to saying that he is unreadable."[43]

Extending those charges, Stein's critics have indicted her for an obscurantism so egregious as to mean hostility toward the reader together with an aestheticism so intransigent as to produce unreasonably autoreferential texts. Pound, with characteristic shrillness, wrote to Cummings that it was "ever a pleasure to have something to decipher that *ain't* dear Jim [Joyce] or oedipus Gertie," and to Wyndham Lewis that "this flow of conquishousness Gertie/Jimmee stuff has about FLOWED long enuff";[44] and Eliot, with characteristic equivocation, portrayed Stein's work as "at once original and obscure" and pronounced it, so Stein reports, "very fine but not for us."[45] Even such an admirer as Edmund Wilson, meanwhile, interrupted his discussion in *Axel's Castle* of Stein's *Making of Americans* to "confess that I have not read this book all through, and I do not know whether it is possible to do so."[46] It is a telling confession from a critic who presumably could read all through *A la recherche du temps perdu*, *Ulysses*, and what then was appearing as *Work in Progress* and soon would become *Finnegans Wake*. Yet Wilson was far from alone in declaring Stein impossible to read but, somehow, significant in spite of this. Indeed, his response so typifies the history of Stein's reception that to read Stein reading James almost would seem an exercise in reading the unread in pursuit of the unreadable.

James and Stein, of course, show neither indifference nor hostility toward their readers, though they do demand of them what Leavis, speaking of James, justly termed "a close and unrelaxed attention, an actively intelligent collaboration";[47] and they show neither an unseemly concern with technique nor a pure aestheticism, though they do reveal in their texts what Marjorie Perloff, speaking of Stein, termed a "tension between reference and compositional game, between a pointing system and a self-ordering system."[48] James and Stein, in other words, differently present acute cases of the dialogic situation inherent in all literature and salient in modernist literature; and they differently present acute cases of the tension between referentiality and autoreferentiality that has haunted formalist aesthetics in music, painting, and literature for more than a century. They are difficult, in sum, for the same general reasons that most modernist writers are difficult. Though James's difficulty does not concern me here, we can see that Stein's may derive in part from her perception of James and, more important, from her conception of the advances she needed to make upon him to bring American writing from the nineteenth century into the twentieth. In any event, we might consider three orders of difficulty in her work: the surface complexity of her texts, the conception of subject in her texts, and the intertextual matrix defined by her texts.

Stein enforced a continual shifting and sliding of the linguistic surface by manipulating semantic and syntactic units within a double movement of phonic and graphic play. And she employed specific devices within this technique to effect dialogue with herself and between herself and her reader: she omitted quotation marks or other punctuation that would indicate direct address and would clarify corresponding shifts in speaker; she introduced personal pronouns with ambiguous, inconsistent, or nonexistent antecedents to confound further any clear discrimination of speaker from auditor and writer from reader; and she often shifted within a single sentence, to the same end, between declarative, interrogative, and imperative voices. Stein also employed equally specific and similar devices to fuse the referential and autoreferential functions of language: she omitted quotation marks or double slashes when analyzing a word's or phrase's function as a sign, thus causing it simultaneously *to* function as a sign; and she often named a text after its subject and omitted quotation marks or italics when using that name, thus causing it to refer to her text and, simultaneously, to her subject. Keeping words constantly in motion with these Cubist devices, she frustrated her reader's interpretations while demanding that reader's interventions. She constructed a polyphonic and polygraphic linguistic surface—a "verbivocovisual presentment," to borrow a phrase from *Finnegans Wake*—that compelled her reader not only to look, listen, and speak, but also to reflect upon his or her doing so.[49]

This polyphonic and polygraphic surface found its necessity in Stein's conception of her subject as including an initiating subject plus her own treatment of it.[50] Whether Stein chose herself as autobiographical subject or chose a subject other than herself, she attempted to apprehend the subject directly and to allow it to pose questions that would govern her treatment of it. When her subject was art, another artist, or herself as artist, those questions were usually questions of art and the point of Stein's treatment to generate by example a theory of art. But Stein came to understand that any subject was already enmeshed in several processes of apprehension. Those included not only the subject's self-apprehension and its apprehension of others, whether the subject was literally conscious or only figured by Stein as such; but also the subject's self-apprehension and its apprehension by others, including Stein and her actual and virtual readers. It follows that Stein's own treatment of the subject became an aspect of subject so defined. Stein needed to develop a style, then, that would accommodate her understanding, that would allow for representation and for the simultaneous analysis of the representational act, and that would allow, even further, for simultaneous second-order analysis of that analysis. Though not coeval in her conception, Stein's initiating subject, her treatment of it, and her analyses of that treatment became coextensive in texts whose apprehensive mesh extended to include the reader's reading.

Those texts, however, also derive much of their meaning from the intertext of Stein's *oeuvre* and from the program implicit in it. However variously stylized or conceptualized, her individual texts form a matrix in which key words, phrases, anecdotes, and structures recur endlessly with minor variations, and in which key ideas, taken up time and again, develop into coherence with extraordinary languor. Often meaningless in isolation, these linguistic features and these ideas become intelligible once the reader cross-references them within the matrix. Yet the reader cannot do so without also negotiating the distortions produced by Stein's remembrances and revisions. Stein, that is, was a highly programmatic writer, and the program she advanced rigorously through five productive decades included not only the formulation of a theory of art but also the fabrication of a portrait of the genius that was Gertrude Stein. In tracing the lines of this theory and self-portrait, the reader must treat Stein's pronouncements on any subject as provisional, and he or she must not take the lure of treating Stein's theoretical and autobiographical writings as definitive, or even "truthful," commentaries upon her work in other genres. Stein's was an *oeuvre* in which theory and practice were everywhere wedded, in which a theory of artistic process could only be in process; yet hers was a program in which this process tended always toward theoretical and autobiographical resolution. She left her reader to negotiate that tension between process and resolution.

Stein created, in sum, complex textual surfaces that manifested an equally complex conception of subject and that took their place within an *oeuvre* and a program marked by internal tension. With respect to surface, Stein orchestrated voices actual and virtual in a way closer to the simultaneity of lyric drama than to the sequentiality of spoken drama; and she manipulated punctuation and other visual indicators with a subtlety more reminiscent of Mallarmé than of the more extravagant typographical experimenters of her own historical moment. That complexity of surface issued from Stein's conceiving her subject to include a subject, her treatment of it, and her first-order and often second-order analyses of that treatment. Though she addressed this multidimensional subject, moreover, from a point of view informed by aesthetic, psychological, and historical interests, she generally intended the form of her address to exemplify her theory of art. Evolving through the intertext of Stein's *oeuvre*, this theory became a process in search of an impossible terminus, as did the equally prominent and parallel evolving self-portrait of Stein. Surface, subject, theory, and self-portrait, finally, together required Stein's reader not only to trace the intertext horizontally but also to extend it vertically. Preoccupied with the problem of mediated perception, Stein included in her texts other, often public, mediations of her subject, and she compelled her reader to take into account not only those mediations but also his or her own reading as yet another one of them.

Though "Henry James" and *Four in America* reflect those three orders of difficulty, they no more defy reading than does Stein's work in general. One must wonder, indeed, why a generation of moderns, their work equally autoreferential and open to readerly intervention, would direct such animus toward Stein and, in effect, direct a generation of critics and reviewers to share in it; why the moderns who found James admirably difficult found Stein only obscurely so; why an Eliot would characterize James as having "a mind so fine that no idea could violate it," by which he meant to compliment James's "superior intelligence,"[51] while a Leo Stein would characterize his sister Gertrude as being "practically inaccessible to ideas," by which he meant to soften without retracting his judgment of her basic "stupidity."[52] One must wonder why Stein could complain justly in *The Autobiography of Alice B. Toklas* that the scarcity of her earlier books had won her a collectorship rather than a readership (301); why the *Autobiography*, a widely disseminated Literary Guild selection, would win her celebrity but neither the publication of her more "difficult" material nor the exegetical attention being given Joyce. One must wonder why sympathetic critics and reviewers such as Edmund Wilson almost invariably would declare Stein's work "important" but still unreadable; why those unsympathetic would produce exhalations such as this, from a review of *Four in America*: "Well, James and Joyce and Sterne are sometimes hard reading, but they make sense for the hard-working reader"—an invocation meant to suggest that Stein makes only, as the review is titled, "Nonsense."[53] Though answers are various, we might conclude by considering briefly Stein's sense of ideas and her sense of tradition, for both reflect her proximity to James and her distance from her fellow moderns.

Stein doubtless would have approved Mallarmé's riposte to Degas, quoted with approval by Valéry, that "one does not make poetry with ideas, but with *words*."[54] But she was no ideologue of the autonomous verbal artifact, and she doubtless would have disapproved MacLeish's dictum that "A poem should not mean / But be." Stein meant her works to mean, but she meant them to mean only those ideas won through her struggle with writing itself. As a poet and portraitist, she was committed to exact representation of the object or person observed, and, as a writer of narrative prose, to exact representation of the event or behavior observed; in each genre, she wished to avoid the intervention of "remembered" conventions, of constituted knowledge, of what often pass for ideas. As we have seen, though, Stein understood representation to mean representation of the thing *being* observed and to entail an autoreferential presentation about that observing and about the writing of it. On the one hand, then, Stein was committed to unmediated representation; but, on the other hand, she perceived representation as a mediation and undertook simultaneous analysis of the representational act. On the one hand, she chose the concrete over the abstract and thus seemed devoid of ideas except those she derived from observing things; but, on the other hand, she wrote things that were analyses of that observing and of themselves as writing and that often appear, as a result, abstractionist. In effect, she adhered to Williams's ambiguous injunction: "Compose. (No ideas / but in things) Invent!" She found in Cubism the method that would serve her both as means of representation and as mode of autoanalysis. She found in it her method not only for developing the ideas she derived from observing things but also for generating and conveying the ideas she was simultaneously developing about the very process in which she was engaged.

This attitude toward ideas reflects the kinds of ideas that Stein tended to develop. She had a coherent view of human psychology derived largely from William James; and she had a coherent view of social relations consistent with it. But Stein the literary practitioner developing ideas about the human psyche and about social relations never departed from Stein the theoretician attempting to demonstrate the fundamental principles of the strictly contemporary twentieth-century writing she determined her Cubism to be. And with this duality of purpose, in turn, she reflected the duality of artistic lineage she claimed for herself. On the one hand, she announced that "one can only have one métier as one can only have one language. [My] métier is writing and [my] language is english" (*ABT* 94); she regarded James as her direct precursor; and she often seemed to consider herself the extension of what Leavis eventually would style the "great tradition" of the English novel. On the other hand, she identified three crucial, lateral influences on her work: Flaubert's self-conscious artfulness, Cézanne's attention to the "realism of the composition" (see TI 16), and Picasso's analytical reflexivity. In short, Stein placed herself in the lineage of Anglo-American realism, but she also claimed that her French tutors had instructed her in extending that lineage toward a still realistic but highly autoreferential Cubist prose. In a sense, Stein countered James's Hawthorne and his Balzac, Flaubert, and Daudet, with James himself and Flaubert, Cézanne, and Picasso.

Without belaboring the point, we can say that Stein's attitude toward ideas, the ideas she developed, and the lineage she claimed form a nexus that distinguishes her from her fellow moderns. At once referential and autoreferential, concrete and abstract, Stein's Cubism also constitutes a method of generating and conveying ideas and conduces to the particular kinds of ideas she developed most fully in her poetry, portraiture, and narrative prose. As such, it shares basic functions with the modernist Symbolism she repudiated, but it differs from it in conception and execution. Marjorie Perloff is correct to contrast the indeterminacy of Stein's Cubism, which frustrates interpretation of deep structure, with the ambiguity of Eliot's symbolism, which precisely invites it. And Perloff is partly correct to argue that Stein's work, unlike Eliot's, "requires no special knowledge on the part of the reader," that Stein's work does not appeal to the myths and mysteries of the European tradition and to the esoteria and arcana of its philosophical thought.[55] Perloff is only partly correct because Stein does require her reader to steep himself or herself in the myths of American culture and in the mysteries of Stein's life among the avant-garde, not to mention the arcana and esoteria of Stein's evolving artistic theory and self-portrait.

Stein's repudiation of modernist symbolism as a compositional and cognitive basis finds its counterpart in her repudiation of the cultural tradition claimed by the modern symbolists. She rejected the "mind of Europe" as Eliot explicitly, Pound and Joyce implicitly, understood that entity; and she rejected Eliot's influential model of the individual talent absorbing the vast European tradition and extending it, in theory at least, through an impersonalized, public writing. Stein refused appeal to a tradition that, needless to say, offered little welcome to a Jewish-American lesbian, and she dwelled instead, however obscurely, on the personal and the private. In fact, Stein portrayed such appeals to tradition as decidedly unmodern and as reasons for the accessibility and the acceptability of the work of her rivals. In the *Autobiography*, she quotes with approval Picasso's characterization of Braque and Joyce as "the incomprehensibles whom anybody can understand" (260), and, extending the characterization to Hemingway, she specifies the reason for that intelligibility: "he looks like a modern and he smells of the museums" (266). Years later, she would elaborate the charge: "You see it is the people who generally smell of the museums who are accepted, and it is the new who are not accepted. You have got to accept a complete difference. It is hard to accept that, it is much easier to have one hand in the past. That is why James Joyce was accepted and I was not. He leaned toward the past, in my work the newness and difference is fundamental" (TI 29).[56] To smell of the museums is to remember the cultural storehouse of symbols rather than to write what one observes; it is to invoke one's prior knowledge and that of one's audience rather than to develop knowledge by writing; it is to practice cultural conservationism rather than to advance a program of strict contemporaneity. No light charge, to smell of the museums is to violate the basic Steinian principles that account, in turn, for the Steinian difficulties.

We would be mistaken, of course, to identify so closely Eliot, Pound, and Joyce, for they differed considerably, and, by the mid-1930s, Pound had extended to Joyce's work the rancor he had for Stein's; but we would be equally mistaken to discount the similarity of their visions of the artist-hero and of the tradition rightfully "his." We also would be mistaken to associate modernism so closely with that trio, for critics such as Perloff, Charles Altieri, and David

Antin have charted for us an alternative modernist tradition that admits Stein; but we would be equally mistaken to discount the effect that the aesthetics of Eliot, Pound, and Joyce, however contrarious, had on subsequent critical practice and continue to have on our definition of modernism.[57] We would be mistaken, finally, to base an analysis of modernism on sibling rivalry among the James progeny; but we surely would be mistaken to ignore that rivalry. As American expatriates and devotees of James, Eliot and Pound not surprisingly dismissed Stein, and she them.[58] Although Joyce seems not to have reciprocated, Stein obviously fixed him as her chief rival for the Jamesian succession, an apt choice, of course, since Joyce, too, was a writer of English prose, one who redefined naturalism in *Ulysses* and prose itself in *Finnegans Wake*.[59] His métier painting and his language Spanish, Picasso was Stein's ideal ally, though, as we have seen, neither her only ally nor only her ally.

Stein differed from her fellow moderns, then, in at least two ways that help account for the animus they showed her. She rejected a broad European tradition in order to claim her place in a narrower Anglo-American lineage of realism, and she repudiated the symbolism she associated with the former in order to practice the Cubism she saw as extending the latter. Moreover, she joined her development of post-Jamesian realism to an original lesbian erotics of writing, and she argued aggressively that a woman, herself, could write so importantly with that combination that she would number among the three first-rate geniuses of Alice B. Toklas's acquaintance and among the few geniuses of the twentieth century. She also appears to differ from us postmoderns, however, in ways that perhaps account for our continued reserve toward her. She anticipated contemporary writing, that is, but her insistence on realism, however redefined, and however assimilable to the theory and practice of a Robbe-Grillet, prevents our *too easily* assimilating her into a postmodernist theory and practice. Likewise, she anticipated contemporary "feminine writing," but the lineage she claimed and the masculinist rank she metaphorically assumed prevent our *too easily* assimilating her into current feminist theory and practice.[60]

It is precisely from that point of reserve, however, that we finally must return to "Henry James" and to *Four in America*. Stein did not write them, obviously, just to solve an aesthetic problem of reconciling modernist portraiture and narration. She wrote them to deconstruct the premises on which American culture had conceived the status of genius and had assigned it to others and to construct the premises on which she could claim that status for herself. Specifically, she freed the roles of spouse, general, and *auctor* from militarist, patriarchal definition and thus subverted the conventional values they had represented; she then redefined those roles from Cubist and lesbian-feminist perspectives and, having done so, adopted them. She had moved from the referential to the autoreferential, that is, but she also moved again from a textualized form of autoreference to an intertextualized form of reference; ultimately, she *was* composing *Four in America* as a study in success and failure. She was addressing not only what it meant to succeed or to fail artistically, but also what it meant to be represented as having succeeded or failed. She staked her claim to success and to the Jamesian succession on the portrait narration with which, circularly, she represented herself as having succeeded; and, in the process, she mooted future attempts to settle whether she had written radical cultural criticism or anxious self-promotion. She had written both at once.[61]

NOTES

Preface

1. In remarks rarely longer than a sentence or two, some critics have noted similarities of style or genre (see White, *Gertrude Stein and Alice B. Toklas*, 2; Loggins, *I Hear America*, 324, 325, 327; Steiner, *Exact Resemblance to Exact Resemblance*, 183, 192); some have noted other similarities (see Sutherland, *Gertrude Stein*, 9, 47, 93, and elsewhere; Michael J. Hoffman, *Development of Abstractionism*, 34–35; Dupee, General Introduction, *Selected Writings of Gertrude Stein*, x; Bridgman, *Colloquial Style in America*, 84–85, 102; Gass, "Gertrude Stein," 83 n. 5); some have linked them metaphorically (see Brinnin, *Third Rose*, 190; Schmitz, "Portrait, Patriarchy, Mythos," 88); and some have linked them as exemplars of literary moments (see Frederick J. Hoffman, *Twenties*, 224; Woodward, *At Last, The Real Distinguished Thing*, ix). Several critics have included James and Stein, and often have treated each superbly, in books devoted to broader topics and covering several writers: Tanner treated their shared stance of wonder in *Reign of Wonder* (1965); Bridgman treated their shared colloquial style in *Colloquial Style in America* (1966); Cooley treated their shared use of the autobiographical genre in *Educated Lives* (1976); and Banta treated their shared manipulation of typal representation in *Imaging American Women* (1987). A few have brought them together in articles: Shaw compared their styles in "Gertrude Stein and Henry James" (1974), and Banta their attitudes toward expatriation in "James and Stein on 'Being American' and 'Having France'" (1979). I first developed their precursor-successor relationship in a much earlier version of chapter 5 of the present study, "Reading Gertrude Stein Reading Henry James" (1985), and Nadel also treated that relationship in his "Gertrude Stein and Henry James" (1988). Even very recent books on Stein, however, continue to ignore the relationship: neither Ruddick's *Reading Gertrude Stein* (1990), Bowers's *"They Watch Me as They Watch This"* (1991), Berry's *Curved Thought and Textual Wandering* (1992), nor Fifer's *Rescued Readings* (1992) mentions Henry James at all, though none particularly needs to; Knapp's life-and-works essay, *Gertrude Stein* (1990), mentions James six times—four of the remarks say very little, the other two retail, inadvertently, conflicting versions of the same anecdote (see 8, 50).

2. I refer here to a 1957 Grove Press reprint.

3. These four works also have had strikingly different histories of reception, each pair of works containing a celebrated example and an ignored one. *Hawthorne* has elicited a critical commentary so extensive, so rich, and so richly interwoven that it forms a distinct strain in American literary and cultural history, with recent analysts of the "*Hawthorne* effect," if I might echo T. S. Eliot, treating the debate itself as a paradigm not only of American cultural studies but also of American culture. *William Wetmore Story*, by contrast, has elicited only scant critical commentary, most of it very recent, most of it sharing the premises that familial and financial pressures caused James to accept an unwanted commission that he executed, at best, indifferently, and virtually all of it trying to sort out whether James was writing biography or autobiography. Stein's publishers advertised *The Autobiography of Alice B. Toklas*, her most celebrated

book, as a documentary account of the Parisian vanguard and American expatriate circles; contemporary reviewers treated it, by and large, as such, and every historian of the "lost generation" retails its anecdotes; and a newer generation of critics has begun to treat it, extensively, as a serious experimental study in genre and in gender. The posthumously published *Four in America* has had a sharply contrasting history: Thornton Wilder provided it a flattering, if rather baffled, introduction; reviewers treated its recently deceased author with an appropriate deference, but the book itself with hostility or bafflement; and serious commentators on Stein, almost without exception, have ignored it altogether. For discussions of these histories of reception, see chapter 2, note 8; chapter 3, note 17; chapter 4, note 12; chapter 5, note 10.

4. For dates of composition for Stein's works, I rely on Haas and Gallup, *Catalogue*, 45–55; Sawyer, "Gertrude Stein," 183; and Bridgman, *Gertrude Stein in Pieces*, 365–85.

Chapter One

1. James, *Painter's Eye*, 227.

2. Nettels has stressed the presence of biographical portraiture throughout James's *oeuvre* ("Henry James and the Art of Biography"), as has Ward ("Portraits of Henry James"); and Steiner has demonstrated "the centrality of the portrait genre within the corpus of Stein's work" (*Exact Resemblance to Exact Resemblance*, 161). Citing Stein, Rosenberg made the crucial link: "'The final test is always the portrait,' [Stein] wrote, having in mind, perhaps, as had Henry James, that in the midst of disintegrated traditions beauty is secondary to grasping the identity of things" ("Paris Annexed," 176).

3. In "The Science of Criticism" (1891), James wrote that the literary critic (or portraitist), unlike the novelist, must take his puppets "as they come" (*LC* 2:99).

4. The latter value figured importantly, for many of the works James reviewed were, in accordance with Victorian conventions, largely archival, their "authors" in fact editors who selected and arranged materials and provided, or failed to provide, connecting narrative. Though James held no strict position on the value of compilation as such, he invariably remarked the type of material compiled, the principle of selection governing the compilation, and the relative obtrusiveness or unobtrusiveness of the editorial hand. Very critical, for example, of "books of 'extracts'" (*LC* 1:817, *LC* 2:1132, 1175), he judged equally harshly books in which "selection, arrangement, elucidation, have been left out of the question" (*LC* 2:1141).

5. Compare, on the one hand, James's reviews of two books on the missionary John Coleridge Patterson in 1875 and of a biography of Count Cavour in 1877, with, on the other hand, his review of James Elliot Cabot's *Memoir of Ralph Waldo Emerson* in 1887. Patterson and Cavour, in James's description of Patterson, belonged to "the noble class of men whose genius has become a matter of the life itself—whose idea and effect have been a passionate personal example," who thereby become "type" (*LC* 2:1386); virtually self-narrating, their lives suit biography. Emerson, however, was "a man of genius, but he led for nearly eighty years a life in which the sequence of events had little of the rapidity, or the complexity, that a spectator loves" (*LC* 2:250); virtually non-narrative, Emerson's life suited the portraitist's art.

6. James did the same with essays on painters for the collection *Picture and Text* (1893).

7. For a sense of the importance James attached to the term "portrait," see his correspondence with Macmillan regarding the title of what would become *Partial Portraits* (*Correspondence of Henry James and the House of Macmillan*, 128–36). Ward has pointed out that James published three books in the 1880s with the word "portrait" in the title—the genres differ and so do the referents of the word ("Portraits of Henry James," 1).

8. In 1877, following some early reviews of Sand, James published (1) an essay on Sand in the *Galaxy*, reprinted in *French Poets and Novelists*, based largely on her *L'Histoire de ma Vie*; in 1897, he published (2) "She and He: Recent Documents," based on the publication of her correspondence with Alfred de Musset; in 1902, he published (3) "George Sand: The New Life," a review of Madame Wladimir Karénine's biography of Sand, volumes 1 and 2; and, finally, some twelve years later, in 1914, he published (4) a review of Karénine's biography, volume 3. The last three items were reprinted in *Notes on Novelists*. These accrue importance because James wrote the first essay shortly before *Hawthorne*, the second and third essays after accepting the commission for *William Wetmore Story* but before executing it, and the last essay (and the compilation of three essays) just after publishing *A Small Boy and Others* and *Notes of a Son and Brother*.

In 1877, James found Sand the autobiographical memoirist to have misplaced her emphasis, because her "real history, the more interesting one, is the history of her mind" (*LC* 1:720); granting the relationship of her personal history to her intellectual history, he dismissed discussion of the former as both artless and unseemly. Exactly two decades later, he used Sand's correspondence and her *Elle et Lui* to explore the transformation of her personal history into art. And, five years after that, he argued that the " 'case' " Sand presented "was definitely a bold and direct experiment, not at all in 'art,' not at all in literature, but conspicuously and repeatedly in the business of living." No longer compelled by the "history of her mind," or by her conversion of "private ecstasies" into "literary material" (*LC* 1:738), James portrayed Sand as a kind of Naturalist autobiographer who lived experimentally and who reported on the experiment: "Her masterpiece consists ... in the mere notation of her symptoms" (*LC* 1:760–61). In 1914, finally, he praised Sand as "the greatest of all women of letters" (*LC* 1:775)—the pun intentional—whose importance lay in her living and in her journalistic and epistolary accounts of it.

For additional Jamesian comments on privacy and literary biography, see *LC* 1:31–32, 756. James explored related issues fictionally not only in "The Aspern Papers" (1888) and in "The Real Right Thing" (1899), but also in two lesser known tales contemporary with the *Story* biography, "The Papers" and "The Birthplace" (both 1903).

9. Reversing terms used in 1877, however, James celebrated Sand in 1914 as "the great fluent artist" (*LC* 1:798).

10. Type of *what* is difficult to say. James had sought to solve the "riddle" of "the irreconcilability of her distinction and her vulgarity." His solution: Sand succeeded "as a man" herself, but "a feminine streak" caused her to seek in her lovers a masculine counterpart, and that *search* produced her vulgarity and comprised "the real moral

tragedy." Nonetheless, Sand gave "her sex, for its new evolution and transformation, the real standard and measure of change": women have aspired to the condition of the "'average' male," even extraordinary women have approximated to the "ordinary man"; but Sand approximated to, indeed surpassed, the "extraordinary" man (*LC* 1:773–75). Sand had dealt with life "exactly as if she had been a man," James repeated in 1914, "had annex[ed] the male identity," and had done so, in James's argument, to the benefit of women *and* men, "so that what we in fact on the whole most recognise is not the extension she gives to the feminine nature, but the richness that she adds to the masculine" (*LC* 1:779–81). Tragic figure, Sand martyrs herself for the benefit of men, man, humanity. For articles variously related to this question, see Daugherty, "Henry James, George Sand and *The Bostonians*"; Miller, "Marriages of Henry James and Henrietta Stackpole"; and Person, "Henry James, George Sand, and the Suspense of Masculinity."

11. The passages to which I refer appear in James, *Portrait of a Lady*, 39–42, 354–64; Hawthorne, *Works* 5:54–56. In the first of them, moreover, Isabel characterizes her father's relationship with his daughters in terms very similar to those that James would use in *A Small Boy and Others* to characterize his father's relationship with his sons. Through Isabel, in effect, James alluded simultaneously to his literary and to his familial progenitors. For a pertinent discussion of Hawthorne's prefaces as an act of autoportraiture, see Timothy Dow Adams, "To Prepare a Preface."

12. James introduced the character/incident dichotomy in his 1883 portrait of Trollope, where he purported to debunk "the droll bemuddled opposition between novels of character and novels of plot," but where he in fact sustained it by assigning character priority over incident: "character in itself is plot, while plot is by no means character" (*LC* 2:1336). Elaborating the dichotomy the following year, in "The Art of Fiction," he debunked "an old fashioned distinction between the novel of character and the novel of incident" as being "as little to the point as the equally celebrated distinction between the novel and the romance"; he now expressly declared picture and novel, character and incident, transposable terms, but he again proceeded to make character the term of privilege: "What is character but the determination of incident? What is incident but the illustration of character? What is either a picture or a novel that is not of character? What else do we seek in it and find in it?" (*LC* 2:55). Though I would not claim that James derived the binary "character/incident" from Hawthorne, the latter had used it in "The Custom-House" and in a key autoreferential passage in *The Blithedale Romance* (Hawthorne, *Works* 5:57, 430).

13. Howells, "James's Hawthorne," 94.

14. In "A Humble Remonstrance" (1887), Stevenson engaged James's argument that the novel must *fuse* character, incident, and dialogue, by countering that there are, rather, three classes of novel. Acknowledging that James had praised *Treasure Island* in "The Art of Fiction" (see *LC* 2:61), Stevenson, nonetheless, objected that the novel of adventure requires plot, not the fine characterization James seemed to demand of it; likewise in the dramatic novel, though for different reasons, "nice portraiture is not required; and we are content to accept mere abstract types." In the middle, Stevenson placed the novel of character, where "Mr. James will recognise the note of much of his own work: he treats, for the most part, the statics of character." Ironically, Stevenson

concluded by reproaching William Dean Howells (*Memories & Portraits*, 275–99; for citations, see 286, 293, 290).

15. In the 1860s, James had rated Dickens for having "created nothing but figure. He has added nothing to our understanding of human character" (*LC* 2:856). He spoke far more highly of Scott as portraitist: "Since Shakespeare, no writer had created so immense a gallery of portraits, nor, on the whole, had any portraits been so lifelike" (*LC* 2:1202).

16. Tinter has shown how James responded in his story, "The Pupil" (1891), to Stevenson's *Kidnapped* and *Treasure Island* (*Book World of Henry James*, 130–41).

17. From *Hawthorne* through the prefaces to the New York Edition (1907–9), James seemed unable to decide whether to attach the romantic/realistic dichotomy to objects, treatment, or sensibility. He was himself, perhaps, as he said of Flaubert in 1902, "formed intellectually of two quite distinct compartments, a sense of the real and a sense of the romantic" (*LC* 1:321).

18. Around 1905, Bridgman tells us, Stein "fixed on the title '*Three Histories* by Jane Sands'" for her then work-in-progress, a title that "remained on the ensuing manuscript until 1909 when her publisher prevailed upon her to change it to *Three Lives*" (*Gertrude Stein in Pieces*, 46). The title page of the first edition carried the subtitle, "STORIES OF THE GOOD ANNA, MELANCTHA AND THE GENTLE LENA"; and testimonials on an unissued dustwrapper for that edition speak, variously, of the "picture of life" represented, of "stories" and "little histories," and of "cases." Stein's change of title may signal a subtle shift from one biographical convention to another, "histories" accenting incident and thus narrative, "lives" accenting character and thus portrait; like her abandoned title, moreover, her retained subtitle echoes French "*histoire*" and thus, perhaps, was meant to signal an affiliation with French Naturalism. Whatever the case, like James's *Portrait*, Stein's *Three Lives* negotiates between incident and character, story and picture, narration and portraiture. For reproductions of the title page and trial dustwrapper, see Robert A. Wilson, *Gertrude Stein*, 2, 4.

19. Several commentators have noted Stein's approval in this period of Otto Weininger's *Sex and Character*; see, e.g., Mellow, *Charmed Circle*, 120–21. On Stein's related theory of "bottom nature," see Stein, *LIA*, 137–46, and Bridgman, *Gertrude Stein in Pieces*, 74–76.

20. Etymologically, triptych means "three-fold," and usually refers to the familiar pictorial form of three hinged panels, the central panel structurally and thematically supported by its two subsidiary wing panels, a form especially favored for altarpieces, with the Crucifixion a frequent theme. Given substantial textual evidence to suggest that Anna is a repressed lesbian, Lena an oppressed lesbian, and that Rose Johnson and Jane Harden initiate Melanctha into lesbian sexuality, and given that Stein recast her earlier autobiographical lesbian novel *Q.E.D.* into "Melanctha," the central panel of this triptych, we might speculate that the Stein who professed a love for *complication*—etymologically, folding things together—used the form of the triptych to create an altarpiece honoring martyred lesbians, an altarpiece whose serial portraits of three women also contained a hidden portrait of Stein herself.

21. In May 1910, James wrote Stein: "Well, I read 30 or 40 pages, and said, 'this is a fine new kind of realism—Gertrude Stein is great! I will go at it carefully when just the right

mood comes' " (*Flowers of Friendship*, 50). Though James could not have known this, the banner " 'A Most Extraordinary Piece of Realism' " appears prominently above title and name of author on the unissued dustwrapper, and the term "realism" dominates one testimonial. Assuming Stein's involvement in this wrapper—she was, after all, footing the bill for publication—we might infer her own interest in locating these "lives" as works of realist portraiture.

22. See, e.g., Boyle and Swale, *Realism in European Literature*; Levine, *Realistic Imagination*; Sundquist, *American Realism*; and, especially, William W. Stowe, *Balzac, James, and the Realistic Novel*. For a discussion of the crisis in Realism as it simultaneously affected writing and painting, see Rosen and Zerner, "What Is, and Is Not, Realism?" and "Enemies of Realism."

23. Fry's standard text *Cubism*, for example, stops before the third step, treats Cubism as concerned only with aesthetics, as though there were apples on the one hand, the bombing of Guernica on the other, and nothing in between. For unpursued intimations of other possibilities, see Richardson, "Picasso's Apocalyptic Whorehouse," and, especially, Golding, "Triumph of Picasso." For a summary of positions of art historians who are advancing, with respect to Picasso though not to Braque, the position I am advocating, see Golding, "Two Who Made a Revolution." For extensive discussions of Stein's work in relation to Cubism, see Steiner, *Exact Resemblance to Exact Resemblance*, especially 131–60, and Dubnick, *Structure of Obscurity*, especially 2–44; see also Michael J. Hoffman, *Development of Abstractionism*, and Steiner, *Colors of Rhetoric*. For a discussion of Stein in relation to Cézanne and to Cubism, see Walker, *Making of a Modernist*, 1–18 and elsewhere.

24. Though "An Elucidation" may have been Stein's "first effort to explain herself" (*ABT* 295), "Composition as Explanation" remains her more accessible and well-known effort.

25. With her reference to "atmosphere," Stein was alluding to a term frequent in James's criticism and ubiquitous in his *Hawthorne*, a term that Hawthorne had used conspicuously, as James knew, when differentiating Novel from Romance in the preface to *The House of the Seven Gables* (Hawthorne, *Works* 2:13).

26. This important solecism, "portrait narration," works perfectly *because* of its grammatical incorrectness. The use of the nominal modifier produces, simultaneously and cubistically, a continuity and a discontinuity, an illusion of highly specified meaning (modifier plus modified) together with a reality of unspecified meaning (two terms, neither term modifying nor being modified by the other).

27. With regard to the first issue, see *Stanzas in Meditation* (1932), "Story of a Book" (1933), "And Now" (1934), "What Are Masterpieces" (1936), *The Geographical History of America* (1936), *The Autobiography of Rose* (composed 1936, published 1939), *The World is Round* (1936); with regard to the second, see *Blood on the Dining Room Floor* (composed 1933, published 1948), "American Crimes and How They Matter" (1934), "A Waterfall and a Piano" (1936), "Is Dead" (1937), "Why I Like Detective Stories" (1937).

28. Stein writes: "You see that is why making it the Autobiography of Alice B. Toklas made it do something, *it made it be a recognition by never before that writing having it be existing*" (*NAR* 62, emphasis added). I interpret that as meaning that Stein made Toklas *never be existing before that writing*.

29. In *Narration*, Stein had listed eight exemplary American writers, beginning with Emerson, including herself, and ending with Dashiell Hammett (*NAR* 10).

30. This might explain why Stein pairs her introductory comments on Hammett and autobiography with comments on Mary Pickford and plans for Pickford to be "photographed together" with Stein (*EA* 6–8). In effect, Stein anticipated the problem that Philip Roth would isolate in "Writing American Fiction" (1961), namely, "that the American writer in the middle of the twentieth century has his hands full in trying to understand, describe, and then make *credible* much of American reality. . . . The actuality is continually outdoing our talents, and the culture tosses up figures almost daily that are the envy of any novelist" (120).

31. In *Lectures in America*, Stein noted that in *The Making of Americans* and in subsequent portraits, "I was doing what the cinema was doing, I was making a continuous succession of the statement of what that person was until I had not many things but one thing." Though she "doubt[s] whether at that time I had ever seen a cinema," she adds that "any one is of one's period and this our period was undoubtedly the period of the cinema and series production" (*LIA* 176–77).

32. Hawthorne, *Works* 6:16.

33. See "Executing the Model," Auerbach's pertinent study of *The Marble Faun*.

34. James placed the *Hawthorne* and *Story* diptych, in effect, within an even more extended polyptych, for the autobiographical self he covertly had represented in 1879 was the embryo of the self he overtly represented, in multiple guises and at multiple moments, in his later phase nonfiction: *William Wetmore Story*, *The American Scene*, the prefaces to the New York Edition, and the two volumes of his "Family Book," *A Small Boy and Others* and *Notes of a Son and Brother*. In these works, James shaped a portrait narration about himself as the exemplary artist of his generation, ultimately perched in 1914 on the edge of the abyss. And he placed that narration, as it were, within an even vaster polyptych that finds its prelude in *Roderick Hudson* (1875) and its postlude in *Within the Rim and Other Essays* (1918). Similarly, Stein extended the *Autobiography* into *Everybody's Autobiography*, into a diptych that frames, conceptually and chronologically, the diptych *Four in America* and *The Geographical History of America*, which, in turn, frames the diptych *Lectures in America* and *Narration*. Writing these texts serially, however, she too created an ongoing portrait narration in which she theorized writing, reading, and narration itself. And she too placed this narration within one even vaster: the three lives of uncelebrated women in *Three Lives* ironically anticipate the four lives of "eminent Americans" (*LGS/CVV* 280) in *Four in America*; and her autobiographies open onto her portrait of genius, *Picasso*, her portrait of place, *Paris France* (1940), and her memoir from her own point of view, *Wars I Have Seen* (1945).

35. Toklas, *Staying on Alone*, 84, 86.

36. Though Stein never explored the linkage between Hawthorne and James, nor proposed one between Hawthorne and herself, she did join Hawthorne and James briefly in the *Autobiography*, and then placed them with herself in lists of exemplary writers in *Lectures in America* and in *Narration* (*ABT* 163, *LIA* 51, *NAR* 10). In a letter to Sutherland, moreover, Toklas characterized James's description of Hawthorne's "democracy" in *Hawthorne* as perfectly applicable to Stein, suggesting that Toklas, at least, knew the text (*Staying on Alone*, 91, 92–93n).

37. See Poggioli, *Theory of the Avant-Garde*, 68–77; for citations, see 72, 75, 76.
38. Ibid., 76.

Chapter Two

1. For a discussion of the English Men of Letters series, see Nadel, *Biography*, 31–47; and see Nadel's comparison of James's *Hawthorne* and Trollope's *Thackeray*, both published in the series in 1879 (131–40). The comment about "representative men," Nadel's, appears on 39; Macmillan's comment is cited on 32.

Morley wrote James in 1878 that "there is no reason why we should not for the purposes of literature consider Americans as English"; and he went on to suggest the appropriateness of Irving or Hawthorne as possible subjects (*Correspondence of Henry James and the House of Macmillan*, 17–18). Nettels notes that *Hawthorne* was "the first book in the series by an American and the first book about an American writer" ("Henry James and the Art of Biography," 112); and Edmund Wilson, Trilling reminds us, had noted that *Hawthorne* was "the first extended study ever to be made of an American writer" (Trilling, "Hawthorne in Our Time," 179).

2. In a footnote appended to the third paragraph of his text, James "acknowledge[s] my large obligations" to Lathrop's work (322); and, in several subsequent passages, he cites or refers to this source (326, 347–48, 371, 379, 387, 396, 448). Though he later wrote his father that he thought *Hawthorne* "gentle and good-natured . . . , and to G. P. Lathrop I pay scarce anything but compliments" (*HJL* 2:263), other correspondence suggests truer feelings. While still finishing the book, he wrote Thomas Sargeant Perry that "G. P. Lathrop will *hate* it, and me for writing it; though I couldn't have done so without the aid (for dates and facts) of his own singularly foolish pretentious little volume" (*HJL* 2:255); and, having finished it, he again disparaged "poor little Lathrop" to Perry (*HJL* 2:274–75).

3. James published pieces on Hawthorne in 1872, 1879, 1896, and 1905, and discussed him as well in *William Wetmore Story* and in *Notes of a Son and Brother*. For a comparative discussion of these texts, see Buitenhuis, "Henry James on Hawthorne." The four autonomous pieces, including *Hawthorne*, appear in *LC* 2 and are cited in this chapter by page number only.

4. Though commentators agree that James mixed biography and criticism, they disagree on the nature of the mixture and on the focus produced. Compare, e.g., Nadel, *Biography*, 134–35; Nettels, "Henry James and the Art of Biography," 112–13; and Goetz, *Henry James and the Darkest Abyss of Romance*, 5.

5. Nettels rightly emphasizes the influence of Sainte-Beuve on James ("Henry James and the Art of Biography," 111); see, for example, James's remark that "the measure of my enjoyment of a critic is the degree to which he resembles Sainte-Beuve," made in his 1884 essay on Arnold (*LC* 2:723). James mentioned Taine in *Hawthorne* (367); and Arnold wrote James in 1879, "When will your Hawthorne be out? . . . That is a man I don't much care for, but I am sure to like what you say of him" (*HJ* 2:394).

6. Morley wrote to Macmillan in October 1878 that "James is working on the Haw-

thorne: but he has not yet answered my questions about biographical material which is a condition since given him" (Nadel, *Biography*, 35–36).

7. James's apparently simple biographical narrative actually breaks down into a governing narrative of Hawthorne as typical antebellum American, comprising subsidiary narratives of Hawthorne as social—or asocial—man and of Hawthorne as artist of genius. In the first, Hawthorne the New England boy, haunted by Puritan ancestors, reaches manhood in an America marked by absences; he finds his first employment as an American governmental official, takes up residence in a characteristically American experimental colony, and writes his central works about America; he has his first brush with antebellum national politics, sojourns abroad as an American consul, and repatriates himself to spend his final years as an "intense American" (448). In the second, Hawthorne the provincial boy with little social contact becomes a provincial and aloof collegian with few but lasting friendships; he matures into a still shy man wanting social relations and therefore being drawn into a communal social experiment, which he despises, and into marriage; and he eventually gains a public post, which he finds uncomfortable, so quits it for a return to private life and, indeed, rural privacy. In the third, Hawthorne the incipient artist of genius grows toward the first, tentative demonstration of his gifts; he experiences one native hiatus that fronts him with an alien philosophy but provides him with material, becomes a romantic artist of brilliance, experiences a foreign hiatus that fronts him with an alien culture but again provides material; and he finally attempts later works both disrupted and dwarfed by cataclysmic public events.

8. From James's moment to our own, distinguished commentators have approached *Hawthorne* as an important statement on American letters and on the American man of letters (see, e.g., Howells, "James's Hawthorne"; Eliot, "On Henry James," 112–19; Trilling, "Hawthorne in Our Time"; Matthiessen, *Achievement of T. S. Eliot*, 24 n. 6 and elsewhere; Matthiessen, *American Renaissance*, 351–68; Fussell, "Hawthorne, James and 'The Common Doom'"; Poirier, *World Elsewhere*, 93–143; Rowe, "What the Thunder Said"; Rowe, *Theoretical Dimensions of Henry James*, 30–57; Anesko, "Friction with the Market," 61–77; and Brodhead, *School of Hawthorne*, 134–39, 154–55, and elsewhere). From Eliot through Poirier, moreover, such commentators often treated the Hawthorne-James succession, and *Hawthorne* as its key document, in terms that anticipated the theoretical model of influence that Harold Bloom would elaborate in *Anxiety of Influence* and elsewhere (see, e.g., Eliot, "On Henry James," 112, 114, and Matthiessen, *Achievement of T. S. Eliot*, 9, 24 n. 6; Fussell, "Hawthorne, James and 'The Common Doom'"; Poirier, *World Elsewhere*, 99). Two major Jamesians have pronounced the Bloomian model inapplicable (see Donoghue, "Portrait of a Critic," 32; Tintner, *Book World of Henry James*, xxii), but that model has informed the best recent commentaries on *Hawthorne*, most explicitly Rowe's (see, e.g., Rowe, *Theoretical Dimensions of Henry James*, 49; Anesko, "Friction with the Market," 61–6; Brodhead, *School of Hawthorne*, 119–20, 139, 154–55).

9. Concluding on the note that "Hawthorne's work savours thoroughly of the local soil—it is redolent of the social system in which he had his being," James employs an analogy that matches vehicle/vehicle (savours/soil) not with tenor/tenor but with

vehicle/tenor (redolent/social system). As a result of this asymmetry, we know that soil stands for social system but we cannot know what "savours" means beyond its equally figurative synonym "redolent." We know only that this "redolence" occurs *because* "the man himself was so deeply rooted in the soil"—as James opens his third paragraph and his biographical chronicle proper (321–22).

10. In the third paragraph of his biography, Lathrop states that "the history of Hawthorne's genius is in some senses a summary of all New England history." He then develops an extended metaphor in which, amidst a practical community, "this fair flower of American genius rose up unexpectedly enough," but in which it also "sprang from seed that rooted in the old colonial life of the sternly imaginative pilgrims and Puritans" (*Study of Hawthorne*, 8). James's metaphor so closely approximates Lathrop's in its point, its construction, and even its phraseology that one is hard put to call it anything but plagiarized. Lathrop seems to have cobbled the metaphor himself, however, from the floral imagery that opens *The Scarlet Letter* together with the arboreal imagery that opens *The House of the Seven Gables*. Finally, as Trilling reminds us, Hawthorne "was at pains to revise his ancient family name [Hathorne] so that it would be more precisely that of a beautiful flower-bearing tree" ("Hawthorne in Our Time," 192).

11. In *Keywords*, Williams characterizes "culture" as "one of the two or three most complicated words in the English language," and proceeds to show how, by the late nineteenth century, it had come to apply not only to the tending of crops and animals but also "to a process of human development." Williams notes that Arnold not only employed, but also importantly elaborated, this latter application in his *Culture and Anarchy* (1867), a book we know James read by 1884 and can suspect he read much earlier. Finally, Williams proposes that the adjective "cultivated" followed the same metaphoric route, and that the adjective "cultural," in its modern usage, dates from the 1870s and was common by the 1890s (76–82). Needless to say, James not only was reflecting this lexical development, but also was advancing it.

12. "Hawthorne took with him to Italy, as he had done to England," James writes in 1896, "more of the old Puritan consciousness than he left behind" (465). Extending the point, he once again depicts a Hawthorne who maintained "aloofness wherever he is," who remained "outside of everything," remained "an alien everywhere," remained a social and "an aesthetic solitary" (467).

13. As James formulates this disemburdening, the Puritan sense of "sin" may have informed Hawthorne's conscience, but seems only an "imported" element in his mind, something employed for literary or artistic purposes, a "pigment" used in his composition. Hawthorne had "converted the very principle of [his ancestors'] own being into one of his toys" (363). Though commentators have noted this theme of aesthetic sportiveness, they have neglected the biographical matrix in which James embeds it: James notes that Hawthorne was lamed as a boy while playing ball (331), and that he was fined while at Bowdoin for playing cards for money—the latter event prompting a letter from Hawthorne to his sister declaring himself a *willing* player, a letter James cites and then glosses with a comment about "the personal character that underlay his duskily-sportive imagination" (334). This all sets up James's theme that Hawthorne's imagination was "always at play" (340). At one level, James was countering the image of

Hawthorne as a gloomy puritan. At a second level, he was linking play to fancy (and fancy to romance) in order to devalue fanciful romance as against serious realism. At a third, related, level, he was shaping the contrast between Hawthorne the amateur—who, James quotes him saying, wrote tales for "nothing but the pleasure itself of composition" (344–45)—and James the professional man of letters. And at a fourth level that I lack space to develop adequately, a level perhaps unconscious, he may have been inserting Hawthorne's leg injury and lameness not only into a cultural mythology that has Philoctetes as its linchpin, but also into a private mythology that has Henry James Sr.'s leg injury and James's own "horrid even if an obscure hurt" (*N* 298) as its linchpins.

14. Brodhead rightly notes that James's "focus is not on America or democracy as such but on the specific phase of cultural development America had attained in the 1830s and 1840s, in effect a post-colonial phase in which it had cut itself off from a foreign cultural center without having yet evolved maturely developed cultural institutions of its own" (*School of Hawthorne*, 136).

15. James's Lewis Lambert Strether, unlike Balzac's Louis Lambert, would "be thrown forward, . . . thrown quite with violence, upon his lifelong trick of intense reflexion" (*AN* 316).

16. James would begin his redaction of 1896 by referring to Hawthorne as a "man of letters" (458). That James neither qualified nor elaborated the phrase there suggests his increasing goodwill toward Hawthorne and his emphasis in the redaction on artistry rather than on critical thought; it also suggests the characteristic ease with which James used ideas as aesthetic touches that, as such, did not demand intellectual consistency.

17. James emphasizes the "absence of the realistic quality" in his opening paragraphs (320–21), and he later repeats that "Hawthorne, to say it again, was not in the least a realist—he was not to my mind enough of one" (369). He goes on to say that Hawthorne was not a realist in *The Scarlet Letter* (404), *The House of the Seven Gables* (412), or *The Marble Faun* (444).

18. James opposes to the "duskiness" of Hawthorne's background the clarity and lucidity of his work, but he quickly converts these terms into "thinness" and, especially, "coldness." "There is in all of [his writings]," he says early on, "something cold and light and thin, something belonging to the imagination alone" (339)—something especially evident in *The Scarlet Letter* (see 403–6). In 1874, James had characterized Flaubert's "picturesque" as "cold-blooded" because simultaneously grotesque and fastidious (*LC* 1:294); and, in 1885, he would characterize George Eliot's later novels as marked by the "coldness" that results when ideas replace experience (*LC* 2:1008).

19. So much commentary has accrued on this passage, and on its relation to its *urtext* in the preface to *The Marble Faun*, that I restrict myself to the observation that readers frequently mistake "American humour" as that which remains. Rather, "American humour" enables—indeed, causes—the American to keep as "his secret, his joke," that which remains. As an American, James himself plays the joke on his English readers.

20. See Howells, "James's Hawthorne" and James's epistolary response (*HJL* 2:266–68); and compare, for example, Howells's assessment of James in this period as a realist perhaps too devoted to the "art" of fiction, with James's assessment of Howells as a

realist perhaps too committed to the proposition "that truth of representation . . . can be achieved only so long as it is in our power to test and measure it" (*LC* 2:502).

21. In a moment of deterministic thinking, James attributes this disposition to "the fact that [Hawthorne] lived in the most democratic and most virtuous of modern communities," Salem "at the beginning of the present century" (330).

22. Lathrop, who was Hawthorne's son-in-law, devotes only one sentence to Hawthorne's engagement and one to his marriage (*Study of Hawthorne*, 181, 199); by contrast, Hawthorne's son Julian would publish *Nathaniel Hawthorne and His Wife* (1884) as well as *Hawthorne and His Circle* (1903). In the shift from critical to intimate biography, the figure of Hawthorne shifted from alienated solitary to integrated social being.

23. James brought this tendency to an extreme in *A Small Boy and Others* and *Notes of a Son and Brother*; and he defended it vigorously in letters to his nephew regarding the latter (see *HJL* 4:793–804, and *Letters of Henry James*, ed. Lubbock, 2:298–92; and see Holly, "'Absolutely Acclaimed,'" 136 n. 10, and, especially, "Family Politics of the 'Family Book'").

24. In 1879, however, James could not have known the very nasty passage about Fuller that Sophia Peabody Hawthorne had excised from her edition of Hawthorne's *French and Italian Note-Books*, but that Julian Hawthorne would include in his *Hawthorne and His Wife* (Hawthorne, *Works* 14:259–62).

25. Specifically, James notes that "the Transcendentalists read a great deal of French and German, made themselves intimate with George Sand and Goethe, and many other writers" (380–81); James had reservations about Sand, though not, apparently, about Goethe (see his 1865 review of Carlyle's translation of *Wilhelm Meister*, *LC* 1:944–49).

26. In his redaction of 1896, James again used "experimental" to refer to literary and to social productions (459 and 464, respectively). Given his ambivalences toward French Naturalism in general and toward Emile Zola in particular, we might note that his use of "experimental" as a literary term differs considerably from Zola's use of it in "*Le Roman experimental*" (1880). James used the term to mean the testing of aesthetic possibilities for the novel, while Zola used it to mean the testing of social-scientific hypotheses in the novel.

27. James must have noticed that Hawthorne's two central acts of human fellowship led directly to the two most public episodes of his life and these, ironically, to his two most intense periods of alienation: his engagement necessitated, for financial reasons, his sojourn at Brook Farm; and his friendship with Pierce enabled his sojourn in Europe. James apparently uses this irony to underscore his depiction of the artist as essential loner whose proper social sphere remains the private rather than the public.

28. In the review essay on Emerson, James repeated several points made in *Hawthorne*; see, e.g., his description of "New England fifty years ago" (*LC* 2:254, 259).

29. James explicitly thematizes partiality of perspective on two occasions; see his comments on Salem (327) and on Bowdoin (332).

30. Lathrop, *Study of Hawthorne*, 7. In the opening chapter, "Point of View," and under the page headline, "Perspective," Lathrop defines his goals in terms strikingly similar to those James would employ: "It is by briefly reviewing that past, then trying to reproduce in imagination the immediate atmosphere of Hawthorne's youth, and com-

paring the two, that we shall best arrive at the completion of our proposed portrait. We have first to study the dim perspective and the suggestive coloring of that historic background from which the author emerges, and then to define clearly his own individual traits as they appear in his published works and *Note-Books*" (13).

31. In his earlier hack period, moreover, Hawthorne had written *Biographical Studies for Children* (1842).

32. Though James claims that antebellum America undervalued artists, he also claims that then, as now, artists were "received on easier terms [in America] than in other countries," that "if the tone of the American world is in some respects provincial, it is in none more so than in this matter of the exaggerated homage rendered to authorship" (342). Quite simply, James has eliminated from the American response the proper middle ground of discrimination.

33. For a discussion of Hawthorne and Trollope as complementary precursors, see Rowe, *Theoretical Dimensions of Henry James*, 29–83. Rowe acknowledges that one would have to add Balzac, "the father of us all," as James famously called him in 1905 (*LC* 1:120).

34. James improved his position, in fact, by subtly undercutting his praise for both Arnold and Taine. Elsewhere remarking Taine's quintessentially French passion for ideas, for example, James then criticized him as a thinker while commending "the literary quality of his genius" (*LC* 1:852).

35. Hawthorne favored the term "actual" and its cognates in his discussions of romance (see, e.g., *Works* 5:55, 321–22; 6:15), and James followed suit in his discussions of realism in *Hawthorne* (see, e.g., 444); each writer used the term to mean not only *real* as opposed to unreal but also, and simultaneously, *current* as opposed to past.

36. Fredrickson treats James's *Hawthorne* in the Prologue of his justly celebrated study; he takes James to task for "viewing Nathaniel Hawthorne as a representative American responding to the crisis," and argues that "James went astray . . . in suggesting that Hawthorne had a typical ante-bellum mentality and that consequently his response to the war was characteristic of 'that earlier and simpler generation.' The fact was that Hawthorne's reaction was unique; he was the only notable writer or thinker who took a detached and critical view of the Union cause" (*Inner Civil War*, 1–2). Though correct to say that James treated Hawthorne as representative of a mentality, Fredrickson misreads James's treatment of Hawthorne's response to the Civil War, and thus fails to see James's inconsistency: James treats Hawthorne's response as atypical, as unpopular, and as needing explanation.

37. My line of thought here was prompted by Buitenhuis's comment that James saw the Civil War as the first American fall, mass immigration as the second (*Grasping Imagination*, 189).

38. On the same day, James wrote Frederick Macmillan that he "was just sending Morley my long-delayed *Hawthorne*," and, two weeks later, he wrote Macmillan that he had, "at last, some days since, consigned my *Hawthorne* to Morley" (*Correspondence of Henry James and the House of Macmillan*, 41, 42). In a long autobiographical journal entry dated 25 November 1881, James referred to having "stayed in London during all August [1879], writing my little book on Hawthorne," and to having "finished the ill-fated little *Hawthorne*" soon after in Paris (*Complete Notebooks*, 219).

39. For an accounting of the many contemporary reviews of *Hawthorne*, see Taylor, *Henry James*, 38–59.

40. Actually, James varied his attributions of difficulty according to subject: Story was too thin (*William Wetmore Story*); America was both too vast and too simplified (*The American Scene*); the origins of his own works were too obscure, and the processes of completing the works too complex (the prefaces to the New York Edition); his childhood was too distant, his memory too uncontrollable (*A Small Boy and Others*, *Notes of a Son and Brother*).

41. Employing Coleridge's distinction, James notes that Hawthorne prefers fancy to imagination, the latter "the larger and more potent faculty" (365). Though Hawthorne has "the genius of a man of fancy" (373), then, though "his most beautiful organ [is] his admirable fancy" (395), both his manhood and his organ seem lacking. More overt in his reactions to his critics, James wrote Charles Eliot Norton on 31 March 1880, that the "very big tempest in a very small tea-pot" produced by *Hawthorne* "seems to me like the clucking of a brood of prairie-hens. My critics, either literally or essentially, seem to me all to have been of the hen-sex" (*HJL* 2:280). For a provocative, though arguably essentialist, reading of Hawthorne's use of notebooks as "female," James's as "male," see Banta, " 'There's Surely a Story in It,' " 163.

42. In the opening line of an essay from 1886, James speaks of Howells as "a man of letters" and refers, in the same paragraph, to his "so called 'campaign' biography of Abraham Lincoln" (*LC* 2:498). Since he wants to portray Howells not as an artist, but as a professional man of letters, he treats this biography without irony.

43. Comparing the conclusions of *Hawthorne* and of the redaction of 1896, however, one can see how James changed Hawthorne from a moralist who employed fancy into a writer of fancy who employed moral themes (*LC* 2:457, 468).

44. *Essays in London and Elsewhere*, 12.

45. Hawthorne, *Works* 5:63.

Chapter Three

1. In notebook entries of 11 December 1904 and of 29 March 1905, James included Story among his small circle of Cambridge ghosts (*Complete Notebooks*, 236, 340); when he converted those notes into the Cambridge section of *The American Scene*, however, he retained references to Lowell, Longfellow, and Howells but dropped those to Story (*The American Scene*, 68–71).

2. James's stress was on "vanity," designated rather preciously as "what an impertinent little word stands for, beginning with *v* and ending with *y*" (*HJL* 1:353).

3. James refers, for example, to dining with Story in London in 1877 and in Rome in 1880 (*HJL* 2:129, 288); he also lacked a high opinion of Story's sons Julian and Waldo (see *HJL* 3:43 and 4:106).

4. In correspondence of this period, James frequently invoked the spectral to figure his nostalgia; he wrote to Sarah Butler Wister, for example, of "the tramping *ghosts* of other years" as his "principal company . . . more numerous now than the present and the palpable" (*HJL* 4:259).

5. James had accepted the *Hawthorne* commission in 1878 despite the prior publication of Lathrop's biographical study, but he argued in 1902 that Horace Scudder's *James Russell Lowell* (1901), Charles Eliot Norton's edition of Lowell's letters (1894), and "the profuse journalistic attention" given Lowell in his lifetime together leave "not much *remainder* of subject, of career and material generally, to treat." With the life already told, a study of Lowell would have to focus on "criticism and 'appreciation,' " and with noted exceptions, Lowell's "few volumes are themselves only critical work, literary and political" (*HJL* 4:262–63).

Scudder's biography had been published by Houghton Mifflin; James did not mention, however, Edward Everett Hale's *James Russell Lowell and His Friends*, also published by Houghton Mifflin in 1901, a group biography more similar in type to *Story* (see Hale, iii). In this volume, Hale cites an anonymous member of the Lowell-Story Harvard circle giving thumbnail sketches of the others, including Story: "W. W. S., versatile and vivacious, a capital mimic, an adept at bright nonsense and gay repartee" (74).

6. Rather than clutter subsequent notes with repeated dates and parenthetical citations, I shall list here recipients, dates, and page references (all letters from *HJL* 4): Francis Boott, 11 October 1895, 23–24; W. E. Norris, 4 February 1896, 26–28; William Blackwood, 28 October 1897, 59; Mrs. Waldo Story, 17 June 1899, 107–8; William Dean Howells, 25 January 1902, 221–25; Sarah Butler Wister, 21 and 23 December 1902, 258–62; Houghton Mifflin and Co., 29 December 1902, 262–64; Henry Adams, 19 November 1903, 288–89; Anne Thackeray Ritchie, 19 November 1903, 290–91; Millicent, Duchess of Sutherland, 23 December 1903, 302–3. Edel omitted an important letter to Mrs. Waldo Story dated 6 January 1903 (*Letters of Henry James*, ed. Lubbock, 1:411–13), and Maves cites another letter from James to her, dated 1914, that refers to *Story* (*Sensuous Pessimism*, 164–65 n. 14). An additional letter concerning *Story*, written to F. Marian Crawford on 19 November 1903, recently appeared on the market; see Batchelder, *Autographs*, unpaginated.

7. On his declining such assignments, see, e.g., a recently auctioned series of letters from James to Robert Underwood Johnson, editor of *Century Magazine*, excerpted in Christie's *Modern Literature*, 61; after mentioning " 'creative work,' " James excuses himself for the "priggish phrase." On James's leasing of Lamb House in 1897 and purchasing of it in 1899, see *HJ* 4:196–200, 319–20, and Gale, *Henry James Encyclopedia*, 373.

James, clearly, no more relished the *Story* assignment than he had the *Hawthorne*. He wrote to Norris in 1896 that the "proposal" from Rome, presumably to visit the Story archive and to fashion the biography, "said little" to him; he could not "give up unremunerated months to a job" he was "not at all keen to undertake," and he had, moreover, "two novels to write before I can *dream* of anything else." When he wrote to Blackwood in 1897 to arrange terms for the book, he added that he would not "get at the business (be at all *able* to) immediately," but would "attack it at my very first leisure." In 1899, however, he was writing Mrs. Waldo Story from Sorrento "to report progress" but also to explain his "delay" in travel arrangements for visits to Rome and to Florence; and in 1903, he wrote her again to explain on technical grounds his considerable delay in producing the book.

8. As the time for writing drew near, James wrote Howells that he had "suffered to be gouged out of me long ago by the Waldo Storys ... a promise first to 'look at' the late W. W. S[tory's] papers and then to write a memorial volume of some sort about him"; and nearly two years later, having completed the job, he wrote Adams of how "the Waldo Storys absolutely *thrust* the job upon me five, six, *seven* years ago." He had written Wister, somewhat more sedately, of "how four or five years ago the Waldo Storys tackled me on the subject of making some use of W.W.S.'s papers"; and he would write to the Dutchess of Sutherland, more sedately still, of "the amiable pressure of his [Story's] children."

9. James wrote Houghton Mifflin that he was "doing my best for *him* [Story]," and hoped to produce "an entertaining book." To Howells he had spoken of the need to "Please the Family too!," but "hope[d] not to be kept Pleasing it more than three or four months"; and he would tell Adams that "someone has just written to ask me if the family 'like it,' and I have replied that I think they don't know whether they like it or not! They are waiting to find out—and I am glad on the whole they haven't access to *you*." He had spoken to Wister of his "putting together a nondescript memorial volume," one that he hoped, nonetheless, might be "sufficiently agreeable and *nourri*"; and to Mrs. Waldo Story, he wrote that the book will be "an agreeable and, in a literary sense, really artistic and honourable" one, and added that "once the Book is out" he should want to see her family and doesn't think he "shall fear to."

10. James likewise wrote Wister that "W.W.S. is, on a near view (as he was from afar!) thinner than thin—as a theme for 'literature and art'"; he wrote Anne Thackeray Ritchie of "the difficult job it was with my so meagre material"; and he wrote the Duchess of Sutherland of his "operation of making bricks without straw and chronicling (sometimes) rather small beer with the effect of opening champagne. Story was the dearest of men, but he wasn't massive, his artistic and literary baggage were of the slightest and the materials for a biography *nil*."

11. For a relevant comment on group biography, see Nadel, *Biography*, 191–92.

12. For Wells's verdict, see "Of Art, of Literature, of Mr. Henry James"; for William James's, see his responses to *The Golden Bowl* and to *The American Scene*, in Matthiessen, *James Family*, 339, 341–42; and see *Letters of William James* 2:277–80. In his correspondence and in his prefaces to the New York Edition, James often alluded to his ability to make a great deal of very little; that, indeed, is the boast implicit in his "germ" metaphor of fictional sources (see, e.g., *AN* 119–22). For a phenomenological analysis of James's absent centers, see Poulet, *Metamorphoses of the Circle*, 307–20; for a structuralist analysis of them, see Todorov, *Poetics of Prose*, 143–89. Todorov, incidentally, focuses on the trope of the spectral.

13. James had used "bookmaking" in precisely this sense in an 1875 review of the compilation, *Thackerayana, Notes and Anecdotes* (*LC* 2:1286). In his correspondence concerning *Story*, he conflated the idea that he had to make a book from archival material with the idea that he had to make an interesting book from essentially uninteresting material. He wrote to Wister, for example, "that one has had to (very artfully and ingeniously) invent a way, a *biais* for doing anything with him [Story]. But some of the materials they have given me *are* interesting." He wrote to Houghton Mifflin that "the subject, owing to its intrinsic slightness, has been all to *make*—to make by a system

of importation of helpful material *into* it, by a system, as it were, of manufactured interest which has really required a diabolical art." And he wrote to Anne Thackeray Ritchie that he "*had* to invent an attitude (of general evocation and discursiveness) to fill out the form of a book at all."

14. James recognized the dangers of an archival biographer's putting herself or himself too much in the foreground. In 1866, he criticized Elizabeth Gaskell's *Life of Charlotte Brontë* because "it tells the reader considerably more about Mrs. Gaskell than about Miss Brontë" (*LC* 2:1019); and in 1874, he criticized Gautier's biographer because "we get a more lively sense of M. Feydeau's own personality than of that of his weightier friend" (*LC* 1:378). Nonetheless, he entertained other possibilities for manipulating the genre. On the one hand, he criticized Anna LeBreton's *Correspondence of William Ellery Channing, D.D., and Lucy Aiken* (1875) on the grounds that "the letters were presumably published for the sake, mainly, of Dr. Channing's memory, but their effect is to throw his correspondent into prominent relief" (*LC* 2:213); but, on the other hand, he praised the Reverend T. P. Hodgson's 1879 memorial volume for his father, the Reverend Francis Hodgson, for having "written his father's life upon a very unusual plan," namely, in the absence of his father's correspondence, he provided that of his father's correspondents, principally Lord Byron (*LC* 2:815).

15. James, *Literary Reviews and Essays*, 237–39.

16. Subsequent references to *Story* in this chapter will cite volume and page number only.

17. Critical commentary on *Story* has been scant, with much of it concentrated in the 1980s. Early articles that comment on the book include Croly, "Henry James and His Countrymen" (1904), and Kenton, "Henry James and the World" (1934). Recent articles focused exclusively or extensively on *Story* include Hynes, "Transparent Shroud" (1975); Nettels, "Henry James and the Art of Biography" (1978); Solimine, "Henry James, William Wetmore Story, and Friend" (1980); Wadman, "*William Wetmore Story*" (1981); Redford, "Keeping Story Out of History" (1985); Jones, "Telling His Own Story" (1987); Marijane Rountree Davis, " 'Fine Bewilderment' " (1988); and Donoghue, "*William Wetmore Story and His Friends*" (1990). Recent books with pertinent commentary include Sayre, *Examined Self* (1964); Buitenhuis, *Grasping Imagination* (1970); Edel, *HJ 4: The Master* (1972); Nadel, *Biography* (1984); Posnock, *Henry James and the Problem of Robert Browning* (1985); and Przybylowicz, *Desire and Repression* (1986).

Examining these and other sources, one is struck by the attention paid to genre, and, particularly, by the constant qualification of the term "biography." Edel and Nadel have expressed opposite views on the quality of biographical research in *Story* (*HJ* 2:89, 5:157; Nadel, *Biography*, 135); Dupee and, especially, Nettels have related *Story* to James's portraiture (Dupee, *Henry James*, 24; Nettels, "Henry James and the Art of Biography," 107); Holly has related it to the autoportraiture of *The American Scene* ("Henry James's Autobiographical Fragment," 175); and Jones has posed the question most frequently on commentators' minds: "Is it, in fact, autobiography, not biography?" ("Telling His Own Story," 241). Sayre was the first to argue that *Story* focuses more on James than on Story (*Examined Self*, 79); a decade later, Hynes reprised the argument in a slightly different context ("Transparent Shroud," 508, 523); and a decade after that, in three consecutive years, Redford, Przybylowicz, and Jones extended the argument—Przybylowicz into overstatement (Redford, "Keeping Story Out of History," 224; Przybylowicz, *Desire and Repression*, 232, 233, 274; Jones, "Telling His Own Story," 246). Taking a different slant, Wadman, Solimine, and Posnock have argued that *Story* attends conspicuously to Browning—Wadman overstating the case (Wadman, "*William Wetmore Story*," 210, 218; Solimine, "Henry James, William Wetmore Story, and Friend," throughout; Posnock, *Henry James and the Problem of Robert Browning*, 32). Dupee and Nettels, finally, have placed *Hawthorne* and *Story* together (Dupee, *Henry James*, 24; Nettels, "Henry James and the Art of Biography," 107 and elsewhere); but only Kenton, in her signal 1934 essay on "dispatriation" ("Henry James and the World"), has developed the connection. No one has explored how James extended the artistic and, especially, political themes of *Hawthorne* into the international context of *Story*.

18. Hynes also made this point in "Transparent Shroud," 512.

19. In 1878, James commented negatively on the absence of such page headings in Frances Anne Kemble's *Record of a Girlhood* (*LC* 2:1069). Of his own works, only *The American Scene* seems also to have had them, and James complained furiously to his agent Pinker of "their [the Harpers'] real *mutilation* of my volume by the perfectly wanton suppression of the page headlines. I had supplied them with all ingenuity and care ... and these indications of the contents and subject of successive pages ... were—and are—an essential element in the readability of the book" (*HJL* 4:448).

20. Only Gale cites James's letter to Mrs. Waldo Story (*Henry James Encyclopedia*, 727).

21. For a case study of how "mid-nineteenth-century editorial practices" differed from ours today, see Hudspeth and Myerson, "Editing Margaret Fuller's Letters"; for a feminist analysis of motives and effects of such practices, in the case of Emily Dickinson, see Martha Nell Smith, *Rowing in Eden*; for evidence of James's employment of such practices, see Habegger, "Henry James's Rewriting of Minny Temple's Letters."

22. For the essay most insistent on *Story*'s "decentralization," see Redford, "Keeping Story Out of History," e.g., 217, 220; for an essay claiming that *Story* finds its "true centre" in Browning, see Wadman, "*William Wetmore Story*," e.g., 210, 218.

23. Very few commentators have noted the degree to which *Story* concerns social and political history, I think, because most commentators attend far more closely to the narrative advanced in James's connective tissue of prose than to the archival materials that actually constitute the bulk of the book. James's narrative primarily explores the artistic and the domestic; the correspondence and journals of the Storys, and the correspondence of the Brownings, the Lowells, Margaret Fuller, Charles Eliot Norton, and Charles Sumner contain much discussion of contemporary social and political issues.

24. Story's was a "rather markedly typical case," albeit "typical with many qualifications" (1:12); James "cannot help" treating Story's "career" as a "case" (1:13); and so on. In a pertinent assessment, James later praises Story's bronze of the Honorable Edward Everett as "happily conceived both as a portrait of the man and as a presentment of the speaker.... No monumental portrait, as I remember this one, could characterise more closely while remaining conscious of the need to generalise nobly" (2:167–68).

25. James used the same romantic language of internal generation when describing Story's friends: "Irresistible in Sumner is the way he gives himself out, irresistible in Lowell the way he . . . keeps himself in" (1:234).

26. At one point, ironically, James cites Lowell writing to Story that their "early associations . . . would seem very poor stuff to most, indeed to all, who had not been actors therein or witnesses" (1:182–83).

27. Despite the negatives, however, James also acknowledges that Story's workshop, containing copies of all his sculptures, presents a "close record of his persistent unfolding. It is pre-eminently the history of a worker, of a man who, whether in felicity or in frustration, required of himself all he had to give" (2:169). As Hynes rightly notes, this "is no mean compliment, coming from Henry James, though it may be the principal compliment he can offer" ("Transparent Shroud," 520).

28. Though Story twice complains about being called an "amateur" (2:74, 171), he also complains about American artists living in Rome who see art as a trade, and says he has no sympathy "with those who are artists merely to make their living" (2:149). The ideal, obviously, was to be a professional who had no financial need to be one.

29. James was echoing something deeply autobiographical with this characterization of Story's "death-blow." See his poignant description of his own father's death, a few months after his mother's, because "nothing . . . was in the least worth while without her" (*N* 178).

30. James constructed *The Golden Bowl*, as he would say in the prefaces to the New York Edition, on the premise that "the Prince, in the first half of the book, virtually sees and knows and makes out, virtually represents to himself everything that concerns us. . . . The function of the Princess, in the remainder, matches exactly with his" (*AN* 329). Obviously, he could not have gone that far with an archival memoir. For a discussion of Story and *The Golden Bowl*, see Marijane Rountree Davis, "'Fine Bewilderment.'"

31. James uses "friends" in various ways: he sometimes refers to persons that he, as a younger man, knew—as when he recalls "friends in common, figures of the Florentine legend" (2:95); he sometimes refers to the ghosts that importune him, that importune the figurative wanderer in the underworld; he often uses the word in the polite, formulaic way epitomized in his final paragraph, where "our friend" takes on a eulogistic cast; and he very often uses the phrase "our friends" in a way that extends his social "circles" to include his reader. Not surprisingly, he evokes Story's nostalgia for friends still at home (see 1:253, 256, 265), and, later, for friends deceased (see 2:61–62, 283).

32. For an illustration of how James, even as a young reviewer, sympathized with biographers facing complex marital issues, see his three reviews of Theodore Martin's serial *Life of His Royal Highness the Prince Consort* (*LC* 2:1158–68).

33. Compare the peripatetic Story with Lady William Russell, one of "the interesting women who have only to sit still to find themselves a centre of life" (2:190).

Story belongs to one circle comprising himself, Lowell, and Sumner and defined by American nationality, and to another circle comprising himself, Browning, and Walter Savage Landor and defined, though less obviously, by Italophilia. The American nationality that puts him in the first circle keeps him anomalous in the second, whose members are British subjects; while his lifelong residence in Italy makes him anomalous not only in the first circle, whose other members are repatriated Americans, but, in fact, also in the second circle, whose other members are cosmopolitan Britons.

34. James likewise characterizes Harriet Hosmer as "destined, whatever statues she made, to make friends that were better still even than these at their best" (1:258).

35. In *The Marble Faun*, Miriam apparently speaks for Hawthorne when she dismisses sculptors as inherently plagiaristic, and when she then goes on to argue how "difficult [it is] to compress and define a character or a story, and make it potent at a glance, within the narrow scope attainable by sculpture!" (Hawthorne, *Works* 4:151). In his writings on Hawthorne, in turn, James advanced the argument that Hawthorne's "curious aversion to the representation of the nude in sculpture" amounted to a failure to appreciate the essentially *formal* quality of sculpture itself (see *LC* 2:311, 441), an argument he directed in *Story* not at a writer who failed to appreciate sculpture, but at a professional sculptor who failed, finally, to appreciate the essence of his own medium: Story's "fondness for the draped body and his too liberal use of drapery" reflected not only a prudery that, like Hawthorne, he shared with his clientele, but also a maladroitness with the elemental human shape (see 2:80–83).

Hawthorne had used Story and his *Cleopatra* as models for *The Marble Faun*, and James used *The Marble Faun*, in turn, as a model for *William Wetmore Story*—referring to Hawthorne's romance in relation to Story, indeed, on two occasions (1:357–58; 2:84–87). James also links Hawthorne and Story as writers of guidebooks to Rome—conjuring "generations of tourists, with Hawthorne's beautiful novel in their hand" (1:343), and conjuring those same tourists, including himself as a young man, clutching Story's *Roba di Roma* (2:130–35); and, in effect, he links them to himself, the biographer who had told Howells, we recall, that he would "make a little volume on the old Roman, Americo-Roman, Hawthornesque and other bygone days, that the intending, and extending, tourist will, in his millions, buy" (*HJL* 4:225).

36. James does credit Story with one clear success, however. He praises Story as sculptor *and* poet, indeed, for the joint success of his "two Cleopatras," statue and verse; in them, Story did "*insist*" (2:217).

37. James rehearses Story's visit to the United States in 1882, for example, and his execution of the John Marshall and Joseph Henry statues (2:268–69); he also notes Story's refusal to enter the competition for the Grant memorial (2:299); and he cites Story's opinion of the Washington Monument as the "ugliest" obelisk in the world, "unable to compete, for anything like beauty, even with many a factory chimney" (2:302). In his most complimentary moment in these passages, James finds that "Story worked bravely on" in the face of "conditions . . . the reverse of inspiring," made "the best of the dire ordeal of the sculptor fighting for his idea, fighting for his life, or for that of his work, with an insensible, an impenetrable, a fatal committee" (2:296–97).

Anyone living in the nation's capital, I think, would remain circumspect about the attitude toward Story expressed by Edel and echoed by most literary commentators, to wit, "Story's sculptures rest in the deepest basements of the art museums, and few pause to look at his public statues" (*HJ* 4:160). Though my point about the relative unimportance of Story's commissions stands, the fact remains that his *Libyan Sibyl* occupies a prominent spot in the National Museum of American Art; his statue of

Joseph Henry stands directly in front of the main building of the Smithsonian Institution, and, consequently, stands prominently on the Mall; and his statue of John Marshall stands as the focal point of the new Judiciary Square (the last placement occurring later than Edel's biography).

38. James not only set a good deal of his fiction in Italy, but also, between 1872 and 1909, wrote twenty-two essays eventually collected as *Italian Hours* (1909). See, for example, Maves, *Sensuous Pessimism*; MacDonald, *Henry James's "Italian Hours"*; Tuttleton and Lombardo, eds., *Sweetest Impression of Life*; and *Italian Hours*, ed. Auchard. As it happens, Story and James appeared back to back in the collection *The Great Streets of the World* (Richard Harding Davis et al., 1892), Story's "The Corso of Rome" followed by James's "The Grand Canal."

39. Though Rome has the same status in *Story* that Paris would have in *The Autobiography of Alice B. Toklas*, James makes it his explicit topic on five occasions only. Speaking first of *The Rome of Other Years* (to use his relevant page headlines), specifically the years before 1871, James begins his treatment of Rome as the background of a canvas, as the stage for dramatic action, or, in a conflation of the tropes, as the subject of a canvas that serves as a backdrop on a stage (1:93–94). He next introduces the important motif of *The Roman Air*, the "golden" air that made Rome "the aesthetic antidote to the ugliness of the rest of the world—that is, of Anglo-Saxondom in especial" (1:331). That air produced *The Roman Spell* that beguiled Story, but that does not constitute, James hastens to keep the touch light, "any analysed treason" (1:333–34). Indeed, James includes himself, in *The Sense of Rome*, as one of the spellbound, one who still must "brave even the imputation of making a mere Rome of words, talking of a Rome of my own which was no Rome of reality" (2:209); and he must brave this, finally, as he intimates in *The Roman Touch*, because, of all cities, "it was only the Roman touch that was fine" (2:211). Having earlier suggested that Rome was "provincial" in comparison to Paris (1:173–74), he here compares its fine touch with the "coarse" touch of London, Paris, and New York (2:209, 211), his point apparently being that Rome before 1871 had a provincial charm lost in its emergence as a modern capital. Though one rarely finds reference to *William Wetmore Story* outside of James scholarship, Tony Tanner aptly used James's passage about writing "a mere Rome of words" as the epigraph to his study of post–World War II American fiction, *City of Words*.

40. The parallel was common in nineteenth-century political thought. Margaret Fuller, in Elizabeth Hardwick's words, changed "her thoughts about political agitation . . . when she began to connect the antislavery movement with the liberation of Italy" ("Genius of Margaret Fuller," 19); and Jane Addams recounts in *Twenty Years at Hull House* (1910) a childhood incident in which she learned "the genuine relationship which may exist . . . between groups of men who are trying to abolish slavery in America or to throw off Hapsburg oppression in Italy" (31–32).

41. Story and Lowell, indeed, appear of one mind. Story finds Holy Week "humbug," the pope engaged in "solemn farce," the crowd "garlic-smelling, fetid," the pilgrims "the rummest set of customers I ever saw, stupid, dirty and bestial in their appearance"; but, Story adds, "To hear Allegri's Miserere in the Sistine Chapel with the awful and mighty figures of Michael Angelo looking down on one from the ceiling, to hear Guglielmi's Miserere in St. Peter's while the gloom of evening was gathering in the lofty

aisles and shrouding the frescoed domes, was no humbug, but a deeply affecting and solemnly beautiful experience" (1:100–101). For his part, Lowell likes the Italian clime and ruins, but adds that "if you mention political changes, Italy has been getting herself born again ever since I can remember," allows that he has two watchmen who "could put to flight the Pope's whole civic guard," and generally finds uninteresting whether "Noodle VI. sits on the throne of the two Sicilies or Loafer XXI. in the grand-ducal chair of Florence." The ancient Romans, evidently like their modern counterparts, were thieves who "stole everything," with the exception of one god, "and he was a two-faced one, an emblem of the treacherous disposition of the people" (1:103–5).

42. The Storys visit Florence during its revolutions, and Emelyn Story finds the Florentines "vulgar and ignorant people" (1:120); soon after in Leghorn: "the people here ... look like pickpockets, knaves, and fools. The women *mere* fools." It is a "purgatorial environment" (1:121). Returning to Rome, they go to watch the "barricade-making at Porta San Giovanni," where "they 'vote the workmen too lazy to live'" (1:134). Story's diary, similarly, begins with an assessment of "the Italian character" as being like the Tiber, "turbulent without depth," and so on, and goes on to note the defeat and abdication of Charles Albert: "What a people! Never is a battle without a *tradimento*" (1:143–45). When the French land at Civitavecchia, Story belittles the response of "the Romans, who are as easily scared as a flock of sheep" (1:151). With these "racial" character studies, of course, the Storys characterize themselves as bigots.

43. One must note, however, that James also ambiguates the revolutionary Princess Belgiojoso in the same way that he ambiguates the radical Sumner, though more harshly. Seeking refuge in the interrogative, James asks, "was she not . . . at once a sincere, a passive crusader and a 'bounder,' . . . of the real bounding temperament?"; then identifying her as "romantic, so to speak, in spite of herself," he ties her to his overarching theme of naive romanticism (1:162). He uses Margaret Fuller toward a related thematic end, one in which the domestic sphere intersects the public. Frequently referring to her as Mme. Ossoli, he ties her marriage to Ossoli (James assumes it) to her work on Italian liberation, both acts depicted as romantic.

44. See Hawthorne, *Works* 4:15.

45. Citing comments by Story critical of abolitionism, identifying them as examples of a contemporary "Northern *malaise* on the Slavery question," James remarks that such malaise took the form "it was still long to keep throughout the conservative north—that of soreness under the great blot on the American scutcheon, cultivating as a counter-irritant a soreness under crude reform." He then advances his defense of a "'quiet' people . . . rather pitifully ground between the two millstones of the crudity of the 'peculiar institution' on the one side and the crudity of impatient agitation against it on the other" (see 1:60–64).

46. Describing the funeral procession of John Quincy Adams in 1848, for example, Lowell chides that "the anti-slavery feeling of New England will bring up the rear of the cortége in a single carriage" (1:107); and a year later, he reminds Story of his fortnightly column in the "Anti-slavery Standard" (1:179).

47. As Story had direct access to Mazzini (1:157), Sumner had direct access to Cavour (2:36); yet both, James intimates, still held rather commonplace and pedestrian views. As Story, in 1849, had assisted at the siege of Rome from a balcony in Casa Dies (1:135),

Sumner, in 1859, assisted at Louis-Napoleon's entry into Paris, "the most imposing spectacle," from "a balcony *au premier*" (2:44). Sumner's scathing comments on Louis-Napoleon in this chapter (2:42), finally, anticipate those of Story in the next (2:125).

48. In a notebook entry for 16 May 1899, James tried out an opening for *Story*: "For W. W. Story. Beginning. 'The writer of these pages—(the scribe of this pleasant history?) is well aware of coming late in the day . . . BUT the very gain by what we see, *now*, in the contrasted conditions, of happiness of old Rome of the old days.' X X X X X" (*Complete Notebooks*, 183). More direct here than in the omnubulatory opening he finally did write, he had found his germ: he placed himself at the beginning, followed by awareness of belatedness; he set *perception in the present of Rome in the past* as one half of an opposition whose elided half was doubtless *perception in the past of Rome in the past*; and, in his initial indecision about nomenclature, he even anticipated his later uncertainty about auctorial role and literary genre.

49. Generally, James characterizes himself as one who "observed" and who now "chronicles" what he observed. More specifically, he becomes the "introducer" or "presenter" of documentary material, that pertaining to events he did not witness and reflecting consciousnesses to which, of course, he lacks other access; he becomes the "embroiderer" of that material, his embroidery consisting, primarily, in the "fancy" he applies to those documents and in the "memories" he invokes with respect to them; and he becomes the "author" or "writer" of all the additional connective tissue that he has supplied, prose going far beyond "introduction" and pertaining to himself as much as to Story and friends (all terms in quotation marks are James's). Though he refers to himself most often as a "chronicler" (1:224; 2:30, 166, 198), he also appears as a "student of manners" (1:5; 2:190), a "historian" (2:196), and a "prose-painter of life" (2:197); he is a "restless critic" (2:247) of the type that would dominate *The American Scene*; and he is the "man of imagination" (1:17) who would dominate all of his later phase nonfiction and whose apotheosis he would effect in *Notes of a Son and Brother*.

James tends not to refer to *Story* as text so directly as he refers to himself as author, but, rather, invokes such generically analogous texts as Story's life of Justice Story (1:20–21, 22, 36); Pearce's life of Sumner (1:42); Raffaello Barbiera's life of the Princess Belgiojoso (1:161); Elizabeth Gaskell's life of Charlotte Brontë (1:354–55); as well as Alfieri's autobiography (2:40), and Story's "Parchments and Portraits," with its "autobiographic" touches (1:242). In most cases, he leaves any intended comparisons implicit, though in a few his comments clearly seem intended to reflect his own endeavors. He speaks of a Mrs. Proctor, for example, as "having been . . . singularly uncommemorated," adds that "she was in an extraordinary degree a subject for portraiture" (1:223), and then gives a set-piece, an extended portrait of the woman (1:224–28). In two cases, James reproduces generically analogous texts, allowing them to function as intended by their authors but, simultaneously, appropriating them for his purposes. He reproduces "an enumeration of primary facts" that Story had prepared for a biographical article on himself (1:29–30); and he reproduces two groups of notes that Emelyn Story had prepared as "Recollections of Walter Savage Landor; with After-Dinner Talk at Siena" (2:17–29). James later argues that the "prose-painter of life" does more justice to his subject than does "the mere enumerator" (2:197); and he then spends considerable time deriding the preference for "facts" to "stories" in London dinner-table talk. Having provided the wanted portrait of Mrs. Proctor, in effect, James next demonstrates his principals' failures to convert facts into stories in order to underscore his own success in doing so.

50. Most of James's briefer recollections of childhood in *Story* likewise concern issues of representation. He recalls many sculptures and paintings seen and much literature, especially popular fiction, read. He also repeats a theme from *Hawthorne*, one he would repeat yet again in *A Small Boy and Others*, namely, that he preserves childhood memories of certain books by refusing to reread them as an adult (1:360). For another memorial version of the encounter with Sumner, see *SB* 50.

51. When James recalls meeting Arnold, "for the first time, at Palazzo Barberini," he neglects to mention Story (2:207–8); and when he later recalls having heard Story lecture on Michelangelo at a fashionable London house, he characterizes the recollection as "an impression with which the presence of Lowell is much mingled" (2:272).

52. James often employs prolepsis toward similar ends; see, e.g., 1:93–94, 258; 2:121, 189, 203.

53. James may have been using something other than fancy. In *Reminiscences of William Wetmore Story* (1897), Mary E. Phillips illustrates a passage on Story's essay with the photograph to which James evidently is referring; she captions it, "W. W. Story and Tommaso Salvini. (Discussing Macbeth.)." James may have seen this book, or James and Phillips each may have seen a pertinent notation in the Story archive.

Not only had James written on Ristori, mentioned above, in 1875, but he had written at length on Salvini, including Salvini's interpretations of Macbeth and Lear, in 1883 and 1884; see *The Scenic Art*, 28–32, 168–91.

54. As a young man, James denigrated photography, invidiously comparing in an 1865 review, for example, "a portrait by Valasquez and a photograph by Brady" (*LC* 1:946). Both James and photography matured, however, and he expressed far more interest in the medium in his letters to Alfred Langdon Coburn concerning the latter's photographic frontispieces for the New York Edition (*HJL* 4:416–18, 426–31), and in his discussions of the frontispieces in the prefaces (*AN* 331–35).

55. For a passage in which James confesses his own guilt for taking a train that blights the landscape, see 1:275–76. This would become an important theme in *The American Scene*; see Caramello, "Duality of *The American Scene*," 458–59, 471 n. 17.

56. As he had done in *Hawthorne*, James characterizes antebellum America in *Story* as "paradisiacal" and as "antediluvian" (1:239; 2:187); he also speaks of the "disconcerting snake" in the "paradise of Italy" and of the "apple" of Europe (1:293, 296); and throughout, he plays on Miltonic imagery of the Fall. Generally speaking, he uses Boston to represent Story's paradise lost, Rome his false or artificial paradise, and Florence his paradise regained.

57. James begins to speak of his stock of documents "dwindling" when his narrative reaches the 1860s and when he is only three-quarters through his book. It seems suspicious that Story's *letters* and *diaries* would dwindle at the moment when James's *recollections* can increase in number. In fact, James uses Story's success of the 1860s to shift from the biographical to the critical, and his own subsequent arrival in Europe to shift from the archival to the memorial. Ultimately, his book concludes overtly with Story's death, but covertly with the trip on which James examined the Story archive.

58. James admits to a "mind addicted to finding more in things than meets the eye" (1:60–61); but he also "likes every little fact of these abnormal hours, every characteristic detail" (1:138), likes the kind of "finishing mark," or "touch," of "*personage*" that would appeal to a Balzac or a Saint-Simon, to "some master of literary portraiture" (2:187). Thus he characterizes himself, in accordance with his definitions elsewhere, as simultaneously a romantic and a realist.

His admitted "addiction," however, prompts the real anxiety. We "read into" reflections on the American initiation, James begins, primarily *as* Americans (1:4); and our "heredity," he adds, informs the "meanings we have read into [the precursors'] names" (1:15). If a typical letter, as he later notes, is "besides being delightful in itself, delightful also in proportion to any old memories, impressions, visions of one's own, that one may read into it" (1:245), that porosity, in effect, means that he sometimes has to "pass over names into which one would fain for the moment read, or at least write, some of the pleasant meaning they have to give" (1:362). This tension between reading (or writing) in meanings and reading out meanings forms a central metadiscourse in *The American Scene* (see Caramello, "Duality of *The American Scene*," 459–62) and also figures prominently in *A Small Boy and Others* and *Notes of a Son and Brother*.

59. James repeatedly starts hares from the underbrush, and spots fish swimming by. "There supremely swims toward me one of those queer reminiscences that take form when we sometimes succeed in looking back hard enough" (1:77), he says at one point, conflating not only tropes but also issues of perspective and agency: if James *looks back* in the sense of *looking backward in recollection*, he encounters an apparition who, if James *looks back* in the sense of *returning the gaze*, takes palpable form. At a later point, James develops an even more fantastic conceit in which a merman who must grasp at piscine subjects floating by him cannot do so with discrimination because *he* is a half-fish sharing the same watery medium. He uses the conceit to show how an expatriate, Story, sharing the medium of Rome, could not choose dispassionately among ancient Roman subjects (2:225–26). At the same time, however, he may be suggesting that his own expatriation makes him half-European, therefore unable to discriminate easily among European subjects, and that his age and his memory make him half-antebellum, therefore unable to discriminate easily among Story's contemporaries: though not of Story's generation, he lived among them and knew them well.

60. See, especially, Beidler, *Ghosts, Demons, and Henry James*. Beidler notes, for example, that in 1890 Henry James read a paper by William James on the subject of ghostly possession to the Society for Psychical Research (154).

61. *Letters of Henry Adams* 2:414. There are curious connections between Boott and Story and between both and *The Golden Bowl*. Edel notes that Boott had emigrated on the same voyage as had Story (*HJ* 2:109–10), and he later suggests Boott and his daughter as possible models for Adam and Maggie Verver (*HJ* 5:211). Citing other connections made by Edel between *Story* and *The Golden Bowl*, Tintner nominates Story and his daughter Edith as possible models for Adam and Maggie (*Book World of Henry James*, 64–65); elsewhere, she proposes Story's son-in-law, the Marchese Simone de Peruzzi de Medici, as the model for Prince Amerigo ("A Source for Prince Amerigo in *The Golden Bowl*"). See, also, William James's eulogy, delivered in 1904, "Francis Boott," *Memories and Studies*, 65–72.

62. "The proof" that biography simplifies, James went on, "is that I wanted to invest dear old Boston with a mellow, a golden glow—and for those who know, like yourself, I only make it bleak—and weak!" (*HJL* 4:289). In fact, though, James had handled his Bostonians with a gentler touch, having spoken, for example, "of the small, select company of the bachelors of Boston, a group so almost romantic in their rarity that their 'note' would suggest, their title verily adorn, a light modern opera" (1:363).

63. Compare the divided Story, for example, with Madame Du Quaire, an Englishwoman married to a Frenchman, "with a home on each side of the Channel" that allowed her to keep "intimacy" with both Paris and London, "which was really to know how to live" (2:121). When James grants that some of "our vanished [American] cosmopolites" living in Paris were surprisingly adept at combining traces of "New England 'at its best' . . . [with] the tradition of France at *its* best" (2:186), he is comparing them, in effect, with the American cosmopolites who failed to negotiate between antebellum America and Italy, Boston and Rome.

64. In 1902, encouraging Wharton "in favour of the *American Subject*," James admonished her, "Profit, be warned, by my awful example of exile and ignorance" (*HJL* 4:235–36). He greatly feared that he had lost that subject, that "the mixture of Europe and America which you see in me," as he apparently told Garland, "has . . . made of me a man who is neither American nor European. I have lost touch with my own people" (quoted in Babiiha, *James-Hawthorne Relation*, 13).

65. As I suggested earlier, James's general distaste for intimate biography, coupled with the familial source of the *Story* commission, precluded his treating the marriages of these real persons as he did those of his fictional creations. His reservations about his own bachelorhood, however, coupled with his general mood at the turn of the century, apparently led him to the morose theme in *Story* that marriage betrays, but primarily because *life* betrays, and that the insidious betrayal of marriage lay precisely in its *not* being the exception to the rule—the only exception imaginable to James . . . beside art.

66. Lowell's loss of two spouses and Landor's and, especially, Browning's traumatic losses of their spouses foreshadow Story's loss of his (see, e.g., 2:9–10, 61–62, 289). The deaths of the Ossoli family by shipwreck (1:129–30), and of Lowell's only son two years later (1:316), foreshadow the death of the Storys' eldest boy at the age of six—the one time "the gods had shown jealousy" for the Storys' happy lives (1:284, 367; 2:188–89).

67. Edel, *Henry James*, 17.

68. In "The Novel in *The Ring and the Book*" (1912), a sustained appreciation of Browning, James virtually would rewrite *The Ring and the Book* as *The Scarlet Letter* (see *LC* 2:791–811). He would characterize Browning's poem, moreover, as achieving the balance he had called for since the 1880s and that, as I have suggested, he implied he too had achieved in *Story*: "We have in the whole thing . . . the element of action which is at the same time constant picture, and the element of picture which is at the same time constant action" (*LC* 2:802).

69. R. Jackson Wilson, *Figures of Speech*, 5.

70. James's reproach may carry a nastier implication: from his commenting that Story was commissioned to sculpt a bust of his father before he became a sculptor (1:82), to his describing Browning's efforts in editing Story and in getting him published (2:142, 145–46), to his reporting Sumner's attempt to secure for Story the Robert

Gould Shaw commission (2:162–63), James implies that Story's familial and social contacts advanced his career perhaps more than did his talent.

71. Stowe tells of how she twice narrated the life of Sojourner Truth to Story, and of how that narrative not only influenced the *Cleopatra*, in progress at the time, but also inspired and informed the subsequent *Libyan Sibyl*. See Harriet Beecher Stowe, "Sojourner Truth, The Libyan Sibyl." For a discussion of Hawthorne, Stowe, Story, and Dickinson, see Crosthwaite, "Women and Wild Beasts."

72. James had less to say about the political events covered in *Story* than one might imagine; he seems less interested in the future of nations than in the salient traits of epochs, less interested in unification or emancipation than in their effects on the social and cultural fabric. This holds for related comments elsewhere. He expressed great admiration in 1874 for "the famous generation of 1830" (*LC* 1:380); and in 1897 for "French life" in "the period from the Restoration to the events of 1848" (*LC* 1:762); but he tended to focus on the literary achievements of the period. Likewise, soon after the events of 1870, he seemed upset equally at Gautier for aestheticizing the conflict (*LC* 1:353) and at the French public for an "almost morbid patriotism" that caused it to lose all sense of artistic discrimination (*LC* 1:206).

73. In August 1914, James wrote Rhoda Broughton of "the tragedy that gathers" and of being "sick beyond cure to have lived on to see it." Broughton and he "should have been spared this wreck of our belief that through the long years we had seen civilization grow and the worst become impossible. The tide that bore us along was then all the while moving to *this* as its grand Niagara—yet what a blessing we didn't know it" (*HJL* 4:713). Two months later, in October 1914, he was writing to Edmund Gosse that "the effect in France of the 1870–71 cataclysm" throws out "analogies verily, I fear, with some of our present aspects and prospects!" (*Letters of Henry James*, ed. Lubbock, 2:410).

74. The concept of the military vanguard had been applied to the aesthetic realm long before 1902; in *The Theory of the Avant-Garde*, in fact, Poggioli dates the application to the same moments James treats in *Story*, i.e., 1848, 1870–71 (see 8–12). James frequently uses military terms in connection with Story and friends (see, e.g., 1:96, 188, 337).

75. In James's "golden age" view of history, however, things actually worsen rather than remain the same. Standing before the Barberini, for example, James comments on "the revolutions of time. It was the name, the race, the power, that, in other days, made the palace; it is the palace that, in our own, has to make ... what it can" (1:338). He must have been struck by his formulation that power once symbolized, whereas symbols must now empower, for he shifts it to the social theme of old world versus new world in *The American Scene*: "In worlds otherwise arranged, ... the occasion itself ... produces the tiara. In New York this symbol has ... to produce the occasion" (*AS* 165).

76. James often speaks pejoratively of Story's "variety of experiment and expression" (1:25), of his numerous "curiosities ... driving him into almost every sort of literary experiment and speculation" (2:84). He directs his more pointed comment, however, toward the painter William Page, who had a "technical theory" that might have translated into application had he settled in Paris rather than in Rome: "His fate represents, after all, clumsy *waste*, unlighted freedom of experiment possible only (for it comes back to that) in provincial conditions" (1:173–74).

77. The rhetorical strategies of *Story*, however, make it difficult to fix where James

stood on the issues he raises. As editor and biographer, he wanted to present not only the precursors' views in their own words but also their actions from their own points of view; and, indeed, he did so by reporting their commentary at length. As a historian and critic, he presumably also would have wanted to judge those views and actions from his perspective; but, in fact, he proffers very little substantive commentary of his own. Instead, he reenacts the very tendencies he denigrates in the precursors: he personalizes and allegorizes public issues; and he adopts a distanced, spectatorial stance toward events of the moment, representing them in terms generally aesthetic and specifically theatrical. This master of novelistic perspective easily could have recovered the precursors' points of view while simultaneously embedding them within, and distinguishing them from, his own point of view. The fact that he did not do so in matters concerning politics, that he remained a disinterested, detached allegorist in these matters alone, suggests that he wished to obscure his position.

With the repeated invocations of theater, moreover, James also was employing a derogatory "racial" stereotype of Italians as naturally theatrical—one that he and Story obviously believed (see James at 1:118 and Story at 1:301–2). He extended the stereotype, indeed, to include Italian affairs: James calls the French siege of 1849 "the first public event at which our special friends were to assist" (1:94), and he underscores his point by repetition: "It was at this battle that foreign visitors 'assisted,' as in an opera-box, from anxious Pincian windows" (1:108). Scores of pages later, he likewise tells us that "public events [in 1860] had hurried over the stage like the contending armies of Elizabethan plays" (2:53). By conflating in such instances the precursors' perspectives and metaphors with his own, however, he again makes it difficult to distinguish the precursors from himself, and so again manages to obscure his position.

78. Though Story had made Europe easy for James, the latter strongly suggests that heredity and circumstances had made *life* much easier for Story. It would not have been lost on James that Story—and Lowell, Sumner, Adams, and the rest—all came from pre-Revolutionary families of homogenous Anglo-Saxon "racial" stock, that all were graduated from Harvard, that all were, in a word, Brahmins; James was not. As a result of his station, Story could indulge his amateurism, could accept or reject commissions from the comfort of his vast apartment in a historically significant Roman palazzo; James, by contrast, could live only as a professional, had to accept a commission like the one for *Story*, say, to maintain his own modest residence in Rye. Story, finally, had not "taken too much of his life to produce too little of his art," as James had said of "poor Dencombe," the artistic saint of renunciation from "The Middle Years" (1893) (*Tales of Writers and Artists*, 195); on the contrary, Story had indulged his gregariousness at the expense of his art. But neither, then, had Story failed to "live all he could," as James was saying of Lambert Strether, and as he was fearing of himself.

79. Some years later, in a letter to Clare Benedict, James alluded to recent "dismal and sinister *Story* tragedies and miseries and follies . . . suicide of Benido Peruzzi [Story's grandson, Edith Story's son], babble of his distracted mother etc." (*HJL* 4:460; and see 4:442–43). The glib remark adds a melodramatic endnote to his book: the misery of the progeny becomes the final price paid for a half-century of parental serenity.

80. *Letters of Henry Adams*, 2:622.

Chapter Four

1. See *EA* 300 and, for Toklas's comment, *What Is Remembered*, 160. Though Stein and Toklas give slightly different accounts, they both characterize the *Autobiography* as a depiction of a circle of people in a given place at a given time—much as James characterized *Story*.

2. See *LGS/CVV* 481 n. 4, 852; Bridgman, *Gertrude Stein in Pieces*, 209; Mellow, *Charmed Circle*, 353. Burns bases his statement on "various materials in the Yale archives" (*LGS/CVV* 852) but elaborates no further. W. A. Bradley, Stein's new agent in Paris, wrote her on 13 November 1932 that he would "be *delighted* to see Miss Toklas' Autobiography," and that Stein "might send it in two installments, so that I can get on with the reading as fast as possible"; he wrote again on 26 November to acknowledge receipt of "the second part of the ms." (*Flowers of Friendship*, 259).

3. On the abridgment and serialization, see letters from Ellery Sedgwick and Edward C. Aswell, *Flowers of Friendship*, 260–62; and see Mellow, *Charmed Circle*, 253–54. On the first edition, see Robert A. Wilson, *Gertrude Stein*, 27–30. On the French translation and its publication, see *LGS/CVV* 291 n. 3, 304 n. 2.

4. Stein obviously perceived *Everybody's Autobiography* as a companion volume, a sequel, to *The Autobiography of Alice B. Toklas*; in June 1936, she wrote Carl Van Vechten about "the new Autobiography" (*LGS/CVV* 505); in February 1937, she reported to Samuel Steward that she was working on "the second volume of the Autobiography" (*Dear Sammy*, 131); and in September 1937 she described *Everybody's Autobiography* to Sherwood Anderson as "the volume following *A. B. Toklas*" (White, *Sherwood Anderson/Gertrude Stein*, 101).

5. See *Dear Sammy*, 146–47; *LGS/CVV* 667–75.

6. See *LGS/CVV* 800–805.

7. See *Dear Sammy*, 185. The other two books, "both ordered by the publishers," were *Picasso* and *Paris France*.

8. See *Flowers of Friendship*, 336, 355.

9. See *Testimony Against Gertrude Stein*. In the introductory comment to this fifteen-page pamphlet, Eugene Jolas characterizes the *Autobiography* as "Miss Gertrude Stein's memoirs," "find[s] that the book often lacks accuracy," and then delivers his indictment: "These documents [that follow] invalidate the claim of the Toklas-Stein memorial that Miss Stein was in any way concerned with the shaping of the epoch she attempts to describe. There is a unanimity of opinion that she had no understanding of what really was happening around her, that the mutation of ideas beneath the surface of the more obvious contacts and clashes of personalities during that period escaped her entirely" (2). He was anticipating Braque's comment that "Miss Stein understood nothing of what went on around her" and "has entirely misunderstood cubism which she sees simply in terms of personalities" (13).

10. Stein, *Appreciation*, 152; Stein, *Journey into the Self*, 148–49. What followed in *Appreciation* were rebuttals of Stein's accounts of such events as the "famous" banquet for Henri Rousseau. For Stein's account, see *ABT* 125–32; for Leo Stein's version, see *Appreciation*, 191; for André Salmon's version, see *Testimony against Gertrude Stein*, 14–

15; for a recent account that relies on the *Autobiography* as equivalent to other documentary sources, see Goldberg, "Banquet for Henri Rousseau."

11. See Hemingway, *Moveable Feast*, 9–31, 115–19, especially 118–19. We fall into the very trap I am discussing, however, if we read *A Moveable Feast* as a documentary account rather than as a novelistic memoir.

12. Virtually every general account of Stein discusses the *Autobiography*, as do the many essays, frequently chapters in more broadly conceived books, on Stein as an autobiographical writer. As I indicated, moreover, several commentators recently have turned to the *Autobiography*, alone, as a perhaps more complex text than it appears to be. For studies that emphasize genre, see Timothy Dow Adams, "Contemporary American Mock-Autobiography," and *Telling Lies*, 17–38; Bloom, "Gertrude Is Alice Is Everybody"; Breslin, "Gertrude Stein and the Problems of Autobiography"; Cooley, *Educated Lives*, 156–78; Couser, *American Autobiography*, 148–63; Fichtelberg, *Complex Image*, 162–208; Jelinek, *Tradition of Women's Autobiography*, 128–47; Merrill, "Mirrored Image"; Schultz, "Gertrude Stein's Self-Advertisement"; and the only book-length study of Stein as autobiographer, Neuman's still authoritative *Gertrude Stein*. For studies that explore problems of representation, see Perloff, "(Im)Personating Gertrude Stein"; and Schmitz, "Portrait, Patriarchy, Mythos," and *Of Huck and Alice*. For studies that address eighteenth-century precursor texts, see Meyer, "Gertrude Stein Shipwrecked in Bohemia"; and Parke, "'The Hero Being Dead.'" For studies that focus on questions of gender and sexuality, see note 46 below.

The idea that Stein's work falls into two distinct categories variously formulated as "serious or popular," "experimental or nonexperimental," "difficult or easy," has such wide currency, indeed such authority, in Stein studies that one cannot isolate its appearances—though one can note that Stein herself fostered the idea with several comments on her work, especially that of the 1930s. The idea sometimes takes the form, pertinently, of opposing the purportedly serious, experimental, difficult *Stanzas in Meditation* to the allegedly popular, nonexperimental, easy *Autobiography*. See, for example, Winston, "Gertrude Stein's Mediating Stanzas," and Dydo, "*Stanzas in Meditation*"; for a take on the *Autobiography* as a book with "its own very real difficulties," one written in response to Dydo's account of the *Stanzas*, see Perloff, "(Im)Personating Gertrude Stein."

13. According to the authors of *The New Painting*, Cassatt's painting is now known as *Portrait of Lydia Cassatt, the Artist's Sister* (277).

14. For Stein's references to Defoe, Boswell, and Clemens, see, respectively, NAR 45, 60, 61.

15. As we explore implications of that mixing, we must honor the basic *donnée* of Stein as author and Toklas as narrator, and we must solve the practical necessity of having subjects for sentences; though I attempt to differentiate the historical Stein and Toklas from their textual counterparts, I sometimes invoke Stein as author, sometimes Toklas as narrator, and sometimes the two jointly.

16. See *Brewsie and Willie*, 114; TI 34. Stein attributes this preference "to a great teacher, William James.... He was a man who always said, 'Complicate your life as much as you please, it has got to simplify'" (TI 34).

17. Inasmuch as the *Autobiography* actually covers events beginning with Stein's and

Toklas's unspecified birthdates (1874 and 1877, respectively), extending through their pivotal union in 1907 and their subsequent years together, and concluding in the present moment of composition in autumn 1932, strict chronology and mimesis thereof would proceed from Stein's birthdate through her moment of arriving in Paris, to the overlapping period from Toklas's birthdate through her years before arriving in Paris, to Stein in Paris from 1903 to 1907, to Toklas's arrival in Paris in 1907—would demand, in short, the reordering four-one-three-two. Had Stein wanted to maintain a chronological order but to parallel, rather than interleave, two lives, she could have chosen the order one-two-four-three. Evidently, however, Stein wanted to follow a memorial order in this fictionalized *memoir* of married life, an order that puts the date of marriage in the pivotal position. If I am right about Stein's locating her union with Toklas in 1907, then she apparently took the same liberties with this part of the historical record that she took with other parts, at least insofar as scholars have been able to reconstruct this part; for one such reconstruction, see Stimpson, "Gertrice/Altrude," 124–26.

18. Though Stein found linear "story" the disappearing element in modern fiction, she neither altogether eliminated it nor, in cases such as the *Autobiography*, altogether attenuated it. In this book *of* gossip that is also, among other things, *about* gossip, she playfully points to this residual linearity: "Lipschitz is an excellent gossip and Gertrude Stein adores the beginning and middle and end of a story and Lipschitz was able to supply several missing parts of several stories" (249).

19. Throughout the *Autobiography*, Stein coordinates gender wars, artistic wars, and the Great War of 1914–1918. See Longenbach, "Women and Men of 1914," for a review of the inseparability of "the battle for women's suffrage, the battle for modern art, and the battle in the trenches" (98); and see Leonardi, *Dangerous by Degrees*, for a discussion of postwar developments in higher education for women and the implications for the aesthetically, though not always ideologically, conservative Somerville College novelists, those who "reject[ed], for the most part, the formal innovation and experimentation of their modernist contemporaries" (6).

20. The first cycle of chapters traces the lives of two young women of good stock from childhood through maidenhood, to departure from the parental home, and to courtship and marriage to each other. The second cycle then traces the course of this now established couple through their—through *its*—middle years. They move in a society of other couples in their neighborhood and city, they adopt progeny under special circumstances, repeatedly becoming godmothers to American doughboys, and they enter their mature years as nurturers of young writers and painters. Though never mentioned, as convention prescribes, their intimate life presumably satisfies.

21. Burns notes that we cannot determine "what prompted Stein to write this book," but, "it is clear . . . that Toklas was pushing her to write a book that would make Stein a popular success and earn a great deal of money" (*LGS/CVV* 261 n. 1). Bridgman speculates at length on the possibility that Stein and Toklas literally collaborated on the *Autobiography* (see *Gertrude Stein in Pieces*, 209–17).

22. Fry, *Cubism*, 14.

23. Toklas seems to be suggesting that she integrated herself into French culture while Stein remained an American devoted to the English language, an American, for exam-

ple, who "rarely read french newspapers, she never read anything in french" (176). In *Testimony against Gertrude Stein*, Matisse and Braque each comment on Stein's inadequacy with the French language (8, 13). This must have prompted Stein's rejoinder in *Everybody's Autobiography*, "I talk French badly and write it worse but so does Pablo" (14).

24. For a related reference to standing, see *ABT* 11. Observable and representable, bodily position and movement provided Stein an important theme in the 1930s.

25. For another reference to pioneering, see *ABT* 255–56; for an account of Stein and Toklas as pioneer Californians, see Rochlin and Rochlin, "Jews on the Western Frontier."

26. For Stein's theory that America was the oldest country in the world, see *ABT* 96 and *Brewsie and Willie*, 50.

27. Henry Ford "declares Emerson's *Essays* to be his favorite reading," Matthiessen would note in *American Renaissance*, 368.

28. More subtly, Stein parallels a scene in which Mildred Aldrich asks Toklas if Picasso and Matisse are "alright," and adds that "Gertrude thinks so and Gertrude knows" (148), with a scene in which Jacques-Emile Blanche asks Stein if the Futurists' painting was "alright," and she replies, "No it isn't" (153). Stein shared with the Futurists the general senses of futurism and of agonism that Poggioli has identified as essential to the classical avant-garde (see *Theory of the Avant-Garde*, 60–77); she also shared with them a particular interest in the relevance of automotive and aeronautical technology to modern art; but she differed from them, on other counts, in ways too complex to address here. For a discussion of those differences, see Perloff, "Call It Marry Nettie."

29. Matisse worked while looking at a Cézanne and a Gauguin, and was "influenced" by Cézanne and then by "negro sculpture" (45); Picasso was "influenced by Cézanne" though not, at first, by "african sculpture"; Matisse, however, then introduced Picasso to Negro sculpture—"drew Picasso's attention" to it—and this African art "affected" Matisse's imagination and Picasso's vision and later "influenced" Picasso's imagination (78).

30. Toklas reports that Stein's being American by nationality, Californian by upbringing, and Parisian by habitation drew her to the style of abstraction, provided her the traditions of American writing and French painting, and informed her vision and aesthetics; and she reports that a Cézanne affected Stein's *Three Lives* (40–41), that William James made a "lasting impression" upon her and "delighted" her, and that Henry James was her "forerunner" (96–97). Stein would not accord Cézanne and Flaubert the specific prestige of "influences," however, until 1946 (TI 15).

31. One thus must read as either ironical or inconsistent Stein's having found a controversial picture by Matisse "perfectly natural" and her having been unable to "understand why it infuriated everybody . . . just as later she did not understand why since the writing was all so clear and natural they mocked at and were enraged by her work" (42).

32. Toklas speaks of Roché as "a translation" of the Cubists (54), of Delaunay as "the founder of the first of the many vulgarisations of the cubist idea" (120), of the Surrealists as "the vulgarisation of Picabia as Delaunay and his followers and the futurists were

the vulgarisation of Picasso"—vulgarizers being those who take "the manner for the matter" (258).

33. Toklas directs the opening remarks of chapter 2, "My Arrival in Paris," to Stein's, Picasso's, and Matisse's innovations of 1907 (7); but she defers discussion of them until chapter 3, "Gertrude Stein in Paris 1903–1907," where she brings a history of their early work to the culmination of 1907 and Picasso's portrait of Stein, Stein's story of Melanctha in *Three Lives*, and Matisse's *Bonheur de Vivre*. In the crucial chapter 5, "1907–1914," Toklas traces in detail Picasso's and Stein's concurrent development of Cubist landscape and portraiture. She recalls that Picasso and Fernande had gone to Spain in 1909 and had returned with landscapes that were "the beginning of cubism" (she repeats the phrase three times: 109, 110, 111); she already has told us, of course, that Picasso had finished his portrait of Stein after a trip to Spain in 1906. In a parallel account, she recalls "how [Stein's] portrait writing began" (139), recalls Stein's sense of the importance of portraiture (146) and later of landscape (146), and recalls Stein's and her trip to Spain in 1912, in which Stein "began to write the things that led to Tender Buttons" (141). Apparently regarding this text as her most painterly, most cubistic, work, Stein would note in *Everybody's Autobiography* that "the later painting of Picasso is writing, just as my middle writing was painting" (180); and she would speak in "A Transatlantic Interview" of *Tender Buttons* as the "apex," the "culmination" of her "middle years" (18).

Stein published her lengthy *Matisse Picasso and Gertrude Stein* in early 1933, some months before the *Autobiography*; and she commented in her notebooks, in an entry troubling to any feminist reading of her, that "Pablo & Matisse have a maleness that belongs to genius. Moi aussi perhaps" (cited in *Picasso: The Complete Writings*, 109).

34. Toklas concludes chapter 3 by telling of Picasso's and Matisse's taking divergent paths and of the disciples who followed them. Having told in chapter 2 of having seen a Braque and a Derain at the vernissage of the independents, and of Stein's having declared that "right here in front of you is the whole story" (22), she now identifies Braque and Derain as the chief Picassoites, as those, in effect, who tell the whole story about Picasso's influence on modern painting and on lesser talents. Stein's first portrait of Picasso, "Picasso" (1909), has others' following Picasso as its central theme and organizing principle.

35. Stein and Toklas so fully shape the first cycle of chapters on conventions of exile and of initiation into the religion of art that I can pause only to sketch an outline. In chapter 1, Toklas recounts her journey to Paris; in chapter 2, she recounts her initiation into modern art in three distinct, ritual moments: her visiting the rue de Fleurus and meeting Stein, her attending the vernissage of the independents with an unnamed woman companion and again encountering Stein, and her accompanying Stein to Montmartre where they visit Picasso's studio and Fernande's apartment. In chapter 3, she recounts how Stein had come to be at the center of the modern movement, not only as the chief collector and interpreter of its painting, but also, more important, as the first practitioner of its writing; and, in chapter 4, she recounts Stein's childhood, adolescence, and young womanhood, telling a tale of vocation similar to that told by James in *A Small Boy and Others* and *Notes of a Son and Brother*, and, especially, by Joyce in *A Portrait of the Artist as a Young Man*.

36. "Painting now after its great moment must come back to be a minor art," Stein had written in "Saving the Sentence" (1929) (*How To Write*, 13).

37. Hemingway later treated the occasion of the "lost generation" remark in *A Moveable Feast*, 29–31. In its time, the phrase primarily meant "lost" as "missing," whereas Stein stresses a secondary meaning of "lost" as "having no direction." For a discussion of "the generation of 1914," its having defined itself according to contemporary generational theories, and its having incorporated its being "lost" into its mythic self-definition, see Wohl, *Generation of 1914*, especially 110–16.

Stein went to great lengths in the *Autobiography*, *Everybody's Autobiography*, and elsewhere to distinguish her work from automatic writing and to distance it from the unconscious; correspondingly, she had little regard for Surrealism (see, e.g., *ABT* 258; *P* 43). Indeed, one might say that her offhand dismissal of Futurism in the prewar chapter of the *Autobiography* finds its counterpart in the postwar dismissal of Surrealism.

38. Toklas had noted that her "life in Paris was based upon the rue de Fleurus and the Saturday evenings and it was like a kaleidoscope slowly turning" (109); and she had added, "It was an endless variety. And everybody came and no one made any difference" (151).

39. Toklas develops the first comparison systematically, through repeated references to Picasso's and Juan Gris's Spanish origins, to Stein's and her trips to Spain with their powerful effects on Stein's aesthetics, and to Stein's argument that America *and Spain* (as she would add in *Picasso*) were the countries that first entered the twentieth century and, thus, produced the writer and artist who went on to create twentieth-century writing and painting; America and Spain, Toklas cites Stein, "are the only two western nations that can realise abstraction" (111).

In the *Autobiography*, Americans appear, variously, as androgynous (60), preoccupied with personal hygiene (82), abstract and cruel (111), enthusiastic (161), generally wealthy (162, 181), organized (188), democratic (198), egalitarian (215), given to concentration (226), charming (291), and, of course, *modern*. For more of this, see *Gertrude Stein's America*.

40. See "Futurist Synthesis of the War," reproduced in Tisdall and Bozzolla, *Futurism*, 187.

41. Stein develops this theme in "An American and France" (1936) (*What Are Masterpieces*, 61–70), and in *Paris France* (1940), 2–3.

42. Toklas organizes events from 1914 to 1918 through a sequence of departures from Paris and returns to it: Paris to London to Paris to Spain to Paris to Perpignan to Paris to Nimes, Avignon, and Alsace to Paris. With these cycles, she parallels public events bearing on the war with Stein's and her increased recognition of the war effort and involvement in it: from reading in newspapers in Paris of increasing tensions to being caught in London by the invasion of Belgium and endorsing England's declaration of war (180–81); from returning "home" to Paris and suffering Zeppelin attacks to decamping to Spain to "forget the war a little" (198); from again returning "home" and deciding "to get into the war" (207) to outfitting and driving a Ford for the American Fund for French Wounded (213), becoming military godmothers (214–15), and endorsing America's declaration of war; from once again returning "home" and meeting "the first piece of the american army" (221) to performing volunteer work for the military

and, following the armistice, relief work for refugees; from finally returning home to a "confused world" (233) to then taking part, nevertheless, in a triumphal procession on the Champs Elysées (236). Throughout this chapter, Toklas subordinates the theme of art to that of war: she depicts Stein, for example, as having abandoned the reading of literature for the reading of newspapers, and as having abandoned the writing of literature for the war effort; she makes only one extended reference to Stein's theories of aesthetics (192); and she otherwise approaches aesthetics only through such martial vehicles as national styles of camouflage (231) and of marching (236).

43. Toklas implicitly contrasts Picasso, whose "struggles" took him and Cocteau to Rome while "everybody was at the war" (212), to Apollinaire, who died of a head wound (73), and Braque, who was a war hero (134); likewise, she contrasts Matisse, to whom an admirer sent a "tribute" after an exhibition, a laurel wreath "To Henri Matisse, Triumphant on the Battlefield of Berlin" (115), contrasts him to Stein, Mildred Aldrich, and herself, all of whom the French government decorated for war service (221, 252–53). Whatever the intention, her specific contrasts serve to depict Stein as the only one of the three modernist "founders" (Matisse, Picasso, Stein) who served the war effort, and she presents the other women in the text, herself included, as having done the same.

With intentions even less clear, Toklas shares Stein's habit of associating artists with generals while also identifying women with that rank. Picasso likens himself to Lincoln (18), for example, but Mildred Aldrich has a George Washington face (147), and Stein, "having been born in February, was very like George Washington" (276). Stein and Toklas are each likened to generals (19, 108), and Stein and Sherwood Anderson "have Grant as their great american hero" and "did not care so much about Lincoln" (303). Finally, though Toklas reminds us that Stein had compared Picasso to Napoleon in an earlier portrait (71), she also points out that one of her own ancestors had raised a regiment for Napoleon (3) and that Fernande has a "Napoleonic forefinger" (23). For more on generals and Napoleon, see my next chapter.

44. For Stein and Toklas's later visiting Duncan in America, see *EA* 255.

45. Enumeration as narration is central to Stein's aesthetics; see, e.g., *LIA* 227.

46. Questions of gender and sexuality, usually but not always in tandem, inform much current Stein criticism and, in many cases, the best of it. For studies focused more on gender than on sexuality as such, and, particularly, on the relationship between gender, literary experimentation, and progressive politics, see Berry, *Curved Thought*; Chessman, *Public is Invited to Dance*; DeKoven, *A Different Language*, "Half In and Half Out of Doors," "Male Signature, Female Aesthetic," "Gertrude Stein," and *Rich and Strange*, 67–84; and Ruddick, *Reading Gertrude Stein*. For studies focusing on Stein's lesbianism and its textual representations, see Benstock, *Women of the Left Bank*, 143–93, and "Expatriate Sapphic Modernism"; Fifer, "Is Flesh Advisable?" and *Rescued Readings*; Gilbert and Gubar, *No Man's Land*, 2:215–57; Gilmore, "A Signature of Lesbian Autobiography"; Sidonie Smith, *Subjectivity, Identity, and the Body*, 64–82; and, especially, Stimpson, "The Mind, The Body, and Gertrude Stein," "Gertrice/Altrude," "Gertrude Stein and the Transposition of Gender," "Somagrams of Gertrude Stein," and "Gertrude Stein and the Lesbian Lie." Of these studies, Gilbert and Gubar's chapter discusses the *Autobiography* (250–56), while Gilmore's essay, Smith's chapter, and Stimpson's last essay focus on it.

With only very recent exceptions, consensus holds that Stein and Toklas enacted heterosexual roles in a marriage based on the heterosexual model, that Stein reinscribed those roles and that model in her texts though also encoding her lesbian sexuality and a lesbian erotics, and that, for all those reasons, Stein and Toklas have become an acceptable lesbian couple and Stein's work acceptable lesbian writing; see, e.g., Rich, "Compulsory Heterosexuality," 156 n. 44; Cook, "'Women Alone Stir My Imagination,'" 730–31; and Stimpson, "Gertrice/Altrude," 126. As Benstock has noted, however, "if there is such a thing as Sapphic modernism, then its philosopher-theorist is Gertrude Stein" ("Expatriate Sapphic Modernism," 194); and some of the commentators mentioned above, especially DeKoven, allow for the subversive tendencies of her work.

When I first drafted this chapter, the consensus was virtually unanimous; since then, Gilmore and Smith have opened up the lines of argument, with respect to the *Autobiography*, that I too am pursuing. Were I to recast this part of my discussion, I would follow theoretical leads suggested by, e.g., Case, "Towards a Butch-Femme Aesthetic"; de Lauretis, "Sexual Indifference"; and Dolan, "'Lesbian' Subjectivity in Realism."

47. Stein and Toklas, for example, create two genealogies of modernist innovators: to the first generation of *European painters* from chapter 3 (Cézanne, Rousseau) and the second generation from chapter 5 (Matisse, Picasso), they add a third generation (Tchelitchev, Bérard, Rose); to the first generation of *American writers* from chapter 4 (James) and the second from chapter 5 (Stein), they add the third (Anderson, Hemingway, Fitzgerald)—throwing in young *American composers* (Thomson, Antheil, Copland) for good measure.

48. Stein's friendships with men may have long history (Juan Gris, Matisse, Picasso), may have less history but deep feeling (Sherwood Anderson, Carl Van Vechten), may be essentially professional (Bernard Fäy, Georges Hugnet, Virgil Thomson), or may be volatile and, ultimately, untenable (Hemingway, McAlmon). Her friendships with women, however, seem more consistently long-lasting and, especially, stable—those with Mildred Aldrich, the sisters Cone, Mabel Dodge, Constance Fletcher, and Janet Scudder, for instance. Toklas intimates the sexual subtext of the homosocial theme when she invokes the companion with whom she had attended the vernissage (19), the companion whom she identifies, only toward the end, as her "friend" Harriet [Levy], with whom she had shared accommodations (251). Toklas had left that friend, of course, for Stein.

49. Toklas mentions any number of heterosexual marriages in passing—Derain's (29), Van Dongen's (33), Uhde's (119–20), Delaunay's (120–21), Henry Gibb's (143), Van Vechten's (168), Apollinaire's (229)—and she makes a motif of Picasso's cohabitations and marriage (e.g., 17, 73, 136, 228). Though Stein and Toklas obviously disapprove of such sexist and heterosexist conceptions of marriage as expressed by Jacob and Picasso (see 29), they do not regard marriage in itself as sexist and sham—a point driven home by the implicit contrast between Uhde's apparent marriage of convenience (119–20) and their own marriage of commitment.

50. Stein repeats this anecdote about Radcliffe in *Everybody's Autobiography* (264–67), again stating her previous dislike of "anything abnormal or frightening" (264). Whether or not Stein subscribed to national types, I would argue, she appears to have

rejected sexual types. For a pertinent comment on Henry James's use of terms such as "abnormal" in *The Bostonians*, see Tintner, *Book World of Henry James*, 265.

51. Stein "liked to read about the suffragettes" in 1913 and 1914 (176); but Toklas, we learn in *Everybody's Autobiography*, not only "felt that when the women writers [in America] asked us to tea we had to go" (7), but she also "is at present most interested in the curtains in all the English houses when we come to England that is what she finds most exciting that and everything else done by women" (*EA* 316). Not trivial in context, Toklas's interest in curtains concludes an extended motif of window treatments in *Everybody's Autobiography*.

52. The title page of the first edition of *The Making of Americans* prominently displays the dates 1906–1908; and Stein reaffirmed the three-year period of composition in "The Gradual Making of The Making of Americans" (*LIA* 152). Leon Katz, however, dates the composition from 1903 to 1911, and Bridgman, concurring, allows that Stein "wrote the first sizable draft" between 1906 and 1908 (*Gertrude Stein in Pieces*, 39n, 59n, 65).

53. In the first two chapters, Stein and Toklas weave the motif of Toklas's initiation into art with a more muted motif of her initiation into lesbian sexuality. In chapter 1, for example, Toklas subtly tells us that her "new full life" differed from her old not in "fullness" but in "ardor" (see 4); and in chapter 2, she describes her first visit to rue de Fleurus as "one of the most important evenings of my life" (19), she encodes into the scene at the vernissage an allusion to Harriet Levy's subsequent displacement by Stein, and she juxtaposes Picasso's studio, with its canvas "of three women, square and posturing, all of it rather frightening" (27), to Fernande's apartment, with its homosociety of three women, none of it frightening. In the second two chapters, as I am suggesting in my text proper, Stein and Toklas similarly weave the motif of Stein's earlier artistic initiation with that of her sexual initiation. In the crucial chapter 5, finally, Stein and Toklas interweave Picasso's and Stein's artistic lives with their domestic lives, Picasso leaving Fernande and moving with Eve (!) to the Edenic Montparnasse, Leo Stein leaving rue de Fleurus to Stein and Toklas and to a Miltonic wedded bliss.

54. Though the contemporary reader of the *Autobiography* could not have known this, Toklas is referring to Stein's *Q.E.D.*, composed in 1903 but not published until 1950 (as *Things as They Are*). Dydo has argued that the real Toklas "had not known about the affair with Bookstaver or about the early novel until the spring of 1932," that Stein's failure to have revealed the affair roused her jealousy, and that this incident, together with others, set off a period of domestic quarreling. In a meticulous analysis, Dydo shows that Stein encoded the incident in *Stanzas in Meditation*; see Dydo, "How to Read Gertrude Stein,'" especially 284–94; and "*Stanzas in Meditation*" (citation on 12). That the real Toklas and Stein were having marital problems during the composition of the *Autobiography* only adds to the book's poignancy, and potency, as a "love letter."

55. For Stein's discussion of "bottom nature," see "The Gradual Making of The Making of Americans" (*LIA* 137–46). Stein cites several relevant passages from the recently published abridgment of *The Making of Americans*; the first of them that contains the phrase "bottom nature" occurs on 128 of the abridged edition, though Stein actually had introduced the phrase in the opening paragraph of that section of her novel (109). In the "complete version," the passages in question appear on 150, 183.

56. For James's use of "stream of consciousness," see *Principles of Psychology*, 1:296.

57. It first might seem that Stein was placing herself in the Symbolist-Formalist tradition passing from Wagner, through Mallarmé and Pater, to Valéry and, eventually, to one of her most ardent present-day admirers, William H. Gass. On closer observation, though, it seems that she was attempting to root herself in eighteenth-century aesthetics and to place herself, in effect, as *beside* the Wagnerian line: she has Toklas depict her, that is, as rejecting not only romantic ideas of writing as an *expression* of emotion, but also symbolist ideas of writing as a *transformation* of emotion.

58. See "Sentences and Paragraphs," whose subtitle or epigraph is "A Sentence is not emotional a paragraph is" (*How To Write*, 23–35). In the *Autobiography*, Toklas reports that "sentences have been Gertrude Stein's life long passion" (50), she mentions Stein's sentences at least three more times (60, 69, 253–54), and she repeats Stein's dictum "that paragraphs are emotional and that sentences are not" (305).

59. Along the way, Toklas tells us that Stein "had a servant named Lena and it is her story that [she] afterwards wrote as the first story of the Three Lives" (99). Conjoining a real Lena's "story" with Stein's "writing" of the "story" that appears in *Three Lives*, Toklas suggests how personal history mediated by writing becomes fictional story—precisely the process suggested in the etymology of Stein's writing Toklas's auto/bio/graphy.

60. In the course of recalling the postwar period, Toklas "look[s] in order to refresh my memory over the bibliography of Gertrude Stein's work" (237). With the parallel formulation, she distinguishes between the prewar Stein known as a collector of paintings and the postwar Stein she is making known as a creator of writings. Whereas some photographs of pictures are said to be missing, moreover, the bibliography of writings seems complete.

61. It is to the point that the *Autobiography* was issued with sixteen photographic illustrations; eight of these feature other texts—seven are of paintings, one is of the first page of manuscript of the *Autobiography*; eight feature principal persons, primarily Stein and Toklas, but are so stylized and allusive as to be, similarly, "about" other representations. References to photography in the *Autobiography*, then, form not only an *indirect* metadiscourse on the text but also a *direct* metadiscourse on its illustrations and on the intertextual relation between text and illustration. For a discussion of these illustrations, see Alkon, "Visual Rhetoric."

62. In an oblique trope of the former, Etta Cone typed the manuscript of *Three Lives* "letter by letter so that she might not by any indiscretion become conscious of the meaning" (64); in a less oblique trope of the latter, Vollard "always wanted to know what everybody thought of everything because in that way he found out what he himself thought" (47).

63. Writing to her military godsons during the war, Toklas had "to remember all their family histories"; she mixed them up once and "deeply wounded" her correspondents—a very pointed phrase in this particular context (216).

64. As a function of the basic conceit of the *Autobiography*, moreover, the first-person pronouns in the sentence in question can be taken to refer, in various combinations, to the real and/or the textual Stein and/or Toklas. The sentence thus anticipates the similar but more complex ambiguation of the opening lines of *Everybody's Auto-*

biography: "Alice B. Toklas did hers and now everybody will do theirs. / Alice B. Toklas says and if they are all going to do theirs the way she did hers" (3). (The first edition has "anybody," incorrectly, in place of "everybody.") Such cubistic transposition of temporal and spatial indicators is common in the *Autobiography* and in Stein's *oeuvre* and finds its perhaps most well known instance in her remark that when she visited Oakland, California, she found "there is no there there," a remark whose context makes memory the key issue (*EA* 289). See Caramello, "Coming Across America," 369.

65. As one consequence, Toklas does not know, and cannot report, some things that Stein does know, and otherwise could report; see, e.g., 260, 265.

66. For an extended discussion of the interplay of fact and fiction in the *Autobiography*, one emphasizing the role of historical error, see Timothy Dow Adams, *Telling Lies*, 17–38.

67. Discussing the evolving conjunction of portrait and narrative in her earlier work, Stein would note in *Lectures in America* that she had made portraits of sites, apparently, as studies for compositions that *could* but *did not yet* contain dramatic action. "That is why painters paint still lives," she says by way of illustration, and "so I began to do this thing, I tried to include color and movement and what I did is what you have all either read or heard of, a volume called Tender Buttons" (*LIA* 189).

68. With her aesthetics of seriality and thematics of celebrity, Stein anticipated Warhol and other Pop Artists; see Steiner, Introduction to *Lectures in America*, xi–xvii. To my knowledge, incidentally, no one has noted that Warhol, in one of his seminal works of serial portraiture, also alluded to Henry Ford as a precursor: "Ten Lizzes" (1963), a portrait of Elizabeth Taylor, directly echoes "tin lizzies," the common term for the Model T.

69. For further discussion of the line in "post-cubist painting," see *EA* 191.

70. Stein later would indicate a desire to collaborate with Lloyd Lewis on a life of Grant (*EA* 235); when Lewis was preparing such a work, many years later, he wrote Toklas to request Anderson's letters to Stein (Toklas, *Staying on Alone*, 95).

71. On Stein's and Toklas's owning a New York Edition, see Toklas, *Staying on Alone*, 86; on the likelihood that Stein had read the prefaces, see Edel, "Correspondence," and Caramello, "Correspondence." On connections between *The Awkward Age*, Thornton Wilder's dramatization of it, and Stein, see Powers, "Thornton Wilder as Literary Cubist," 35–36, 42–43.

72. In fact, Toklas alludes to the connection much earlier; having twice suggested "My Twenty-five Years with Gertrude Stein" as a possible title for her book (17, 309), she echoes Defoe's subtitle, "Who lived Eight and Twenty Years, all alone in an uninhabited Island... [etc.]." The relevant, hidden joke is that Stein and Toklas inhabit not only a figuratively insular *quatier*, but also a literally insular city—Paris having been founded on the Isle de Cité.

73. Indeed, Stein may be sighting *through* James's preface to *The Portrait of a Lady*, with its Stevensonian allusions to maritime adventures and pirates, *to* Defoe's titular and subtitular references to "Strange Surprizing Adventures" and to "Pyrates."

74. Bridgman notes that "Stein originally ended the manuscript as Mark Twain had the *Adventures of Huckleberry Finn*—'Sincerely yours, Alice B. Toklas,'—then canceled it" (*Gertrude Stein in Pieces*, 219n); Clemens, however, actually ended *Huck Finn*—"The End. Yours Truly, Huck Finn."

75. I have characterized the entire theme of war as ambiguous, however, and the reference to Duchamp proves no exception. Toklas describes him as "looking like a young norman crusader," thus tying him to the motif of romantic and religious warriors. She then notes that he went to New York "in the early years of the war. His brother had just died from the effect of his wounds, his other brother was still at the front and he himself was inapt for military service. He was very depressed and he went to America" (164). If the first reference is ironic, the second seems far more sympathetic and, indeed, anticipates the passage about Duncan. All in all, she seems to be saying, on the one hand, that war is necessary, but, on the other hand, that war only kills, maims, and shames people.

76. Toklas reports that Coburn "was a queer american who brought with him a queer english woman," and, with the slightly deceptive "just finished," uses him to link James to Stein: she is referring, evidently, to Coburn's frontispiece photographs for James's New York Edition, which he executed in 1906-7, some six years before photographing Stein (see *HJL* 4:416-18, 426-31). Given her desire to forge this link, Stein not surprisingly "forgets," as it were, to mention her failure to secure an introduction to James via Coburn (see my next chapter; Edel, "Correspondence"; Caramello, "Correspondence"). For Coburn's appreciative remarks on James and Stein as subjects, see *Alvin Langdon Coburn, Photographer*.

77. Stieglitz already had published Stein's portraits of Matisse and Picasso in the August 1912 issue of *Camera Work*; see Robert A. Wilson, *Gertrude Stein*, 123-24.

78. See, for example, the many reviews of *Tender Buttons* excerpted in White, *Gertrude Stein and Alice B. Toklas*, 4-10.

79. For schematic purposes, I am simplifying a more complicated set of associations. Toklas notes that "in looking and looking at [Cézanne's *Portrait d'une Femme*], Gertrude Stein wrote Three Lives," she reiterates the point on the next page (40-41), and she thus anticipates Stein's unmediated acknowledgment of Cézanne's influence in "A Transatlantic Interview." Earlier, Toklas had identified with 1907 the already completed *Three Lives*, the ongoing *Making of Americans*, *The Portrait of Miss Gertrude Stein*, Picasso's "strange complicated picture of three women," and Matisse's *Bonheur de Vivre* (7); and, somewhat later, she reassociates the portrait of Stein, "Melanctha," and *Bonheur de Vivre* (66). With respect to genealogy, she is identifying Cézanne as the father of Picasso, Stein, and modern art; with respect to gender, she seems to be recalling the initiatory scene at Picasso's studio, where she saw *Les Demoiselles* and *Three Women*, and to be associating *Three Lives* and *Three Women* while also juxtaposing them.

80. Though the real Stein's calling card read, conventionally, "Miss Gertrude Stein," Toklas refers to Stein throughout the *Autobiography* as "Gertrude Stein." Given the theme of marriage, given Toklas's feminism, and given Picasso's *Portrait of Miss Gertrude Stein*, Stein and Toklas would not want to use "Miss"; given the rejection of intimate memoir, the inclination against familiarity, and the desire to have Stein regarded as a person of letters, they would not want to call her "Gertrude." With the endless repetition of the name "Gertrude Stein," moreover, they follow a basic rule of advertising for achieving product recognition, but in so doing, of course, they also commodify Stein.

81. Richardson has identified the "skull-like head of Josep Fontdevila, a nonagenar-

ian smuggler" and innkeeper, whom Picasso painted and drew repeatedly, as "the principal inspiration for the formidable Gertrude Stein portrait" ("Picasso's Apocalyptic Whorehouse," 43); indeed, there is a striking resemblance between a drawing of Fontdevila (reproduced by Richardson, 45), the portrait of Stein, *and* Picasso's *Self-Portrait* of 1907. This does not contravene Katz's association of the face with the exhibition of pre-Roman Iberian sculpture at the Louvre in 1906, an exhibition that everyone agrees influenced Picasso enormously in, for example, *Les Demoiselles* (see "Matisse, Picasso, and Gertrude Stein," 50–63).

82. For relevant discussion of the general issue, see Armstrong, "Edgar Degas and the Representation of the Female Body," and, especially, Duncan, "Virility and Domination in Early Twentieth-Century Vanguard Painting."

83. There are dangers, unfortunately, in reading things back into the *Autobiography*. In *Picasso*, Stein notes that "Picasso a Spaniard is never fantastic, he is never pornographic" (41).

84. The problem is not nudity as such, since Stein was no prude; but rather the cultural context for nudity and the implications of that context. It is not stretching too far, perhaps, to say that Stein figures these implications through a seemingly offhand, and otherwise meaningless, automotive reference. Max Jacob had spoken of "possessing" women, and Stein later says that when an American mechanic throws his tunic over the radiator, "the car was his" (230). By way of contrast, Stein names her second, her postwar, Ford "Godiva because she had come naked into the world and each of our friends gave us something with which to bedeck her" (235). As opposed to covering the nude to "possess" her, "bedecking" the nude to make a communal, celebratory act; as opposed to Futurist automotive phallicism, Steinian automotive feminism.

The Futurists actually despised the genre of the nude, but for very different reasons. The five authors of "Futurist Painting: Technical Manifesto" (1910) concluded by denouncing the nude in painting "as nauseous [sic] and as tedious as adultery in literature"; though they went on to claim an aesthetic rather than a moral basis for the denunciation, they also ranted that "artists obsessed with the desire to expose the bodies of their mistresses have transformed the Salons into arrays of unwholesome flesh!" (see Chipp, *Theories of Modern Art*, 293). Disclaimers notwithstanding, they disliked the nude, in part, for reasons reflecting their evident misogyny.

85. There is hearsay: Matisse, for example, tells Stein about Vollard (47), everybody talks about Eliot before they meet him (246), and Stein tells a story of a public affront and retraction between Picasso and Cocteau—a story about stories (273). And there is gossip, at which some are better than others: Matisse (83), Braque (229), Lipschitz (249).

86. In the opening paragraph of the first, epistolary, part of his autobiography, Franklin speaks of "having emerg'd from the Poverty and Obscurity in which I was born and bred, to a State of Affluence and some Degree of Reputation in the World" (1).

87. On the one hand, Stein's publications: her first fugitive piece (36), first publication (95), first little magazine publication (169), and, importantly, *Elucidation* as her first effort to explain her own work (256–57, 295). On the other hand, her reputation: Toklas mentions the first time anyone quotes Stein's work to her and Stein's first international recognition (123), the first time anyone photographs Stein as a celebrity

(171–72), Cocteau as "the first french writer to speak of her work" (250), Elliot Paul as the author of "the first seriously popular estimation of her work" (293).

88. Beside Picasso's *Portrait of Miss Gertrude Stein*, for example, Toklas also mentions Coburn's and Man Ray's photographic portraits (171–72, 242–43), Lipschitz's and Jo Davidson's sculptural portraits (249, 251), and finally Francis Rose's portrait (308). Similarly, she first mentions Bernard Fäy's and Madame Seillière's current (1932) translation of *The Making of Americans* (69), mentions a German translation of Stein's portraits (123), mentions *The Making of Americans* translation again in conjunction with a French translation of her portraits (283), and yet again in conjunction with the French translation of *Three Lives* [for *Ten American Novelists*] (307–8).

89. This theme begins with the first publication of *Three Lives* (83–84), with John Lane's plans to republish the book (173, 177–79), with Elliot Paul's reprinting of *Tender Buttons* in *transition* (296), and with Brewer's publication of *Useful Knowledge* (297–98); and the theme carries through the history of the publication of *The Making of Americans*: Toklas's out-of-chronology mention of McAlmon's later printing it (246), Hemingway's arrangement for it to appear in *Transatlantic* (264–65), its being printed (270), and its appearing (276). Though T. S. Eliot, however, had solicited a portrait from Stein for the *Criterion*, he "naturally" had not printed it (247).

90. Though men may have helped Stein into print, they also tended to abandon her. Toklas ends her appreciative commentary on Elliot Paul thus: "In the last numbers of transition nothing of hers [Stein's] appeared. Transition died" (see 293–96). And she links Brewer's failure to publish additional works of Stein directly to her own founding of Plain Edition (297–98). As Toklas sees the problem, French picture-dealers are adventurous (hence the success of Picasso and others) but American publishers are not (hence the obscurity of Stein).

91. The joke at the expense of Ford also works nicely at the expense of Stein, who does only *one* thing—write—and who insists, in fact, that "one can only have one métier" (94).

92. When Toklas recalls first meeting Picasso, for example, she cleverly describes him as wearing overalls that make him look simian—an homage to a Picasso motif turned against him (26); much later she recalls Picasso's mother and Stein together teasing him and, in effect, making him seem childish (271–72); and, throughout, she casts his attitudes toward women in a dubious light. Far harsher toward Hemingway, she (with Stein) depicts him as an artist who cannot distinguish "remarks" from literature (94, 270), who writes an "inevitable" first novel (261), and who, overall, is not a creator but a follower—specifically, a "pupil" of Stein's and Anderson's "who does it without understanding it" (266). As a person, he seems even worse: Toklas portrays him as a whining adolescent when faced with fatherhood (262), Stein and Anderson call him "yellow" (265), and a friend (!) of his says he is "fragile" and "breaks" easily (267–68)—which suggests that Stein's admitted "weakness" for him (271) merely follows from her weakness for breakable objects in general. Ultimately, Toklas brings Hemingway's failings as an artist into line with his flaws as a man. Stein and Anderson agree on the value of a book that "would be the real story of Hemingway, not those he writes but the confessions of the real Ernest Hemingway" (265–66); and Toklas later quotes Stein wishing he could, or would, "only tell his own story" (270). Though Stein may be turning those

very comments against herself at some level, Toklas essentially suggests that Hemingway lies as an artist because he lacks courage as a man. The critique of Picasso seems to have eluded readers to the extent that Braque and other missed it altogether; that of Hemingway eluded the mass audience, but was not lost on its subject.

93. According to Samuel Steward, Stein later said that Hemingway would " 'really attack all those he thinks had anything to do with his "greatness," Fitzgerald and Zelda and Alice and me and all the rest, just the way he attacked Sherwood' " (*Dear Sammy*, 65–66).

94. In a nasty review of *Staying on Alone*, Virgil Thomson notes that Toklas "hated" Hemingway, that her efforts to protect Stein were also ways of "protecting her own monopoly on Gertrude's sentimental life," and that, with respect to the broken friendship, Hemingway knew "that Alice, not Gertrude, was the enemy" ("Wickedly Wonderful Widow," 12, 14). Toklas's dislike hardly seems unjustified, given, for example, Hemingway's later claim to W. G. Rogers: "I always wanted to fuck her [Stein], and she knew it and it was a good healthy feeling and made more sense than a lot of the talk" (cited in Sheed, "A Farewell to Hemingstein," 8). Stein seems to have taken the matter up in references to Ida and "Ernest" in the brief "Ida" (1937) (Stein, *How Writing Is Written*, 43) and in references to Ida and the man from Omaha in the longer *Ida* (1941) (Stein, *Writings and Lectures: 1911–1945*, 324). For Steward's very different version of the Stein-Hemingway breakup, see *Dear Sammy*, 95–96.

95. In *Everybody's Autobiography*, Stein writes: "There is too much fathering going on just now and there is no doubt about it fathers are depressing. Everybody nowadays is a father, there is father Mussolini and father Hitler and father Roosevelt and father Stalin and father Lewis and father Blum and father Franco.... Fathers are depressing" (133). Given the context of her personal and familial history in *Everybody's Autobiography*, Stein is making a point almost identical to one Virginia Woolf elaborated in the same year in *Three Guineas*, namely, that the father in the patriarchal family strongly resembles the dictator in the fascist state (see Woolf, 53, 142).

96. My argument here owes much to Schmitz's insight and to his elaboration of it in "Portrait, Patriarchy, Mythos." Schmitz ultimately argues, however, that Picasso's appropriation of Stein is replayed in Stein's appropriation of Toklas, that Stein's revenge on Picasso *with* the *Autobiography* gets replayed in Toklas's revenge on Stein *in* the *Autobiography*; he argues, put differently, that the *Autobiography* reads as *Huckleberry Finn* as told from the perspective of Jim, *Robinson Crusoe* from the perspective of Friday. Though I find this argument suggestive, I remain committed to the view that Stein neither appropriated Toklas's voice in the way that Picasso appropriated her image (in fact or in fiction), nor constructed Toklas as a subordinate wife or partner.

97. Toklas found Stein, in 1907, "deep in The Making of Americans" and Picasso, at the same time, having "just finished his portrait of her" (7); when Toklas told Picasso that she liked the *Portrait*, he responded, "everybody says that [Stein] does not look like it but that does not make any difference, she will" (14). Neither Picasso nor Stein, Toklas later reports, remembers "how [the portrait] came about" (55), but someone, obviously, remembers what happened after the reportedly ninety sittings it took. Toklas reports, that is, that Picasso "painted out the whole head" before taking a trip to Spain (64–65); when Stein, soon after, returned from a concurrent trip to Florence, it

was "to her finished portrait," because Picasso, on the day he had returned, had painted in the masklike face mentioned above (70). Since "no one thought of taking a photograph of the picture as it was," no one, including Picasso and Stein, remembers "what it looked like" (57, repeated on 70). Toklas remembers, though, a related "charming story": many years later, when Stein had her hair cut short, Picasso at first grew angry and then added, "mais quand même, tout y est, all the same it is all there" (70). She finds this so charming, apparently, that she repeats it near the closing passage of the *Autobiography* (304). For Stein's further comments on the *Portrait*, see *P* 7–8, 21, 39.

The anecdote about Stein's hair is only one of several accounts or comments repeated exactly or almost exactly in the *Autobiography*; see, e.g., 62/259/306–7, 70/304, 87/300, 94/270.

98. Following the publication of *Picasso*, William Cook wrote Stein that she had "done the Picasso legend and it will stay that way," that she "made Picasso, . . . made him Picasso," an obviously figurative comment that perhaps alludes to the theme in the *Autobiography* that Picasso had done the Stein image (*Flowers of Friendship*, 327).

99. Stein wove the theme of sainthood throughout her *oeuvre*, beginning very covertly with martyrdom in *Three Lives*, as I have suggested, and reaching a peak of overtness in *Four Saints in Three Acts* (1927). In the *Autobiography*, Toklas names Stein's and her "favourite saints" (107–8; and see 142); she quotes Stein distinguishing between hysterics and saints and associating the latter with true creators (280); and she twice identifies Stein as looking like she belongs to a religious order (142, 304). Strictly speaking, Stein the creator cannot be beatified while still alive, so she appears as a monk who will be beatified.

100. As Stein has Toklas put it in the *Autobiography*, Stein and Picasso demonstrated "simple affection" in a "long friendship with all its sometimes troubled moments and its complications" (18–19).

101. Stein appears to be echoing this phrase, and extending its meaning, when she says in "Henry James," "I am I not any longer when I see," and then repeats the phrase with a small but significant variation (*FIA* 119, 125).

In a further complication of this theme, Stein notes in *Picasso* that Picasso "painted in the head without having seen me again and he gave me the picture and I was and I still am satisfied with my portrait, for me, it is I, and it is the only reproduction of me which is always I, for me" (8).

102. Stein seemed disinclined, for example, to loan the painting for the Picasso retrospective at the Museum of Modern Art in the winter of 1939–40 (see *Flowers of Friendship*, 340; *LGS/CVV* 658 n. 1). Shortly after war broke out in 1939, according to Kahnweiler, Stein and Toklas took only two pictures from Paris to their country home in Bilignin: Cézanne's portrait of Madame Cézanne and Picasso's portrait of Stein (Kahnweiler, Introduction, *Painted Lace*, xvii–xviii). Finally, Stein bequeathed to Toklas her paintings (and the bulk of her estate) except for the Picasso portrait, which she willed to the Metropolitan Museum of Art in New York (*LGS/CVV* 835, 837 n. 3). In a final irony, the Metropolitan Museum soon loaned the painting to the Museum of Modern Art as part of an extensive exchange; Toklas then wrote the president of the Met that Stein "was not interested in the Museum of Modern Art," and, after enumer-

ating Stein's reasons, appealed to him and the trustees on "ethical" grounds to reconsider their actions (Toklas, *Staying on Alone*, 82–83; and see 76–78). For photographs showing the portrait hanging in different locations in rue de Fleurus, see *Four Americans in Paris*, 91, 93, 94.

103. Murder as allegory for artistic representation seems connected to the *Huckleberry Finn* motif in the *Autobiography*, owing, I presume, to the symbolic patricide/faked suicide with which Huck Finn starts his adventure. See Stein's extremely brief and elliptical piece, "Mark Twain Centenary" (*Painted Lace*, 316) and her comments on Clemens and *Huckleberry Finn* in EA 110, 269–70.

104. For the uncropped version, see *Four Americans in Paris*, 91.

105. See Banta, *Imaging American Women*, 287–338. One could do a far more extensive and detailed comparison of the two texts than it would serve my purpose to do here.

106. Though perhaps only serendipity, Hawthorne's use of "phantasmagoric" in the preface to *The Blithedale Romance* recurs in James's use of the word in a key passage about romance in *Story*; and James's description of Isabel Archer's first extended reverie as "kaleidoscopic" recurs in Stein's use of that word in a key passage about Toklas's early reaction to life at rue de Fleurus (Hawthorne, *Works* 5:321; James, WWS 1:348, and *Portrait of a Lady*, 44; Stein, *ABT* 109).

107. The *Autobiography* was published, almost simultaneously, in a Literary Guild edition and a trade edition. Literary Guild editions of this period, I infer from several examples, seem to have had dustwrappers with a constant design (an abstracted bird) executed in variable color combinations; the *Autobiography* was no exception. The dustwrapper of the trade edition, however, featured the title above a differently cropped version of the frontispiece photograph; Stein's name appears neither on it nor on the title page. In fact, the internal gag about authorship extends to the testimonial back cover of the dustwrapper, where Van Vechten and two other signatories rebuke the purported claim that Toklas does not exist. And the gag continues on the inside front-flap, where Stein is presented as subject but not as author (the inside rear-flap, with a nice appropriateness from our present point of view, carries an advertisement for Virginia Woolf's *Flush: A Biography*).

108. Since we know that Stein owned a New York Edition, we can surmise that she would have read the version of *The Portrait of a Lady*, and especially of the penultimate scene, that I am citing.

109. In a concurrent allusion to Lewis Carroll, Toklas enters as *Alice through the Looking Glass*; the allusion has real resonance with respect to the confusion of realms (both the model *and* the character in each book being named Alice) and with respect to the implicit theme in each book of feminine sexual initiation (the latter immediately echoed in the allusion to *The Awkward Age*).

110. In *What Is Remembered*, Toklas indicates that Stein sold Picasso's *Woman with a Fan* (1905) to finance the Plain Edition (136). See, also, *Flowers of Friendship*, 246; LGS/CVV 207 n. 1; Kellner, *Gertrude Stein Companion*, 240; Mellow, *Charmed Circle*, 348–49.

111. The first installment, "Autobiography of Alice B. Toklas-I," appeared in May 1933;

according to Wilson, "The newsstand copies bore a pasted-on black and blue label reading 'My friend Picasso by Gertrude Stein.'" The fourth installment was titled "Ernest Hemingway and the Post-War Decade Autobiography of Alice B. Toklas. IV" (see Robert A. Wilson, *Gertrude Stein*, 132).

112. Toklas, *Staying on Alone*, 357.

Chapter Five

1. In *Charmed Circle*, Mellow presents evidence suggesting that, in 1913, Stein may "have tried to get a copy of *Three Lives* to Henry James" (146). In correspondence with Donald Sutherland, however, Toklas remarked that "no word of his [James's] about Gertrude ever came to us—though it is probable that William James spoke to him of her" (*Staying on Alone*, 91); this seems, in fact, less than probable. On Coburn's unsuccessful attempt to arrange a meeting between James and Stein, see Coburn's two letters to Stein, each dated 28 July 1914, in *The Flowers of Friendship* (98); and see James's telegram to Coburn, apparently sent on the same day, the text of which Mellow quotes (212).

2. See "Henry and I," *Painted Lace*, 273–74; and "James Is Nervous," *Bee Time Vine*, 208. Stein mentions "Henry James Winner" in "Scenery," *Bee Time Vine*, 217–18; and she remarks in "A Circular Play," *Last Operas and Plays*, 139–51, "We are all agreed that we like the letters of Henry James" (143). Bridgman surmises that these latter two references owe to the publication in 1920 of *The Letters of Henry James* (*Gertrude Stein in Pieces*, 161–62). One should note, however, that the second section of the earlier "Henry and I" is headed "WRITING LETTERS."

3. Stein must have read James when a young woman, however, since a character in her *Q.E.D.* (composed 1903) quotes by name Kate Croy from James's *Wings of the Dove*.

4. Sutherland likened Stein's use of the term "disconnection" to James's use of it in *The Ivory Tower* (*Gertrude Stein*, 93); I would be inclined to trace her use of it to passages in James's prefaces to the New York Edition, especially the final paragraph of the final preface (see *AN* 347–48).

5. Stein did not restrict to James such speculations about consciousness of intention; see her comment on Whitman: "He wanted really wanted to express the thing and not call it by its name.... I do not at all know whether Whitman knew that he wanted to do this but there is no doubt at all but that is what he did want to do" (*LIA* 241).

6. Stein's analysis of Jamesian characterization echoes T. S. Eliot's in his "On Henry James" (1918), 110, and in his essay "A Prediction" (1924), 55–56.

7. Stein also claimed James as her authority for her use of the split infinitive; see Toklas, *What Is Remembered*, 115, and *ABT* 247. Toklas commented on her own ability to type the "complicated sentences" of *The Making of Americans*: "Of course my love of Henry James was a good preparation for the long sentences" (quoted in Sprigge, *Gertrude Stein*, 81).

8. Though Haas and Gallup list 1933 for the composition of *Four in America* and 1934 for that of *Lectures in America* (*Catalogue*, 54), the record suggests otherwise.

Lincoln Kirstein wrote Stein on 7 October 1933 to solicit a contribution for the Henry James number of *Hound and Horn*, mentioning Stein's comments on James in *The Autobiography of Alice B. Toklas* and adding that "in this country [James] is almost completely forgotten by our younger writers" (*Flowers of Friendship*, 269–70); but the editorial preface to this number, *Hound and Horn* (April–May 1934), in noting the absence of contributions from Eliot, Pound, and Stein, explains that "Miss Stein's study is not finished at this date." I assume that study to have been the "Henry James" section of *Four in America*. In a letter of 15 October 1933, immediately following a cryptic reference to "Washington," Stein commented to Carl Van Vechten, "I am doing a book all about 4 eminent Americans and the first one is Grant it is beginning well" (*LGS/CVV* 280); in April 1934, in lines I have quoted as the epigraph to this chapter, she wrote Sherwood Anderson, "I have just been writing about four Americans" (*Sherwood Anderson/Gertrude Stein*, 85); and on 4 May 1934, Lansing Warren reported in the *New York Times Magazine* that "Miss Stein *is engaged in writing* a book on four Americans" ("Gertrude Stein views Life and Politics," 23; emphasis added). Stein obviously completed the book in the summer, since Van Vechten acknowledged receipt of the manuscript on 5 August 1934—judging it, incidentally, to be "one of your major works" (*LGS/CVV* 328). Finally, in *Lectures in America*, composed in late July through late August 1934 (see *LGS/CVV* 327, 332), Stein twice implied (24, 172) and once stated (206) that she had "finished" *Four in America*.

I detail that record to make the following point. Bridgman also questions Haas and Gallup, commenting that "the date of *Four in America*'s composition is still unclear" (*Gertrude Stein in Pieces*, 238n). He refers to Stein's comment in *Everybody's Autobiography*: "I had just before I wrote the Autobiography written Four in America" (*EA* 91); he cites a letter from Stein to Thornton Wilder, dated 1935, in which she says, "it was all written 4 years ago"; and he notes that a portion of the Washington section had been published in *Hound and Horn* in 1932. The record suggests that Stein wrote part of the eventual Washington section of *Four in America* in 1931 (Dydo convincingly sets the date of composition in autumn 1931; see "Gertrude Stein," 49, 59 n. 7); but it also suggests that she composed the book itself between autumn 1933 and summer 1934. Claiming in 1937 to have written it "all" in 1931, then, Stein again was fictionalizing her autobiography and mythologizing her self—in this case, I assume, to exaggerate the distance between the composition of a book she deemed important and any publication of it.

9. Responding to Van Vechten's letter of 5 August 1934, Stein concurred a few days later that *Four in America* was "one of my major works" and then went on to explain that "I will not give my lectures to anybody who will not print the Four in America and then later a portrait book." She apparently refused the lectures to Harcourt, Brace and Company "on that issue," but she eventually dropped the demand when dealing with Bennett Cerf, who published *Portraits and Prayers* and *Lectures in America* at Random House, but not *Four in America* (see *LGS/CVV* 329).

10. See "Not for the Tired," 110, 113–14; and Hart, *Library Journal*, 1468. Such assessments have not abated altogether: in *Henry James*, McColgan characterizes the James section of *Four in America* as "A 'Steinish' discussion. . . . Impressionistic ramblings

about James' name and artistic identity" (141). For the only recent commentaries of substance, see Schmitz, "Doing the Fathers," and "*Four* (and Then Some) *in America.*"

11. Warren, "Gertrude Stein Views Life and Politics," 23. Warren reports this particular information in indirect quotation.

12. See Steiner, *Exact Resemblance to Exact Resemblance*, 130, 163.

13. Stein seemed to have meant that these novels emphasize character over plot, picture over narrative, that they correspondingly emphasize circular structure over linear, and that they emphasize the ongoing story of their own composition over the incidents they relate. Her choice of these three novels doubtless derives, in part, from their being the prose works Edmund Wilson had discussed at length in *Axel's Castle*; for evidence that Stein read *Axel's Castle* before 1934, see LGS/CVV 239.

14. Gray, "Competent Priestess," 30.

15. Pearson, "Gertrude Stein," 744, 745.

16. Stein notes in *Everybody's Autobiography* that she has "just bought [Grant's *Memoirs*] to *read again*" (235, and see 260; emphasis added), and she retails in her Grant composition incidents that appear in his *Memoirs*; she mentions the site of the Wright monument twice in her Wright composition (84–85, 95) and mentions the monument itself four additional times (100, 109, 111, 116); she weaves her Washington composition around the general remark that Washington was "the father of his country" and around Lee's particular remark that Washington was "first in war, first in peace, and first in the hearts of his countrymen"; and she seems to have in mind throughout her James composition her precursor's later phase memorial writing.

17. James mentions Napoleon in the opening paragraph of *Notes of a Son and Brother*, and, as I noted earlier, he characterizes Grant as "no light-handed artist" at the opening of the crucial four-page paragraph in which he associates the Civil War with his back injury, Lincoln's assassination with Hawthorne's death, and those two associations with each other (*N* 439, 477–78).

Scholars have compared many authors with Napoleon, and many authors have invoked his name, but the Napoleonic connections with James and Stein seem especially strong. In her memoir, "Henry James at Work" (1924), for example, James's amanuensis Theodora Bosanquet noted of the novelist's visage: "He might well have been a merciful Caesar or a benevolent Napoleon, and a painter who worked at his portrait . . . was excusably reminded of so many illustrious makers of history that he declared it to be a hard task to isolate the individual character of the model" (245). In the delirious deathbed dictation that Edel has retrieved for us, moreover, James imagined himself Napoleon (see *HJL* 4:808–9). Apparently an homage to the deceased novelist, Stein's "Henry and I" contains the line "He is dead"; and she seems to echo it in "A Circular Play," in which she explicitly names James, with the line "Napoleon is dead." Given that parts of Bosanquet's memoir appeared serially in 1917 and 1918, and given that the passage I cited resonates with the themes of *Four in America*, I am tempted to think that Stein knew of the memoir in 1920 or, more likely, by the early 1930s. Though she could not have known of James's deathbed dictation in 1920, moreover, she might have known of it and, if only vaguely, of its contents by the early 1930s (see Edel's discussion, cited above). Whatever the case with respect to James, Stein constructed her second portrait of Picasso, "If I Told Him, A Completed Portrait of

Picasso" (1923), on an extended metaphor of Picasso as Napoleon (see Stein, *Picasso: The Complete Writings*, 99–103); and she traced her own family name to "the time of Napoleon" in the paternity-obsessed *Everybody's Autobiography*—in a passage followed immediately by a one-line paragraph that points to issues already explored in *Four in America*: "Identity always worries me and memory and eternity" (115).

Both James and Stein, finally, admired not only Grant the general, but also Grant the memoirist. In his column on "American Letters" for the 16 April 1898 issue of *Literature*, James praised the "hard limpidity of [Grant's] strong and simple Autobiography" (*LC* 2:661). In *The Autobiography of Alice B. Toklas*, Toklas reports that Stein and Sherwood Anderson had Grant "as their great american hero" and "even planned collaborating on a life of Grant" (303–4); Stein actually did attempt to interest Lloyd Lewis in such a collaboration in 1935, luring him with the manuscript of *Four in America* (see *LGS/CVV* 404–5 n. 6; *Flowers of Friendship*, 321–22); and she spoke favorably of Grant's *Memoirs* in *Everybody's Autobiography* (225, 260).

18. With reference to James's Napoleonic identification, coincidentally, Edel notes on the final page of his five-volume *Henry James*: "He had indeed planned a career and carried it out as a general plans his campaigns and wins his victories" (*HJ* 5:564).

19. José Ortega y Gasset, "Dehumanization of Art," 31. Assuming Stein is employing this pun, she may have arrived at it independently, or she may have derived it from Ortega's essay, first published in Spanish in 1925. I think the former more likely. Despite Stein's extended visits to Spain (1912) and to Spain and Mallorca (1915), I find no evidence that she read Spanish.

20. Stein, *Bee Time Vine and Other Pieces*, 208.

21. See chapter 10 of *Principles of Psychology*, 1:291–401.

22. In another possible level of reference, Stein may want her reader to consider not only the paternal, fraternal, and filial relations between Henry James Sr., William James, and Henry James Jr., but also, and more specifically, the memorial writing generated from those relations: William edited Henry Sr.'s papers as *The Literary Remains of the Late Henry James* (1885); Henry Jr. opened his memoirs, at once autobiographical and biographical, with a reference to William and incorporated into their second volume letters from William and Henry Sr.

23. The opposition that governs all of these, and that commentators find central to Stein's work of the 1930s, is that between "entity" and "identity"—one that closely echoes the relationship that William James had postulated between the particle and the flux in his model of the stream of consciousness. If Stein understood the dialectical nature of James's model, however, as I feel certain that she did, then her commentators are mistaken in their efforts to have her "choose" between entity and identity, entity-writing and identity-writing, and, by implication, such allegedly "difficult" texts as *Stanzas in Meditation* and such allegedly "simple" texts as *The Autobiography of Alice B. Toklas*. Stein could not choose between two interdependent, mutually constitutive aspects of the psyche any more than she would choose between such aspects of literary representation as, say, picture and story, portrait and narrative; she could only *be* both ways at once, just as she would only *write* both ways at once—that was her central point about Henry James, herself, and his lesson for her.

In correspondence with Donald Sutherland, interestingly, Virgil Thomson suggested that Stein, a few others, and he might have picked up the term "identity," at Harvard, from "Henry James via William" (cited in Dydo, "Gertrude Stein," 58–59 n. 4). For treatments of intellectual connections between Henry James and William James, see (among others) Hocks, *Henry James and Pragmatistic Thought*, and Posnock, *Trial of Curiosity*; for a treatment of such connections between William James and Stein, see Bush, *Halfway to Revolution*.

24. If my analysis is correct, then Stein would be on unstable ground with respect to sources: generally based on earlier oral or written materials, that is, Shakespeare's plays would seem more obviously translated and more obviously conventional than his sonnets. She appears to have other things in mind, however: with respect to composition, Shakespeare invented dramatic forms while only employing sonnet forms, that is, generated the former internally while applying the latter externally; with respect to reception, an audience experiences his plays, like any others, in unmediated time but a reader experiences his poems, like any other, in mediated time—or so Stein argues in *Lectures in America*. In any event, this case serves to illustrate problems in reconstructing Stein's logic.

25. Neuman, *Gertrude Stein*, 34. See, also, Neuman's bio-bibliographical account of the circumstances surrounding *Before the Flowers* (14) and her comments on generic distinctions in Stein's theory of audience (35–36).

26. Stein wrote *Before the Flowers* in 1930, she quarreled about the translation with Hugnet, Bravig Imbs, and Virgil Thomson for some time afterward, and she saw her source-text, Hugnet's *Enfances*, published in 1933 (see, e.g., LGS/CVV 226–27 n. 2). References in the *Autobiography* suggest that she was reading James around 1931 and 1932, and epistolary evidence cited above (note 8) certainly suggests that she was thinking about him in 1933. These accidents of timing caused *Before the Flowers* and her reading of James to "coincide" in her mind, hence the second coincidence.

27. In a letter to Carl Van Vechten of 17 January 1936, Stein expressly identified *Four in America* as the book "out of which [*The Geographical History of America*] came" (LGS/CVV 474).

28. In fact, Stein was reworking language she had used in "Ada" (composed before 1912) to describe how Ada and "some one who was loving" told stories to each other and listened to each other (*A Primer for the Gradual Understanding of Gertrude Stein*, 45–47); as we recall, Stein and Toklas had identified "Ada," in the opening passage of the *Autobiography*, as being about Toklas. Stein would rework related issues about Toklas in "Ida" (1937) and *Ida* (1941).

29. Stein seems to have been playing a verbal game with James's predilection for marriage as a metaphor for the fusion of content and form in literature. See, for example, AN 115–16: "They ["substance and form in a really wrought work of art"] are separate before the fact, but the sacrament of execution indissolubly marries them, and the marriage, like any other marriage, has only to be a 'true' one for the scandal of a breach not to show. The thing 'done,' artistically, is a fusion, or it has not *been* done." As preoccupied with proper relations between content and form as were James and her fellow post-Jamesians, Stein introduced into her art the alternative marital model she practiced in her life; what James feared as possible "scandal," Stein welcomed sexually and textually:

not "fusion" but, as she puns, purposeful "diffusion." As I argued in chapter 4, Stein was advocating, sexually and textually, alternatives and experimentation—not adultery.

30. For discussions of Stein in relation to "feminine writing," see Gibbs, "Hélène Cixous and Gertrude Stein," and DeKoven, *A Different Language*.

Bridgman traces Stein's first use of "Rose is a rose is a rose is a rose" to "Sacred Emily" (1913) and indicates its variations in other texts (*Gertrude Stein in Pieces*, 138–39); he also suggests its pertinence to Stein's "Autobiography of Rose" (1936) and to *The World Is Round* (1938) and reminds us that Stein used a linked circle for the rose device on the cover of the *Autobiography* (*Gertrude Stein in Pieces*, 299–300). Charles Demuth echoed the pun on "a rose" and "eros" in his poster portrait, *Love, Love, Love (Homage to Gertrude Stein)* (c. 1928), a pun that employs the obvious yonic connotations of the rose as a flower and of *rose* as French for the color pink. In a sense, Stein anticipated by seven years Duchamp's adoption of the pseudonym Rrose Sélavy (*Eros c'est la vie*), a pseudonym related to themes of androgyny and transvestism in his work. (Actually, Duchamp began using Rose Sélavy in 1920 and Rrose Sélavy in 1921; see Schwarz, *Complete Works of Marcel Duchamp*, 587.) For commentary on the rose as symbol for female sexuality and for lesbian eroticism, see, e.g., Cramer, "Notes from Underground," 183–84.

31. Stein's sense of Freud is difficult to fix. As a protégé of William James and a thinker preoccupied with consciousness, as an ally of Picasso and a foe of Surrealism, she predictably ignored Freud, at least explicitly, in her work; she mentions him briefly, but negatively, for example, in *Everybody's Autobiography* (28). Rudick argues, however, that Stein owed more to Freud than we heretofore have recognized.

32. Stein's use of the word "volume" throughout *Four in America* to characterize a very small unit of writing, then, seems more than just a parody of literary convention; it also functions as a pun that points to her Cubism, her small volumes being like the small volumetric shapes that constitute a Cubist painting.

33. Some slippage enters Stein's view of this. In *The Autobiography of Alice B. Toklas*, Toklas quotes Stein on "America as being now the oldest country in the world because by the methods of the civil war and the commercial conceptions that followed it America created the twentieth century . . . in the sixties of the nineteenth century" (96). In *Brewsie and Willie*, however, Pauline quotes Stein on "America that is the United States of America [as] the oldest country in the world because she went into the twentieth century in eighteen ninety, when all the others were way behind" (50).

34. That Picasso and, by implication, Stein produced Cubist perspectivalism without actually having flown suggests their true genius. That, at least, is the argument of Stein's epilogue to *Picasso*, its key sentence: "When I was in America [1934–35] I for the first time travelled pretty much all the time in an airplane and when I looked at the earth I saw all the lines of cubism made at a time when not any painter had ever gone up in an airplane" (50).

35. The preceding phrase in the James composition, "Prepare for flight," simply may be a notation of the subject Stein next will consider or may be an imperative to herself and to her reader. Given the themes of expatriation and of remembrance in *Four in America*, Stein also may be suggesting that James had prepared inadequately for his

flight from America, that he remembered in exile either too little or too much of his American sensibility—a point she also makes about Picasso and herself.

Like so many of Stein's tropes, however, this one opens onto a complex intertext—whether by auctorial intention or by readerly intervention. James had used Shakespeare's *Tempest* as a source-text for his tale "The Middle Years" (1893), and, as had Prospero, James's protagonist Dencombe "takes his flight" (for an elaboration of this textual connection, see Tintner, *Book World*, 49–50); some years later, James wrote the introduction to *The Tempest* for a new edition of Shakespeare (1907), an introduction that concludes with his pondering how Shakespeare's genius could have "contrive[d], in such perfection, the arrest of its divine flight." It is hard to imagine that Stein did not draw on this essay for her James composition, given James's *donnée* of Shakespeare's "genius" (he repeats the word endlessly); given his comment that Shakespeare in *The Tempest* was the artist "so generalized, so consummate and typical," that he paradoxically almost revealed himself as a man; given his central theme that, however, "we shall never touch the Man *directly* in the Artist"; given Stein's remark, allegedly made to Robert McAlmon in 1925, that "nobody has done anything to develop the English language since Shakespeare, except myself, and Henry James perhaps a little"; and given, finally, her triangulation of Shakespeare, James, and herself in "Henry James" (for citations, see James, *LC* 2:1219, 1209, 1220; McAlmon, *Being Geniuses Together*, 228).

Were that not enough, in articles on "The Younger Generation" in the *Times Literary Supplement* (1914)—combined and revised as "The New Novel" for *Notes on Novelists* (1914)—James described Conrad's narration with a tortured trope involving shadows cast by the flight of an "aeroplane" (*LC* 2:149), a trope Edel traces to James's having seen, "one day at Rye, Blériot's plane over the Channel" (*HJ* 5:55). In fact, James had noted his distaste for the noisy "ravage of the motors & the aeroplanes" on Sussex even earlier (letter to Hamlin Garland, 30 July 1909; excerpted in Christie's *Modern Literature*, 67); a distaste he apparently also had for the Matisses and Picassos he saw at about the same time (see Toklas, *Staying on Alone*, 92).

36. Some slippage also enters Stein's view of this. In *Everybody's Autobiography*, she wrote: "The 1914–1918 war was bigger and had different arms but eventually it added nothing to what had been imagined in the Civil War" (246). A year or so later, however, she wrote in *Picasso*: "Really the composition of this war, 1914–1918, was not the composition of all previous wars, the composition was not a composition in which there was one man in the centre surrounded by a lot of other men but a composition that had neither a beginning nor an end, a composition of which one corner was as important as another corner, in fact the composition of cubism" (11). And some years after that, in *Wars I Have Seen* (1945), she again would describe the 1914–1918 war as "after all . . . a nineteenth century war" (80–81).

37. The plural admits Juan Gris, "after Pablo Picasso Gertrude Stein's dearest friend" (*ABT* 24) and the illustrator of her *Book Concluding With As A Wife Has A Cow[:] A Love Story* (1926).

38. In *Wars I Have Seen*, Stein would claim: "I belong to the generation who born in the nineteenth century spent all the early part of my life in escaping from it, and the rest of it in being the twentieth century yes of course" (80).

39. Simplified and shorn of its Cubist dimensions, *Four in America* looks like this:

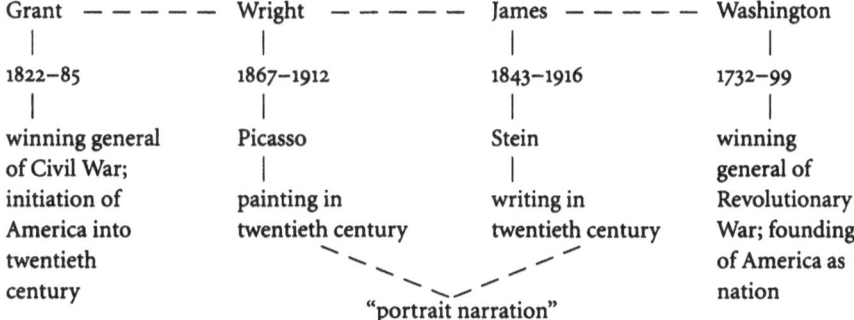

40. See Pound, "Henry James"; the first citation appears on 298.

41. Eliot, "On Henry James," 110.

42. See Forster, *Aspects of the Novel*, 153–64; and Leavis, *Great Tradition*, 154–72.

43. Spender, "Henry James and the Contemporary Subject," 104.

44. Quoted in *Pound/Joyce*, 255, 256; the letter to Cummings appears in full in *Letters of Ezra Pound*, 227.

45. The first citation appears in Eliot's review of *Composition as Explanation*, 162; Stein reports the second remark in *The Autobiography of Alice B. Toklas*, 248.

46. Edmund Wilson, *Axel's Castle*, 239. Interestingly, Leavis observes that "several of the contributors to the Henry James number of the *Hound and Horn* (April–June 1934) [sic] . . . expose themselves as not having read, or having not been able to read, the works they write about" (*Great Tradition*, 155).

47. Leavis, *Great Tradition*, 156.

48. Perloff, *Poetics of Indeterminacy*, 72.

49. Stein perceived the essence of genius as "being one who is at the same time talking and listening," a combination she extended to include "looking" (*LIA* 170, 188–94; and see *NAR* 34, *What Are Masterpieces*, 84).

50. With fine discrimination, Steiner isolates autoreference as a feature of Stein's "second-phase portraits" (*Exact Resemblance to Exact Resemblance*, 105). Without disputing Steiner's typology, I maintain that varieties of autoreference were pandemic in modernist portraiture.

51. Eliot, "On Henry James," 110.

52. See Leo Stein, *Journey into the Self*, 142, 149, 298.

53. Sloper, "Nonsense," 17.

54. Valéry, "Poetry and Abstract Thought," 63.

55. Perloff, *Poetics of Indeterminacy*, 72.

56. Stein similarly criticized the Surrealists for still "see[ing] things as every one sees them," for practicing a twentieth-century "complication" of an essentially nineteenth-century "vision" (*P* 43). Though she greatly admired Proust and argued that he did the novel "the best" in the twentieth century, she nonetheless added that he "made an old-fashioned thing of it" (TI 21–22).

57. Antin goes so far as to argue that "Gertrude Stein was our only pure modernist" ("Some Questions about Modernism," 11).

58. Scholars often have followed suit. In the opening sentence of *The Pound Era*, for example, Kenner invokes James, and in his opening chapter, "Ghosts and Benedictions," he focuses on James as the great precursor of Pound and, by implication, of Pound's era; in six hundred pages, he mentions Stein only twice in passing.

59. For a discussion of Joyce's perception and repression of James as the "father" of "the Modernist sensibility that created *Ulysses*," see Fogel, *Covert Relations*, 26–53. In a nice formulation in *Finnegans Wake*, Joyce has "Jacobiters," including the Eliot-figure Shaun, attack the Joyce-figure Shem (also identified with Jacob) (111). In the early years of the James revival, Jamesians were tagged Jacobites.

Toklas wrote to Sutherland, in November 1947, that Joyce "was for several years a grievous thorn in [Stein's] side" (*Staying on Alone*, 91); and Hemingway, in *A Moveable Feast*, remarked: "If you brought up Joyce twice, you would not be invited back. It was like mentioning one general favorably to another general. You learned not to do it the first time you made the mistake" (28).

60. In Stimpson's apt words, Stein was "an anti-patriarchal writer, with strong moorings to the patriarchy" ("Somagrams of Gertrude Stein," 39 n. 7).

61. Though I stand by the conclusions reached in the latter half of this chapter, I must qualify them. Following the publication of *The Autobiography of Alice B. Toklas*, as I discussed in chapter 4, Stein did achieve celebrity in America, to a degree that she developed a severe writer's block. She worked through it, slowly, by writing *Four in America*, among other texts, and, not surprisingly, she focused there on relevant questions about the assignment and acquisition of fame. She had complained *in* the *Autobiography* that she had become notorious for her life, while others had become famous for their art; and she seemed to be thinking in *Four in America* that nothing had changed—that she now was notorious *because of* the *Autobiography* but still was not famous because of *The Making of Americans*. She would extend this theme, and treat it more explicitly, in *Everybody's Autobiography*, her account of her lecture tour as a "lion" in 1934–35, her examination of the relation between fame and mass-cultural celebrity and between celebrity and identity.

WORKS CITED

Primary Texts

HENRY JAMES

James, Henry. *The American Scene.* 1907. Reprint. Bloomington: Indiana University Press, 1968.
———. *The Art of the Novel.* New York: Charles Scribner's Sons, 1934.
———. *The Complete Notebooks of Henry James.* Edited by Leon Edel and Lyall H. Powers. New York: Oxford University Press, 1987.
———. *The Correspondence of Henry James and the House of Macmillian, 1877–1914.* Edited by Rayburn S. Moore. Baton Rouge: Louisiana State University Press, 1993.
———. *Essays in London and Elsewhere.* New York: Harper & Brothers, 1893.
———. *Hawthorne.* 1879. In *Literary Criticism: Essays on Literature,* pp. 315–474.
———. *Henry James Letters.* 4 vols. Edited by Leon Edel. Cambridge: Harvard University Press, Belknap Press, 1975–84.
———. *Italian Hours.* 1909. Reprint, edited by John Auchard. University Park: Pennsylvania State University Press, 1992.
———. *The Letters of Henry James.* 2 vols. Edited by Percy Lubbock. New York: Charles Scribner's Sons, 1920.
———. *Literary Criticism: Essays on Literature, American Writers, English Writers.* Edited by Leon Edel. New York: The Library of America, 1984.
———. *Literary Criticism: French Writers, Other European Writers, The Prefaces to the New York Edition.* Edited by Leon Edel. New York: The Library of America, 1984.
———. *Literary Reviews and Essays: On American, English and French Literature.* Edited by Albert Mordell. 1957. Reprint. New York: Grove Press, 1979.
———. *The Middle Years.* New York: Charles Scribner's Sons, 1917.
———. *Notes of a Son and Brother.* New York: Charles Scribner's Sons, 1914.
———. *The Painter's Eye: Notes and Essays on the Pictorial Arts.* Edited by John L. Sweeney. Cambridge: Harvard University Press, 1956.
———. *The Portrait of a Lady.* 1881. Reprint, edited by Robert D. Bamberg. New York: W. W. Norton, 1975.
———. *The Scenic Art: Notes on Acting and the Drama, 1872–1901.* Edited by Allan Wade. 1948. Reprint, New York: Hill and Wang, 1957.
———. *A Small Boy and Others.* New York: Charles Scribner's Sons, 1913.
———. *William Wetmore Story and His Friends.* 2 vols. Boston: Houghton, Mifflin, 1903.

GERTRUDE STEIN

Stein, Gertrude. *The Autobiography of Alice B. Toklas.* New York: The Literary Guild/Harcourt, Brace, and Co., 1933.
———. *Bee Time Vine and Other Pieces [1913–1927].* The Yale Edition of the Unpublished Writings of Gertrude Stein, Vol. 3. New Haven: Yale University Press, 1953.

———. *Brewsie and Willie*. New York: Random House, 1946.
———. "Composition as Explanation." In *What Are Masterpieces*, pp. 23–58.
———. *Everybody's Autobiography*. New York: Random House, 1937.
———. *Four in America*. New Haven: Yale University Press, 1947.
———. *The Geographical History of America*. New York: Random House, 1936.
———. *Gertrude Stein's America*. Edited by Gilbert A. Harrison. 1965. Reprint. New York: Liveright, 1974.
———. *How To Write*. Plain Edition, 1931. Reprint. New York: Dover, 1975.
———. *How Writing Is Written*. Edited by Robert Bartlett Haas. Los Angeles: Black Sparrow, 1974.
———. *Last Operas and Plays*. New York: Rinehart, 1949.
———. *Lectures in America*. New York: Random House, 1935.
———. *The Making of Americans: Being a History of a Family's Progress*. 1925. Reprint. New York: Something Else Press, 1966.
———. *The Making of Americans: The Hersland Family*. Abridged Version. New York: Harcourt, Brace and Company, 1934.
———. *Narration*. 1935. Chicago: University of Chicago Press, 1969.
———. *Painted Lace and Other Pieces [1914–1937]*. The Yale Edition of the Unpublished Writings of Gertrude Stein, Vol. 5. New Haven: Yale University Press, 1955.
———. *Picasso*. London: B. T. Batsford, 1938. New York: Charles Scribner's Sons, 1939.
———. *Picasso: The Complete Writings*. Edited by Edward Burns. 1970. Reprint. Boston: Beacon Press, 1985.
———. *A Primer for the Gradual Understanding of Gertrude Stein*. Edited by Robert Bartlett Haas. Los Angeles: Black Sparrow Press, 1971.
———. *Stanzas in Meditation and Other Poems, 1929–1933*. The Yale Edition of the Unpublished Writings of Gertrude Stein, Vol. 6. New Haven: Yale University Press, 1956.
———. *Three Lives*. 1909. New York: The Modern Library, 1933.
———. "A Transatlantic Interview." Excerpt from "Gertrude Stein Talking—A Transatlantic Interview." In *A Primer for the Gradual Understanding of Gertrude Stein*, 13–35.
———. *What Are Masterpieces*. 1940. Reprint. New York: Pitman, 1970.
———. *Writings and Lectures 1911–1945*. Edited by Patricia Meyerowitz. London: Peter Owen, 1967.

Secondary Texts

BOOKS

Adams, Henry. *Letters of Henry Adams*. 2 vols. Edited by Worthington Chauncey Ford. Boston: Houghton Mifflin, 1938.
Adams, Timothy Dow. *Telling Lies in Modern American Autobiography*. Chapel Hill: University of North Carolina Press, 1990.

Anesko, Michael. *"Friction with the Market": Henry James and the Profession of Authorship*. New York: Oxford University Press, 1986.
Babiiha, Thaddeo K. *The James-Hawthorne Relation: Bibliographical Essays*. Boston: G. K. Hall, 1980.
Banta, Martha. *Imaging American Women: Idea and Ideals in Cultural History*. New York: Columbia University Press, 1987.
Batchelder, Robert F. *Autographs*. Catalog 67, 1988. Unpaginated.
Beidler, Peter G. *Ghosts, Demons, and Henry James: "The Turn of the Screw" at the Turn of the Century*. Columbia: University of Missouri Press, 1989.
Benstock, Shari. *Women of the Left Bank: Paris, 1900–1940*. Austin: University of Texas Press, 1986.
Berry, Ellen E. *Curved Thought and Textual Wandering: Gertrude Stein's Postmodernism*. Ann Arbor: University of Michigan Press, 1992.
Bosanquet, Theodora. *Henry James at Work*. The Hogarth Essays. London: The Hogarth Press, 1924.
Bowers, Jane Palatini. *"They Watch Me as They Watch This": Gertrude Stein's Metadrama*. Philadelphia: University of Pennsylvania Press, 1991.
Boyle, Nicholas, and Martin Swales, ed. *Realism in European Literature: Essays in Honour of J. P. Stern*. Cambridge: Cambridge University Press, 1986.
Braque, Georges, et al. *Testimony against Gertrude Stein*. Transition Pamphlet No. 1. The Hague: Servire Press, 1935.
Bridgman, Richard. *The Colloquial Style in America*. New York: Oxford University Press, 1966.
———. *Gertrude Stein in Pieces*. New York: Oxford University Press, 1970.
Brinnin, John Malcolm. *The Third Rose: Gertrude Stein and Her World*. Boston: Little, Brown and Co., 1959.
Brodhead, Richard H. *The School of Hawthorne*. New York: Oxford University Press, 1986.
Buitenhuis, Peter. *The Grasping Imagination: The American Writings of Henry James*. Toronto: University of Toronto Press, 1970.
Burns, Edward, ed. *The Letters of Gertrude Stein and Carl Van Vechten, 1913–1946*. 2 vols. New York: Columbia University Press, 1986.
Bush, Clive. *Halfway to Revolution: Investigation and Crisis in the Work of Henry Adams, William James and Gertrude Stein*. New Haven: Yale University Press, 1991.
Chessman, Harriet Scott. *The Public is Invited to Dance: Representation, the Body, and Dialogue in Gertrude Stein*. Stanford: Stanford University Press, 1989.
Chipp, Herschel B. *Theories of Modern Art: A Source Book by Artists and Critics*. Berkeley and Los Angeles: University of California Press, 1968.
[Coburn, Alvin Langdon]. *Alvin Langdon Coburn: Photographer, An Autobiography*. Edited by Alison Gernsheim and Helmut Gernsheim. 1966. Reprint. New York: Dover, 1978.
Cooley, Thomas. *Educated Lives: The Rise of Modern Autobiography in America*. Columbus: Ohio State University Press, 1976.
Couser, G. Thomas. *American Autobiography: The Prophetic Mode*. Amherst: University of Massachusetts Press, 1979.

Davis, Richard Harding, et al. *The Great Streets of the World*. New York: Charles Scribner's Sons, 1892.

Defoe, Daniel. *Robinson Crusoe*. 1719. Reprint, edited by Angus Ross. Harmondsworth: Penguin, 1965.

DeKoven, Marianne. *A Different Language: Gertrude Stein's Experimental Writing*. Madison: University of Wisconsin Press, 1983.

——. *Rich and Strange: Gender, History, Modernism*. Princeton: Princeton University Press, 1991.

Dubnick, Randa. *The Structure of Obscurity: Gertrude Stein, Language, and Cubism*. Urbana: University of Illinois Press, 1984.

Dupee, F. W. *Henry James*. 1951. The American Men of Letters Series. New York: Delta/Dell, 1965.

Edel, Leon. *Henry James*. 5 vols. Philadelphia: J. B. Lippincott, 1953–72.

——. *Henry James*. Pamphlets on American Writers, no. 4. Minneapolis: University of Minnesota Press, 1960.

Edel, Leon, and Dan H. Laurence. *A Bibliography of Henry James*. 3d ed. Oxford: Clarendon Press, 1982.

Fichtelberg, Joseph. *The Complex Image: Faith and Method in American Autobiography*. Philadelphia: University of Pennsylvania Press, 1989.

Fifer, Elizabeth. *Rescued Readings: A Reconstruction of Gertrude Stein's Difficult Texts*. Detroit: Wayne State University Press, 1992.

Fogel, Daniel Mark. *Covert Relations: James Joyce, Virginia Woolf, and Henry James*. Charlottesville: University Press of Virginia, 1990.

Forster, E. M. *Aspects of the Novel*. 1927. Reprint. New York: Harcourt, Brace & World, 1954.

Four Americans in Paris: The Collections of Gertrude Stein and Her Family. New York: The Museum of Modern Art, 1970.

Franklin, Benjamin. *Autobiography*. Reprint, edited by J. A. Leo Lemay and P. M. Zall. New York: W. W. Norton, 1986.

Fredrickson, George M. *The Inner Civil War: Northern Intellectuals and the Crisis of the Union*. New York: Harper & Row, 1965.

Fry, Edward F. *Cubism*. 1966. New York: Oxford University Press, 1978.

Gale, Robert L. *A Henry James Encyclopedia*. New York: Greenwood, 1989.

Gallup, Donald, ed. *The Flowers of Friendship: Letters Written to Gertrude Stein*. New York: Alfred A. Knopf, 1953.

Gilbert, Sandra M., and Susan Gubar. *No Man's Land: The Place of the Woman Writer in the Twentieth Century*. Vol. 2, *Sexchanges*. New Haven: Yale University Press, 1989.

Goetz, William R. *Henry James and the Darkest Abyss of Romance*. Baton Rouge: Louisiana State University Press, 1986.

Haas, Robert Bartlett, and Donald Clifford Gallup, comp. *A Catalogue of the Published and Unpublished Writings of Gertrude Stein*. New Haven: Yale University Library, 1941.

Hale, Edward Everett. *James Russell Lowell and His Friends*. Boston: Houghton, Mifflin, 1901.

Hawthorne, Nathaniel. *The Works of Nathaniel Hawthorne*. 15 vols. Boston and New York: Houghton, Mifflin and Company, 1882–84.
Hemingway, Ernest. *A Moveable Feast*. New York: Charles Scribner's Sons, 1964.
Hocks, Richard A. *Henry James and Pragmatistic Thought: A Study in the Relationship Between the Philosophy of William James and the Literary Art of Henry James*. Chapel Hill: University of North Carolina Press, 1974.
Hoffman, Frederick J. *The Twenties: American Writing in the Postwar Decade*. Rev. ed. New York: The Free Press, 1965.
Hoffman, Michael J. *The Development of Abstractionism in the Writings of Gertrude Stein*. Philadelphia: University of Pennsylvania Press, 1966.
"Homage to Henry James, 1843–1916." *Hound & Horn* 7 (1934).
James, William. *Memories and Studies*. New York: Longmans, Green, and Co., 1911.
———. *The Principles of Psychology*. 2 vols. 1890. Reprint. New York: Dover, 1950.
Jelinek, Estelle C. *The Tradition of Women's Autobiography: From Antiquity to the Present*. Boston: Twayne/G. K. Hall, 1986.
Joyce, James. *Finnegans Wake*. New York: Viking, 1939.
Kellner, Bruce, ed. *A Gertrude Stein Companion: Content with the Example*. New York: Greenwood, 1988.
Kenner, Hugh. *The Pound Era*. Berkeley: University of California Press, 1971.
Knapp, Bettina L. *Gertrude Stein*. Literature and Life: American Writers. New York: Continuum, Frederick Ungar, 1990.
Lathrop, George Parsons. *A Study of Hawthorne*. 1876. Riverside Pocket Series. Boston and New York: Houghton, Mifflin and Company, 1886.
Leavis, F. R. *The Great Tradition: George Eliot, Henry James, Joseph Conrad*. 1948. New York: New York University Press, 1973.
Leonardi, Susan J. *Dangerous by Degrees: Women at Oxford and the Somerville College Novelists*. New Brunswick: Rutgers University Press, 1989.
Levine, George. *The Realistic Imagination: English Fiction from Frankenstein to Lady Chatterly*. Chicago: University of Chicago Press, 1981.
Loggins, Vernon. *I Hear America: Literature in the United States Since 1900*. New York: Thomas Y. Crowell, 1937.
MacDonald, Bonney. *Henry James's "Italian Hours": Revelatory and Resistent Impressions*. Studies in Modern Literature, No. 106. Ann Arbor, Mich.: UMI Research Press, 1990.
Matthiessen, F. O. *The Achievement of T. S. Eliot: An Essay on the Nature of Poetry*. 3d ed. New York: Oxford University Press, 1958.
———. *American Renaissance: Art and Expression in the Age of Emerson and Whitman*. 1941. New York: Oxford University Press, 1968.
———. *The James Family: A Group Biography*. New York: Alfred A. Knopf, 1961.
Maves, Carl. *Sensuous Pessimism: Italy in the Work of Henry James*. Bloomington: Indiana University Press, 1973.
McAlmon, Robert. *Being Genuises Together: An Autobiography*. 1938. Reprinted as *Being Genuises Together, 1920–1930*. San Francisco: North Point Press, 1984.
McColgan, Kristin Pruitt. *Henry James, 1917–1959: A Reference Guide*. Boston: G. K. Hall, 1979.

Mellow, James R. *Charmed Circle: Gertrude Stein & Company*. New York: Praeger, 1974.

Modern Literature from the Library of James Gilvarry. New York: Christie's, 1986.

Moffett, Charles S., et al. *The New Painting: Impressionism 1874–1886*. Burton and The Fine Arts Museums of San Francisco, 1986.

Nadel, Ira Bruce. *Biography: Fiction, Fact and Form*. New York: St. Martin's Press, 1984.

Neuman, S. C. *Gertrude Stein: Autobiography and the Problem of Narration*. ELS Monograph Series No. 18. Victoria, B.C.: English Literary Studies, University of Victoria, 1979.

Perloff, Marjorie. *The Poetics of Indeterminacy: Rimbaud to Cage*. 1981. Reprint. Evanston: Northwestern University Press, 1983.

Phillips, Mary E. *Reminiscences of William Wetmore Story*. Chicago: Rand, McNally & Company, 1897.

Poggioli, Renato. *The Theory of the Avant-Garde*. Translated by Gerald Fitzgerald. 1952. New York: Icon/Harper & Row, 1971.

Poirier, Richard. *A World Elsewhere: The Place of Style in American Literature*. New York: Oxford University Press, 1966.

Posnock, Ross. *Henry James and the Problem of Robert Browning*. Athens: University of Georgia Press, 1985.

———. *The Trial of Curiosity: Henry James, William James, and the Challenge of Modernity*. New York: Oxford University Press, 1991.

Poulet, Georges. *The Metamorphoses of the Circle*. Translated by Carley Dawson and Elliott Coleman. Baltimore: Johns Hopkins University Press, 1966.

Pound, Ezra. *The Letters of Ezra Pound*. Edited by D. D. Paige. New York: Harcourt, Brace, 1950.

———. *Pound/Joyce: The Letters of Ezra Pound to James Joyce*. Edited by Forrest Read. New York: New Directions, 1967.

Przybylowicz, Donna. *Desire and Repression: The Dialectic of Self and Other in the Late Works of Henry James*. Tuscaloosa: University of Alabama Press, 1986.

Rowe, John Carlos. *The Theoretical Dimensions of Henry James*. The Wisconsin Project on American Writers. Madison: University of Wisconsin Press, 1984.

Ruddick, Lisa. *Reading Gertrude Stein: Body, Text, Gnosis*. Ithaca: Cornell University Press, 1990.

Sayre, Robert F. *The Examined Self: Benjamin Franklin, Henry Adams, Henry James*. Princeton: Princeton University Press, 1964.

Schmitz, Neil. *Of Huck and Alice: Humourous Writing in American Literature*. Minneapolis: University of Minnesota Press, 1983.

Schwartz, Arturo. *The Complete Works of Marcel Duchamp*. 2d rev. ed. New York: Harry N. Abrams, 1970.

Smith, Martha Nell. *Rowing in Eden: Rereading Emily Dickinson*. Austin: University of Texas Press, 1992.

Smith, Sidonie. *Subjectivity, Identity, and the Body: Women's Autobiographical Practices in the Twentieth Century*. Bloomington: Indiana University Press, 1993.

Sprigge, Elizabeth. *Gertrude Stein—Her Life and Work*. New York: Harper & Brothers, 1957.
Stein, Leo. *Appreciation: Painting, Poetry and Prose*. New York: Crown, 1947.
——. *Journey into the Self*. Edited by Edmund Fuller. New York: Crown, 1950.
Steiner, Wendy. *The Colors of Rhetoric: Problems in the Relation Between Modern Literature and Painting*. Chicago: University of Chicago Press, 1982.
——. *Exact Resemblance to Exact Resemblance: The Literary Portraiture of Gertrude Stein*. New Haven: Yale University Press, 1978.
Steward, Samuel M., ed. *Dear Sammy: Letters from Gertrude Stein and Alice B. Toklas* [to Samuel M. Steward]. New York: St. Martin's Press, 1977.
Stowe, William W. *Balzac, James, and the Realistic Novel*. Princeton: Princeton University Press, 1983.
Sundquist, Eric J., ed. *American Realism: New Essays*. Baltimore: Johns Hopkins University Press, 1982.
Sutherland, Donald. *Gertrude Stein: A Biography of Her Work*. New Haven: Yale University Press, 1951.
Tanner, Tony. *The Reign of Wonder: Naivety and Reality in American Literature*. Cambridge: Cambridge University Press, 1965.
Taylor, Linda J. *Henry James, 1866–1916: A Reference Guide*. Boston: G. K. Hall, 1982.
Testimony against Gertrude Stein. Transition Pamphlet No. 1. Supplement to *Transition* 1934–35. The Hague: Servire Press, 1935.
Tintner, Adeline R. *The Book World of Henry James: Appropriating the Classics*. Ann Arbor, Mich.: UMI Research Press, 1987.
Tisdall, Caroline, and Angelo Bozzolla. *Futurism*. New York: Oxford University Press, 1978.
Todorov, Tzvetan. *The Poetics of Prose*. Translated by Richard Howard. Ithaca: Cornell University Press, 1977.
Toklas, Alice B. *Staying on Alone: Letters of Alice B. Toklas*. Edited by Edward Burns. New York: Liveright, 1973.
——. *What Is Remembered*. New York: Holt, Rinehart and Winston, 1963.
Tuttleton, James W., and Agostino Lombardo, eds. *The Sweetest Impression of Life: The James Family and Italy*. New York: New York University Press, 1990.
Walker, Jayne L. *The Making of a Modernist: Gertrude Stein from "Three Lives" to "Tender Buttons."* Amherst: University of Massachussets Press, 1984.
White, Ray Lewis. *Gertrude Stein and Alice B. Toklas: A Reference Guide*. Boston: G. K. Hall, 1984.
——. ed. *Sherwood Anderson/Gertrude Stein: Correspondence and Personal Essays*. Chapel Hill: University of North Carolina Press, 1972.
Wilson, Edmund. *Axel's Castle: A Study in the Imaginative Literature of 1870–1930*. 1931. New York: Charles Scribner's Sons, 1935.
Wilson, R. Jackson. *Figures of Speech: American Writers and the Literary Marketplace, from Benjamin Franklin to Emily Dickinson*. Baltimore: Johns Hopkins University Press, 1990.
Wilson, Robert A., comp. *Gertrude Stein: A Bibliography*. The Phoenix Bibliographies, Vol. 7. New York: The Phoenix Bookshop, 1974.

Wohl, Robert. *The Generation of 1914*. Cambridge: Harvard University Press, 1979.
Woodward, Kathleen. *At Last, The Real Distinguished Thing: The Late Poems of Eliot, Pound, Stevens, and Williams*. Columbus: Ohio State University Press, 1980.
Woolf, Virginia. *Three Guineas*. 1938. New York: Harcourt Brace Jovanovich, 1966.

ARTICLES

Adams, Timothy Dow. "The Contemporary American Mock-Autobiography." *Clio* 8 (1979): 417–28.
———. "To Prepare a Preface to Meet the Faces That You Meet: Autobiographical Rhetoric in Hawthorne's Prefaces." *ESQ* 23 (1977): 89–98.
Alkon, Paul K. "Visual Rhetoric in *The Autobiography of Alice B. Toklas*." *Critical Inquiry* 1 (1975): 849–81.
Antin, David. "Some Questions about Modernism." *Occident* 8 (1974): 7–38.
Armstrong, Carol M. "Edgar Degas and the Representation of the Female Body." In *The Female Body in Western Culture: Contemporary Perspectives*, edited by Susan Rubin Suleiman, pp. 223–42. Cambridge: Harvard University Press, 1986.
Auerbach, Jonathan. "Executing the Model: Painting, Sculpture, and Romance-Writing in Hawthorne's *The Marble Faun*." *ELH* 47 (1980): 103–20.
Banta, Martha. "James and Stein on 'Being American' and 'Having France.'" *The French-American Review* 3 (1979): 63–84.
———. "'There's Surely a Story in It': James's Notebooks and the Working Artist." *Henry James Review* 9 (1988): 153–64.
Benstock, Shari. "Expatriate Sapphic Modernism: Entering Literary History." In *Lesbian Texts and Contexts: Radical Revisions*, edited by Karla Jay and Joanne Glasgow, pp. 183–203. New York: New York University Press, 1990.
Bloom, Lynn Z. "Gertrude Is Alice Is Everybody: Innovation and Point of View in Gertrude Stein's Autobiographies." *Twentieth Century Literature* 24 (1978): 81–93.
Breslin, James E. "Gertrude Stein and the Problems of Autobiography." *Georgia Review* 33 (1979): 901–13.
Buitenhuis, Peter. "Henry James on Hawthorne." *New England Quarterly* 32 (1959): 207–25.
Caramello, Charles. "Coming Across America: Stein and Federman." In *Autobiographie & Avant-garde*, edited by Alfred Hornung and Ernstpeter Ruhe, pp. 367–75. Tübingen: Gunter Narr Verlag, 1992.
———. "Correspondence." *Henry James Review* 10 (1989): 214–19.
———. "The Duality of *The American Scene*." In *A Companion to Henry James Studies*, edited by Daniel Mark Fogel, pp. 447–73. Westport, Conn.: Greenwood, 1993.
———. "Reading Gertrude Stein Reading Henry James, or Eros Is Eros Is Eros Is Eros." *Henry James Review* 6 (1985): 182–203.
Case, Sue-Ellen. "Towards a Butch-Femme Aesthetic." *Discourse* 11 (1988–89): 55–73.
Cook, Blanche Wiesen. "'Women Alone Stir My Imagination': Lesbianism and the Cultural Tradition." *Signs: Journal of Women in Culture and Society* 4 (1979): 718–39.
Cramer, Patricia. "Notes from Underground: Lesbian Ritual in the Writings of Vir-

ginia Woolf." In *Virginia Woolf Miscellanies*, edited by Mark Hussey and Vera Neverow-Turk, pp. 177–88. New York: Pace University Press, 1992.

Croly, Herbert. "Henry James and His Countrymen." In *The Question of Henry James: A Collection of Critical Essays*, edited by F. W. Dupee, pp. 28–39. New York: Henry Holt and Company, 1945.

Crosthwaite, Jane. "Women and Wild Beasts: Versions of the Exotic in Nineteenth Century American Art." *Southern Humanities Review* 19 (1988): 97–114.

Daugherty, Sarah B. "Henry James, George Sand and *The Bostonians*: Another Curious Chapter in the Literary History of Feminism." *Henry James Review* 10 (1989): 42–49.

Davis, Marijane Rountree. " 'A Fine Bewilderment': The Influence of Henry James's *William Wetmore Story* on *The Golden Bowl*." *Henry James Review* 9 (1988): 17–34.

DeKoven, Marianne. "Gertrude Stein." In *The Gender of Modernism: A Critical Anthology*, edited by Bonnie Kime Scott, pp. 479–88. Bloomington: Indiana University Press, 1990.

———. "Half In and Half Out of Doors: Gertrude Stein and the Literary Tradition." In *A Gertrude Stein Companion: Content with the Example*, edited by Bruce Kellner, pp. 75–83. New York: Greenwood, 1988.

———. "Male Signature, Female Aesthetic: The Gender Politics of Experimental Writing." In *Breaking the Sequence: Women's Experimental Fiction*, edited by Ellen G. Friedman and Miriam Fuchs, pp. 72–81. Princeton: Princeton University Press, 1989.

de Lauretis, Teresa. "Sexual Indifference and Lesbian Representation." In *Performing Feminisms: Feminist Critical Theory and Theatre*, edited by Sue-Ellen Case, pp. 17–39. Baltimore: Johns Hopkins University Press, 1990.

Dolan, Jill. " 'Lesbian' Subjectivity in Realism: Dragging at the Margins of Structure and Ideology." In *Performing Feminisms: Feminist Critical Theory and Theatre*, edited by Sue-Ellen Case, pp. 40–53. Baltimore: Johns Hopkins University Press, 1990.

Donoghue, Denis. "Portrait of a Critic." Review of *Literary Criticism*, by Henry James. *The New Republic* (1 April 1985): 29–33.

———. "*William Wetmore Story and His Friends*: The Enclosing Fact of Rome." In *The Sweetest Impression of Life: The James Family and Italy*, edited by James W. Tuttleton and Agostino Lombardo, pp. 210–27. New York: New York University Press, 1990.

Duncan, Carol. "Virility and Domination in Early Twentieth-Century Vanguard Painting." In *Feminism and Art History: Questioning the Litany*, edited by Norma Broude and Mary D. Garrard, pp. 292–313. New York: Harper & Row, 1982.

Dupee, F. W. General introduction to *Selected Writings of Gertrude Stein*, edited by Carl Van Vechten, pp. ix–xvii. 1946. New York: Modern Library, 1962.

Dydo, Ulla E. "Gertrude Stein: Composition as Meditation." In *Gertrude Stein and the Making of Literature*, edited by Shirley Neuman and Ira B. Nadel, pp. 42–60. Boston: Northeastern University Press, 1988.

———. "How to Read Gertrude Stein: The Manuscript of Stanzas in Meditation." In *Text: Transactions of the Society for Textual Scholarship*, Vol. 1, edited by D. C. Greetham and W. Speed Hill, pp. 271–303. New York: AMS Press, 1981.

———. "*Stanzas in Meditation*: The Other Autobiography." *Chicago Review* 35 (1985): 4–20.

Edel, Leon. "Correspondence." *Henry James Review* 9 (1988): 224.

Eliot, T. S. "A Prediction." Excerpted from "A Prediction in Regard to Three English Authors." *Vanity Fair* (February 1924). Reprinted in *Henry James: A Collection of Critical Essays*, edited by Leon Edel, pp. 55–56. Englewood Cliffs, N.J.: Prentice-Hall, 1963.

——. "On Henry James." 1918. In *The Question of Henry James: A Collection of Critical Essays*, edited by F. W. Dupee, pp. 108–19. New York: Henry Holt and Company, 1945.

——. Review of *Composition as Explanation*, by Gertrude Stein. *The New Criterion* 5 (1927): 162.

Fifer, Elizabeth. "Is Flesh Advisable? The Interior Theater of Gertrude Stein." *Signs* 4 (1979): 472–83.

Fussell, Edwin. "Hawthorne, James, and 'The Common Doom.'" *American Quarterly* 10 (1958): 438–53.

Gass, William H. "Gertrude Stein: Her Escape from Protective Language." In *Fiction and the Figures of Life*, pp. 79–96. New York: Vintage, 1972.

Gibbs, Anna. "Hélène Cixous and Gertrude Stein: New Directions in Feminist Criticism." *Meanjin* 38 (1979): 281–93.

Gilmore, Leigh. "A Signature of Lesbian Autobiography: 'Gertrice/Altrude.'" In *Autobiography and Questions of Gender*, edited by Shirley Neuman, pp. 56–75. London: Frank Cass & Co., Ltd., 1991.

Goldberg, Vicki. "The Banquet for Henri Rousseau: Pablo Picasso Throws a Wild and Woozy Party." *Connoisseur* (August 1988): 41–45.

Golding, John. "Two Who Made a Revolution." Review of *Picasso and Braque: Pioneering Cubism*, exhibition and catalog. *New York Review of Books* (31 May 1990): 8–11.

——. "The Triumph of Picasso." *New York Review of Books* (21 July 1988): 19–26.

Gray, James. "Competent Priestess." Review of *Four in America*, by Gertrude Stein. *Saturday Review of Literature* (22 November 1947): 30–31.

Habegger, Alfred. "Henry James's Rewriting of Minny Temple's Letters." *American Literature* 58 (1986): 159–80.

Hardwick, Elizabeth. "The Genius of Margaret Fuller." *New York Review of Books* (10 April 1986): 14–22.

Hart, H. W. Review of *Four in America*, by Gertrude Stein. *Library Journal* (15 October 1947): 1468.

Holly, Carol. "'Absolutely Acclimed': The Cure for Depression in James's Final Phase." *Henry James Review* 8 (1987): 126–38.

——. "The Family Politics of the 'Family Book.'" *Henry James Review* 10 (1989): 98–100.

——. "Henry James's Autobiographical Fragment: 'The Turning Point in My Life.'" *Harvard Library Bulletin* 31 (1983): 40–51.

Howells, William Dean. "James's Hawthorne." *The Atlantic Monthly* (1880). In *Discovery of a Genius: William Dean Howells and Henry James*, compiled and edited by Albert Mordell, pp. 92–97. New York: Twayne, 1961.

Hudspeth, Robert N., and Joel Myerson. "Editing Margaret Fuller's Letters." *Manuscripts* 39 (1987): 242–47.

Hynes, Joseph. "The Transparent Shroud: Henry James and William Story." *American Literature* 46 (1975): 506–27.
Jones, Marnie. "Telling His Own Story: Henry James's *William Wetmore Story*." *biography* 10 (1987): 241–56.
Kahnweiler, Daniel-Henry. Introduction to *Painted Lace*, by Gertrude Stein, pp. ix–xviii. Translated by Donald Gallup.
Katz, Leon. "Matisse, Picasso and Gertrude Stein." In *Four Americans in Paris: The Collections of Gertrude Stein and Her Family*, pp. 51–63. New York: The Museum of Modern Art, 1970.
Kenton, Edna. "Henry James in the World." *Hound & Horn* 7 (1934): 506–13.
Longenbach, James. "The Women and Men of 1914." In *Arms and the Woman: War, Gender, and Literary Representation*, edited by Helen M. Cooper et al., pp. 97–123. Chapel Hill: University of North Carolina Press, 1989.
Luhan, Mabel Dodge. "Speculations, or Post-Impressionism in Prose." 1913. In *Intimate Memories*. 4 vols. Vol. 3, *Movers and Shakers*. New York: Harcourt, Brace, 1936.
Merrill, Cynthia. "Mirrored Image: Gertrude Stein and Autobiography." *Pacific Coast Philology* 20 (1985): 11–17.
Meyer, Steven J. "Gertrude Stein Shipwrecked in Bohemia: Making Ends Meet in the *Autobiography* and After." *Southwest Review* 77 (1992): 12–33.
Miller, Elise. "The Marriage of Henry James and Henrietta Stackpole." *Henry James Review* 10 (1989): 15–31.
Nadel, Ira. B. "Gertrude Stein and Henry James." In *Gertrude Stein and the Making of Literature*, edited by Shirley Neuman and Ira B. Nadel, pp. 81–97. Boston: Northeastern University Press, 1988.
Nettels, Elsa. "Henry James and the Art of Biography." *South Atlantic Bulletin* 43 (1978): 107–24.
"Not for the Tired." Review of *Four in America*, by Gertrude Stein. *Time* (17 November 1947): 110, 113–14.
Ortega y Gasset, José. "The Dehumanization of Art." 1925. Reprinted in *The Dehumanization of Art and Other Essays on Art, Culture and Literature*, pp. 3–54. Translated by Helen Weyl. Princeton: Princeton University Press, 1968.
Parke, Catherine N. " 'The Hero Being Dead': Evasive Explanation in Biography (The Case of Boswell)." *Philological Quarterly* 68 (1989): 343–62.
Pearson, Norman Holmes. "Gertrude Stein." Review of *Four in America*, by Gertrude Stein. *The Yale Review* 37 (1948): 743–45.
Perloff, Marjorie. "Call It Marry Nettie: Modern Poetry and the Politics of the Image." Lecture delivered at University of Maryland, College Park, April 1993.
———. "(Im)Personating Gertrude Stein." In *Gertrude Stein and the Making of Literature*, edited by Shirley Neuman and Ira B. Nadel, pp. 61–80. Boston: Northeastern University Press, 1988.
Person, Leland S., Jr. "Henry James, George Sand, and the Suspense of Masculinity." *PMLA* 106 (1991): 515–28.
Pound, Ezra. "Henry James." *The Little Review* (1918). In *Literary Essays of Ezra Pound*, edited by T. S. Eliot, pp. 295–338. New York: New Directions, 1968.

Powers, Lyall H. "Thornton Wilder as Literary Cubist: An Acknowledged Debt to Henry James." *Henry James Review* 7 (1985): 34–44.

Redford, Bruce. "Keeping Story Out of History: Henry James's Biographical *tour de force*." *American Literature* 57 (1985): 215–25.

Rich, Adrienne. "Compulsory Heterosexuality and Lesbian Existence." In *The Signs Reader: Women, Gender and Scholarship*, edited by Elizabeth Abel and Emily K. Abel, pp. 139–68. Chicago: University of Chicago Press, 1983.

Richardson, John. "Picasso's Apocalyptic Whorehouse." *New York Review of Books* (23 April 1987): 40–47.

Rochlin, Harriet, and Fred Rochlin. "Jews on the Western Frontier: An Overview." *Arizona Highways Magazine* 61 (1985): 2–11. Exerpted from Rochlin and Rochlin, *Pioneer Jews*. Boston: Houghton Mifflin, 1984.

Rosen, Charles, and Henri Zerner. "Enemies of Realism." *New York Review of Books* (4 March 1982): 29–33.

———. "What Is, and Is Not, Realism?" *New York Review of Books* (18 February 1982): 21–26.

Rosenberg, Harold. "Paris Annexed." In *The De-definition of Art*, pp. 167–77. New York: Collier/Macmillan, 1973.

Roth, Philip. "Writing American Fiction." In *Reading Myself and Others*, pp. 117–35. New York: Farrar, Straus and Giroux, 1975.

Rowe, John Carlos. "What the Thunder Said: James's *Hawthorne* and the American Anxiety of Influence: A Centennial Essay." *Henry James Review* 4 (1983): 81–119.

Sawyer, Julian. "Gertrude Stein: A Bibliography 1941–1948." *Bulletin of Bibliography* 19 (1948): 152–56; 19 (1948): 183–87.

Schmitz, Neil. "Doing the Fathers: Gertrude Stein on U. S. Grant in *Four in America*." *American Literature* 65 (1993): 751–60.

———. "*Four* (and Then Some) *in America*: Gertrude Stein's Studies in Classical American Literature." Paper delivered at the convention of the Modern Language Association, Washington, D.C., December 1989.

———. "Portrait, Patriarchy, Mythos: The Revenge of Gertrude Stein." *Salmagundi* 40 (1978): 69–91.

Schultz, Susan M. "Gertrude Stein's Self-Advertisement." *Raritan* 12 (1992): 71–87.

Shaw, Sharon. "Gertrude Stein and Henry James: The Difference Between Accidence and Coincidence." *The Pembroke Magazine* 5 (1974): 95–101.

Sheed, Wilfrid. "A Farewell to Hemingstein." *New York Review of Books* (12 June 1986): 5–12.

Sloper, L. A. "Nonsense." Review of *Four in America*, by Gertrude Stein. *Christian Science Monitor* (22 November 1947): 17.

Solimine, Joseph Jr. "Henry James, William Wetmore Story, and Friend: A Noble Mistake?" *Studies in Browning and His Circle* 8 (1980): 57–61.

Spender, Stephen. "Henry James and the Contemporary Subject." *The Destructive Element*. 1935. Reprinted as "The Contemporary Subject" in *Henry James: A Collection of Critical Essays*, edited by Leon Edel, pp. 102–10. Englewood Cliffs, N.J.: Prentice-Hall, 1963.

Steiner, Wendy. Introduction to *Lectures in America*, by Gertrude Stein, pp. ix–xxvii. Boston: Beacon Press, 1985.
Stevenson, Robert Louis. "A Humble Remonstrance." In *Memories and Portraits*, pp. 275–99. London: Chatto and Windus, 1887.
Stimpson, Catharine R. "Gertrice/Altrude: Stein, Toklas, and the Paradox of the Happy Marriage." In *Mothering the Mind: Twelve Studies of Writers and Their Silent Partners*, edited by Ruth Perry and Martine Watson Brownley, pp. 122–39. New York: Holmes & Meier, 1984.
———. "Gertrude Stein and the Lesbian Lie." In *American Women's Autobiography: Fea(s)ts of Memory*, edited by Margo Culley, pp. 152–66. Madison: University of Wisconsin Press, 1992.
———. "Gertrude Stein and the Transposition of Gender." In *The Poetics of Gender*, edited by Nancy K. Miller, pp. 1–18. New York: Columbia University Press, 1986.
———. "The Mind, the Body, and Gertrude Stein." *Critical Inquiry* 3 (1977): 489–506.
———. "The Somagrams of Gertrude Stein." In *The Female Body in Western Culture: Contemporary Perspectives*, edited by Susan Rubin Suleiman, pp. 30–43. Cambridge: Harvard University Press, 1986.
Stowe, Harriet Beecher. "Sojourner Truth, The Libyan Sibyl." *The Atlantic Monthly* (1863). Reprinted in *Narrative of Sojourner Truth*, edited by Olive Gilbert and Francis Titus, pp. 151–72. Battle Creek, Mich.: n.p., 1878.
Thomson, Virgil. "Wickedly Wonderful Widow." Review of *Staying on Alone*, by Alice B. Toklas. *New York Review of Books* (7 March 1974): 12–15.
Tintner, Adeline R. " 'Dear and Venerable Circe': An Unpublished Henry James Letter." *Manuscripts* 39 (1987): 156–61.
———. "A Source for Prince Amerigo in *The Golden Bowl*." *Notes on Modern American Literature* 2 (1978): 23–25.
Trilling, Lionel. "Hawthorne in Our Time." In *Beyond Culture: Essays on Literature and Learning*, pp. 179–208. New York: Viking, 1965.
Valéry, Paul. "Poetry and Abstract Thought." In *The Art of Poetry*, pp. 52–81. Translated by Denise Folliot. The Collected Works of Paul Valéry, Vol. 7. Bollingen Series 45. New York: Pantheon Books, 1958.
Wadman, Karen L. "*William Wetmore Story and His Friends*: Henry James's Portrait of Robert Browning." *The Yearbook of English Studies* 11 (1981): 210–18.
Ward, J. A. "The Portraits of Henry James." *Henry James Review* 10 (1989): 1–14.
Warren, Lansing. "Gertrude Stein Views Life and Politics." *New York Times Magazine* (6 May 1934): 9, 23.
Wells, H. G. "Of Art, of Literature, of Mr. Henry James." 1915. Reprinted in *Henry James and H. G. Wells: A Record of Their Friendship, Their Debate on the Art of Fiction, and Their Quarrel*, edited by Leon Edel and Gordon N. Ray, pp. 234–60. Urbana: University of Illinois Press, 1958.
Winston, Elizabeth. "Gertrude Stein's Mediating Stanzas." *biography* 9 (1986): 229–46.

INDEX

Adams, Henry, 92–93, 100–101
Addams, Jane, 221 (n. 40)
Aldrich, Mildred, 154, 158, 160, 168, 232 (n. 28), 235 (n. 43), 236 (n. 48)
Anderson, Sherwood, 149, 160, 170, 235 (n. 43), 239 (n. 70), 242–43 (n. 92), 243 (n. 93)
Apollinaire, Guillaume, 135, 154, 235 (n. 43)
Armory Show, 126, 153–55
Arnold, Matthew, 23–24, 26, 48, 57, 208 (n. 5); *Culture and Anarchy*, 210 (n. 11)
Autobiography: GS on, as modern genre, 13–16; and *William Wetmore Story and His Friends*, 84–88, 217–18 (n. 17); and *The Autobiography of Alice B. Toklas*, 123–24, 143–44, 148, 157, 230 (n. 12)

Balzac, Honoré de, 28, 47, 213 (n. 33)
Belgiojoso, Princess, 81, 222 (n. 43)
Bergson, Henri, 146
Biography: HJ on, 4–6, 92–93, 202 (nn. 4, 5), 217 (n. 14); GS on, 13–16; and *Hawthorne*, 45–47, 52–53; and *William Wetmore Story and His Friends*, 58–60, 63–64, 215 (n. 5), 217–18 (n. 17); and *The Autobiography of Alice B. Toklas*, 123, 124, 149–50; and *Four in America*, 173, 188
Bookstaver, May, 140, 237 (n. 54)
Boott, Frank, 58, 92, 225 (n. 61)
Bosanquet, Theodora: "Henry James at Work," 248 (n. 17)
Boston, 92–93, 224 (n. 56), 226 (n. 62)
Boswell, James: *Life of Johnson*, 14, 121
Braque, George, 120, 198, 229 (n. 9), 232 (n. 23), 233 (n. 34), 235 (n. 43), 243 (n. 92)
Brewster, H. B., 55–56
Brook Farm, 37–40, 43, 48, 49
Brown, John, 42

Browning, Elizabeth Barrett, 42, 68, 70
Browning, Robert, 61, 64, 68, 71, 72–73, 75–76, 93, 94, 226 (nn. 66, 68, 70)

Carlyle, Thomas, 57
Carroll, Lewis: *Alice through the Looking Glass*, 245 (n. 109)
Cerf, Bennett, 120, 247 (n. 9)
Cézanne, Paul, 12, 163, 165, 190, 232 (nn. 29, 30), 240 (n. 79); *Portrait d'une Femme*, 148, 156, 165, 240 (n. 79), 244 (n. 102)
Clemens, Samuel L.: *A Connecticut Yankee in King Arthur's Court*, 121; *The Adventures of Huckleberry Finn*, 152, 239 (n. 74), 243 (n. 96), 245 (n. 103)
Coburn, Alvin Langdon, 154, 169, 240 (n. 76), 246 (n. 1)
Cocteau, Jean, 135, 242 (n. 87)
Cosmopolitanism: HJ on, in *Hawthorne*, 33–34, 47; HJ on, in *Notes of a Son and Brother*, 55–56; and *William Wetmore Story and His Friends*, 62, 93, 226 (nn. 63, 64). See also Expatriation
Cubism, 10–12, 197–98, 206 (n. 23); and *Three Lives*, 10–12; and *The Autobiography of Alice B. Toklas*, 124–26, 134–35, 141, 145, 151–53, 153–57, 229 (n. 9), 232–33 (n. 32), 233 (n. 33); and *Four in America*, 188–92, 251 (n. 32), 252 (n. 36); and *Tender Buttons*, 233 (n. 33); and *Picasso*, 251 (n. 34)

Daudet, Alphonse, 8
Defoe, Daniel, 124, 125; *Robinson Crusoe*, 14, 121, 151–52, 239 (nn. 72, 73), 243 (n. 96)
Dickens, Charles, 9, 205 (n. 15)
Dodge, Mabel, 148–49, 153–54; "Speculations, or Post-Impressionism in Prose," 154
Duchamp, Marcel, 154, 240 (n. 75), 251

(n. 30); *Nude Descending a Staircase*, 126, 153–57

Eliot, George, 8, 9, 10, 47, 211 (n. 18)
Eliot, T. S., 192, 193, 196, 198–99, 241 (n. 85), 242 (n. 89), 246 (n. 6)
Emerson, Ralph Waldo, 48, 54, 129, 170, 207 (n. 29)
English Men of Letters, 21, 32, 37
Expatriation: and *Hawthorne*, 47–48, 53–56; and *William Wetmore Story and His Friends*, 62–63, 65–67, 72–76, 82, 225 (n. 59); and *The Autobiography of Alice B. Toklas*, 128, 154, 233 (n. 35); and *Four in America*, 190–91. See also Cosmopolitanism
Experimentalism: and *Hawthorne*, 34, 37–41, 43, 49; and *William Wetmore Story and His Friends*, 72–73, 100, 227 (n. 76); and *The Autobiography of Alice B. Toklas*, 121, 142, 230 (n. 12); and *Four in America*, 173–74; and George Sand, 203 (n. 8); and Emile Zola, 212 (n. 26)

Flaubert, Gustave, 12, 205 (n. 17), 211 (n. 18), 232 (n. 30)
Ford, Henry, 15, 129, 131, 239 (n. 68)
Franklin, Benjamin, 124; *Autobiography*, 157, 241 (n. 86)
Freud, Sigmund, 251 (n. 31)
Fuller, Margaret, 38, 80, 81, 212 (n. 24), 221 (n. 40), 222 (n. 43)
Futurism, 130–31, 134, 232 (nn. 28, 32), 234 (n. 37), 241 (n. 84)

Gender: and *The Portrait of a Lady*, 2, 164–67; and *Three Lives*, 3, 10; and George Sand, 6, 203–4 (n. 10); and *The Autobiography of Alice B. Toklas*, 121, 125–27; and war, in *The Autobiography of Alice B. Toklas*, 135–36, 231 (n. 19); and feminism, in *The Autobiography of Alice B. Toklas*, 139, 162, 237 (n. 51); and portraiture, in *The Autobiography of Alice B. Toklas*, 153–57, 162–67; and publication, in *The Autobiography of Alice B. Toklas*, 159–61; and *Four in America*, 191, 199; and *Hawthorne*, 214 (n. 41); and the nude, 220 (n. 35), 241 (n. 84); and GS scholarship, 235–36 (n. 46); and GS's name, in *The Autobiography of Alice B. Toklas*, 240 (n. 80). See also Marriage; Sexuality
Genealogy, 18–20, 47–48, 152–53, 197, 236 (n. 47). See also Influence; Precursivity/succession
Grant, Ulysses S., 54, 55, 149, 173, 174, 175, 189, 190, 191, 192, 235 (n. 43), 239 (n. 70), 247 (n. 8); *Personal Memoirs*, 174, 248 (n. 16), 249 (n. 17)
Gris, Juan, 161, 252 (n. 37)

Hale, Edward Everett: *James Russell Lowell and His Friends*, 215 (n. 5)
Hammett, Dashiell, 14, 207 (n. 29)
Hawthorne, Julian, 51; *Hawthorne and His Circle*, 212 (n. 22); *Nathaniel Hawthorne and His Wife*, 212 (nn. 22, 24)
Hawthorne, Nathaniel, 7–8, 9–10, 18, 19, 21–56 passim, 71, 94, 95, 96, 152, 207 (n. 36), 208–14 passim; *Atlantic Monthly* article of 1862 ("Chiefly about War Matters"), 42; *The Blithedale Romance*, 35, 38, 39, 48, 204 (n. 12); "The Custom-House," 7, 56, 204 (n. 12); *The House of the Seven Gables*, 25, 35, 210 (n. 10); *Life of Franklin Pierce*, 41, 53; *The Marble Faun*, 16, 18, 35, 70, 75, 76, 79, 81, 220 (n. 35); Note-Books, 21, 26, 44, 46, 212 (n. 24), 213 (n. 30); *Our Old Home*, 42; preface to *The Blithedale Romance*, 245 (n. 106); preface to *The House of the Seven Gables*, 206 (n. 25); preface to *The Marble Faun*, 17, 36, 81, 211 (n. 19); *The Scarlet Letter*, 25, 35, 48, 49, 210 (n. 10), 211 (n. 18), 226 (n. 68); *Septi-

mus Felton, 42; *Twice-Told Tales*, 45; "Young Goodman Brown," 35
Hawthorne, Sophia Peabody, 30, 37, 38, 212 (n. 24)
Hemingway, Ernest, 126, 138, 157, 161, 168, 198, 242 (n. 89), 242–43 (n. 92), 243 (nn. 93, 94), 246 (n. 11); *A Moveable Feast*, 120, 230 (n. 11), 234 (n. 37); *The Sun Also Rises*, 133
Hound and Horn, 247 (n. 8), 253 (n. 46)
Howells, William Dean, 7–8, 36, 47, 205 (n. 14), 211–12 (n. 20), 214 (nn. 42, 1)
Hugnet, Georges: "*Enfances*," 177, 184, 250 (n. 26)

Influence, 23–25, 26–27, 94–95, 131, 169–72, 232 (n. 29). *See also* Genealogy; Precursivity/succession

Jacob, Max, 126, 137
James, Henry: *The Ambassadors*, 54; *The American*, 98; *The American Scene*, 50–51, 54, 214 (n. 40), 214 (n. 1), 218 (n. 19), 223 (n. 49), 224 (n. 55), 225 (n. 58), 227 (n. 75); "The Art of Fiction," 7, 8, 204 (n. 12); "The Aspern Papers," 95; *The Awkward Age*, 150; *The Bostonians*, 237 (n. 50); "The Death of the Lion," 95; "Family Book" (*see* HJ: *Notes of a Son and Brother; A Small Boy and Others*); *French Poets and Novelists*, 23; *The Golden Bowl*, 67, 219 (n. 30), 225 (n. 61); *Hawthorne*, 7, 9, 18, 19, 21–56, 59, 89, 94, 96, 98, 206 (n. 25), 207 (n. 36), 208–14 passim; introduction to *The Tempest*, 252 (n. 35); *Italian Hours*, 221 (n. 38); *The Ivory Tower*, 246 (n. 4); "The Jolly Corner," 93; "The Lesson of the Master," 93; "Letter to the Hon. Robert S. Rantoul: The Hawthorne Centennial, 1904," 53–54; "The Life of George Eliot," 8; "London," 54; "The Madonna of the Future," 93; memoirs (*A Small Boy and Others, Notes of a Son and Brother, The Middle Years*), 174, 175–76, 178, 182, 183–88, 249 (n. 22) (*see also* HJ: *Notes of a Son and Brother; A Small Boy and Others*); "The Middle Years," 136, 228 (n. 78), 252 (n. 35); "Nathaniel Hawthorne" (1896), 21, 30, 46, 53, 210 (n. 12), 211 (n. 16), 212 (n. 26), 214 (n. 43); "The Next Time," 95; *Notes of a Son and Brother*, 54–56, 64, 68, 93, 100–101, 184, 186, 212 (n. 23), 214 (n. 40), 223 (n. 49), 225 (n. 58), 248 (n. 17); *Notes on Novelists*, 6; "The Novel in *The Ring and the Book*," 226 (n. 68); *Partial Portraits*, 7, 9, 203 (n. 7); *The Portrait of a Lady*, 2, 6–7, 8–9, 10, 26, 51, 127, 151, 164–67, 245 (n. 106), 245 (n. 108); preface to *The Awkward Age*, 150; preface to *The Golden Bowl*, 167, 219 (n. 30), 246 (n. 4); preface to *The Portrait of a Lady*, 8–10, 165; "The Real Thing," 152; review of Cabot, *A Memoir of Ralph Waldo Emerson*, 39, 43–44, 202 (n. 5), 212 (n. 28); review of Hawthorne, *French and Italian Note-Books* (1872), 21, 26, 31, 32, 52; review of Nordhoff, *The Communistic Societies of the United States*, 39, 40; review of Story, *Nero*, 61; *Roderick Hudson*, 93; *A Small Boy and Others*, 100, 204 (n. 11), 212 (n. 23), 224 (n. 50), 225 (n. 58); "The Turn of the Screw," 91; *William Wetmore Story and His Friends*, 18, 19, 54, 57–101, 151, 214–28 passim, 245 (n. 106); *The Wings of the Dove*, 246 (n. 3); *Within the Rim*, 19; writings on George Sand, 5–6, 203 (n. 8). *See also* New York Edition
James, Henry, Sr., 50, 84–87, 96, 184, 204 (n. 11), 211 (n. 13), 219 (n. 29); *The Literary Remains of the Late Henry James*, 249 (n. 22)
James, William, 3, 10, 50, 60, 84–85, 91, 96, 127, 138–39, 142, 146, 169, 197, 205–6 (n. 21), 225 (n. 60), 230 (n. 16),

232 (n. 30), 246 (n. 1), 249 (n. 22), 249–50 (n. 23); *The Principles of Psychology,* 176, 238 (n. 56)
Jolas, Eugene, 229 (n. 9)
Joyce, James, 126, 143, 193, 196, 198–99, 254 (n. 59); *Ulysses,* 174, 193, 199; *Finnegans Wake,* 193, 199

Kahnweiler, Daniel-Henry, 132, 154
Kemble, Frances Anne, 86–87

Lathrop, George Parsons: *A Study of Hawthorne,* 21, 29, 33, 37, 38, 45–56, 208 (n. 2), 210 (n. 10), 212 (n. 22), 212–13 (n. 30)
Lee, Henry: *Funeral Oration on the Death of General Washington,* 174–75, 248 (n. 16)
Lewis, Lloyd, 239 (n. 70), 249 (n. 17)
Lincoln, Abraham, 55, 235 (n. 43)
Literary Guild, 245 (n. 107)
London Exposition of 1862, 69, 82
Lowell, James Russell, 54, 58, 66, 68, 74–75, 80, 81–82, 86, 214 (n. 1), 215 (n. 5), 219 (nn. 25, 26), 221–22 (n. 41), 222 (n. 46), 224 (n. 51), 226 (n. 66)

McAlmon, Robert, 242 (n. 89)
Macmillan, Alexander, 21
Marriage: and *Hawthorne,* 37–41, 43, 50, 212 (n. 22); and *William Wetmore Story and His Friends,* 67–68, 93–94, 226 (nn. 65, 66); and *The Autobiography of Alice B. Toklas,* 121, 124, 125, 127, 136–40, 155, 166–67, 184, 186–87, 231 (nn. 17, 20), 236 (n. 49), 237 (n. 54); and *The Portrait of a Lady,* 166–67; and *The Golden Bowl,* 167; and *Four in America,* 183–88, 190–91, 250–51 (n. 29). *See also* Gender; Sexuality
Matisse, Henri, 120, 132, 137–38, 151–52, 232 (n. 23), 233 (nn. 33, 34), 235 (n. 43), 252 (n. 35); *Bonheur de Vivre,* 137, 156, 233 (n. 33), 240 (n. 79); *Femme au Chapeau,* 148, 155–57, 163–64

Memoir: and *William Wetmore Story and His Friends,* 62, 83–84, 88–92; and *The Autobiography of Alice B. Toklas,* 123–24, 146–47, 231 (n. 17); and *Four in America,* 176. *See also* James, Henry: memoirs
Modernism/modernity, 16–20, 192–200; and *William Wetmore Story and His Friends,* 63, 78–79, 97–99; and *The Autobiography of Alice B. Toklas,* 124–36 passim, 151, 231 (n. 19); and *Four in America,* 187–88
Morley, John, 21, 25, 208 (n. 1), 208–9 (n. 6), 213 (n. 38)

Napoleon, 175, 235 (n. 43), 248–49 (n. 17), 249 (n. 18)
Narration: GS on, 13–14, 181–82; and *Hawthorne,* 25–26; and *William Wetmore Story and His Friends,* 90, 94–95; and *The Autobiography of Alice B. Toklas,* 121–22, 144–48, 150–53, 183–85; and *Four in America,* 172–74; and "Henry James," 184–86
Naturalism, 10, 205 (n. 18), 212 (n. 26)
New York Edition (*The Novels and Tales of Henry James*), 54, 150, 239 (n. 71); prefaces to, 214 (n. 40), 216 (n. 12), 246 (n. 4); photographic frontispieces to, 224 (n. 54), 240 (n. 76)
Norton, Charles Eliot, 68, 215 (n. 5)
Novel: HJ on, 4, 7–8, 204 (n. 12); GS on, 13–16, 248 (n. 13); and *The Autobiography of Alice B. Toklas,* 150–51; and *Four in America,* 174–75; Robert Louis Stevenson on, 204–5 (n. 14)

Ortega y Gasset, José, 175

Palazzo Barberini; 77–79, 224 (n. 51), 227 (n. 75)
Paris, 124, 128, 132, 147, 154, 226 (n. 63), 227 (n. 76), 234–35 (n. 42), 239 (n. 72)
Paul, Elliot, 145, 158, 242 (nn. 87, 89, 90)

Phillips, Mary E.: *Reminiscences of William Wetmore Story*, 224 (n. 53)
Picabia, Francis, 1, 125, 149, 150, 232 (n. 32)
Picasso, Pablo, 3, 8, 18, 120–32 passim, 135, 137, 138, 145, 154–57, 158, 160, 161–62, 168, 188–89, 190–91, 206 (n. 23), 232–44 passim, 251 (n. 34); *Les Demoiselles d'Avignon*, 11, 126, 154–57, 241 (n. 81); *Nude Girl with Basket of Flowers*, 156; *Portrait of Miss Gertrude Stein*, 122, 125, 126, 127, 138, 148, 155–57, 162–64, 233 (n. 33), 240 (nn. 79, 80), 240–41 (n. 81), 243 (n. 96), 243–44 (n. 97), 244 (n. 101), 244–45 (n. 102); *Self-Portrait*, 241 (n. 81); *Three Women*, 154, 240 (n. 79); *Woman with a Fan*, 245 (n. 110)
Pickford, Mary, 207 (n. 30)
Pierce, Franklin, 30, 37, 41–43, 46–47, 55
Plain Edition, 127, 160, 168, 242 (n. 90), 245 (n. 110)
Poe, Edgar Allan, 33, 48
Portrait narration, 3, 13, 121, 171, 172–74, 182
Portraiture, 1–13 passim, 17, 20, 141–42, 181, 202 (n. 2), 203 (n. 7), 205 (n. 15); and *Hawthorne*, 22–23, 34–35; and *William Wetmore Story and His Friends*, 83–84, 90; and *The Autobiography of Alice B. Toklas*, 121, 125–27, 134, 148–61; and *Four in America*, 173–74, 188–92; and *Picasso*, 188–89
Pound, Ezra, 192, 193, 198–99, 254 (n. 58)
Precursivity/succession, 7, 12, 18–20, 199–200, 204 (n. 11); and *Hawthorne*, 31, 44, 46, 47–48, 49, 50, 54, 213 (n. 33); and *William Wetmore Story and His Friends*, 61–62, 63, 74, 81, 83, 85–86, 89, 92, 100, 227–28 (n. 77); and *The Autobiography of Alice B. Toklas*, 128, 161–62, 164; and *Four in America*, 169–72, 182–83. See also Genealogy; Influence

Proust, Marcel, 253 (n. 56); *A la recherche du temps perdu*, 174, 193

Realism: and HJ, 6–10, 36, 211–12 (n. 20); and GS, 10–13; and Cubism, 11–12, 145; and *Hawthorne*, 28–29, 34–35, 211 (n. 17); and *The Autobiography of Alice B. Toklas*, 151, 152–53; and *Three Lives*, 205–6 (n. 21)
Ristori, Adelaide, 81, 224 (n. 53)
Romance: and HJ, 6–10; and novel, 7–8, 206 (n. 25); and realism, 9–10, 76, 205 (n. 17), 213 (n. 35); and *Hawthorne*, 22, 27, 28–29, 35–36, 44–45, 52–53; and *William Wetmore Story and His Friends*, 70; and *The Autobiography of Alice B. Toklas*, 152–53
Romanticism, artistic and political: and *Hawthorne*, 27, 47; and *William Wetmore Story and His Friends*, 65–66, 70, 74–75, 76, 96–100
Rome, 58, 61–62, 65–66, 73, 76–79, 93, 97–98, 99, 166, 175, 220 (n. 35), 221 (n. 39), 223 (n. 48), 224 (n. 56), 227 (n. 76), 235 (n. 43)
Rönnebeck, Arnold, 120, 145–46, 156
Roth, Philip: "Writing American Fiction," 207 (n. 30)
Rue de Fleurus, 140, 234 (n. 38), 237 (n. 53)

Sainte-Beuve, Charles Augustin, 23, 48, 208 (n. 5)
Salvini, Tommaso, 87, 224 (n. 53)
Sand, George, 5–6, 52, 203 (nn. 8, 9), 203–4 (n. 10)
Sargent, John Singer, 1
Scott, Sir Walter, 9, 205 (n. 15)
Scudder, Janet, 146
Sexuality: and communes, in *Hawthorne*, 38–41; and *The Scarlet Letter*, 48; and *The Autobiography of Alice B. Toklas*, 138–39, 236 (n. 48), 237 (nn. 53, 54); and writing, in *The Autobiography of Alice B. Toklas* and *Four in America*,

186–87, 250–51 (n. 29); and *Three Lives*, 205 (n. 20); and GS scholarship, 235–36 (n. 46); and GS's motto ("Rose is a rose is a rose is a rose"), 251 (n. 30). *See also* Gender; Marriage

Shakespeare, William, 9, 71, 84–85, 87, 176–77, 179–81, 250 (n. 24), 252 (n. 35)

Sitwell, Edith, 158

Stein, Gertrude: "Ada," 141, 143, 148, 150, 250 (n. 28); *The Autobiography of Alice B. Toklas*, 13, 14, 15, 16, 18, 19, 119–68, 169–70, 172, 173, 183–88, 191, 196, 198, 206 (n. 28), 229–46 passim, 247 (n. 8), 251 (n. 30), 254 (n. 61); *Before the Flowers of Friendship Faded Friendship Faded*, 177, 179–81, 182, 183–84, 250 (n. 26); *Brewsie and Willie*, 19, 123; "A Circular Play," 248 (n. 17); "Composition as Explanation," 11–12, 130; "An Elucidation," 206 (n. 24); *Everybody's Autobiography*, 13, 14–16, 119, 120, 156, 157, 167, 172–73, 229 (n. 4), 237 (n. 51), 238–39 (n. 64), 247 (n. 8), 249 (n. 17), 254 (n. 61); *Four in America*, 18, 19, 172–92, 196, 199–200, 246–53 passim, 254 (n. 61); *Four Saints in Three Acts*, 13, 244 (n. 99); *The Geographical History of America*, 180, 250 (n. 27); *Geography and Plays*, 158; "Henry and I," 169, 248 (n. 17); "Henry James," 175–88, 196, 199–200, 244 (n. 101), 247 (n. 8), 247–48 (n. 10), 248–51 passim, 251–52 (n. 35); *How To Write*, 142–43, 160; "Ida," 243 (n. 94), 250 (n. 28); *Ida*, 243 (n. 94), 250 (n. 28); "If I Told Him: A Completed Portrait of Picasso," 235 (n. 43), 248–49 (n. 17); "James Is Nervous," 169, 176; *Lectures in America*, 13–14, 15, 170, 172, 173, 178–79, 181, 183, 184, 246–47 (n. 8), 247 (n. 9); *Lucy Church Amiably*, 160; *The Making of Americans*, 11, 13–14, 15, 125, 132, 140, 141, 143, 148, 149, 150, 154, 156, 158, 160, 170, 174, 193, 207 (n. 31), 237 (nn. 52, 55), 242 (nn. 88, 89), 243 (n. 97), 246 (n. 7), 254 (n. 61); *Matisse Picasso and Gertrude Stein*, 233 (n. 33); "Melanctha," 143, 205 (n. 20); *Narration*, 13–14, 170, 172, 173, 181–82, 184, 185; *Operas and Plays*, 160; *Paris France*, 229 (n. 7); "Picasso," 233 (n. 34); *Picasso*, 171, 188–89, 191, 229 (n. 7), 244 (n. 98); *Portrait of Mabel Dodge at the Villa Curonia*, 148, 153, 154, 156–57; *Q.E.D.*, 140, 205 (n. 20), 237 (n. 54), 246 (n. 3); *Selected Writings of Gertrude Stein*, 120; *Stanzas in Meditation*, 121, 160, 230 (n. 12), 249 (n. 23); *Tender Buttons*, 13, 141, 142, 174, 233 (n. 33), 239 (n. 67); *Three Lives*, 3, 10–13, 125, 140, 143, 154, 156, 160, 165, 205 (n. 18), 207 (n. 34), 238 (n. 59), 240 (n. 79), 242 (n. 88), 244 (n. 99), 246 (n. 1); "A Transatlantic Interview," 12–13, 123, 165, 170–71, 182, 183; *Wars I Have Seen*, 19

Stein, Leo, 140, 196; *Appreciation*, 120; *Journey into the Self*, 120

Stevenson, Robert Louis, 8, 9, 10; *Treasure Island*, 9, 204–5 (n. 14), 205 (n. 16); "A Humble Remonstrance," 204–5 (n. 14)

Stieglitz, Alfred: *Camera Work*, 154, 240 (n. 77)

Story, Edith (Countess Peruzzi), 58, 225 (n. 61), 228 (n. 79)

Story, Emelyn, 60, 67–68, 80–81, 86, 222 (n. 42)

Story, Julian, 58, 214 (n. 3)

Story, Justice Joseph, 66, 74, 81

Story, Waldo, 58, 214 (n. 3), 216 (n. 8)

Story, William Wetmore, 17, 18, 19, 47, 57–100 passim, 214–18 passim; *Cleopatra*, 17, 69–70, 96, 220 (n. 36), 227 (n. 71); "Distortions of the English Stage," 87; *Fiammetta*, 87, 88; *The Libyan Sibyl*, 69–70, 96, 220 (n. 37), 227 (n. 71); *Nero*, 57, 61, 71, 85, 86–87, 94; *Roba di Roma*, 220 (n. 35); statue of Edward Everett, 218 (n. 24); statue

of John Marshall, 220–21 (n. 37); statue of Joseph Henry, 220–21 (n. 37)
Stowe, Harriet Beecher: *Uncle Tom's Cabin*, 86; "Sojourner Truth, The Libyan Sibyl," 96, 227 (n. 71)
Sumner, Charles, 68, 71–72, 74–75, 76, 82, 86, 96, 219 (n. 25), 222–23 (n. 47), 224 (n. 50), 226–27 (n. 70)
Surrealism, 133, 232 (n. 32), 234 (n. 37), 253 (n. 56)
Symbolism, 197–98, 238 (n. 57)

Taine, Hippolyte, 23–24, 26, 48, 52, 208 (n. 5), 213 (n. 34)
Temple, Minnie, 184, 186
Testimony against Gertrude Stein, 120, 229 (n. 9), 232 (n. 23)
Thoreau, Henry David, 33
Toklas, Alice B., 14, 18, 119–68 passim, 169, 183–85, 188, 191, 206 (n. 28), 207 (n. 36), 229–46 passim, 254 (n. 59); "Fifty Years of French Fashion," 168

Transcendentalism, 38, 48, 212 (n. 25)
Trollope, Anthony, 47

Van Vechten, Carl, 120, 154, 245 (n. 107), 247 (nn. 8, 9)
Vollard, Ambroise, 132, 156, 238 (n. 62)

Warhol, Andy: "Ten Lizzes," 239 (n. 68)
Washington, George, 173, 174, 189, 190, 191, 192, 235 (n. 43)
Wells, H. G., 60
Whitman, Walt, 246 (n. 5); *Democratic Vistas*, 36
Wilson, Edmund: *Axel's Castle*, 193, 248 (n. 13)
Woolf, Virginia: *Three Guineas*, 243 (n. 95)
Wright, Wilbur, 173, 174, 189–92; memorial at Le Mans, 174, 248 (n. 16)

Zola, Emile: *Le Roman experimental*, 212 (n. 26)

www.ingramcontent.com/pod-product-compliance
Lightning Source LLC
Chambersburg PA
CBHW020300010526
44108CB00037B/274